MW01196632

IN ME WE TRUST:

A DISCOVERY OF SELF AFTER SEXUAL TRAUMA

By: Anna Gulden

FOR SURVIVORS

Please take comfort and care of yourself while reading my story. It is one of hope...*and* it chronicles pain and suffering that may be relatable and potentially triggering. Advanced readers who are also survivors offered these suggestions:

- Tell your support system that you are reading this book so they may help you process it

- Read in small doses

- Pick a time of day to read that won't interfere with your sleep

- Journal, draw, sculpt or do another form of creative expression

- Skip sections that are triggering

- Call the RAINN National Sexual Assault Telephone Hotline (800) 656-HOPE (4673)

- Call the National Suicide Prevention Lifeline (800) 873-TALK (8255)

In Me We Trust:

A Discovery of Self After Sexual Trauma

Anna Gulden

Mental Health Education Press
Seaside, California

Cover design by Valkyri Design (https://valkyri.design)

Printed & distributed by BookBaby (https://www.bookbaby.com/)

Print ISBN: 978-0-96000-510-9
eBook ISBN: 978-0-96000-511-6

Dedicated to

Survivors of sexual violence and those
who love and support them.

Also to my daughter, nieces and nephew.

*May we heal ourselves so that we
heal our communities.*

TABLE OF CONTENTS

LETTER FROM AUTHOR

Dear Readers,

I began writing this story as part of my recovery in July 2016. Writing is something I enjoy, and can be a therapeutic tool. As the words poured out of me onto the computer screen, I wondered if others would find my story helpful. I thought about my frustration when I searched for books about the aftermath of sexual trauma. Don't get me wrong, there are myriad books and resources about sexual trauma and trauma in general. Many focus on early childhood sexual abuse, stranger rape, PTSD due to military service or living through a natural disaster, and self-help or technical guides to recovery. For me, none of these resources helped when I was alone trying to make sense of what I was going through. I needed a story that captured what it is like to live after being raped by a friend.

I attempt to describe in present tense what I went through before I knew I had PTSD, and the healing process I embarked on after planning a suicide attempt. I knew something wasn't right, but I felt isolated, confused and uncertain about what to do about it. I wasn't sure how to begin talking about it with others. The stigma around mental health kept me suffering in silence.

My road to recovery includes adaptive and maladaptive attempts to heal. I've tried illicit drugs, work-a-holism, suicidal ideation, alcohol, and unhealthy relationships to name a few self-destructive methods. I've also engaged in EMDR, Al-anon, individual and group talk therapy, sand tray techniques, spiritual counseling, meditation, yoga, massage therapy, self-defense training, dream groups, medication, Internal Family Systems, Dance/Movement Therapy, art therapy, and an in-patient mental health retreat. A combination of a ten-day in-patient mental health retreat, weekly sessions with a board-certified dance/movement therapist who regularly incorporates Internal Family Systems, bi-weekly massage therapy, meditation groups, daily medication, and a support system with knowledge of PTSD helped me heal. It has taken a commitment to these practices since 2014, a willingness to invest time and financial resources in my healing, and an understanding of neuroplasticity. Knowing that my efforts literally change my brain motivates me to continue my efforts to heal.

I can say with confidence that I am well on the road to recovery. Panic attacks that used to haunt me weekly now occur once or twice a year. The few panic attacks I've had since 2016 last less than ten minutes compared to 30 minutes or more before. I sleep throughout the night now and have little difficulty falling asleep. I haven't had suicidal ideation in two years. I meditate regularly. Most relationships with family and friends have improved. I met an incredible man. I did not sabotage our relationship like I would have in the past. Instead, we've bought a house, started a family and gotten married (in that order). Our relationship continues to grow stronger. Perhaps most importantly, I have learned how to be a leader of the many parts of me through the use of Internal Family Systems. We - I and my Parts - now trust in me to keep us safe and loved.

I have three main objectives in sharing my story.

1. The first is to bring comfort to victims and survivors who may relate to my experiences. You are not alone. You are not crazy. You are not a burden. You are a beautiful human being who has been violated in horrific ways. My story may offer hope for healing. It shows the importance of breaking through stigmas that can silence us. It illustrates what can happen when you are ready to reach out and get help.

2. The second objective is to demonstrate ways in which friends and family of survivors may help on the healing journey. Readers will meet a handful of friends who supported me in a variety of ways. Some gently encouraged me to seek help. Others were there when I was suicidal. Others were there via text message and voicemail, never giving up on me even when I couldn't be there for them. Readers will meet family members who actively engaged in counseling and supported me simply by being physically present to experience daily life. Finally, readers will briefly meet my husband who has become my pillar of strength and love.

3. The third objective is to destigmatize mental health through showcasing the therapeutic process. My story offers guidance for appropriately integrating multiple healing practices. In addition to being a survivor of sexual trauma, I am also a licensed mental health counselor and hold a PhD in a mental health field. I have a strong knowledge base of the ethical standards, legal regulations, counseling theories, helping skills, diagnosis and assessment, therapeutic techniques, and general appropriate behavior that underscore a clinician's work in mental health settings. Perhaps in reading my story, the secrecy that often clouds what happens in a counselor's office may diminish. Whenever possible, readers will also find links to resources related to specific therapeutic techniques, massage therapy, mindfulness and meditation, and other alternative healing practices.

Mental health professionals may find my story insightful, particularly in seeing one way in which PTSD can be treated. For instance, pre-practicum students and graduate interns may find this story useful as they prepare for the practical portion of their training. The Clinical Foundation section and Appendix B may be useful for graduate counseling coursework and mental health practitioner professional development.

Policymakers who read this story may use it as a spring board to learn more about the need to de-stigmatize mental health through policies that support access to on-going, high quality treatment across income levels; and to prevent sexual violence through policies that promote healthy sexual development, social and emotional learning, and adequately punish and rehabilitate perpetrators and those who enable perpetrators by turning a blind eye.

My intention in publishing my story does not include publicly calling out my perpetrators and bystanders. Names and locations of people and places in my story have been changed, including my own, to protect the anonymity of those involved. I wish no harm to anyone.

I do not intend to promote these techniques and activities as the *only* way to heal from sexual trauma. My story is simply a story of one white, heterosexual, cisgender woman's recovery. It is not the only way, or even the most effective way for a survivor of sexual trauma to engage in healing. The techniques and activities described in this book may not work for everyone.

I am a qualitative researcher by training and at heart. I applied heuristic inquiry[1] to the writing and editing process and incorporated trustworthiness strategies[2] to build credibility of my story. Data sources included my personal journals, notes from my therapist and massage therapist, binders from the mental health and dream retreats, a review of the timeline with family and friends, relevant books and online resources. To check for accuracy of the events and therapeutic interventions, adequate anonymity and relevance to my objectives

---

1 Heuristic Inquiry is a qualitative research method pioneered by Dr. Clark Moustakas, a psychologist. It is based on introspection of the researcher to focus on an area of personal interest, puzzlement or challenge. I did not go through institutional review, which is required by law for research using human subjects, so this memoir is not formal heuristic inquiry research.

2 For a review of trustworthiness strategies in qualitative research please read "Qualitative Inquiry in Clinical and Educational Settings" by Drs. Danica G. Hays and Anneliese A. Singh.

noted above, I asked family and friends who know me and many of whom are survivors of sexual violence; my therapist; massage therapist; the founder of Internal Family Systems; and mental health students, educators and practitioners to read and provide feedback on the manuscript.

In total, 16 people gave feedback that informed the final manuscript. Readers will see footnotes throughout each chapter that capture most of their feedback. The Clinical Foundations section took shape based on their feedback. Reflection boxes were added at the end of each chapter in printed copies based on feedback about the emotional response these readers had while absorbing my story. The epilogue was added based on their feedback.

Please read with caution as I include details of my sexual trauma, as well as details of suicidal ideation, anxiety, panic attacks, flashbacks, re-enactments and triggers. For readers who do not like profanity, please be advised the words shit, fuck and asshole are used to tell my story.

I hope my story helps you recognize that you are not alone. You matter. There is hope.

Much love,
Anna

FOREWORD
FROM MY THERAPIST

This book was written with the highest of intentions. As the therapist engaged in the healing process of Anna, the author, I have been the witness of this remarkable journey into the shadows and back again. I have been very curious of late what it is exactly that entails the shift into recovery from trauma. As I watched this shift occur in Anna, I wanted to be extra focused and observant, so that I could use this information to help other clients and to give them hope. Healing from trauma can feel like a war.

It turns out, writing this book was one of the main components in her shift into release from her symptoms. The Internal Family Systems (IFS) work we did, paired with Dance/Movement Therapy interventions, along with applying concrete coping skills to sooth herself, and just plain telling her story with caring audience, as a combined whole, seemed to have the most profound impact on her ability to come back to Self. Writing this book seemed to be a way of organizing her thoughts around the various components to make sense of what was happening to her internally. This kind of cognitive shift is essential in healing the brain, and is what we are referring to, at least in part, when we talk about neuroplasticity. I witnessed a profound shift in her ability to manage her memories, her life, her psyche, and to enjoy her marriage, her baby, and herself as a human being. Anna is now thriving, no longer afraid of her outer and inner lives.

But this shift was not Anna's main intention in writing this book for publication. She was so moved by the changes she was experiencing that she decided to share this experience so that others suffering the devastating symptoms of sexual abuse would know that there is a way out. She wanted to share her map of recovery, which is so deeply personal, so that others would know there is indeed a way out to the other side and life can be enjoyed again.

I want to emphasize the personal aspect of this map. Anna knew she wanted to do body-based therapy. She was experiencing somatic symptoms and sought out a therapist who could work with her in this way. The specific combination of models we used were carefully chosen with curiosity and openness. Any journey of recovery will require this kind of attention to what works and what does not work. Anna has been very sensitive to this as she has shared her story. Her way out might not be everyone's way out, as any therapist worth their salt will tell you. And they will adjust their skill base appropriately. This may be the main ingredient in her story of recovery. Yes, these methods are highly effective, but we came in and out of how we used them with her specific needs in mind and remained very communicative with one another about their efficacy in each moment. And yet, in terms of evidence-based practices, we do know at this point, that using embodied work combined with a model shown to be effective for trauma, will have the most impact. We were both excited about her sharing her story so that clients, clinicians, and loved ones alike, would have a resource of hope, inspiration, and some direction, in understanding that recovery from the trauma of sexual abuse is indeed possible.

I want to emphatically state that a skill base in trauma work is essential for any therapist thinking of embarking on this journey with clients. I have had teachers with great integrity and scholarship, clinical directors, and supervisors, who taught me what they knew with the same emphasis. As therapists, we are entering a world fraught with pain. Deep caring about this suffering partnered with a honed skill base are two essential ingredients for any therapist interested in doing this work. You must be able to tolerate the level of emotions that will erupt and understand that this is not personal. It's part of the recovery process. I like to warn my clients ahead of time that this may feel like a war and there may be times when they resent me for embarking on this road with them…and that this is normal for the process and we will traverse it together. I will be with them every step of the way. They may come to therapy angry and resistant or just cancel altogether. I have a great deal of necessary respect for this part of the process. And I was in constant awe at Anna's courage and commitment.

She was determined to get through to the other side. She told me how she felt every step of the way, which made her unusually brave and able to face whatever blockage came up. It is also necessary to have great respect for the walls that are there. They are there for good reason. We must love them as well, as painful as they may be to face. I have found that IFS work is especially helpful in understanding this and remaining present. It gives the therapist a place to rest, i.e. in Self, when the painful stuck places appear. Then we can both listen carefully and move forward only when it is time to do so.

I am so moved by Anna and her recovery. I am so honored to write this foreword and be able to share in the joy of her recovery, and to hopefully inspire others who are suffering to take that journey back to Self. The Self is in there awaiting your return with a loving cushion to land in. And your Parts will be very relieved to be seen and understood. You get to have You back again. What a wonder.

With Great Love and Great Respect,
Jennifer

CLINICAL FOUNDATION*

This section grounds my story from a clinical mental health standpoint. I've attempted to use language, charts and tables that bridge clinical knowledge to non-clinically trained readers. It includes definitions of key terms to which readers may refer back. I've bolded the Post Traumatic Stress Disorder diagnostic criteria that readers will see in action beginning with the Prologue. A chart and table show readers how I perceive changes to interventions that helped me cope with trauma since January 2002 when I was raped by a friend. Finally, I include a table that lists the characters in my story and summarizes ways in which they supported me throughout my recovery.

Readers who are not interested in the clinical underpinnings of my story may skip this section.

Definition of Key Terms & Treatments*

Unless otherwise noted, these definitions are based on the author's experience, knowledge gained from professional training and personal beliefs.

Active Consent	All persons involved in a sexual interaction say "yes" based on their exacting desire to participate. In other words, they do not say "yes" because they are forced, coerced, manipulated or in any other way are obligated to say "yes" against their will.

Cisgender	A person's gender identity matches the biological sex with which they were born. In other words, I was born with a vagina and I identify my gender as female. My experience with sexual trauma, treatment and recovery may be different than transgender, gender queer and other non-normative gender identities because systems like healthcare are set up by and for cisgender people. Cisgender people do not have to contend with stereotypes, prejudice and discrimination that likely complicate trauma treatment and recovery for non-gender normative people.
Clinician	A professional title for people who have specialized training in an area, such as mental health, psychology or massage.
Consent	All persons involved in a sexual interaction agree to it, preferably with active consent. A person may change their consent at any time during a sexual interaction.
Counselor	A protected professional title for someone who meets state board requirements to practice counseling. In California, the complete protected professional titles include, but are not limited to Licensed Professional Clinical Counselor (LPCC), Licensed Marriage and Family Therapists (LMFT), Licensed Clinical Social Workers (LCSW), and Licensed Clinical Psychologists. See also therapist.

Destigmatization	Efforts to breakdown stigmas such as through education and awareness campaigns, changes in policy, and confronting stereotypes, prejudice and discrimination.
Dissociation	A sense of leaving one's body. Could be described as floating and/or watching one's self on a movie screen in real time.
Heterosexual	A person's sexual orientation when they are attracted to the opposite sex from a binary standpoint. In other words, I am a woman attracted to men. As a heterosexual person, I do not have to contend with stereotypes, prejudice and discrimination that may complicate recovery from sexual trauma for Lesbian, Bisexual, Gay, Queer, Questioning and other non-hetero sexual orientations.
Intervention	In this story, the term intervention is a general category that may consist of a variety of treatments and activities. Interventions include professional and non-professional activities.
Neuroplasticity	The brain's ability to build new neurological nets and pathways. In other words, the ability to change the way a brain is wired.
Non-consent	When any person involved in a sexual interaction says "no" and/or is incapacitated and cannot consent.

Objectification	A person is perceived as an object devoid of emotions, feelings, intellect, spirit and all the beauty that comes with being human. In this story, objectification is based on a human becoming an object for sexual satiation.
Panic Attack	A physiological response that involves flooding your bodily systems with stress hormones, such as cortisol, adrenaline, and nor-adrenaline. It could include shortness of breath, paralysis, loss of sense of safety, blurry vision, and dry mouth. It could be invoked by environmental triggers that are real or perceived threats to survival.
Passive Consent	When any person involved in a sexual interaction consents without saying "yes" or "no." A person may go along with a sexual interaction without actually wanting to.
Posttraumatic Stress Disorder	Mental illness with diagnostic criteria in the DSM-5. See the next page of this book for more detail.
Rape	The Center for Disease Control (CDC) defines rape as a subset of sexual assault when oral, anal, and/or vaginal penetration occurs without consent through the use of force, threat of bodily harm, coercion, manipulation, or when incapacitated and unable to give consent.

Rape Culture	Values, norms, beliefs and behaviors that reinforce, perpetuate, and influence sexual violence. Rape culture may be promoted actively, such as using language that condones and encourages sexual violence; and, passively such as by turning a blind eye and remaining silent when confronted with sexually violent language and behavior.
Sexual Assault	The United States Department of Justice defines sexual assault as any nonconsensual sexual act proscribed by Federal, tribal or state law, including when the victim lacks capacity to consent.
Sexual Harassment	Any sexual advance that is unwelcome, such as requests for sexual favors and other verbal or physical conduct of a sexual nature.
Sexual Trauma	One or more sexual violations that result in significant distress (Yuan, Koss & Stone, 2006). Sexual violations could include rape, sexual assault and sexual harassment experienced directly or witnessed.

Sexual Violence	The CDC states sexual violence is any completed or attempted contact between the penis and the vulva or the penis and the anus involving penetration; contact between the mouth and the penis, vulva or anus; penetration of the anus or genital opening by penis, finger, or object and intentional touching of the genitalia, anus, groin, breast, inner thigh or buttocks. The CDC also includes non-contact acts such as voyeurism and verbal and behavioral sexual harassment.
Stigma	Negative, harmful, misguided beliefs about something that causes shame and secrecy. Mental health stigmas include, but are not limited to being labeled crazy if you have a mental illness, shrinking your mind by going to see a "shrink," and extreme selfishness when one takes their own life.
Suicide	Ending one's own life; killing oneself.
Suicidal Ideation	Thinking about ending one's life including, but not limited to making plans to kill oneself.
Survivor	A person who survives an act of violence, such as rape.
Therapist	A professional title that implies specialized training in a field of study. For instance, massage therapist, physical therapist, speech therapist, or marriage and family therapist.

Treatment	For the purpose of this story, a treatment falls under the umbrella of an intervention. For instance, an intervention may be medication and the treatment may be a specific type of medication like an antidepressant.
Victim	A person who was violated in a criminal act committed by another person or persons.
White	A racial identity. In the United States, all systems were designed to privilege and benefit White People at the expense of the safety, dignity and humanity of People of Color. As a White person, I do not have to contend with stereotypes, prejudice and discrimination that People of Color may experience when seeking access to quality mental healthcare.

309.81: Posttraumatic Stress Disorder*

*I've **bolded** the diagnostic criteria that I experienced after being raped by a friend. A quick glance at the amount of **bold text** indicates my distress, pain and suffering.*

Diagnostic Criteria: The following criteria apply to *adults, adolescents, and children older than age 6 years.*

1. ***Exposure to actual or threatened death**, serious injury, or **sexual violence** in one or more* of the following ways: **Directly experiencing the event**; witnessing, in person, the event happening to others; **learning that the event happened to a close family member or close friend** (for actual or threatened death, the event must be violent or accidental); and/ or experiencing repeated or extreme exposure to details of such an event (the latter does not apply to exposure through electronic media, TV, movies, or pictures, unless it is work related).

2. *After* the traumatic event, the **person exhibits new (or worsening) symptoms** from *each* of the following four clusters:

 a. *One or more intrusion symptoms:* (1) **Recurrent, involuntary, and intrusive upsetting memories of the event** (in children older than age 6, there may be repetitive play related to the event); (2) **recurrent upsetting dreams related to the event** (in children, there may be frightening dreams without recognizable content; (3) **dissociative reactions (e.g., flashbacks) in which the person feels or acts as if the event were recurring** (in children, reenactment may occur in play); (4) **intense or prolonged psychological distress when exposed to internal or external cues that symbolize or resemble an aspect of the event**; and/or (5) **intense physiological reactions to internal or external cues that symbolize or resemble an aspect of the event.**

 b. *Persistent avoidance of stimuli* associated with the event as demonstrated by *one or both* of the following: **Avoidance of, or efforts to avoid, upsetting memories, thoughts, or feelings about or closely related to the event**; and/or **avoidance of, or efforts to avoid, external reminders that trigger upsetting memories, thoughts, or feelings about or closely related to the event.**

 c. *Negative changes in cognitions and mood* associated with the event as demonstrated by *two or more* of the following: (1) Inability to remember an important aspect of the event (usually due to dissociative amnesia rather than head injury, alcohol, or drugs); (2) **persistent, exaggerated negative beliefs or expectations about self, others, or the world**; (3) persistent, distorted cognitions about the cause or consequences of the event that lead to blaming self or others; (4) **persistent negative emotional state (e.g., fear, anger, guilt, shame)**; (5) markedly reduced interest or participation in significant activities; (6) **feelings of detachment or estrangement from others**; and/or (7) persistent inability to experience positive emotions.

d. *Marked changes in arousal and reactivity* associated with the event as demonstrated by *two or more* of the following: (1) **irritable behavior and angry outbursts (with little or no provocation) often expressed as verbal or physical aggression toward people or things**; (2) **reckless or self-destructive behavior**; (3) **hypervigilance**; (4) **exaggerated startle response**; (5) **problems with concentration**; and/or (6) **sleep disturbance.**

3. **The duration of the disturbance is** *more than 1 month.*

4. **The disturbance causes clinically significant distress or impairment in important areas of functioning and is not attributable to the**

psychological effects of a substance or another medical condition.

The following specifiers may apply when diagnosing *adults, adolescents,* or *children of any age.*

Specify whether: *With dissociative symptoms*- in addition to meeting criteria for PTSD, the person experiences persistent or recurrent symptoms of either of the following in response to the traumatic event:

1. *Depersonalization:* **Feeling detached from and like an observer of one's body or mental processes (e.g., feeling as though one is in a dream, feeling a sense of unreality of self or body or of time moving slowly).**

2. *Derealization:* **Feeling as though one's surroundings are unreal, dreamlike, distant, or distorted.**

Note: Dissociative symptoms must not be attributable to the physiological effects of a substance (e.g., blackouts) or another medical condition.

Specify if: *With delayed expression* (full diagnostic criteria are not met until at least 6 months after the event, although onset of some symptoms may be immediate).

Note: Comprehensive evaluation of PTSD must include assessment of cultural concepts of distress.

Reference

American Psychiatric Association. (2013). *Diagnostic and statistical manual of mental disorders* (5th ed.). Washington, DC: Author.

> *Author note*: Criteria for children ages 6 and younger were omitted as they do not pertain to this story.

Intervention Change Over Time

I've thought a lot about how to explain my recovery efforts in a way that makes sense to people who are unfamiliar with mental health. Consider this analogy: When you have allergies (or several other physical health ailments), you may go to the pharmacy for Claritin, Zyrtec, Benadryl or other types of allergy medicine. They consist of different ingredients.

I think of my recovery efforts in a similar way. In Chart 1, each column is like a pill. Within each pill, there are a variety of ingredients indicated by different shades. The ingredients are interventions. Over time, the dosage of those ingredients changed. Instead of pills treating my allergy symptoms with different ingredients, the "pills" shown in Chart 1 reflect a time period when my PTSD symptoms were treated with different doses of interventions.

The first "pill" represents interventions from January 2002 when I was raped until June 2014 when I considered attempting suicide (i.e., Prologue thru Chapter 7). The second "pill" represents interventions from July 2014 to February 2015 when I lived with my dad and step-mom and began regular, sustained trauma recovery efforts (i.e., Chapters 8 thru 21). The third "pill" represents interventions from March 2015 when I moved into my own apartment to present day (i.e., Chapter 22 thru Epilogue).

Chart 1. Comparison of the Change in Intervention Dosage Over Time

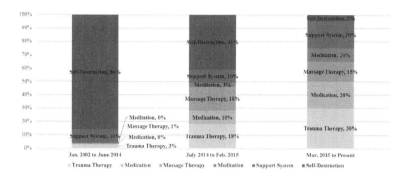

This chart comparison is based on my own self-report data. In counseling, client self-report is an important measure of progress, or lack thereof. I identified interventions that I use regularly for the specific intention of trauma recovery. For instance, Trauma Therapy includes individual and group counseling, a dreamt retreat and an in-patient program. Meditation includes self-guided and group experiences. I purposefully placed trauma therapy and medication on the bottom to represent the foundation of my healing. Self-Destruction is on the top because these activities can crush other interventions. Massage therapy, meditation and support system interventions grow out of trauma therapy and medication while keeping self-destruction at bay. *All interventions are necessary for me to thrive in my daily life.* Table 1 summarizes these interventions.

I grappled with including exercise and spirituality as separate interventions, which are important to me and are known to protect against mental health challenges. I decided not to include those separately because I don't engage in them with the expressed purpose of trauma recovery. Furthermore, exercise became a trigger at one point during my recovery. Feeling out of breath during a jog reminded me of being suffocated by pillows during my rape. Exercise as a trigger could be categorized under self-destruction.

The percentages in Chart 1 reflect my perspective about the doses of each intervention I regularly employed to live with PTSD. In other words, how much self-destruction was I using to cope with PTSD during a given timeframe? How much trauma therapy and medication did I use to cope with and heal from PTSD during a given timeframe? Obviously, these percentages are not an exact science. They accurately reflect my perception of changes in interventions to heal from sexual trauma.

I also want to point out that the interventions represented by different shades imply that they are separate from one another. This chart comparison works for the purpose of portraying an at-a-glance picture of what changed in my trauma recovery efforts. It does not work to show how the interventions are connected. The intentional coordination to integrate these interventions continues to be crucial to my recovery. This integration between interventions is described throughout the chapters of this book.

There are many important conclusions from this comparison. First, I survived because and in spite of my self-destruction from 2002 to 2014. I want to be clear that while self-destruction is dangerous, it cannot only be viewed as "bad" or "wrong." For instance, work-a-holism kept me pursuing advanced degrees and professional opportunities that gave me a daily purpose. Cigarettes gave me a reason to go outside and get fresh air when I started feeling panicky. Second, over time I've learned how to integrate healthy, life promoting activities in place of many self-destructing ones. I've developed strong and lasting relationships in my support system that help me maintain my recovery efforts. Third, while trauma therapy continues to be the highest dosage, the other interventions are just as important. They simply aren't employed as frequently to specifically address trauma recovery. Again, I need *all* of these interventions to thrive in my daily life. Finally, healing takes time. At the time of publication, 16 years has passed since I was raped. I've actively engaged in recovery for 4 years and counting.

Table 1: A Description of Interventions Displayed in the Chart 1

Intervention	Column 1: Jan. 2002 to June 2014	Columns 2 & 3: July 2014 to Present
Trauma Therapy	• Approximately 64 hours including: • EMDR • Self-defense class • CBT • Dreams groups	• 308 hours at time of publication including: • 10-day in-patient mental health retreat • weekly sessions with board certified dance/ movement therapist, Ph.D. in clinical psychology, trained in Internal Family Systems and has a Canine Good Citizen

Medication	None	Daily 50 milligrams of Sertraline (generic for Zoloft) from September 2014 to October 2015 and March 2016 to September 2016; 25 milligrams from September 2016 to present.
Massage Therapy	Infrequent sessions with different massage therapists	• 3 90-minute sessions with massage therapists trained in trauma recovery at mental health retreat • Bi-weekly or monthly 90-minute sessions with the same massage therapist from September 2014 to March 2017; as needed to present

Meditation	Found meditations on YouTube, iTunes and Podcasts to assist in sleep	• 2 4-week groups lead by licensed practitioner certified in Hakomi and Mindfulness-based Stress Reduction • 2 4-week introductory and 3 weekly advanced groups lead by certified clairvoyant facilitator • Weekly self-guided practice for connection to inner child • Daily self-guided practice for pregnant women while pregnant • Sleep meditations as needed
Support System	• Limited to a few close friends and sister, none of whom had formal training, education or understanding of trauma and trauma recovery • I did not utilize support with the intention to assist in trauma recovery	• Expanded to include everyone in my immediate family, a few extended family, and close friends • Support system attended counseling sessions to learn about PTSD and trauma recovery • I learned how to utilize support system with the intention of assisting in trauma recovery

Self-Destruction	Main form of coping with trauma was through the use of illicit drugs, binge drinking, cigarettes, work-a-holism, nail-biting, avoidance, re-enactments, unhealthy relationships, rage and suicidal ideation	• Stopped engaging in most self-destruction activities with the exception of cigarettes and alcohol. • Smoked cigarettes until July 2016 • Abstained from alcohol while pregnant and breast-feeding • Today, alcohol and the occasional nail-biting persist.

Summary of Support People
in Alphabetical Order

Support Person	Relationship to Me	Years in My Life
Ben	Step-Dad; Family	25
Camille	Friend; mental health retreat	4
Catherine	Friend; master's degree	15
Charlie	Dad; Family	39
Dusty	Friend; mental health retreat	4
Elizabeth	Friend; kindergarten	34
Frank	Husband; Family	3
Franz	Brother-in-law; Family	16
Grandma Ophelia	Maternal mom; Family	39 (15 years in memory/spirit)
Grandma G	Paternal step-mom; Family	37
Jennifer	Board-Certified Dance/ Movement Therapist	4

Kate	Cousin; Family	30
Lindsey	Step-mom; Family	15
Melanie	Mom; Family	39
Pansy	Canine Good Citizen Dog	4
Phora	Massage Therapist	4
Samantha	Friend; doctoral program	8
Sasha	Friend; mental health retreat	4
Tessa	Aunt; Family	39
Violet	Sister; Family	37

Characteristics of Support People

Open-minded * Willing to shift perspective about masculinity, oppression, patriarchy, sexism * Common experiences with mental health challenges and recovery * Available via text message, phone, video, social media and in-person * Encouragement * Willing to be wrong * Willing to learn and change * Don't give up * Initiate difficult·conversations * Observe & share when my behavior seems off * Don't take personal when I can't be there like usual * Have fun * Don't always dwell on PTSD * Acknowledge the anniversary of my rape * Acknowledge other potentially-triggering events * Willing to step outside of your comfort zone * Financial assistance * Bring me dinner * Celebrate milestones * Go for hikes * Advocate for me with people who don't believe me * Go to meditation groups with me * Unconditional love * Give reassurance and encouragement * Acknowledge ways you've seen me change for the better * Act as my litmus test to help me recalibrate experiencing danger * Give me the benefit of the doubt when I'm not being myself * Build me a pillow fort * Know yourself * Be a safe and trustworthy person * Forgive * Help with crisis response * Dance * Laugh * Give hugs * Create art with me * See Me first and not sexual violence or PTSD * Compassion * Say sorry * Gratitude * Offer to hear about sexual violence & PTSD without pushing for details * Stay calm * Find resources for healthy living * Have patience * Empathy * Adaptable * Keep me connected to how life could be * Remind me who I am

PROLOGUE: 2007

My eyes are closed. They move from left to right to left to right following the beep. Images emerge. *The brown wood furniture. The streetlight through the microblinds. The red clock numbers reflecting in the vanity mirror. A musty salt-air smell, like all ocean apartments.*

My heart starts racing. My fingers clinch. *STOP.* My mind screams. Eyes bolt open. Blink a few times. Pause the beeps.

"You're o.k. You are in my office. Describe what happened." My therapist's gentle voice brings me back to the present. I take a deep breath and walk through what happened in that round of EMDR[3].

"Are you ready to go back in?" she asks.

I nod.

"Take a deep breath. When you are ready close your eyes. Start the beeps. Try to pick up the imagery where you left off. Open your eyes when the memory gets too intense."

---

3 EMDR stands for Eye Movement Desensitization and Reprocessing and was discovered by Dr. Francine Shapiro in 1987. Research supports the efficacy of EMDR in trauma treatment. Visit www.emdria.site-ym.com.

I'm back in my room. I see the brown dresser with the vanity to my left. The tall brown dresser to my right. I'm asleep in the double bed on the side closest to the door. He is next to me. Now I'm face down. He's pulling my drawstring gray pants down. Now my underwear. I can't breathe. Why can't I breathe? Something is thrusting inside me. My vagina screams as it tears. I'm disoriented. Why can't I breathe? Suddenly my lungs force me to turn my head. I gulp in musty salty air. WHAT THE FUCK I say out loud. Blackness. Nothing. The sun through the blinds. I reach for my pants. They are up, but not tied. He sleeps next to me.

My heart races. Fear tingles through my body. Palms sweat. I open my eyes and pause the beeps. My breathing is shallow. My whole body is tense. That's the most remembering I've done.

"You are o.k. You are in my office. Describe what happened." After I recall the details, my therapist asks, "Where were you in the room?"

"I was floating in the doorway into my old bedroom looking down on the bed."

"If you could tell her anything, what would you tell her?"

I begin to cry without sound. "I'd tell her 'you are not alone.' And then I'd go to her and hold her hand through it all."

Reflections ∞ Reactions ∞ Responses

_____

_____

_____

BEFORE THE RAPE

RAINN stands for Rape, Abuse & Incest National Network. RAINN operates the National Sexual Assault Hotline (800.656.HOPE), collects data to inform policy and action, and engages in preventive programing.

According to RAINN, 15% of rape victims were 12 to 17 years old and 54% were 18 to 34 years old. Also, most rapes are perpetrated by someone known to the victim. In my case, I met the man who raped me when I was 14 years old. I was raped at 22 years old. These ages fall within the lifespan when 69% of rapes occur.

CHAPTER 1

THE RAPIST & ME IN 1997

Senior year is almost over. My high school buzzes with prom, college acceptances, and summer plans. I look forward to leaving Santa Maria, a small agriculture town in California for some place totally different.

I've been accepted to my top three schools: Georgetown, University of Washington aka U-Dub, and Cal Berkeley. Berkeley is closest to home and one of my best friends is going there. But after visiting with my step-mom, Lindsey, last week, I realize the Bay Area is not the place for me.

Never one to make a decision easily, I fret over Georgetown and U-Dub for a few days. The deadline to accept an offer is around the corner. My dad, Charlie, took me on a college tour trip last year during spring break. Washington DC and Seattle are cities where I can see myself living. But making this decision without input from my mom just doesn't feel right. My mom, Melanie, knows me best. After she and Dad separated in 1986, my sister and I lived primarily with her. We live on a fixed income because she decided not to return to work following their divorce.

I walk down the hallway from my room to the living room where Mom sits folding laundry. "Mom," I call before reaching the living room. "I have a question. I feel bad about asking, but I'm going to anyway. Do you think you can go with me to see U-Dub and Georgetown? I know last minute airfare will be expensive. I just can't make this decision without you. I don't know where I am going to fit in best." I feel bad asking her because we've already talked about using financial aid for her portion of college tuition.

She sighs and looks down at the laundry basket. "I'll see what I can do Anna. I want to see where my first baby is off to." She looks up with a sad smile on her face. She's trying to not show me her stress over finances.

∞∞∞

A few weeks later we're on our way to Washington DC with an extended layover in Seattle. Evan, a friend from home, is finishing his second year at U-Dub. He has always been like a big brother to me. Some of our friends dated him or hooked up with him, but I've never been attracted to him in that way. He is going to show Mom and me around campus and have dinner with us at a popular restaurant nearby. He threw wild parties in high school and was always the life of the party, so I'm sure he will give us the inside scoop on the social life at U-Dub.

A short visit to Seattle, tour of the campus, and great pizza at a local college hang out with Evan is enough for me. I can't see myself living there for 4 years. Plus the idea of rain most of the time does not suit me.

I fret. "What if I don't like DC either, Mom?" I watch rain pelt the window of our airplane readying for takeoff.

"Well, you have acceptances from four other schools. You can go to the community college for a year. You have options." She always reminds me that I'm not trapped.

"But I have to get away from Santa Maria. I want to see the world. I'm tired of how gross all those produce men are. I just have to like Georgetown."

I shake my head as my mind recalls all the times I've felt uncomfortable around my dad and his friends. They are so vulgar. And going to their offices makes me gag because the secretaries are all women and the managers are all men. Not to mention my dad and all his friends grew up in Santa Maria, too, like their parents. Their maturity is the same as the guys at my high school. I mean, I learned the hand gesture for cunnilingus when dad flashed it to his crony at work while talking about what he did the night before with his then girlfriend. So gross. I feel suffocated by it all.

Somewhere over Illinois, I silently talk with my mom's mom. *Please, please, please let me like DC. Let Georgetown be the place for me. Let Mom like it, too.* Even though she died 4 years ago, I know Grandma still listens to me.

It's late when we arrive at Dulles International Airport and catch a cab to our bed and breakfast. I can't sleep. Mom's snores and sneezes interrupt my racing mind. *Will I like it?* Sneeze. *I hope I like it.* Snore. *I have to get away.* Sneeze. She is allergic to something in our room. *Thank God we are only staying two nights.*

"Annie, get up. We have to get breakfast and head to campus." I must have fallen asleep at some point.

"Mom, you snored and sneezed all night." I groggily roll out of bed.

"I know. I'm sorry honey." We smile at each other in the mirror as we brush our teeth.

The moment I step foot on campus, I know Georgetown is the place for me. Mom goes with other parents to a morning session while I join other accepted seniors facing the same decision. I ask questions like where do we do laundry? And do you have retreat programs for students? Others ask about nightlife, athletics, housing options, the gym, favorite professors, and registering for class. I feel at home.

At lunch, we rejoin our parents. I see Mom walking up the stairs. "Mom, Mom, I love it here. I want to go here. I just know in my gut this is the place for me." Excitement bubbles in my voice.

Her face erupts in a smile. "Really Annie? You feel like this is the place for you?"

"YES."

"That is so great. I like it, too. I can see you here."

Later that night, we recount details of our day. We crack up over the lady from Rhode Island in the perfect polk-a-dot dress who was shocked that Georgetown students drink alcohol before they turn 21.

Mom imitates her New England accent. "'My son does not drink and we don't want him in an environment that allows it.' I mean really. Are there college students anywhere that don't at least try a beer once before turning 21? And she was dressed perfectly to the nines."

Suddenly, Mom gets serious. "Annie, I know you've had drinks at high school parties. We've talked about how alcohol ruined my marriage. I just want you to be safe. Don't walk alone in this big city. When you do drink, use the buddy system. Stay together with your friends. I'm scared about you coming all this way, but I know you have a good head on your shoulders. I know you are responsible and you don't let a party get in the way of your commitments. Just be safe when you go to parties here." She reaches out to give me a hug. "You are my first baby and I don't want anything to happen to you."

∞∞∞

Back home, I excitedly share my big decision with Dad. We're sitting around the island at his and Lindsey's house.

He looks down, a hint of sadness in his eyes. "You know if you want to get away from us you can go to the University of Soledad and we promise we won't bother you."

Soledad is a small farming community north of Santa Maria. We drive through it when we visit my grandparents. It is the home of a high security prison, not a university. I don't think it even has a community college. Why would he say that? I wonder. It dawns on me that he's trying to say he wants me closer, not that he wants me in prison.

"DA-aad. You know how much I want to get out of this town and go someplace totally new. You took me to DC in the first place last year. Please be happy for me." I try to tone down my desperation for his approval.

"I know A," he said. "It's just that DC is so far. I didn't think you'd actually go."

I remind him that he always preaches about dreaming big and taking risks. Don't let fear of the unknown get in the way of going places.

His eyes twinkle when he looks up at me. "And don't forget that your academics should not get in the way of your college education." He and mom are so opposite. "I'm really proud of you A and happy for you. It was your reach school. Plus, DC has great international cuisine and will be fun to visit."

"Much better than visiting the prison," I say.

He looks at me quizzically and breaks into laughter. "Yes, that wasn't the best metaphor. I should have said Cal Poly in San Luis Obispo instead of University of Soledad. I don't think there is even a college in Soledad."

I chuckle and pat his arm. "I know what you meant Dad. It took me a second, but I figured it out."

Reflections ∞ Reactions ∞ Responses

_____

_____

_____

RESISTING HELP

About 2 out of 3 sexual assaults go unreported, which could mean victims suffer alone; despite 70% of rape and sexual assault victims who experience moderate to severe distress, a larger percentage than for any other violent crime (www.rainn.org/statistics/victims-sexual -violence, 2018).

I did not report my rape to police. Nor did I seek professional help for about five years[4].

---

4 An advanced reader suggested including statistics about perpetrators resisting and seeking help. My story is not focused on perpetrator recovery, but I did briefly search for related information. I did not come across specific statistics. I found information about sex offender treatment. Visit www.stopitnow.org and www.atsa.com.

CHAPTER 2

NIGHTMARES AND FLASHBACKS 4 YEARS AFTER BEING RAPED

Why are these dreams happening again? My breath is shallow. The morning summer sun peers through the blinds. My eyes are puffy. My body aches. I am not rested.

Downstairs I hear Jessica making breakfast. We worked together as in residential life at a public university this past academic year. Jessica's position was interim and ended when spring quarter came to a close. Our compensation package includes housing, so she had to move out of her apartment when her contract ended. She is staying with me for a few weeks this summer before moving to a new city and job. My accommodation is a two-bedroom, two-bath townhouse. My bedroom overlooks a small canyon surrounded by eucalyptus trees. The front door is directly under the balcony, which means the back of the house is closer to my office and the residence halls. It is one of the most coveted housing units on campus for live-on staff because of the privacy due to the canyon and trees.

Reluctantly, I head downstairs and ask her if I did that sleep walk thing again. I knew she'd say yes.

"You didn't leave your room, but I heard your door slam a few times. It sounded like you were trying to keep someone out." She hands me some toast and a cup of coffee.

I sip coffee and the nightmare floods my mind. A man dressed all in black without a soul trying to get in my room. I slam the door repeatedly to keep him out. I shake my head because it's so real, as if that man was really in our house at my bedroom door last night.

"Was it the same one?" she asks. "It seems like you're having these nightmares more and more often."

"I know. Two nights ago I dreamt that I was walking home around the front of our house. Instead of mulch, the ground was covered in bright green grass and there was a small tree without any leaves. Scattered around the grass and hanging from the branches were dead horses. They were perfectly butchered into parts with their skin, muscles, hair, eyes…everything still intact. But they were cut in chunks. My heart started racing and I was scared. I wanted to turn and run, but I couldn't stop walking towards them. I had to get to our front door. It was dusk. The sunlight was dim." I shudder. "What do you think that means? I'm honestly not sure."

She looks at me with care and concern. "Honestly, do you think it's time to talk to someone about your sexual assault? Like a professional?"

"No," I say dismissively. "I already took care of that in grad school last year. I told you. We had to write papers and go to 15 hours of our own counseling. I've dealt with it."

My master's degree in counseling required reflection papers, clinical supervision and personal counseling. Those activities were enough to confront issues related to my rape. One class even dedicated a few weeks to the treatment of trauma.

"I know you've said that before. But we had to respond to two sexual assault calls in the last few months and you've been really involved in bystander intervention training[5]. That training is preventative and I know you're passionate about it. But sexual assault is still the focus. Maybe something's been churned up in you." She hasn't pushed this hard for me to seek help before.

I give her a sad smile. "I'll think about it. I'm glad you are sharing your thoughts with me. It's just not something I like to think about." I change the subject. "How's your new place coming along?"

Later that day, I listen to a voicemail from Catherine. We met in August of 2003 during our pre-practicum course for our master's degree. I think about that day we met at a coffee shop after class to study. Instead of studying, we shared about our lives up to that point. She was the first person in my class I disclosed about my rape. At the end of that conversation, her mom called and I'll never forget what Catherine said into the phone while looking directly at me. "Mom, I'm sitting with my new life-long friend Anna. Can I call you back?" I knew she was right about our life-long friendship. Catherine is my friend because she is matter of fact, takes no bull shit, and puts the F-U-N in fun. She is always there, even when she isn't. She moved to northern California after we graduated. Now our conversations take place mainly via voicemail because we are in a perpetual game of phone tag.

I play her voicemail again. "Hey Annie Bananie. So I was driving the other day and Pearl Jam came on. Remember how much we loved listening to Pearl Jam. God those were the days. With Grey's Anatomy. You are my person, just like Meredith and Cristina. Anyway, I also tried a caramel chocolate coffee shake the other day. It was super sweet. I'm not sure you would like it. So how's the job?

---

5 Bystander intervention training started at colleges and universities. It aims to help students learn to intervene when they see sexual assault or other forms of violence in safe and respectful ways. www.stepupprogram.org.

Any news in the love department? Nothing really new here. Just wedding planning. You know…a LOT goes into planning a wedding. So many details. So many. My head is spinning. You would be much better at these details than me. Like when you re-wrote the syllabus for that one professor…which one was that? It was so confusing until you cleaned it up. O.K. going to sign off now. Tag you're it."

I love hearing Catherine's voicemails. They take me back to the first conversation we had in the coffee shop. No matter how much time passes between our in-person meet-ups, we are still in an on-going conversation. I decide to call Catherine and get her input on my nightmares. I think to myself *She probably won't answer. I can't really leave a voicemail that says I have nightmares that cause me to sleep walk…call me back.*

To my surprise, she picks up. "Howdy friend," she quips. "How's it going down there?"

"I can't believe you answered. I thought for sure you'd be rocking a presentation for transfer students or something."

"Well, funny you should say that. I'm walking over to one right now, which is why I could answer."

"O.K. I'll keep this quick." My stomach knots and a wave of nausea passes over me. "I'm having nightmares. A soul-less man without a face, almost a shadow, is trying to get in my room. I sleep walk…literally…and slam my bedroom door open and closed repeatedly according to my friend Jessica who is staying with me right now. She thinks they are about my sexual assault and that maybe I should talk to someone."

Catherine's tone fills with compassion and concern. "Whoa Annie. That is a lot and really scary. I don't think it will hurt for you to talk to a counselor. I wish I had more time to talk with you right now. I could help you find someone if you want."

Sadness in my chest replace the knots in my stomach. "I thought that's what you'd say. I don't know. Am I really ready for that? Do I really need that? I know you have to go. I want to hear about your life and help with the wedding details."

"I'll call you later, I promise. Just think about it. You don't have to make any decision right now." She is calm and firm. Her compassion mixes with the sadness in my chest.

Catherine calls later that evening. I do not want to talk about nightmares, sexual assault and therapy. I also do not want to talk about wedding details. Both topics remind me that I'm damaged and broken…tarnished and weak. Sadness balloons across my body. I wish I could talk about love and weddings. I feel guilty for not being able to express the happiness I feel for her. Happiness is an emotion I have to force myself to feel these days. I don't answer her call.

∞∞∞

A few weeks after Jessica moved out, my sister Violet moved in. She's attending a local university to earn her MBA. I'm happy to have her live with me rent-free while she's in school. Vi is my one solid, steady person in life. She is the only other person who knows what it was like living in our two different houses, shifting between families, dad's girlfriends, and girlfriends' families. We grew even closer during and after college, but haven't lived together since 1997. That year I went to Georgetown, which was five years before my rape.

Since I live and work on campus, my commute is quick. Tonight the brisk October air quickens my pace. I try the slider, but the security bar is down. Grudgingly I walk around to the front of the house. Ever since the horse dream, I avoid the front at all costs.

Tonight I am running late, so I have no choice. Vi is at class and I'm meeting Dad and Lindsey for dinner downtown with some of their friends. They're in town for an annual produce convention. I know the drinks will be flowing, so I decide to take a cab to meet them. Better not to drink and drive. I call Yellow Cab while I quickly change my clothes. The cab arrives in ten minutes.

The familiar racing heart, shallow breath, and sweaty palms increase the closer I am to downtown. I ask myself, *why is this happening?* No answer. I coach myself. *You've done this a million times. You grew up with these people. Dinner downtown is no big deal. You'll be with Dad and Lindsey.* I try to take deep calming breaths. *Seriously, what's wrong with me? Why can't I just get it together? I feel crazy.* My heart pounds as I pay the cab driver and step on the sidewalk. *Maybe I should go home?* I chastise myself. *Don't even think about it. You'll have fun. Besides Dad and Lindsey aren't here very often. Don't be a wimp. You can do this. Put on your happy face. Have fun.* This internal dialogue happens almost every time I go out. It frustrates me because I'm in constant battle with myself to seem normal in social settings. *I used to not have this battle. That was before you-know-what happened to you.*

I stand on the sidewalk in front of Dad and Lindsey's hotel for a brief moment. I look at what I'm wearing. The usual- cute jeans, heels, black shirt that is fitted, but not tight, covers my waistline and hips, and isn't too low, a jacket and scarf. *Not too showy or revealing.* I take a deep breath and push open the lobby door.

I flash a huge grin as soon as I see them. "Hi guys. It's so great to be here with you!" I say with as much exuberance as I can muster.

"Annaaaaaaaa." Dad bear hugs me. "It's so great to see you honey."

"You, too, Dad. Where are we going for dinner?" I make sure to plaster the perfect smile on my face. The one that exudes calm-cool-collected; and that hides my growing distress.

We take the hotel elevator to the pool-side lounge to have a drink while waiting for the rest of our dinner group. Every person who comes by seems to know Dad, per usual. He's been in the produce industry since high school, and before that other family members were well-known in the industry, too. Rumor has it that Evan works in the produce industry now, too.

Dad greets everyone with friendly hellos and small talk. He's in his element. In contrast, every person who comes by seems to quicken my heart beat and shallow my breath. I chastise myself, *what the hell is wrong with me?* Somehow, I manage to keep my calm-cool-collected mask on.

After dinner and several bottles of wine, Dad and Lindsey invite me to go with them to a dance club down the block. A bunch of their produce friends are going.

"Sure, why not? I'm not driving and it's only 10." I'm pretty buzzed, so I don't hear the voice in my head shout *GO HOME* or notice my heart pounding harder.

We continue drinking. Dad and Lindsey introduce me to some customers from South America. One asks me to dance. I love dancing. It's one activity that quiets my mind. I'm not sure how much time has passed. I'm actually enjoying myself.

My dance partner looks directly at me. He moves closer toward me. "Your eyes are beautiful." He tries to kiss me.

All air is sucked from the room. I am caught off guard. My thoughts race. *I don't want to kiss him. Did I send the wrong signal? I thought we were just dancing and having fun.*

"Oh, no thank you." I pull away to look for Dad and Lindsey. "I have to use the bathroom."

I try to look calm-cool-collected as I walk with my head held high to the bathroom. Only my darting eyes give away my increasing panic. They aren't where I left them. They aren't anywhere in sight. I start seeing only men. I can't find the exit. I have to pee.

My mind instructs me. *Get to the bathroom and you will be O.K. Just get to the bathroom.*

As the stall door closes, I burst into tears. *What is wrong with you? Why are you acting like this?* I ask myself repeatedly. I can't breathe. I try to muffle my sobs by covering my mouth tightly with one hand and wiping tears away with the other. At some point, I calm down enough to consider an exit strategy. *Get to the door. You can do this. Once you're outside, you will feel better. You will be able to breathe. The air will be cool. You can catch a cab.*

I wish I could pee forever so I don't have to give up my bathroom stall, but someone is knocking. I take the deepest breaths possible. Pause the tears. I pull out the eye drops I keep in my purse for moments like these to decrease the redness. I blow my nose. At least it's dark in the club. Maybe no one will notice.

Upon exiting the bathroom, the loud room closes in on me. Everyone here is a man with a clown face jumping out at me. Smiling and jeering as I search for the exit. The music pounds so loud. Someone grabs my arm. I shake them off and speed toward the door. I don't look back to see who grabbed me.

"Have a nice evening ma'am." The bouncer does a double take. "Are you o.k.?"

"Yes, I'm fine." I put my head down and keep walking. My lungs gulp up air as if I've been under water and run out of oxygen.

My pulse calms the further I get from the club. The air is cool. Normal city noise surrounds me. *It's time to catch a cab…whoa not that one. That guy has the clown face.* My pulse quickens and my mind races. *What if he's a rapist? He will take you to TJ and gang rape you.* My eyes blur, but not because of tears. They just won't focus. I'm becoming hysterical. *Every cab driver could hurt you. No cabs are safe. You're stuck downtown. Call your Dad. NO, don't call him. He will think something's wrong and wonder why you always have these outbursts. Walk towards his hotel then. At least the lobby is safe.*

The next thing I'm aware of is Violet's familiar voice in my ear. I sit on a bench in the lobby of Dad and Lindsey's hotel. The lighting is really bright. I wish it was dim so I could hide.

"Anna is that you?" Violet's concern jumps through the phone. "What happened? Where are you? I'm coming to get you right now."

Bell captains and front desk clerks ask if I'm O.K.

"Yes. I'm O.K. My sister is coming. Can I wait here?" I can't bring myself to make eye contact.

My inner battle wales on. *This is unbearable. Why is this happening to me? What is wrong with me? I can't hold it together for much longer. Hurry Vi.*

Somehow we are home. I sob hysterically in my bed, as I've done hundreds of nights since January 2002 when I was raped. Snot running down my face at the same rate as my tears. Hiccup breathing. Body tingling. Paralyzed. It's dark. Night lights shine through the blinds.

Tonight is different than all the others. Tonight Violet lies next to me. Her little arms hold me tight, her t-shirt absorbing my hysterics.

"I'm so scared all the time. I just don't know what's wrong with me. I'm petrified to leave the house. You have no idea how afraid I am. It's not like me. I don't understand why this is happening. This is going to kill me. You have to promise you will take care of Mom and Dad for me. You have to make sure they are O.K. I'm crazy. Something is so wrong. I hate all men. All men are violent. All men hate women. All men are rapists. We aren't safe."

Violet's arms never loosen around my body. She holds me. She listens. She tells me that it's O.K. That I'm O.K.

"I'm in so much pain. I don't want to die, but I want this pain gone. Like if I could just cut open my veins, the pain would bleed out. I'm so scared all the time." I try to explain what I go through most nights without frightening her. I really don't want to end my life. The pain is unbearable.

"You are not alone in this Annie." She is calm, yet firm. "I'm here with you now. You are not alone."

I feel myself come back into my body as my hovering view of us evaporates with a deep inhale of Violet's recently laundered shirt drenched in my snot and tears. My eyes focus on her shirt. Suddenly I breathe a normal breath. My legs can move. I feel the bed beneath us. I cling to her. I silently pray. *Thank you for my little sister. Keep her safe.*

Reflections ∞ Reactions ∞ Responses

_____

_____

_____

CHAPTER 3

RAGE IN 2010

My head throbs. My eyes are swollen. I had an outburst last night and my younger cousin took the brunt of it. Kate recently graduated from college. I am ten years older than her. She and her friend are driving with me from the West Coast to my new home on the East Coast. I've accepted an offer to earn a PhD in a mental health field in the South and they're tagging along for their post-graduation adventure. We've decided to drive through the South and stay with locals using the online platform, Couch Surfing. I'd never fathom staying with strangers if I were traveling alone. But we are three. Like Mom said when we visited Georgetown before I accepted the offer to enroll, there is safety in numbers.

Last night in Las Vegas, we went out with our Couch Surfing host. It was great right up to the point when Kate was nowhere to be found. Frantically, I searched the club with her friend. We couldn't find our host either. Our host was older than me, so way older than Kate.

I was really pissed she'd left without telling us. At the same time, I prayed that she actually left and was not in a dark alley passed out with that creep-of-a-host on top of her. My mind points out, *he isn't really a creep though Anna. He even apologized for separating from the group.*

I have only hazy memories of what transpired after we all got home. I'm so ashamed and sad that I did that to Kate and said those things about Aunt Tessa, her mom. It was venomous, hateful, disgust. Rage poured from my body as I yelled at her, packed my belongings and threatened to leave them in Las Vegas. I sat in my car for several hours to sober up enough to drive away. At some point I fell asleep.

Things are understandably awkward between us this morning. I didn't imagine this trip going like this. I apologized immediately when we woke up. Now I'm sitting on a hammock chair in the back yard. They took the car to get coffees and breakfast sandwiches.

My mind continues talking. *The rape creeps up on you, Anna. You have to learn how to control your outbursts. Not every club is bad. Not every older guy is going to take advantage of younger girls. Kate isn't destined to be raped even if she's about the same age as you were. Get it together.*

I'm exhausted. I take deep breaths and adjust myself in the hammock so I can write in my journal[6]. I want to understand why these outbursts happen. I title this entry "Patron & the Buttery Nipple" because Patron is a clear liquid and a Buttery Nipple is a shot that consists of a creamy liquor and butterscotch schnapps. Plus, alcohol is involved in most outbursts, so the title seems fitting. I mainly write in stream-of-consciousness style[7] because I can't formulate complete sentences when reflecting on my emotional state.

---

6 Unless otherwise noted, journal entries were copied directly from my journals including formatting to reflect how I wrote throughout this time period.

7 Stream-of-consciousness style of writing intends to capture flowing thoughts as they occur without a need to write proper sentences, complete thoughts, etc.

Anger
I have to face it
embrace it
understand it
generations of it
Sits somewhere
　　　w/in
locked up
caged
like a racehorse
at the gates
Raging to be
let out
And when it is
It is vicious
biting
attacking
Aimed to hurt
　　　to wound
　　　　　to inflict
　　　　　　　pain
　　　　　　　suffering
It hits w/
the force of
a poisoned arrow
straight in the
heart
Is it envy?
　　　Greed?
　　　Insecurity?
　　　Jealousy?

Right now
I think
Envy
Bitter realization
that my life
isn't as full
as I want
It is half
full
balancing on little old me
I need
a stronger base
Instead of a
      shot of Patron
I need a
      Buttery Nipple
Clear separation
w/ a solid base of
      Baileys &
a clear top half
      Of Schnapps.
Not that I
      need alcohol
But I need
comfort that comes with Baileys (or a glass of milk)
My life is half full
      w/ purpose, change, & empowerment
I need the other half
      love, comfort, security, family
How can I let go of Anger
      once and for all so I
      can let love 100% in?

Exchange a little anger
>For a lot of love.
Patron for Buttery Nipple
I wonder if I start over
…Rewind to 21
My choices might be different
My priorities might have emerged
More balanced
>Looking for independence
>Fulfilling my ambitions
AND
>Looking for love
>Strength in family
I suppose this means
I needed/need to believe
in that kind of love
in order to make it
a priority
Like all my other goals
>Loving & letting love in
The priority of my
>30s
Perhaps Anger comes
from the fear
that accompanies this goal
Rather than the goal
This way of being in the world.
That Patron took away from me.

>I put the pen down and re-read my stream-of-con-
>sciousness. The rapist poisoned me, like too much
>alcohol poisons the body. I recall friendships, romantic

and professional relationships that ended because of this rage, this poison that condemns me to a life without love.

Reflections ∞ Reactions ∞ Responses

_____

_____

_____

CHAPTER 4

CAN'T SLEEP IN 2011

My mind battle is in full effect. It's 1:00AM. I'm in my bed at the apartment I rent while earning my doctorate. I'm a graduate assist, which means I teach one undergraduate course and assist a faculty member with research while carrying a full-time course load. It's a lot, but I like to be busy.

Fuck...it's 1AM. Come on Anna. You need to sleep. You have a long day tomorrow...teaching in the morning and class in the evening. You're safe in this apartment. You and Dad picked it because of the security. No one can break in. It is like Fort Knox. I roll over. But what if someone does break in? Who would hear you? The walls are sound proof. Maybe it's too secure. You'd be left to fend for yourself. It will take Mom, Dad, Lindsey, and everyone at least a day to come ID your body. Violet would have to come from Europe.

I throw the covers off and sit up to turn on the light. I say out loud, "OH MY GOD. Be. Quiet." I know my mind won't be quiet though. Once racing thoughts like these start, they rarely stop on command. With a sigh I reach for my journal on the night stand. *Maybe this will help.*

Sleep is
the most
challenging
part of my day
A battle fought
    every night
Dreaded w/
    each moment
where my physical
being simply
can't continue
    OR
The calls of
tomorrow force
me to bed
because @
least rest
is better than
nothing
Last night
    I
    cried
See, when I close my eyes
there is no
distraction
from the pain
in my mind
There isn't
anything to focus on
except the thoughts
    memories
    playback

fears

guilt

anger

I wish I would haves

or

I wish I could haves

There is no defense

against the

cinema of my pain

my hurt

my sadness

There are always

movie trailers

like checklists of what I have tomorrow

or

deep breathing 2 in 6 out

or

tensing & relaxing each muscle group head to toe & back

or

urging mantras

"Please sleep"

"Mind just shut up"

"Don't do this to me"

Every night The Opening Scene

usually doubt

followed by something

horrible I've done

followed by something horrible

been done to me

inevitably Evan's face comes in

And I imagine my body

lying there lifeless

And I imagine my mom's child
      lying there in pain
And I imagine my dad's child
      crying out in pain
My heart aches for her
      Because she will never know
A product of extreme sexism &
      Male privilege her whole life
      Being undervalued by men
      Therefore never fully developing
Her whole life never knowing or
      Believing that she deserves more
And now I can't get an image
      out of my head
It's late. I'm young, like 8 or
      9 and it is after we've all gone
      to bed. We shared a bed, my
      mom, Violet & I because we
      were scared. I came around
      the corner of the hall & my mom
      was closing the front door. The porch
      light was on. A man w/ gray
      greasy hair, long mustache
      w/ handle bars in jeans &
      a flannel shirt is staring
      at me w/ a salivating
      look. My mom is tense
            I can tell. She tells me
      to go to bed this man is
      lost & confused.
I haven't thought of that in a
long time. Was it a dream

or was it real? Was it one
of my dad's friends? Did
he hurt my mom?
These are the types of things that go through my mind.
Then I think
"I'm crazy"
"You for sure dreamt that."
Then I wonder why I'm
        conversing with myself in
        first & second person.

Each night is a battle
The chaos of my life re-enters
The doubt in my judgment returns
The lack of trust in my self haunts

I think about Violet
And hope I did enough
To keep the chaos away from her
I believe she is my best accomplishment
Somehow, as the most steady person in her life
I tried to make it so she didn't
feel the chaos like me
I gave her a chance to develop
        A sense of self-worth
        A belief in herself
        A trust in her judgment
I kept her from the chaos
        As best as I could

But I also created chaos for her
I mistreated her in some ways
Somedays I just couldn't help it

I simply couldn't stand it
Anymore
It being the chaos, the
disregard of my needs
The comforting forgotten
The misplacement of nurture
The verbal bashing
        Or
Complete ignoring
Of my needs
My request for downtime
For help
For understanding
I learned that my needs were unreasonable
and
The expectation is that I
Must bend or completely
disregard my needs for those around me.
My needs don't matter
They are laughable
They are unreasonable or extreme
My needs are undeserving
And so…I grew up watching
My mom be alone or w/ men who treated her
        like dirt
Watching my dad treat women
        like shit
Watching alcohol take King of the home.
It was anything but quiet,
        Except when I read my books
        After everyone went to bed.

And so now as I get ready
        for bed
As the day winds down
And my body screams and begs for sleep
I gear up for a battle
        that reminds me
        every day that
I am not worth it
Except when I drink…
        @ least then I simply pass out

So let the battle begin…2:01AM

> I lean back against my pillows. My mind is quiet. My body is tired. I close my journal and return it to the night stand. I turn the light off and burrow into my covers. Sleep finally comes.

Reflections ∞ Reactions ∞ Responses

_____

_____

_____

CHAPTER 5

CAN'T CONCENTRATE
AND DREAM RETREAT IN 2011

My friend Lucy and I went to Al-Anon together earlier this evening. Lucy is one year ahead of me in the doctoral program. She is one of the kindest, most thoughtful, authentic, and honest people I've ever met. She reminds me of home.

Lucy is taking a class on addictions this semester. Attending Al-Anon is an assignment for that class. I went to Al-Anon during my master's degree for an assignment. But that was over six years ago, so I offered to go with her. I can't decide if it was a good idea to go or a bad one.

My mind continues the monologue. *It's nice to be reminded that I'm not alone. At the same time, I haven't thought about the emotional starvation that plagued my childhood in a long time. It pisses me off that most of us growing up with alcoholic parents are often denied consistent emotional support and safety.*

I sit at my dining room table, which doubles as my desk. I have an assignment due tomorrow, but I can't concentrate. I push back my chair and walk to the sliding glass door. My hand touches it to see how cold it is outside. The glass is like an icicle. *Yep, too cold to sit out there and journal.* I return to the table and open a new Microsoft Word document on my computer. I type a journal entry titled "I always feel better eventually."

Why are my shoulders so tight?

They have been this way since the woman shared at Al-Anon

"He said walk"[8]

I am so tired of being on my own. I am so tired of feeling bad for needing love and needing help. Why is it so much to ask for someone to say "ok I'll pick you up"?

Because you know they do that for their friends.

People are asking me to speak up. Why don't I? I say it is because I can't be bothered. Most people don't want to be changed. So why bother? But what I am really doing is letting my place as a victim dictate how I am in groups. My shoulders are tight. My body is yearning. But there is no one I can call without a suggestion being in the air. I just want to be able to say "I am tired and need to feel safe. Will you please come over and hold me without needing anything from me?" I just can't give all the time, but I really don't know how to ask for what I need. Because I don't trust that people are out there to hear it genuinely the way I hear those types of requests. It is a constant battle. If it were me receiving those pleas, I would come over simply to hold my friend

---

8 The woman at Al-anon told of an experience where a person close to her directed her to walk as a way to help her take steps toward healing. I don't remember the specifics of her story except those words- "He said walk"- because they were so simple yet so profound to me. Recovery and healing happens one step at a time.

or sister or brother or lover. I would sleep on the couch, hit repeat on iTunes, listen, dance, be there. Please just help me like I would help you. Please just make me feel safe. Let me sleep and feel safe. Don't wonder why it is easy to change the subject or smoke or submit to you. It is ultimately what you want. Let me be selfish. Let me sleep without worrying that I am indebted to you and you deserve my body. Let me believe that my body is not what you desire and instead you desire to be with all of me. Which means that I don't always have to give myself to you. Just let me be safe. Just let me be held. Just help me be o.k. I am so not o.k. Let me be in pain. Let me listen to music over and over. Don't blame it on the alcohol. Don't look at me like I am crazy. Let me just be crazy. I will feel better tomorrow. I always feel better eventually.

Fatigue hits me like a ton of bricks. I hit save and close out of Microsoft Word. I decide to finish my assignment tomorrow.

I check my calendar for the week and feel excited because the dream group retreat[9] is next weekend. Lucy and I are attending together. She is doing her dissertation on dreams and asked me to be on her research team. It will be a nice change of pace from my grad assistantship and coursework. I power off my computer and push the chair back to get ready for bed. I beg myself, *please let me sleep tonight.*

∞∞∞

The following Tuesday, Samantha and I are eating breakfast at our favorite café. Samantha is my best friend here. We met on the day

---

9 I attended the Mindful Dreaming Retreat, which was based on Mindful Dreaming: A Practical Guide for Emotional Healing Through Transformative Mythic Journeys by Dr. David Gordon. Carl Jung is a pioneer in the utility of dreams in modern psychology. He authored many books and articles on this topic.

we interviewed for the program. We kept in touch and were happy to learn that we were both accepted and decided to attend this program. I'm bubbling with excitement from my experience at the dream retreat.

"Wow buddy!" She grins. "You look…different. Happy and joyful. Not like our usual stressed-out doc student look."

I smile with a twinkle in my eye. "You know I had that dream retreat with Lucy this past weekend?" I don't wait for her to respond. "It was really amazing. I've always been into dreams. I used to keep a dream journal and at one point had a book about interpreting dreams."

"Yes, and you still look up dream definitions because you text them to me all the time," she chuckles. "Some of them are a little bit off the wall."

"I know! That's what I love about them." I pause for a bite of my omelet. "So anyway, this was a 2 day retreat. It was in a big room with couches, chairs, floor-back-rest-mat-things. The lighting was soft. There was lots of artwork on the walls and sculptures. Oh, and a water effect. It was really peaceful."

"How many people were there? Did you know anyone besides Lucy?"

"No, I didn't know anyone else. I'd say there were about 15 of us. Give or take a few. There were 2 facilitators, both licensed. People had varying degrees of formal dream work. Everyone had interest in working dreams."

"Was it structured?" Samantha asks between sips of orange juice.

"Yes it was. The facilitators are trained in a specific method. I forgot what it's called. But basically, we all went around and shared a brief summary of a dream we'd like the group to work with. Then the group selected the dream we would work. The person with the dream would describe it in detail for a set period of time. I think it was like 6 or 8 minutes. Next the group would ask questions to clarify details. The facilitators were strict on not asking questions or comments based on interpretation during this round. So things like what color was fill-in-the-blank? Was it cold or hot? What was the lighting like? Were there other people there? Where were you in relation to other people or other things in the dream? Things like that."

She nods and I sip my coffee.

"After all those questions are done, or after like 15 or 20 minutes, the facilitators instructed the group to ask meaning-making questions. So like, does that color have a particular meaning to you? What does that person represent in your life? Things like that. Like the previous round, this round lasts about 15 to 20 minutes. The next round everyone in the group finishes this statement: If this was my dream, I would…fill-in-the-blank. Finally, the person who had the dream is asked to share up to 3 things that stood out for them while the group worked the dream. The person is also asked how they might honor the dream work over the course of the week. Like they might do something symbolic. And group members are also asked to share how they might honor the dream over the next few days in a way that memorializes their learning."

She is thoughtful. "That sounds actually really cool. Did your dream get picked?"

"How'd you guess?" I say while chewing my last bite of omelet.

"Because you are beaming and I sense that you learned something big." She chuckles again. "You know your eyebrows say a lot and they are bouncing all over your face like they are doing a little happy jig."

I move my eyebrows up and down purposefully to the beat of the song playing at the restaurant. She laughs louder.

"So, are you going to tell me about it or do I have wait until next breakfast?" She settles into her chair anticipating that I'm going to share with her.

"Of course!" I exclaim. "I'm not going to make you wait. Plus my eyebrows need a break from all their dancing. So I had this dream last week that included my sister. Violet was at my apartment. The one I live in now. You know how my apartment building has internal hallways that are windowless and there are trash chutes near the elevators?" She nods. "So, Vi and I were in our workout clothes and we were walking down the hallway. When we got to the elevator, I pushed the button to go down. I turned to look at her and she was opening the trash chute door. She was super playful and excited. I was super confused. Like 'what the hell is she doing?!' Anyway, before I could blink, she was crouched down in a ball, like the fetal position but on her feet. You know, not lying down. And she somehow jumped to the chute opening, turned and waved at me and said 'Come on Annie, it will be fun.' She went down the chute, as if it was a slide at the park. I rushed over to the chute and peered in. It was only darkness. I could see the bottom. Vi was gone. I was so confused. And I woke up."

"So that was the dream the group chose to work?" I nod. "That's a good one. A lot of symbolism there."

"Yes, there was." I slowly nod.

"Did you tell them about your sexual assault?" Her question was more of a statement.

"Yes, I did. It was hard. I paused before I shared and had to will myself to say it. But I figured it can't hurt and I thought the dream had something to do with it."

"That's good. I think it does, too." Her face fills with compassion while she waits for me to continue.

"So during the clarifying question round, someone asks what was at the bottom of the chute? I clarified that couldn't see it. It was like a never ending tunnel into darkness. Another person asked if it smelled like trash? I said no, it didn't really smell like anything. It felt cool, almost like pure, crisp air. Which added to my confusion in real life about the dream. At the next round, someone asked what my sister means to me? I said she is the one person I truly trust who has been with me through thick and thin. Another person asked if she would ever misled me? I said no. Then another person asked what I thought was at the end of the chute. And I said I wasn't sure. That logically it would be a dumpster. That same person asked a follow up- if it wasn't a dumpster what else could it be. That one stumped me. I said I wasn't sure. Then a few more interpretive questions came up. I don't really remember all of them. Those were the ones that stuck with me."

A kind smile rests on her face when I pause and focus on her. She waits patiently for me to continue. I take a sip of water and stir the ice cubes while I rest in the memory of this retreat.

I continue. "So during the interpretation round a few things stood out. One person said 'if this was my dream, I would explore the possibility of a different end to the chute. Like maybe it is meant to actually be a slide at a park and at the end is beautiful green grass, trees and kids playing in the sunshine.' Another person said 'if this was my dream, I'd trust that my sister is leading me out of the prison-like windowless building, through the clean, pure air down the slide to something magnificent.' Another person said 'if this was my dream, I'd recognize that she crouched into the fetal position and was showing me a path to rebirth.' It was really so powerful. I told the group I would honor the dream by waking up each morning and spending time in the child's pose from yoga. One woman came up to me at lunch and thanked me. She said she lost her virginity by rape when she was 18 traveling through the Mediterranean coast. She said she had never told anyone that before and that she felt a lot of healing through the work we did with my dream. I was speechless because I didn't realize others would be so impacted. Mine was the first dream we worked, so I hadn't had a chance to be impacted by another dream."

Samantha speaks after a brief pause. "I imagine when you do share about your rape, depending on the audience, other people feel empowered to open up about their experiences with sexual assault."

"You know, I guess you're right." Several faces flash in my mind of women and men who disclosed about their experience with sexual violence after learning of mine. "Most times when I share, at least one other person says they've had the same or similar experiences. I don't always know how to respond. Like it's great because we aren't alone in it. And it sucks because it happens so frequently. And I feel tongue-tied because I want to be able to say something that will make it all O.K., but I know from personal experience that there isn't anything anyone can say that will make it all O.K."

She nods. "Yeah, that's a tough one. Like you don't want to be left hanging, dangling really when you disclose something like that. So you want to say something, but what to do say?"

"Exactly!" I exclaim. "I think for me it helps when people acknowledge what I disclosed. Like saying something like 'that is a terrible thing you had to go through. I wish it didn't happen to you, or anyone really. Please tell me if I can do anything to help you.' Or some-thing like that. But, I haven't come up with a response that feels right. Either to give to others or to receive from others."

"You know, Anna, I've not thought about that this deeply before. It is really hard to hear that information. Most people don't know what to do with it and they might even be processing their own experience with sexual trauma. So it might be re-traumatizing for them in those moments, too."

The server comes over with the check. "Can I clear your plates? You seemed in a deep conversation, so I didn't want to interrupt."

We smile at her. "Yes," Samantha confirms.

I dig around my bag for my wallet. Samantha knows exactly where hers is. She giggles.

"Anna, your bag is so messy. How do you find anything in there?"

"I know! Catherine, you know my friend from my master's degree, she cleans it out every time I see her. Which I love because I don't take the time to do it very often."

"I want to meet her," Samantha says.

"Oh you will someday. You two will like each other."

We split the bill and walk to the parking lot. She's heading to campus and I'm heading back home. I teach later tonight. We are both looking forward to the end of the semester, which marks the end of our first year of the doctoral program.

"Thank you for sharing all that Anna." She reaches out to give me a hug.

"You're welcome. Thanks for letting me dominate breakfast. Next time it is your turn." I hug her back.

Reflections ∞ Reactions ∞ Responses

_____

_____

_____

CHAPTER 6
ALONE WITH CLICHÉS IN 2012

I'm nearing the end of my second year in the doctoral program. Last summer I decided to move to a new apartment. This apartment is not as safe as the first one. It's in a gated community, but all apartments face outside. My previous apartment entrance was inside a secured hallway. I have a roommate now, which I like better than living alone. He's a doctoral student in a different program at the same school. We rarely see each other and have similar cleanliness habits, so it's worked out well. We're both smokers, which means we mainly meet on the balcony at odd hours when taking breaks from assignments.

He isn't home right now, so I am working at the dining table. I need a break from the final project for a research class. My eyes gaze out the slider at the pine tree right outside our balcony, across the Opera House parking lot, and to the city skyline. I decide to smoke a cigarette. My mind takes inventory of the last few years. *School has gone well overall. I am progressing. It is really stressful. I'm All But Dissertation now and will collect my data later this summer. I have a small group of friends at school and recently met some people outside of school. It's nice to have a group out of school to talk about things other than research, manuscripts, publications, dissertations, assistantships, etc.*

Last week I went to an annual festival with some of the non-school people. I met someone intriguing. There is something different about him. But I can't tell if I really like him romantically. He has texted a few times since. Most recently he invited me to go swimming at a local members-only pool. I pull on the last drag of my cigarette. *Maybe you should write in your journal. You haven't done that in a while.* My mind surprises me because I haven't heard it in a while. I've been all consumed with preparing my dissertation proposal defense and passing comprehensive exams. I put my cigarette out in the jar that used to hold marinara sauce and now overflows with butts. *Disgusting!* I cringe and make a mental note to throw that in the dumpster next time I leave the apartment.

Instead of returning to the table, I go to my room and pull my journal out of my night stand drawer. I walk back to the living room. I wonder, *Hmmm…should I sit on the couch or the chair?* I decide on the oversized chair that faces the slider. I like the view of the skyline. I open my journal and begin to write an untitled entry.

I don't know the last time I wrote. When I think about what to say next, clichés come to mind…well there have been some ups and downs these last few weeks. Then I think I've visited the depths of darkness. Then I think why am I using clichés? What are they protecting me from? In undergrad I bought a poster "It is always darkest before dawn." Another cliché. I am afraid of being honest because I don't want to burden anyone. I don't want to cause pain. Or dis-ease. I'm not sure how to ask for help. I'm angry that I'm alone. I'm undeserved of help or something. "Maybe you should get help." "Maybe you have a problem." "The hatred is in you." It's so pointed at me most of the time. Even Violet said it, well spat it really in my face. There wasn't a "we can figure this out together" or "we have a problem." So much of what I do I do because alone-ness is a dis-ease in our world and I want to stop that. I don't want anyone to feel alone. It is a "we." Maybe my family has already been there enough, already given what they can. Where is my "we"?

I look up from my journal toward downtown. The intriguing guy I met at the festival works in one of those buildings. I wonder: Can he handle my burden? I'm conflicted. He likes to do many of the same things that I like. Like going to the beach, listening to live music, eating out, hanging out with friends. His house seems really put together. Like it is an adult person's house. He has a really cool garden. I've always wanted a garden.

Reflections ∞ Reactions ∞ Responses

_____

_____

_____

CHAPTER 7

FRAGILE SHELL
RAMBLINGS IN 2012

Untitled journal entry, July 10, 2012

A fragile shell. I feel like if I drop I will shatter. My vision of cigarettes → they feed the evil. They keep her calm, tame. This shell...this is who I think I was meant to be. Who I am, the solid root to the core is not nice. Evil. Angry. Hateful. Not to be trusted. Not caring. Apathetic. Passionless. Alone. She haunts me. She says, she whispers "you know you aren't pure." "You know you aren't good." "You know you are just a fragile fake shell of greatness." Only this shell illustrates the face. Of the 3 faces I drew, he[10] thought the most skeleton-like one was beautiful (third picture).

---

10 Several advanced readers questioned who "he" is. He and I briefly dated during the period of time I wrote this journal entry. We parted on amicable terms.

Is that who I really am? A skeleton of pain? Heavy, weight filled, dense, hot, hatred. And a cigarette keeps it, keeps her calm.

Maybe I need happy pills. Maybe this will solidify the shell. Maybe this will turn hate to beauty. Maybe that is what he always meant. When he said to get to the bottom of why I don't like them. Their unhappiness won. I don't want that to happen. Yet it is so exhausting. And all I do, all that works is to throw myself into work & calm my nerves w/ cigarettes. Maybe if we can get to the bottom of pain, really pain then we can be done w/ all these addictions and just be in fun.

Will marriage and a baby do this for me? Intuition says no way jose!

I envision a practitioner life, part time, kids, garden, teaching, philanthropy.

Follow this Anna.

The shell needs to shatter, but when that happens I will be in bad shape. If I never finish anything I won't have to shatter the shell. How can I not wear my hatred and be smoke-free?

Reflections ∞ Reactions ∞ Responses

SHATTERED, BUT NOT ALONE

"Using the idea of 'empowerment through empathy,' me too. was ultimately created to ensure survivors know they're not alone in their journey." – https://metoomvmt.org

Ms. Tarana Burke created 'me too.' in 2006. I heard Ms. Burke at Wisdom 2.0 in February 2018. I saw her raw, genuine passion and compassion that underscores her belief that sexual violence can end with an empowered and empathic community. Survivors are not alone.

She is one of my role models and heroines.

CHAPTER 8

POST SHATTER VISIT FROM
A LIFE SAVING FRIEND IN 2014

I did shatter. Only a couple months ago, in July. I broke. I crumbled. I almost took my life. Earlier this year, the last two weeks of June.

I ended up marrying that guy I met at the festival during my doctoral program. We were living in Santa Barbara, which is just over an hour south of Santa Maria. Our marriage happened fast. And it ended just as quickly. I was suicidal for ten days prior to moving out of our apartment. Now I live with Dad and Lindsey. Up until the day I moved in with them, I never imagined myself returning to Santa Maria and living at their house. Fortunately, our bedrooms are on opposite sides of the house and all of us travel frequently. So far it's working out O.K.

Samantha flew in yesterday evening from the East Coast. She got me through my marriage, suicide crisis, and now divorce. We got each other through our doc program. Dad and Lindsey are out of town, and Violet and her family returned to Europe earlier this week. Samantha and I have the house all to ourselves. I'm grateful she is here because I don't want to be alone in this big house.

We wake up around the same time. "Good morning, Samantha. How'd you sleep?"

She is groggy. "O.K. This house creaks a lot."

I chuckle. "Yes, it does. And it is really quiet outside which is very different than what you are used to. It's like the country out here compared to the cities you've lived in."

Now she chuckles. "Yes. It. Is." She changes the subject. "Are we going with your mom to drive along the coast today and stop in to my favorite breakfast place?"

"Yes, she will be here in an hour to pick us up."

I'm at peace with Samantha. She helps me feel grounded. As I get ready for the day, I think about all the times she was there for me during school. She really was my only family when I lived in the South. One time when I was too drunk to drive home and couldn't get a cab after a pub crawl, she picked me up. Then there was that other time when my ex-boyfriend crashed his car with me and two others in it. I begged him to stop driving like a maniac and he wouldn't listen. Samantha was out of town, but I called her and she stayed on the phone with me while I walked home from the accident.

I shake my head as I brush my teeth. I look in the mirror and sigh. *Thankfully I made it out alive. So much destruction around me. Thank God for Samantha.*

I remember when she pointed out that when my ex-husband offered me drugs and alcohol to help me through a rough patch, that this was actually unsafe. I recall telling her that I'd never thought of that interaction as unsafe because he was only trying to help.

I shake my head again and give myself a perplexed look as I apply mascara. *How did I think that was safe?* I'm perplexed by my lack of knowing that, especially given my training. Samantha reminded me that I grew up with addiction in my family, so it is familiar. I sigh again and fight back tears. I repeat to myself, *I'm so grateful for you Samantha.*

Later that night we sit on the patio. The sun light rises up the hills in front of us as the sun sets into the Pacific Ocean 15 miles west. It is breathtaking. We see two vultures in the distance that usually come out for dinner this time of night. The water effect near the door is soothing. The air is not too warm and not too cool. A perfect early Fall evening to be with my best friend.

She's been quiet for a while and I can tell she's thinking about something important. I know her well enough not to push and to trust she'll tell me when she's ready. Instead I say, "So I'm not ready to date, but when I am, I'll need some good selfies."

She bursts out laughing. "Oh lordy. Selfie's aren't your strong suit. Here let's try." She reaches for her phone. "O.K. now don't smile too much. Sort of smile. Look at the camera and make your eyes say 'I'm confident and sexy.'"

She snaps a couple of shots and cracks up. "Anna, you look like you're smelling a fart in one and like you're a cheesy news broadcaster in the other. Here, let's go over there where the sun light is a little brighter." She directs me to sit on the patio ledge and gaze toward the vultures. "Good. Don't move. Maybe it's better if you don't look at the camera. Then you can't ham it up." She snaps a few before I burst out laughing.

I turn to face her. "Let me see them."

We walk back to the patio chairs. Most of the photos are definitely not natural and my expression is pretty cheesy. "Here's a good one. Look how serene I look." I can't remember the last time I felt as peaceful as I look in that photo.

She grows quiet again and looks down. "Anna, I have to tell you something." She looks up with tears brimming in her eyes. "When you called to tell me you were suicidal, I have never been more scared in my life. I couldn't get to you. If you died, I honestly do not know what I would do. A piece of me would be gone. I did not want to tell you that then because I knew you had so much you were coping with and I didn't want to make it about me. But you have to know that my world crashed down on me that day knowing you were in such pain." Tears spill down her cheeks.

"I know. I'm sorry Samantha. My mom said almost the exact same thing a few days after I gave her the no-harm contract[11]. Her eyes filled with tears, too and she was really quiet. I'm really sorry I scared you so much. You really were one of the few who got me out of that situation." I reach out and hold her hand.

She shudders. "Once you told me you were fighting against enacting a plan to take your life, I kept my phone ringer on at all hours during those weeks until I knew you moved out. That night you called…the night before you separated, you did not sound like yourself. I swear I almost got in my car to drive to you because it was too late to get a flight."

"That night was scary, but in a different way. I wasn't suicidal. I was exhausted. He said horrible things to me. I don't think he really believed- when he said he didn't want kids with me- that I would leave him. That night it became real for him because the next day was the day. He was nasty. He asked if I was going to get gang raped right away so I could get pregnant. He repeatedly tapped my leg with his foot. I finally asked him to stop when it got harder. No bruise or anything, but it was aggressive. I went in the guest room, locked the door, curled up under the covers and called you.

11 A no-harm contract is used in therapeutic settings when a client is thinking of or actively engaged in self-harm behavior. Usually, it lists alternative ways to get help in those moments including naming support people.

I remember you said, 'Anna, you don't sound like yourself.' And I said 'Samantha am I crazy?' And you said, 'No, you are not crazy. You are in a crazy situation right now, but you are not crazy.'"

She squeezes my hand tighter. "I remember. You sounded like your soul was gone. I waited to hang up until I could tell you were drifting off to sleep. He really wasn't good for you. I'm so sorry you had to go through that."

I look at her, my heart bursting with gratitude and love. "I'm so lucky to have you as a friend. Thank you for being there. For believing in me even when I was so lost. For helping me remember who I am." We're both crying now.

"You've helped me, too, Anna. More than you know. I never went out to eat or on an airplane before I met you. I never imagined actually leaving my hometown, even though I dreamed about it. You helped me break through so many of my fears. I think my mom brought us together." Samantha's mom had died from cancer in 2009, a few months before we met.

"I think you're right about that. I love that our moms have the same name, only spelled differently." I squeeze her hand tighter now.

"Are you going to try to see a counselor now that you're back from the retreat?" she asks. "Your sister and everyone left, and your normal routine is back."

Silence settles around us. The water effect comes into focus. I think about the mental health retreat[12]. Three weeks after my suicide crisis, I went to a 10-day mental health retreat specializing in trauma recovery. Those 10 days in late July 2014 changed my life. In addition to talk therapy in individual, small, and large group settings, we also engaged in meditation, yoga, art, movement, psychoeducation and massage therapy. Groups counseling included one on grief and one based on 12-step. We had access to a pool, a labyrinth and horses. The facilitators emphasized creating a healing plan to continue what was started upon returning home. My healing plan included yoga, individual therapy with a dance/movement certified licensed clinician, art, meditation, massage therapy, and to stay in touch with my small group. It was an ambitious and expensive plan[13]. It's already been 5 weeks since the retreat.

I turn my attention back to Samantha. "Yes, I guess. I know it will help. Especially since I'm starting this new mental health counseling program at work. There is something a bit comical about the fact that I'm in the worst mental health breakdown of my life while embarking on building this state-wide mental health program from the ground up. Did I tell you I started working with a clinical

---

12 The organization website that facilitated the mental health retreat referred to it as an intensive in-patient recovery program and mental health retreat. These types of programs are available in a variety of settings with different duration, amenities and interventions. For instance, some are closed programs, like the one I completed where the same participants start and complete the program together; whereas others are open programs meaning participants' start and completion dates vary. In choosing an intensive program, I looked for evidence-based interventions, number of licensed staff, closed vs. open participation, cost, and schedule. One person who reviewed this manuscript suggested I include a separate chapter about the mental health retreat. I choose not to because my experience was intertwined with other retreat participants and I want to honor confidentiality.
13 To date, I've spent over $30,000 and my family has spent over $6,500 out of pocket on trauma-related recovery efforts. This amount does not include lost wages, costs associated with maintaining connection to my small group, costs of the self-destructive ways I used prior to the mental health retreat, or moving expenses. In the 12 years since being raped, I'd moved 14 times.

supervisor?" She shakes her head. "Yeah, I know I need support and I want to minimize the impact of my personal life on my work with counselor trainees and clients. He is absolutely fabulous! I see him every other week."

"That's so great, Anna. I loved working with my clinical supervisor. I should start doing that again. Good idea."

We binge-watch Married At First Sight, which gives us a lot of fodder to analyze our failed relationships. We eat great food and spend time with my family. Mostly, we hang out together. There are only a few other people in this world that I can simply be in the moment with. I'm sad to say goodbye when she leaves a few days later.

Reflections ∞ Reactions ∞ Responses

CHAPTER 9

ENACT MY HEALING
PLAN IN 2014

"Hello. My name is Anna Gulden." I start a voicemail for a potential therapist. "I'm interested in trying Dance/Movement Therapy and found your name and number on the American Dance Therapy Association[14] website. Most recently, I left my husband and am going through a divorce. I have a PhD in the mental health field and am a state licensed counselor. Please call me back so we can see if this might be a good fit." I click the red circle to end the call.

I stare out the window of my room at Dad and Lindsey's house. The big oak tree is beautiful this time of day in the September sun. It is home to some beautiful birds. I sigh and think about how I ended up back in Santa Maria at their house. *Oh well. At least you have a family who takes you in and their house is big enough that you aren't on top of each other.*

---

14 Finding the right therapist can be difficult. One way is through professional associations for mental health professionals in general or with specific expertise. Examples of general: American Counseling Association, American Psychological Association, American Association for Marriage and Family Therapists. Examples of specific expertise: American Dance Therapy Association, The Center for Self Leadership for IFS Therapists.

I've just made my third call of the day in search for a local therapist. My family's therapist from high school was there for me during my suicide crisis in July, but I know she's not the one for my healing plan. At that session in July when I expressed suicidal ideation, she read me the diagnosis for Borderline Personality Disorder out of the DSM[15]-IV and insisted I'd need to get on medication. She had me sign the no-harm contract and give a copy of it to Mom and Violet. She also encouraged me to tell Dad and Lindsey.

After all my advanced degrees in mental health, I was annoyed that she diagnosed me with a personality disorder in our first session in almost 20 years and one in which I was suicidal. Plus she used the DSM-IV. The DSM 5[16] was released last year! I was also annoyed that she used the no-harm contract. Anyone who stays current on best practice research knows results on the effectiveness of no-harm contracts in stopping suicide are inconsistent at best. Plus, she didn't take a full background since she'd worked with me in the past. A lot has happened in the 20 years since I was in high school. That session did give me comic relief. In spite of my suicidal ideation, I couldn't turn off my years of training.

The back door slams and footsteps echo from the T.V. room.

"Hi honey," Lindsey yells on her way to her home office near my bedroom.

I walk to the office doorway. "Hey. How was your day?"

Stress seeps through her voice. "It was busy. We have a lot going on." She sits in front of three monitors.

---

15 The Diagnostic and Statistical Manual of Mental Disorders (DSM) is used in the United States of America to diagnose mental health disorders. The most recent edition, DSM 5 was released in 2013.

16 For reasons unknown to me, the most current version of the DSM switched from Roman to Arabic numerals.

I know to make it quick. "What was the name of that massage therapist you said was great, but wouldn't give you her contact information because of her contract with the spa?"

"Zephora Crane," she says without looking up. "Z-E-P-H-O-R-A I think. Google her."

I return to my room and search "Zephora Crane, massage, Santa Maria" on my computer. One listing comes up that seems like it could be her. I dial the number.

"Hello." She answers after a few rings.

I stammer. "Uh. Hi. Are you a massage therapist in Santa Maria that has a private practice and also works for a local spa?" I'm not prepared for the first live person to enact my healing plan.

"Yes. That's me."

"O.K. I got your name from my step-mom who told me you couldn't give her your number because she saw you at a spa and you have a contract, so I looked you up and found you." I pause for a quick breath before rambling on. "I'm going through a really difficult time with a lot of changes and I just moved back in with my parents and I'm 35 and my ex-husband…well on the way to being ex-husband and I are getting divorced…that was obvious. Anyway, I'm rambling now. I need help. Lindsey said you gave her one of the best massages she's ever had. Are you taking new patients? Err, clients?" I'm so glad she isn't in front of me because my cheeks are bright red. *That's weird…why am I blushing? And why did I ramble?*

"O.K. I have time on September 20th. How long do you want to come?" Her voice is serene and reassuring.

"Maybe 90 minutes?" I'm still stammering.

"Perfect." A peaceful feeling washes over me as I write down her office address.

I stare out at the oak tree after we hang up. This is real. I'm actually doing it this time. I'm taking charge of my care. I take a fragile, yet deep breath. It fills my chest. I feel hope.

The back door slams again.

Dad's voice bellows through the house. "Annnnn-IIIIEEEEEE."

"Hi Dad." I come out of my room. "How was your day?"

"It was great. I got some swordfish for the grill. Sound good?" He's all smiles.

Lindsey joins us in the kitchen. I'm cleaning lettuce, she's making rice, and he's marinating the fish. Tunes are playing on Pandora radio throughout the house. Lindsey opens a bottle of wine and pours a glass for her and Dad. She pours me sparkling water in a wine glass. I stopped drinking after the suicide crisis. I'm grateful that they've acclimated to my decision to abstain from alcohol for a while because wine is a big part of our family life.

"They paved paradise/ And put up a parking lot/ With a pink hotel, a boutique/ And a swinging hot spot/ Don't it always seem to go/ That you don't know what you've got 'til it's gone/ They paved paradise/ And put up a parking lot…" Adam Duritz's voice fills the house with Counting Crows' hit Big Yellow Taxi. I learned on retreat that hearing Counting Crows' songs trigger[17] a trauma response.

I take a deep breath. Grip the counter. My mind begins to race. *The song will be over soon. It's not even THE song Evan blasted at every high school party. Just hang in there.* My heart rate increases

---

17 A trigger is anything that reminds a trauma victim of a traumatic experience. Triggers lead to trauma responses, which could include flashbacks, anxiety attacks, use of alcohol and drugs, and suicidal ideation, to name a few. For the record, I really enjoy music by Counting Crows. I've seen Counting Crows in concert and at one point could sing along to almost every song on the August and Everything After album. This trigger is one of the most frustrating ones because they used to be a source of happiness and joy for me. In contrast, another trigger was seeing pornographic magazines at a convenient store. I didn't like those magazines before being raped.

and breathing grows shallower. I struggle to focus on cleaning lettuce. *Hopefully, Dad and Lindsey don't see me having a moment.* I
channel my calm, cool, collected mask. I remember the mantras I
learned at the mental health retreat. *This moment will pass. This will
not last forever. It has gripped you in the past until now. Breathe.
Good. Nice slow breath. Good. You will be O.K. It's just a song.*

"So what'd you do today Annie?" Dad's question briefly
interrupts my thoughts.

My mind continues to chatter. *Did he notice something is
wrong? My back is to him. Maybe he sensed it.*

My words seem to tumble out. "I worked all day and then
came home and called some counselors and a massage therapist."
S*hoot I'm talking too fast. Steady.*

"Good for you honey. Any luck with the counselors and massage therapist?"

"I left three voicemails for the counselors and scheduled an
appointment with the massage therapist for later this month."

The song ends. I feel my body normalizing.

"That's GRA-eat! Let us know if you like the massage therapist. We are always looking." He exclaims after a moment, "We
could probably use a counselor, too."

' We all chuckle. Adam Levine's voice floods the house with
one of my favorite songs. Lindsey and I sing along to the chorus.
The moment passed. I say to myself, *I feel hope.*

∞∞∞

"Hi. Is this Anna? This is Jennifer Lazar. I'm sorry it has taken
me a few days to return your call. You called about doing therapy
together." Her voice is kind and confident.

"Yes. Thank you for calling me back. I'm interested in learning more about your approach to therapy. To give you a little background about me, I'm a licensed counselor with a master's and PhD in counseling. My education and professional experiences create a challenge in finding a therapist for myself. I need someone who I can trust, learn from, and not be able to analyze for quality of work." I wonder if I'm coming off too strong. "I don't mean I know everything. I've just had a few experiences with counselors in the past where I could see what they were doing before they did it and it wasn't helpful."

"You aren't coming off strong. You are giving clues for what you need in a therapist. I appreciate that. What do you want to work on in therapy?" Her reassurance eases my concerns.

"Well, there is a lot. Most recently, I was suicidal for ten days. I've never experienced anything like that. It really scared me. I've had suicidal thoughts before, but never anything like that. I was in a really destructive relationship that I left shortly after I got help from the suicide crisis. So, I'm going through a divorce and I've recently returned to my hometown. I'm living with my dad and step-mom. I never thought I'd be in this position. Also, I was raped when I was 22 by a friend. He and I never dated. In fact, I never found him attractive. He was almost like a brother. That was 13 years ago. I've done some counseling since then. Like I worked with a certified EMDR specialist in 2007-ish. That really helped reduce the intensity of my hatred toward all men and my ability to block out some everyday triggers, like seeing Maxim and Playboy at the store. Immediately following my 10 suicidal days, I went to a 10-day mental health retreat. I learned a lot there and want to continue the work. When I returned from that, my sister and her family were in town visiting. My niece and nephew are 3 and 1. Every time I was with them, I started crying. We were supposed to be having kids now, not getting divorced. Anyway, I went on Zoloft and that has really helped me function. That's a lot of information and I could keep going. I'm interested in long-term therapy focused on trauma recovery." I feel relief. "Oh one more thing, my parents divorced when I was 8. My dad is an alcoholic. Our home growing up was really chaotic."

"Thank you for sharing all of that Anna. I've worked with a lot of women struggling with trauma. I was a professional dancer and have found movement to be healing in my own life. Because of that, I got certified as a dance/movement therapist, which you saw on the website. My PhD is in clinical psychology. So we can do talk therapy and movement. I'm interested in working with you."

"O.K. great. What's your rate? And when are you available?" I hold my breath because I do not want to use insurance.

"I don't take insurance. Is that going to be O.K. for you?"

"Yes," I exhale with relief. "I actually don't want to use my insurance. I know with ObamaCare we don't have to worry as much about being denied coverage, but I have a funny thing about having my mental health care on my health record. I know it's the stigma[18]. At any rate, not using insurance works."

"O.K. The other thing is I can only meet on weekends. On Sunday actually. I could do 8 in the evenings on Tuesday, but it would be challenging because I work at a residential treatment facility, too."

"That's also great for me. I travel almost every week for work, so Sundays are perfect." I can't believe my luck.

"My rate is $125 an hour. If that's too high…"

I cut her off. "No that rate works for me."

---

18 Mental health stigma is a primary reason people do not seek assistance for mental health challenges. Prior to the Affordable Care Act aka Obamacare, third-party payers penalized people with pre-existing conditions, including mental health disorders, by denying coverage or charging high premium rates. Other stigmas reinforced by society and de-stigmatization efforts may be found on www.eachmindmatters.org.

"Really?" She sounds surprised. "We can meet this Sunday at 3. I need to identify a space to meet, so I'll let you know before Sunday. Is this the best number to reach you?"

"Yes, call or text anytime."

"I look forward to meeting you Anna. Oh one more thing. Are you allergic to dogs? I have a dog. Her name is Pansy and she likes to come with me on the weekends if that's O.K. with you."

"That's fine with me," I say with a huge smile. "I have one more question. Are you by chance Jewish? I'm wondering because of meeting on Sunday and not Saturday."

"Yes, I am," she replies.

"I converted to Judaism[19] last year. It is the greatest gift to come from my marriage." I feel suddenly shy.

"Well that will make our work together even more interesting! Great. I'll see you Sunday." I think I hear her smiling, too.

That night I sleep through until morning for the first time in years.

Reflections ∞ Reactions ∞ Responses

_____

_____

_____

---

19 Spirituality, including but not limited to organized religion, has been shown to be a protective factor that can aid recovery efforts in therapeutic settings when utilized appropriately. In other words, when a client shares that spirituality has helped them in the past and/or they are interested in learning about spirituality for the benefit of their healing, a counselor may incorporate spirituality into the treatment plan. Ethical guidelines explicitly state that counselors are not to push their own beliefs, including beliefs about spirituality and religion on their clients.

CHAPTER 10

MEET JENNIFER AND PANSY

My nerves are jittery as I pull into the office park to meet Jennifer. *It's very industrial up here. The views are beautiful though.* At the parking lot, I veer to the right per her instructions. Her office building is at the far end with a view across the regional airport runway. Beautiful bougainvillea wrap up and around a pergola near the front entrance shading a round patio table with four chairs. I like it here.

Jennifer waits inside the front door. Pansy bolts around the corner when she hears me approach. She is the cutest little rescue dog I've ever seen. Wiry fur, wagging tail, purple bandana fashioned around her neck, and all smiles. She barks and jumps for joy as I come in.

"Pansy. Pansy. That's enough," Jennifer says. "I'm sorry. She obviously really likes you. I'm Jennifer. You must be Anna."

I feel nervous and shy. "Yes, I'm Anna. No worries about Pansy. I like her bandana." I didn't tell Jennifer that I'm not much of an animal person. If she had a cat, I would've told her because I'm not a cat person. Ever since Camille helped me pet the horses at the retreat, I've been intrigued by the power of healing with animals[20]. Camille was in my small group on retreat. I grew up with a dog until I was 12, so dogs are basically the only animal I half-way like.

This space is part of the residential treatment facility where Jennifer works during the week. The group room isn't used on the weekends and is large enough for movement.

Jennifer says, "We'll meet here for the foreseeable future." She locks the door behind me. "I lock the door when I'm the only one here," she explains. "This area isn't dangerous, but I lock it any way for safety."

She points out the restroom on our way to the group room. We also pass a kitchen. "If you ever need a snack, let me know."

Helium balloons dot the ceiling in the group room. A collection of chairs and couches form a circle; pillows and blankets line a wall; there are white boards with group guidelines written in different colors, and cabinets presumably holding art supplies along another wall.

I look around the room to decide where to sit. I choose a couch that is opposite a wall with big windows overlooking hills across the airport. It's a beautiful late afternoon day with few clouds in sight. Jennifer explains that they had a celebration last week for the clients, so there are balloons. I feel comfortable here. I can tell she runs her groups like I run mine. It's not dry and sterile. Instead it is full of life and creativity. It's familiar.

She formally begins our session. "So it is really nice to finally meet you in person. I have a few papers for you to complete. We can

---

20 Pansy is a certified Canine Good Citizen, a training program by the American Kennel Club. She is not a certified therapy dog, so my therapeutic treatment does not include Animal Assisted Therapy (AAT). For more information on AAT, visit https://psychcentral. com/lib/the-truth-about-animal-assisted-therapy/ or https://www.americanhumane.org to learn about post-traumatic stress service dogs for military service members.

do them now or you can take them home to review and complete later, whichever you prefer."

I look them over. The informed consent and basic intake form[21] seem typical to me. I complete them and consider listing Lindsey as my emergency contact. She's really good under pressure, whereas my parents might be too emotional. When I told her and Dad about my suicide crisis, she moved to sit next to me on the couch and put her arms around me like Violet did that night I had a panic attack after being with her and Dad at the produce convention. Understandably, Mom and Dad were a bit frozen in shock when I told them I was suicidal.

I think to myself, *not that I plan to use the emergency contact. You never know though. Ever since the suicide crisis anything is possible.* I decide to list Mom. Mom knows my whole history and, if it is ever used, she'll call Dad and Lindsey.

Jennifer asks if I have any questions about the forms when I hand them back to her.

"No," I answer. "I do have a question about movement. How does it happen?"

Her voice is soft and kind. "Well, I will ask if you want to try a movement when it seems appropriate. Movement can include dancing, stretching, lying on the ground, walking. We can go outside if you like. Or any other kind of movement you want to make. You never have to do anything I suggest, so it is always up to you."

"O.K. Do we move together?" I'm nervous.

---

21 Informed Consent is completed at the start of working with a therapist. It outlines confidentiality, voluntary participation, and other information relevant to counseling. Most therapists or mental health facilities also include intake forms that collect demographic, health, family, presenting concerns and other information relevant to client situations. Visit American Counseling Association, www.counseling.org, American Psychological Association, www.apa.org, or the American Association for Marriage and Family Therapy, www.aamft.org, for more information about these documents.

"We can move together, I can witness you moving, or I can go in another room while you move alone. It's up to you." She emphasizes that I am in the driver's seat. I really appreciate this client-centered[22] approach.

"Do you have any other questions before we start the initial interview?" I'm surprised she uses clinical jargon, but I also really appreciate it. She knows I know what she is doing. Plus, she is orienting me to what comes next, which limits surprises. I don't like surprises, which I am sure relates to the surprise attack I survived in 2002.

"Not right now. I'm sure more will come up. My friends and colleagues have put me on a daily question quota in the past." I smile as I recall my colleague and friend in residential life who introduced that concept to me 11 years ago.

She writes something on her notepad. "O.K. Where do you want to start? From our conversation on the phone, I know there's a lot going on."

"I've been thinking about where to start, too," I begin tentatively. "I guess with the most recent stuff. From a clinical perspective, I'd guess the suicide crisis is high on your list."

She redirects. "That is important to talk about, but we do not have to start there. We can start wherever you want. Remember

---

22 In the context of this story, client-centered refers to Jennifer's emphasis on giving me options to direct how we spend our sessions. Throughout our work together, Jennifer empowers me to determine if and how I want to integrate different therapeutic tools and techniques. She gives guidance and direction without telling me explicitly what to do. This approach empowers me to be in sync with myself and state my needs. It helps build my connection to self. In this instance, I am not referring to the specific theoretical approach, called Person-Centered Therapy founded by Carl Rogers, which is also referred to as Client-Centered Therapy.

you're the client in here. You aren't alone in this to play counselor and client to yourself." Her voice is reassuring and firm, but not pushy.

"O.K." I take a deep breath and begin…

"I'm not suicidal at the moment. I haven't had thoughts of suicide since I got back from the retreat and started taking Zoloft. I've thought a lot about what sent me into that dark place. On retreat, I told my small group it was like I was sunburned living in a tanning bed. Everything hurt and nothing soothed. I was a zombie. A shell of myself. Everything in that time seemed so desperate. Liam, my ex-husband and I moved to California to escape our dissatisfaction with life on the East Coast, which I thought would ease the dissatisfaction in our marriage. He stopped smoking pot and cut way back on the prescription drugs. He started a program at the local community college to change careers. I had two job offers to choose from. Things were going better. But I was angry. I was so filled with resentment and rage. I went on a 3-day blackout rage and I wasn't even drinking. I said awful things to him and threw my rings across the room. It was a rage that scared me."

Jennifer asks, "About when was that Anna?"

"That was around February. We'd been living with my Aunt Tessa for about six weeks."

She asks for clarification, "In California?"

"Yes. Aunt Tessa offered to let us live with her until we could find our own place. I was desperate to get out of where we were living and closer to home, so I took her up on it. I was surprised Liam went for it, but also grateful that he did."

"Tell me more about the resentment, anger and rage," she probes[23]. "Where do you think that stems from?"

I'm pensive. "I've wondered that, too. Like why then did that rage come out?"

"Have you ever experienced blackout rage before?" she asks.

"Not like that," I reply. "I've had angry outbursts before, mostly when drinking. I think this one happened in part because of how I was raised. The way I saw my dad treat my mom is a lot like how Liam treated me. There was an unpredictability in our house like I remember when my parents were still married. Like when I first moved into Liam's house, I was organizing the kitchen. He wasn't home from work yet. I had my favorite playlist on and was dancing and singing around the kitchen. He came storming in and yelled at me to turn it off. He said something like 'How dare you blast that music in my house. It gives me a headache. Turn it off.' I was so caught off guard. It seemed so innocuous to me. I wondered why he couldn't see how happy I was in that moment. I rationalized that he must have had a bad day or something. That was the same with Dad. You could never tell what would set him off. Rage runs in our family on my dad's side."

She paraphrased and probed deeper. "So your marriage had similar patterns to your family of origin and there is a generational precedent for rage on your Dad's side. What else about the rage and resentment in February?"

"I gave up so much for him. I pulled out of a national faculty search after I graduated from the PhD program. I put off moving out of that city. I moved in with a cat. He only gave me one-fourth of

---

23 Probe is a basic helping skill meant to invite a client to share more information about a topic (Egan, 2002). Other basic helping skills include, but are not limited to paraphrase, reflection, summarize, confront, and active listening. These skills are taught in graduate counseling programs. The Council for Accreditation of Counseling and Related Education Programs (www.cacrep.org) has more information on required learning outcomes.

the closet. My clothes were scattered throughout the house. Then, about 2 weeks after we returned from our honeymoon, I came home from my part-time assistantship that was supposed to end soon and he was crying. He was crying and pacing around the kitchen. When I asked what was wrong, he said 'It's all your fault. You don't like my parents. You made me stop asking them for money. Now I have nothing.' I was so confused. He went on 'I can't tell you. I'm too ashamed. You will never look at me the same. It's all over.' I went into crisis response mode. I asked what he meant when he said it's all over and asked him to tell me what was going on. After about ten minutes of back and forth, he finally told me that his company cut off his draw on future commissions, which essentially meant his net paycheck was about $250 per month." I pause and come back to the present for a moment. I don't like thinking about that memory.

She asks, "Why was that hard for you? I mean, I get that $250 isn't close to enough to live on, but why did that impact you so much?"

I continue. "Well, Mom and Dad both always taught me not to rely on anyone but myself for financial stability. They both always encouraged Violet, my sister and me to be independent. I've worked since I was 15. My parents have helped me financially at different points in my life, but for the most part I have been financially independent from them since 2001. I paid for both graduate degrees and some of my undergrad. I worked in jobs that covered my housing expenses, like when I was a live-in nanny or when I worked in residential life at two different universities. Liam told me in 2008 when the bubble burst, that he like many brokers had to take draws off of future commissions. He said he was paying it back and had built his business back up. I had no reason to suspect otherwise. That spring, after consulting with Liam, I turned down a summer adjunct faculty position because I was so worn out after my doctoral program and life in general. I remember distinctly he said it would be O.K. for one summer for me not to work. He couldn't understand why I felt so betrayed when I found out that he lied about his income. There was no remorse. Fortunately, my part-time assistantship supervisor was able to extend the position through the summer. So, I became the primary income earner with a part-time hourly job. I felt so... bamboozled."

Jennifer interjects. "Anna, I can see how that was shocking. Did you consider leaving the marriage?"

"Yes. I called my best friend from childhood the day after I found out. Her name is Elizabeth. She encouraged me to annul the marriage. I remember her vividly saying 'A, that sucks. You need to get out now.' I also told my mom. She sounded like the wind was knocked out of her and her voice was really small, almost a whisper. She said something like 'The betrayal. The hardest part is there was no way to know before you were married. He put on a good show.' I could almost hear her re-living her own experience with my dad. In the end, I decided to stay because I also heard from a lot of people that the first year of marriage is hard and we may be . lucky to be going through a lot of obstacles at once. I did change my direct deposit to go to my personal bank account and not our joint account." I stop for a moment. "Where was I...?"

She glances at her notes. "We started talking about your black-out rage. You talked about how your marriage reminded you of your parent's marriage. You also described the betrayal and resentment you felt when confronted with his real income. What else led to that kind of rage?"

I feel silly. "I got my period."

She uses silence to wait for me to carry on.

I am crying now. "I wanted to have a baby. He and I agreed that we would start trying in the fall. But with everything that happened, and then he did 30 days of detox and that was great, but really hard. I was so angry. I did not get married to be a mom. I wanted to have a baby with him and be a mom. When I got my period that February, I was just consumed with anger that this was my life. I felt such remorse and guilt after those three days. We both talked to our couple's counselor on the East Coast who encouraged us not to make any permanent decisions until we were settled. I begged for forgiveness. He finally gave my rings back. I felt so awful. At that point, I was desperate to find us a place to live on our own."

Jennifer asks, "May I offer an insight?" I nod. "You've mentioned the word desperate a few times. I do get that sense that you were running, escaping from something, and almost blindly pushing on. Do you think some of your desperation at this point was to get settled so you could leave the marriage since your couple's counselor encouraged that?"

I look up and consider her question. "You might be on to something there. Somewhere in my subconscious I knew once we were settled, I could move on." I continue. "We moved to our own place in March of 2014. It was a really cute unit about a mile from the beach in Santa Barbara. Far enough from home that I didn't feel like I was in Santa Maria, but close enough that my family was there if I needed them. Once we got all moved in, things settled down between us for a month or so. Liam wasn't smoking pot because he was looking for a job, which he got a part-time one in his new career field. He made some friends through work. I enjoyed the month of April before starting my job. Violet, her husband Franz and their kids visited from Europe. We all took a trip to Santa Catalina to celebrate Mom's birthday. That's where Liam started smoking pot again. When we got back, I started my job. His first class was coming to an end and I inquired about his summer school plans. He blinked a few times and said he didn't think he was going to do Summer School. I was like 'O.K. then you are going to get another job or increase your hours?' And he was really angry with me. He carried on that he'd been through so much with the move and our relationship, that he needed this down time. I said 'O.K., as long as you can continue paying your part of the rent and monthly expenses.' He didn't speak to me for the rest of the day. I felt like his mother. He used to give her the silent treatment if she denied his requests for money."

"It sounds like his drug use coincided with more challenging times," Jennifer points out. "You mentioned your dad was also an alcoholic and used drugs. This pattern was familiar to you."

"Yes, it was," I concur.

"What happened next?" she asks.

"How much time do we have left?" I ask.

"About 20 minutes. Would you like to do some movement instead of continuing with the story?"

The words catch in my throat. I dread talking about this part. I feel so ashamed that I let this happen. I can't look at her. I hear Samantha's voice in my head. *You can do this, Anna. Get this off your chest.* I take a deep breath and exhale slowly.

"Not yet. I want to get this part out. At some point in early June, Liam texted me from work. It said something like 'Last night was hot.' I texted back 'What are you talking about?' He texted back 'You don't remember? I thought you woke up.' I texted back 'No I don't remember and did not wake up.' He texted 'Nothing bad. I fondled your hot ass and jacked off.' I didn't respond. My stomach knotted. I felt myself leave my body. I walked around like a zombie the rest of the day. When he got home, I confronted him. I said something like 'You know what happened to me.' Meaning the rape. I told him 'It happened in my own bed while I was asleep. And you did something similar in our bed. Why would you do that?' Tears streamed down my face. My eyes pleaded with him to say something to acknowledge how traumatizing that was for me. Instead he said 'I didn't mean it like that. I thought you would like hearing that I think your ass is hot and you turn me on.' He looked exasperated. He begged me to forget about it and not be mad at him." I look up at Jennifer and take a deep breath.

"And that is what led to your suicide crisis?" She asks intuitively.

"Yes." Sadness settles on me. My eyes strain trying to focus on anything. "The thing is, he did like my ass. Every morning in the beginning of our relationship, he caressed it and jacked off. I thought that was O.K. since I wasn't always in the mood to have sex. When I wasn't in the mood to let him touch my ass, he'd get mad. He'd say 'What am I supposed to do?' And I'd shoot back 'Watch your porn.' He used to tell me that on some days he would masturbate to porn 2 or 3 times a day. Once he said he did it 7 times in one day. I don't know why, with all of my training, I didn't realize he really struggled with addiction of many types.

"After that night that he texted me about fondling me while I slept, I stopped sleeping. I don't think I slept more than a couple hours for about a week. The suicidal thoughts started creeping in. I'd say things to myself like 'You're in such pain. You are in a hopeless situation. You can't get out of this. The only way out is to kill yourself. It's not his fault he married a crazy person. Don't penalize him for doing that just because you were raped. That's what husbands and wives do. If you don't want to do that, then you must not be marriage material. You are broken. You are trash. You will always be this way. Don't burden people anymore.'

"Then I was on a work trip and was eating alone at a restaurant. I didn't realize that sitting at the bar, eating a roast chicken dish and sipping a glass of white wine while reading a book meant I was open for business. I was in my workout clothes and had my wedding rings on. A middle-aged man with an accent came up from behind me and firmly put his hand in the middle of my back. When I looked at him startled, he asked 'What's wrong?' I told him to take his hands off me. He increased the pressure on my back and gave me a strange look. I said 'Do I know you?' For a second I thought maybe it was someone from college. My friends always have to remind me who people are because I can't ever remember. So I thought, maybe I'm being rude or something. He backed away with the dirtiest look on his face. Obviously I didn't know him. The restaurant was across the street and down the block from my hotel. It was one I went to on my first work trip with other colleagues, so I thought it was safe. I was so scared to walk home that I actually ran back to the hotel. I called Liam to tell him about it and he said he was sorry that happened, but encouraged me not to think too much about it. I know he was just trying to help, but didn't know how."

She gently asks, "What was your plan?"

"Well, the next day at my work meeting, I tried to talk to my boss about what happened, but I could tell the severity of the incident didn't resonate the same with him. Once I got home, every time I went to bed, Liam would be snoring, and I'd relive my rape. It felt like hundreds of times a night for the first few nights. Then I began researching ways to kill myself on my phone. I didn't want it to be too messy, like a gun. Plus I knew I would chicken out. I wanted it to be more likely to work than say driving my car off a cliff or into a tree. I started reading blogs about how to complete[24] suicide by ingesting something. You'd be surprised what's out there. I found

---

24 Several advanced readers questioned my word choice- "complete suicide" vs "commit suicide." In an effort to de-stigmatize suicide, I intentionally say "complete" or "died by" suicide instead of "commit." Criminals commit crimes. Unfaithful spouses commit adultery. These acts are shame-bound and stigmatizing. We don't say someone with cancer, "commits to cancer" when they die from cancer.

very few that said 'get help,' or 'call the national hotline'[25]. Not that I would have read them anyway. I was more interested in what people recommended in terms of pills.

"On the tenth night, it was about 3 or 4 in the morning. I found a website that sold the pill concoction I'd landed on. It wasn't that expensive. I knew Liam had to work that weekend, so I was planning to do it then. I think it was a Thursday, or actually early Friday morning. I could get the pills overnighted to arrive on Saturday. A voice…it sounded like my own voice maybe off in the distance…or maybe it was my Grandma's voice. I'm not sure. A voice said 'put your phone down. Tell your family tomorrow what's going on.' I don't know why, but I listened to it. I slept for a few hours and got an emergency appointment with my high school therapist. She had me sign the no-harm contract, which I agreed to give to my mom and sister. Well, I took a picture of it and texted it to my sister since she lives in Europe. I went to Dad and Lindsey's house and told them. Lindsey was a rock. A kind and warm rock. She held me and said it will be O.K. She asked if I wanted to stay with them that weekend. I was relieved because I didn't want to go home. That's the weekend I decided to leave my marriage." I'm suddenly exhausted.

Jennifer's expression is full of warmth and gratitude. "Thank you for sharing with me, Anna. That sounds so hard. I want to check in about how you're feeling now?"

"I'm really tired, but I feel surprisingly peaceful."

"Are you thinking about suicide now?" She asks like any astute clinician would in this case.

"No. I do not want to die." A memory from the mental health retreat flashes through my mind. "In fact, the first time I really felt

---

25 The National Suicide Prevention Lifeline provides a 24-hour free hotline or chat for anyone in distress or looking for resources to help someone in distress. Call or visit (800) 273-8255 or https://suicidepreventionlifeline.org.

like I didn't want to die was at that mental health retreat I told you about over the phone. We did a guided meditation that asked me to visualize myself as a young child, then as an elementary-aged child, then teenager and then present day. In each visualization, we were asked to go to that version of ourselves as the adult we are today. We journaled immediately following the meditation. I remember sobbing because I saw my littlest self all alone playing in my childhood bedroom, trying to keep quiet. Little Me looked at my adult self with such big innocent and confused eyes. Like she was saying 'why am I alone?' One of the facilitators sat with me and comforted me. She kept telling me that I am a fighter and I won't let suicide take my life. It was powerful."

"O.K. I'd like to share a few thoughts if that's O.K. with you." She continues when I nod. "It seems your family messages about gender roles and sex may have been destructive and unhealthy. These gender role messages also could be confusing since your parents encouraged you and your sister to be independent and financially stable, which is not typical for traditional female gender roles. It also seems that addiction, being that it is familiar to you, is a pattern that has played out in your adult relationships. I want to be clear on one point- none of the sexual stuff- the rape, the experience with your ex-husband- none of that was your fault. Just because you let Liam masturbate while touching you once doesn't mean he was allowed to do that any time he wanted. I want to make sure we establish that starting now, O.K.?" She stares at me intently. "I was impressed at how you told that man to take his hand off you. A lot of people who have been traumatized freeze or cause a scene. It sounds like you were firm in your boundaries. I'm sorry that you had to go through that. Even if you were dressed in something more provocative, that still doesn't give anyone the right to touch you without your permission."

"O.K." I know she's right. If I was the therapist, I'd be saying the same thing, but for some reason I'm having a hard time believing it.

"The experience you had with that meditation on retreat does sound powerful. We'll continue that work. I want you to know that if at any time you feel suicide creeping up, you can contact me. O.K?" She waits for me to nod. "We have a few more minutes. Are you interested in doing a little movement?"

"I'm pretty tired, but yeah, let's try something. What do you have in mind?" I'm really reluctant. I've been very vulnerable today.

"I sense you feel a bit raw and exposed, so I'd like to do some self-soothe movement." She stands up and gets a mat. "If you want to do this, you can lie on the mat in a comfortable position."

I lie on my back.

"O.K., now tell me where I can put a pillow that would make it more comfortable for you."

I look at her quizzically and take a deep breath. *What would make me more comfortable? That's a new thought.*

"I guess under my head. And maybe under my bum." As she hands me pillows and helps me position them, I realize what we're doing. I think to myself, *this feels really good.* "Let's do another one behind my back and neck. And also my knees."

She's smiling. "Anywhere else?"

I shake my head. *My elbows and heels are sort of uncomfortable on the mat, but no need to bother her for more pillows.*

"You sure? I can get more pillows." I nod my head. "What about a blanket? Or soft music?"

I nod again. "A blanket and soft music is nice. What now?"

She says, "Lie there and feel what it feels like to be taken care of. If you want you can close your eyes. We have a few minutes. I could also leave the room if you want."

Pansy nuzzles at my side. Jennifer giggles, "Pansy obviously wants some comfort, too. Do you want me to get her?"

My eyes are closed and I'm smiling, too. "No that's O.K. This feels good. Different, but good."

After a few minutes, she says "Anna, we're about at time. Open your eyes when you're ready."

I slowly open my eyes. The clock is over time by a few minutes. She sees me looking.

"You seemed so at peace, I let us go a little longer. I hope that was O.K. Next time I will ask you. How was that?"

"I don't feel as exhausted and raw. Thank you for listening to me verbal vomit this whole time." I smile cheekily.

She looks at me with uncertainty. "I did not think you verbal vomited at all. It was beautiful what you shared and how open you were in our first session."

I back track. "Verbal vomit is a funny term some of our clients came up with at work about what counseling is like. It isn't that pretty of a metaphor though."

She hesitates. "I also sensed some self-deprecation?"

Damn she's good. The thought pops in my mind out of the blue. I lie to Jennifer. "Oh no. Just making light after a heavy session."

Her facial expression tells me that she doesn't quite believe me, but lets it go. "O.K. Do you want to continue to work together?"

"Yes," I say. "The only thing is I can't come back until the beginning of next month because I've got stuff each weekend this month. I know I said weekends are good for me, and I honestly don't know how this happened. Well two weekends I have to leave on Sunday for work. Anyway, can we start weekly then?"

"Sure," she hesitates. "That is an awful lot of time and you just shared a lot with me. Please call me or email me if anything comes up before we meet next."

The sun is setting as I walk to my car. I have a good feeling about this.

∞∞∞

That night in bed, I position pillows all around me like Jennifer did earlier today. I think to myself, w*ow. I can't believe I've never thought to do this before.* I reminisce about the retreat. They said we have to think about ourselves as newly developing beings. I tell myself, *I guess I'm in infancy…this almost feels like a swaddle.*

I really appreciated the emphasis the retreat facilitators placed on understanding the impact of trauma on the brain[26]. Essentially, my primitive brain has been in charge for a long time. According to my small group facilitator, I have a really high functioning executive brain that helped me maintain a somewhat normal life despite the trauma I've experienced.

I ask myself, w*ith all my training, how did I not know that?* I shake my head.

A voice answers. *You read about the impact of trauma on the brain and how that impacts behavior, but you obviously didn't get it. It didn't sink in.*

I stare at the pictures of my niece and nephew, Leah and Max on my dresser. I shake my head again. Instead of writing in my journal or watching Homeland On Demand, I decide to read my journal

---

26 Dr. Bessel van der Kolk is a leader in providing scientific evidence of the connection between trauma, the brain and the body, and on effective treatments for post-traumatic stress. For additional information, please read his book titled The Body Keeps The Score.

from the time right after I moved out of our apartment in Santa Barbara. One entry stands out. I wrote it on the day I registered for the mental health retreat.

July 9, 2014

Prayers answered
Hope
Living my potential
Peaceful
Not exhausted
Looking forward
Open arms
How much I've hid in the bathroom
         To avoid crisis
Fearful of closeness
Afraid of myself
Want to feel worthy
Want to know me

I rest the journal on my lap and think about Catherine, my best friend from my master's degree. I ask myself, *remember when she put you to work 'harvesting' the cilantro leaves for the guacamole because 'your family is in ag'?* I giggle out loud. My mind wanders back to our telephone conversation that afternoon on July 9th, the same day I registered for the retreat. I was driving to one of my work sites...

"Hi Catherine. I have news," I say. "I've left Liam."

"Really? Honestly, I'm not surprised," she said. "I'm all ears."

"Well, I was really suicidal for like 10 days. I just couldn't take it anymore and didn't see any way out of my life. When I was younger I used to hide in the bathroom when the going got tough at home. Pictures of Leah and Max used to give me solace. Nothing was working. It's not his fault. He didn't get it. I didn't really even get it. He wants me to move back in. He wants me to go back to counseling with him and reconcile. He wants…"

"Whoa. Whoa. Whoa!" she interrupts. "To be clear, it doesn't matter what he wants at this point. You are struggling for your life and he doesn't help. He made it worse. It doesn't matter what he wants. What do you want?"

Her words hit me like a ton of bricks. They play back in my head. *You are struggling for your life…*

"To stop hiding in bathrooms."

She chuckles. "Yes, you've been hiding in bathrooms a long time. You don't have to do that though. You owe nothing to anyone, except yourself. You owe yourself a chance to come out of that bathroom and live in the world."

I remember driving by a field that had recently been tilled. *It smelled like a bathroom at that moment in the drive, too.* I close my journal, adjust the pillows, and have no problem falling asleep.

Reflections ∞ Reactions ∞ Responses

CHAPTER 11
PANIC AT THE AIRPORT

The following Sunday I sit in one of the black pleather chairs at my gate in the airport. I'm flying up north for work. My chest is really tight. I have trouble breathing. I can't focus. I think to myself, *ugh… not again. Why is this happening?*

I review in my mind what happened in the last few days and what's upcoming in the next few days that could cause this anxiety flare up. *The divorce attorney meeting was last week. Liam can't understand why I am going through with the divorce.*

A voice reminds me, *you were pretty deflated after you talked to him last week.*

An announcement comes over the loud speaker asking for emergency responders in baggage claim. I think, *great, now the airport is going to blow up.* My thoughts become sarcastic. *Stop being so dramatic Anna and breathe. You are o.k. You've flown a million times. This is nothing new.*

I decide to text Jennifer to see if we can talk for a moment. Relief floods over me when her response comes back within seconds. She can talk for about 15 minutes.

She picks up after the first ring. "Hi Anna. I'm glad you reached out. What's going on?"

"I'm at the airport on a work trip and feeling really anxious. I tried deep breathing and talking myself out of it, but it isn't working." I feel so lame explaining my current state to Jennifer.

The sarcastic thoughts continue. *This is ridiculous. You are a grown woman, Anna.*

Her voice drowns out my inner critic. "Well, Anna you were really raw last weekend. Even though you have traveled alone, and are very capable of traveling by yourself, you are raw right now. And that rawness can make you extra vulnerable. Did anything happen that could have triggered this?"

My chest loosens. "I talked to Liam and a divorce attorney this week," I state bluntly. "I liked the divorce attorney. But when I talked to Liam, I felt like I got caught up in a vortex. Like swept into his guilt-trip, sob story. I felt so bad and so angry all at the same time. I shut down. I've kind of been in a daze ever since he and I talked."

"And now you are on a work trip, going to an unfamiliar place, by yourself. It is understandable that your anxiety would be higher right now." She normalizes my experience. "What you described with Liam, the vortex, is also somewhat common with loved ones of addicts. Addiction makes people manipulative and it's easy to get sucked into that vortex. My hunch is you've experienced that vortex before when you have left feeling dazed and wondering 'what just happened?' You disrupted the pattern this time by reaching out to me."

The more she normalizes what I am experiencing, the calmer I feel.

Her next question prompts me to use my phone. "You mentioned you have a meditation on your phone about grounding and centering?"

"Yes," I respond excitedly, nodding my head.

"Do you have time to listen to that before you get on your flight?" She offers a suggestion without telling me what to do.

I think to myself, *she is really good pointing to coping tools that I already have.*

"Jennifer, thank you. You just reminded me that I can do this." As soon as we hang up, I play a grounding meditation. I feel my feet solidly on the floor, the chair under my body. My breath is back to normal by the time I board my flight.

Reflections ∞ Reactions ∞ Responses

_____

_____

_____

CHAPTER 12

MOM, NATURE, MUSIC AND RELIGION

Home again! I'm happy to be sleeping in my own bed. Fortunately, after the anxiety I felt at the airport and talking with Jennifer, I didn't have any other flare ups this week. My phone buzzes on the night stand. I roll over with an annoyed huff. *I really need to remember to put that on Do Not Disturb.* Who's calling me so early on a Saturday? My screen reads ICE[27]-Mom-Melanie and says it is 10:15. My annoyance softens. *O.K. I guess it's not that early.*

"Hi Mom." My voice is flat like my mood.

"Hi Anna. What are you doing today?"

I think to myself, *she sure sounds chipper today.*

"No plans." I suddenly feel really sad.

"Want to go for a hike? It's beautiful today. We could go to the Sanctuary." We call the Bluff Trail the Sanctuary.

I stifle a groan. *Her chipper-ness has got to stop.*

---

27 ICE stands for In Case of Emergency. At some point in the past, I read an email forward about using ICE in my phone contact list to indicate who to call if something happens to me.

120

Reluctantly, I agree to meet her in 30 minutes. I look at myself in the bathroom mirror as I brush my teeth. *Dark circles and sunken in eyes. You look sick.* It takes a lot of effort to put my hiking clothes on. I don't hear Dad and Lindsey, which is a saving grace. I don't actually want to interact with the world today.

What song can I put on to match this crappy mood? That thought makes me smile. *Nothing like wallowing in sadness.* This thought makes me chuckle.

Florence and the Machine is already in my car stereo. It doesn't match my mood, but there is a darkness to their lyrics that comfort me. I scroll to number 4 and turn the volume up to 26. Never Let Me Go is one of my favorite songs. I put my sunglasses on and shift the car into reverse. I feel less curmudgeon-like. *It is nice out today. Mom was right.* I feel my heart stir as the song opens. I turn the volume up again so I can sing at the top of my lungs without ruining the song. I start soft, like Florence does.

My mind wanders to childhood summers at Grandma's house. *I loved playing in the waves with Elizabeth and Violet. Diving under the waves. Life was so care-free on those summer days.*

My mind daydreams with the second verse. *Now I'm older, floating on my back. It's low tide. The sun is beginning to go down. I'm peaceful as my legs begin to sink.* I feel the fog lift as I take a deep breath and belt out the chorus. *The warm ocean surrounds me. The currents gently rock me.* Even though I shouldn't be able to breathe under water, I am very much alive in my daydream. *That's a little weird. Maybe it is my mermaid self.* I giggle at myself and recall the many hours in the ocean and neighborhood pools I spent playing mermaid with my friends.

I'm filled with joy. *I love this song!* I drive past the lupine field. The purple flowers aren't in bloom, but I imagine my grandma bending over to smell the lupines when she visited us in the early

80s. *Mom always reminds me that those flowers were in bloom when she brought me home from the hospital after my birth.*

I join Florence again, "But the arms of the ocean deliver me/ And it's over and I'm going under." My mind returns to an image of me floating on my back and slowly sinking under. I sing along, "But I'm not giving up/I'm just giving in."

I can sense the comfort of the ocean around me. *I don't want to die,* I think to myself. *I just want to surrender and let the ocean carry me, rock me, cocoon me, protect me, cleanse me.* I'm still singing along with Florence. My favorite part is the last verse. I think about the words in that verse. *God it would feel so good to have my sins released.* I stop my sing a-long and listen to Florence wrap up the song. *Please ocean, don't ever let me go.*

Mom sits on the front brick ledge as I pull up to my childhood home. The front yard hasn't changed much in the last 30 plus years. Mom nurtures her garden. She loves being outside with Mother Nature. She always tells us that Mother Nature is our church. We head up to the trail. On a clear day, we can see up and down the coast for miles. We reach the Sanctuary in about 30 minutes.

Mom asks, "Anna, have you thought about doing anything for the High Holidays?" She came to the East Coast for my Beit Din and Mikveh[28]. She isn't Jewish, but she knows Judaism is important to me.

Tears well up as I think about my limited Jewish network in California. "I really want to do something. It makes me really miss Liam. When we did Jewish things together…that's when I felt like we were true partners. I don't really know anyone out here. I mean Elizabeth's sister's husband is Jewish, but they're busy with their kids this year."

---

28 A Beit Din and Mikveh are the final steps to convert to Judaism.

"Have you looked at any of the temples in the area? Maybe you can get involved?" Mom puts her arm around me. "Liora needs a home."

Liora is my Hebrew name. The Rabbi who worked with me during my conversion helped me pick her name. It means "I have light."

That evening I reflect on my conversion. I wish my rabbi was closer. I miss Liam and our faith community. My thoughts get louder in my head. *Maybe I should just look up the local shuls*[29]. *I'm sure they are doing something for Rosh Hashanah*[30]. *It starts in two days. But do I really want to go alone? I feel like such an imposter.* I click on Internet Explorer and type the name of the local shul. *Hmmm…Tashlich. That could be interesting. Maybe Mom could go with me. It's at the beach.* The website says Tashlich means "casting off" in Hebrew and it is a ritual to symbolically "cast off" sins from the previous year in a flowing body of water. I think, *Yeah, I want to do that.* It is scheduled in a few days. Luckily I'm not traveling this week for work. I text mom to see if she can go with me.

Of course she responds yes.

∞∞∞

The coastline is breathtaking on the afternoon of Tashlich. A light breeze, salty fresh air, white sands, medium waves. I'm really nervous. I don't know anyone. They gather in a circle around the rabbi. Mom and I stand on the outside. We take a copy of the program. I notice each person has a bag of bread. I feel embarrassed that I am unprepared. I didn't bring anything. My toes grip the sand. Mom is calm. She smiles and says hi to those standing near us.

The rabbi begins with a prayer in Hebrew. "Baruch Atah Adonai Eloheinu Melech Ha-Olam…"

---

29 A shul is a synagogue.

30 Rosh Hashanah, the Jewish New Year is the first of the High Holy Days.

A wave of nostalgia washes over me. I fight back tears. It's been so long since I heard those words. I don't hear the rest of the prayers or the story of the origin of Tashlich. I feel warmth. My nerves calm down. I realize I feel safe in this group of strangers. We sing a few songs from the program. Everyone laughs when the rabbi excuses us from the rest of the songs "to get to the good part." We roll up our pant legs and walk to water's edge. I stand back and watch everyone rip pieces of bread. Some throw them from where they stand. Others walk into the shallows of the waves and set their bread in the water. Some say a prayer out loud and others don't. I'm struck by how personal, yet communal this ritual is. I think about my sins of the past year. I ask myself, w*here do I begin?*

A woman offers me some bread. I accept with thanks. I break it into two pieces as I wade in the shallow waves. The water's chill does not bother me. It feels purifying. I wonder what to say. Then a prayer comes softly from my heart. *God forgive me for wanting to take my own life.* I drop a piece of bread in the wave and watch it wash away from me. Louder I hear my next prayer come from my heart. *God forgive my sins and help me find value and purpose in my life. Help me want to live.* Tears flood my eyes. My heart opens. *I'm so sorry I wanted to die. I'm so sorry for this pain.* I toss the last piece of bread at the next wave and watch the foam swallow it. I stare out to sea and feel the sand wash out from under my feet with each receding wave. I talk to Grandma, which I haven't done in a long time. *Grandma I'm going to be O.K.* For the first time I actually believe that I will be O.K.

Reflections ∞ Reactions ∞ Responses

_____

_____

_____

CHAPTER 13

RECOGNIZE SOMATIC RESPONSES TO TRAUMA

I've been looking forward to my second session with Phora all week. I smell essential oils in the hall outside her office. The building has big orange Spanish tile floors, stucco walls, and exposed beam. It feels sturdy, warm, and safe. I remember my first session...it was also in the evening. Phora walked me to my car after it ended so I wasn't alone. I didn't even have to ask her. She is incredibly intuitive and thoughtful.

"Hi there Beautiful." She embraces me in a warm hug. "How are you doing?"

I know Phora genuinely wants to know how I am doing, so the "I'm fine" answer won't fly.

"I'm doing O.K. I had my first session with that movement therapist I told you about last time. It went really well. I think she will really be able to help me. We are meeting again this upcoming weekend. My ex-husband sent me a long letter. I honestly haven't read it. I just can't yet. Work has been a bit stressful. We are launching the counseling program right now. I'm really glad to be here. I've been looking forward to it all week." I settle into the chair that sits to the right of the door.

She sits on a stool facing me. "Where is your body feeling all of it?" Posters of the body's muscular and skeletal systems on the wall behind her punctuate her question.

I think for a moment because I haven't thought of my body all week. "The base of my skull, my wrist and elbow joints. My hips are really tight. Oh and my jaw is constantly achy."

"So it sounds like your joints are carrying a lot of your stress." She pauses and gazes up toward the ceiling before continuing. "I know deep tissue is what many people think of as the best kind of massage. Last time you shared that you haven't felt your hips and legs for as long as you can remember. You told me about the massage therapist who worked on you at the retreat. You described that she worked on blending your energy because it was all in the upper half of your body. I'd like to continue that work. There may be sessions where we don't go deep tissue, but that doesn't mean it isn't effective. Does that sound O.K. with you?"

"That is O.K. with me. You are the expert and I trust you."

She steps out so I can get ready. As I lie on the table waiting for Phora, I remember Claudia, one of two massage therapists who worked on me at the mental health retreat. After my first massage with her, Claudia said "I need to tell you something about your energy. You can be feminine and masculine at the same time. You don't have to hide your femininity. Just because someone took advantage of you and the messages you received about being a woman may seem like femininity is weak doesn't mean that is true. You do not have to hide yourself. You can be strong and feminine. Your feminine energy has been locked away, which has helped you survive until now. My wish for you is to unlock it and embrace it." I hugged her as I wept. Actually it was more like I clung to her. This woman had just given me such a gift. She made me aware of a mystery I'd been trying to unlock for a long time- I can be masculine *and* feminine and both energies are strong. A flood gate came down in that moment. I felt something in my heart that was not panic or pain. It had been so long since I felt something else. I couldn't name the feeling.

I ran into Sasha on my way back to my room that day. Sasha was in my small group. She is the epitome of feminine. Beautiful, tall, fit, great smile, tan. She exudes confident woman. Sasha had her tennis skirt and bikini top on as she headed to the pool. She leaned down and swept me into a bear hug. "Annie-girl, you are beautiful." And she was off. *Wow, the universe was right on par that day. Did I feel self-compassion?*

Phora's knock on the door brings me back to the present. "Anna are you ready?"

"Yes." I hear the door open and close. "What aroma do you have under my nose today?"

"It is a blend from Young Living called Clarity. Clarity promotes a clear mind and mental alertness. Rosemary and peppermint found in the blend have been used for years to improve mental activity and vitality." I hear her near the shelves where she keeps her lotions, towels, neck pads, and other tools. "Inhaling peppermint oil can increase mental accuracy. It also relieves toxic buildup and could help those who get headaches." She opens and closes a door with a gentle click. "Clarity may also keep one from going into shock during times of trauma. It's known to be uplifting, refreshing and invigorating. And it may be beneficial for clearing confusion. I use the oil on you so that when we are talking about any stresses you might have, you may be able to relive them with focus, but also feel supported. Is it O.K. for you? I can also change it if you like."

I am at ease knowing why she selected that scent for me and appreciate that she checks in with me regularly to make sure everything is O.K. I take a deep breath in through my nose and feel calm enter my body. "Yes, I like it."

"How is the temperature?" She inquires.

"Very comfortable. My feet are cold, but what's new."

I hear a soft click again and soon feel a warm pad on my feet.

She whispers, "This should help until we get your energy flowing through your body."

I smile as best I can in the face cradle. "You are a magician Phora. Where did that come from?"

"I have a couple towel warmers in here just in case." She begins by gently placing her hands on my back outside the sheet that covers my body. She moves her right hand down to my hamstrings while her left hand stays on my back. Her left hand joins her right only after her right hand is gently and firmly on my leg. She repeats this pattern until she covers all of my body.

She must sense that I am tracking her move. "I do that because it is important for your body to feel my touch before I actually begin the massage. It shows respect and allows your body to acclimate to my touch. It also helps me see where your energy flows and where it is stuck."

I mumble, "Thanks for sharing Phora. I really like learning about what we are doing."

"I can tell your body has been touched in hurtful ways. A body holds memories of healthy and harmful experiences[31]. If you ever

---

31 The connection between mind and body is well documented in research. For more information, please visit http://www.besselvanderkolk.net, http://www. traumacenter.org/, https://www.sensorimotorpsychotherapy.org and https://adta.org/american-dance-therapy-journal/.

feel like I am doing something that isn't comfortable, or reminds you of a painful experience, please let me know. It is important that you tell me so we can make adjustments. Your comfort is most important, O.K. Anna?"

"O.K. Phora. I will."

This experience is another new one for me. Her words settle over my body like the blanket Jennifer laid over me in our last session. Suddenly, in my mind I'm sitting on Grandma's lap in the mid-80s. The summer morning sun lights up the kitchen and dining room. Coffee and peaches fill the air. Her blue velour robe is soft against my check as she cradles me and rubs my back while I slowly wake up. *Wow I haven't thought about that memory in a long time. Grandma's house was so calm. The birds chirped and the ocean breeze danced through the house. Never a shortage of love and so predictable.* My breath is steady and full. As Phora continues long flowing strokes on my right side, I begin to see beautiful swirling colors in my mind.

"I'm having a light show Phora."

"Really? What colors are you seeing?"

"Blues, yellows, reds, greens, oranges. All swirling around. It's really pretty." She places more hot pads on my right side before transitioning to the left.

"Phora my left side is totally black." I'm alarmed.

She is calm. "That's O.K. Anna. That happens sometimes. Pay loose attention to it and try not to focus on it too much. We will see if we can open it up."

I grow aware of drum beats filling the room. The drum beats help me pace my inhales and exhales. Phora works on my left back and arm. Speckles of white and yellow light begin to appear as if I am floating in outer space. They are faint. Blackness swallows them when she moves to my left leg. Seeing those faint stars give me hope. *My left side isn't dead.*

After the massage, Phora checks in. "How was that?"

I feel scared. "Phora, why was the left side black?"

"Well, there could be a number of reasons. One that may resonate though is feminine energy is associated with the left side and masculine energy with the right side. Given what you've shared, I think it is a blessing that your feminine energy began to sparkle. I was working on blending your energy today and that means opening blocked channels." She is wise, like Claudia. "Like the massage therapist from the retreat, I was trying to open your feminine side with long, gentle movements."

My mind tunes in to the drum beats. "O.K. What was that music? I liked those drum beats."

She shows me the CD cover. "Do you want me to write down the name?"

"No," I say. "Hold it up and I'll snap a picture of it."

She smiles and shakes her head at the same time. "That's a great use of technology! I would have never thought to do that."

I thank her as she walks me to my car. "I'll see you in two weeks."

∞∞∞

I wake up Sunday morning with itchy arms. I inspect my skin for a rash, but there isn't one. I try lotion without relief. *Maybe a Benadryl?* That doesn't help either. The skin on my shins begin to itch, too. *What the hell is going on?* I throw lotion in my bag as I run out the door to meet Jennifer.

We settle on the floor instead of the couch this time. Pansy chews on a toy. I'm trying not to itch my forearms, but can't help it.

Jennifer raises her eyebrows. "Your arms are itchy."

"I know," I say exasperated. "I'm not sure why. I've tried everything that I could think of to stop them from itching. There aren't any bumps or hives. I can't find any mosquito bites. I was afraid of bed bugs since I've been traveling so much, but so far no symptoms of those either. Just itchy. And it's only my arms and shins. Isn't that weird?"

She nods. "Yes that is strange."

"You know what it actually feels like?" It suddenly dawns on me. "When I was little I spent most days at the pool, beach, in the backyard sprinklers, and running around the neighborhood with friends. We were mostly good about sunblock, but sometimes we forgot. Anyway, I'm blessed with my dad's and grandma's fair skin. The Swedish, English, and Irish side. I've had some pretty bad sunburns. This itch feels like it felt when my skin peeled after a really bad sunburn."

"Have you been out in the sun lately?" she asks.

"Not really. Not enough to get a sunburn." I'm quiet for a moment. "Do you think my body is healing? I told my small group at the retreat that I felt like I was sunburned living in a tanning bed during the suicide crisis. Am I somehow actually experiencing that?"

"It's possible, or maybe there is another medical condition going on. The mind and body are connected though." She shifts gears. "How have you been since we talked on the phone?"

"I've been really busy with work for the most part, so I haven't really had time to get anxious." For some reason, I don't feel like talking as much today.

"Do you want to talk about anything today?" She must sense my reluctance.

"Nothing really new has come up. The divorce is moving along. I'm still at my dad and Lindsey's house." I'm grappling for something to say. "Oh, here is something you might appreciate. Mom and I went to Tashlich at the beach with the local shul. It was an incredible spiritual experience. And very cleansing."

She smiles. "That's a lovely ritual. Do you want to tell me more about it?" I feel a lump catch in my throat and tears well up. "Oh, it seems like it was powerful. Where in your body do you feel it right now?" She is calm with a steady gaze.

I swallow. "I didn't expect to feel anything like that." My voice quivers. "I feel it in my chest and jaw."

"What do you feel?" Pansy barks and bolts towards the windows. "Pansy. Pansy. Be quiet. It's just a bird. Pansy." Jennifer chuckles softly. "I'm sorry about that."

I smile. "That is quite alright. Saved by the bark." Now I chuckle.

Silence settles around us. Pansy walks back over and perches her front paws on a pillow facing my direction, as if she is waiting for me to go on.

"I've got the feeling." I look at Pansy and start crying. "I'm just really sad. I'm sad that I don't have a strong faith community. I'm sad that I was so close to dying. I'm sad I put my family and friends through such a scare. I'm sad for the little girl I used to be. Where did she go? I've been thinking about my grandma a lot and all the times we spent down at the beach with her and my grandpa. It was so predictable, calm, quiet, peaceful. We had so much fun. We were carefree. Standing out in the waves with my piece of bread, I felt that carefree young girl. I'd lost touch with her and I didn't even realize it. I'm just sad. And I miss my grandma and those summer days. I don't remember being scared there." I pause as a memory flashes through my mind. "Well, actually, I used to be scared at night. Violet and I used to sleep with Grandma in a queen bed. Poor Grandma would have to sleep in the middle because both of us wanted to be closest to her. I don't know what Violet was scared of, but I was convinced that Michael Jackson's Thriller zombies were going to come out of the carpet on my side of the bed. One time when we were in our early twenties, Mom, Violet and I were staying with Grandpa. My grandma died in 1993 on my 8th grade graduation day. That's another story. Anyway, we were too grossed out to sleep on the pull out couch in the den because Grandpa didn't keep the house very clean and we found mice droppings in there. So, the three of us shared that same queen bed, only this time Violet had to sleep in the middle because she is the youngest. Anyway, I thought my mom had dozed off, so I whispered 'Violet, do you remember when I thought Michael Jackson Thriller lived under the bed?' All of a sudden, the bed started shaking and my mom started snort laughing. Pretty soon we were all laughing that deep belly laugh. It was a glorious moment."

Jennifer's expression is amused. "Your relationship with your mom, sister and grandma seem like they were really strong. Not everyone has even 1 family member to share deep belly laughs."

"Yes, I'm grateful for them. I know I would not be here if it wasn't for them. I mean grounded. Well, not that I am that grounded anymore either. But you know what I mean." I struggle to find the right words to express the impact they've had on my life.

"I know what you mean. They've helped mold and shape you by sharing in moments like the one with Thriller. They've created calm and stable environments where you could be carefree and in the moment. Is that right?"

"Yes, exactly." Now I feel guilty because I didn't mention Dad. "My dad helped mold me, too, but in different ways. Not just in those assholic-alcoholic ways that were scary and unpredictable. He also taught me to do math, and encouraged us to read. He bought us books and paid us a dollar for every book we finished. I went through all the Nancy Drew's in like a week! I still love reading to this day. He was great at all-time quarter-back in the neighborhood two-hand touch football games. Dad always encouraged us to dream big and take advantage of every opportunity that comes our way. He was famous for saying 'keep as many balls in the air as possible.' I've always said my mom grounds me and my dad sets me free."

Jennifer is thoughtful. "That's beautiful. Even though your dad struggled with alcoholism, he was still your dad. He still did fatherly things that showed his love for you and Violet. You mentioned when we first started that you were feeling emotion in your chest and jaw. Did you share about the feeling that was in your jaw? You said sadness, I think in connection with your chest."

Now it's my turn to be thoughtful. "When I was on the retreat, there were two massage therapists. One was Claudia and the other was Julia. Both helped me a lot. Anyway, when Julia was massaging me, I did something I'd never done before during a massage. I was lying on my back, and I had an overwhelming urge for her to massage my jaw. She was working on my wrists. So I asked her if she could please move to my jaw. She asked if I meant right then or after she was done with both wrists. I said right then. I never directed a massage like that. Anyway, as soon as she started gently rubbing my jaw, tears flowed out of the sides of my eyes, down my temples." I gesture with both hands from the outer corner of my eyes down my temple to my hair line to show Jennifer what I meant. "She began gently massaging my tears into my jaw. I heard a voice say 'Violet saved your life.' It was so clear and distinct. It had such firm resolve. Like a very articulate voice. I remember my chest opened a little after that." I say softly, "I think I felt love."

Jennifer asked, "Is that what you felt in your jaw earlier today?"

"Honestly, I'm not sure. The feeling in my chest was sadness. My chest felt very similar to that day on the massage table with Julia. Like there was movement. And somehow my jaw is connected to it."

Jennifer offers insight. "It could mean that love and sadness are connected. That would make sense."

"Yeah, maybe." I'm suddenly tired.

"You seem tired. Are you interested in doing some movement?"

"O.K." I nod. "What do you have in mind?"

"Well, I was thinking we could do a body scan. Have you ever done one?" Her voice is tentative.

"I've done some guided meditations on YouTube that do body scans, but I'm not sure if it is the same as what you are talking about. The ones I've done are to help relax tense muscles for sleep."

She stands and begins to walk toward the cabinets. "O.K. This is similar, but a little different. You'll lie on your back again and put one hand over your head and stretch it and the same leg in opposite directions. Then you do the other side. We will see if there are any blocked spots." She returns with a yoga mat and places it on the ground. "I'm going to hold Pansy for this because I don't want her to interrupt you."

I lie on my back and stretch my right arm up and over my head. Simultaneously, I stretch my right leg away from my hip.

Jennifer says, "Good. Now take a deep breath and see if there are any areas that seem blocked or stuck on your right side."

After a moment, I shake my head. "Seems pretty good to me."

I repeat with my left arm and leg. Immediately my left hip locks up. I continue stretching my arm and feet away from each other, but can't seem to get my left hip to budge.

She asks, "Are you feeling any blocks?"

"Yes, in my left hip." *Isn't that interesting...what would Phora and Nanette say?*

"Can I do a light hands on?" she asks.

I look at her quizzically. I've never known a mental health therapist who asks to touch a client.

"We haven't done that yet, have we?" I shake my head. "I will put one hand under your hip bone and apply slight pressure. Then I will ask you what you are feeling, or seeing, or hearing. If you don't want to that is O.K., too. Sometimes light pressure can help move the block."

"Let's try it." I wait while she applies slight pressure and take a deep breath. "An image just appeared in my mind of a dead tree. But it's not really dead. It just doesn't have any leaves. I don't think it is dead. The grass around it is green. It is on a rolling hill." *What is that word I am looking for? It isn't really dead, but it doesn't have leaves, but it looks dead.*

She removes her hand. "Good Anna. You have a barren tree in your hip. It will be interesting to see if anything grows around it or if it gets leaves over the course of our work together. If you have time over the next week, try writing about it, or anything we talked about today with your left hand."

I make a face and bolt up. "I forgot to tell you I can't meet for two weeks."

Jennifer looks concerned. "That's a lot of time to miss. Are you sure Sundays are the best days for you?"

I'm apologetic. "I know. I'm really sorry. I meant to talk to you about it at the beginning. Next weekend my small group from the retreat are coming in. After that, I will not miss another Sunday until I go to Europe for Christmas."

Her face softens. "O.K. The women from the retreat are coming in? That will be great."

My mind focuses on the tree image as I leave our session that day. *Does that tree have roots even though it doesn't have leaves?* I pick up some aloe vera on my way home because that used to soothe my peeling sunburned skin when I was young. I apply it in the car before leaving the parking lot. To my surprise, the skin on my arms and shins soak up the aloe vera and stop itching. *Unbelievable!* I shake my head before turning the ignition.

Reflections ∞ Reactions ∞ Responses

_____

_____

_____

CHAPTER 14

REGULAR, NORMAL FUN
WITH THE SMALL GROUP[32]

Another long travel week is coming to a close. I peer out the window of the airplane as the runway comes up to greet us. Despite my fatigue, I'm all smiles. Sasha, Camille, and Dusty are coming this weekend. We haven't all been together since the retreat. I can't believe this part of my healing plan is actually working out! Sasha is flying in from the East Coast later tonight. Camille arrived from the Midwest a few hours ago. Dusty is driving in from Ontario county tomorrow evening. They are my go-tos whenever I have anxiety, panic attacks and suicidal ideation. They've made it easier for me to talk about what I'm feeling without being judged. Plus, we can also simply hang out and be together doing regular, normal activities that friends do together. Like go out to dinner, talk about dating, and giggle and joke about life. I have such gratitude that we've remained close since the mental health retreat.

---

32 Many advanced readers suggested this chapter was too long and unnecessary. I changed the chapter title to reflect why this chapter is important. I relished times when I had fun with friends without having to wear a mask, when I felt normal doing everyday regular things. For these reasons, I did not change the content of this chapter.

I see Camille across baggage claim sitting at a Starbucks tables. It reminds me of the first time I saw her, which also happened to be sitting in the baggage claim where we flew in for the retreat. Like then, she has her earbuds in while scrolling through her phone. Unlike then, she looks up and smiles when she sees me.

"Hiiiiiiiiiiiii," I shout across baggage claim.

I run-walk to give her a bear hug. We are like the actors at the beginning of Love Actually, the 2003 movie set in London's Heathrow international arrivals hall.

After stopping by Trader Joes and In and Out, we arrive at the beach house. Dad and Lindsey offered it to us this weekend instead of all of us staying at their house. The beach house is in Arroyo Grande, about 20 minutes from Santa Maria. It has a balcony that overlooks the ocean and four bedrooms, so we all have our own space. We plan to hike along the coast and have a cooking class at Aunt Tessa's house. Grandma G, my dad's step-mom and Mom are going to be there, too. Even though Yom Kippur[33] was last weekend, Aunt Tessa and I crafted some menu items based on traditional Yom Kippur dishes.

"Camille, how are you really?" We chit chatted in the car on the way home. Now it is time to go deeper.

Worry flashes across her face. "I'm really overwhelmed. I'm supposed to finish my junior year in May and have no idea how I'm going to do that. I'm thinking of medically withdrawing from school because my depression is just really bad right now."

---

33 Yom Kippur is often thought of as the holiest of the high holidays in Judaism. It is the Day of Atonement and is celebrated with a day of fasting from sundown the day before to sundown the day of. Break the Fast, which involves lots of food, family, friends and conversation closes the holiday.

"Oh no Camille. I'm so sorry to hear that. I know you've had a hard time but I didn't realize you are considering taking time off from school."

Her voice is monotone. "Yeah. I just don't know what to do. I'm switching up my medications and I've talked with our counselor from the retreat on the phone regularly. But I just feel like everything is closing in on me."

"What will you do if you take time off?"

"Oh, I don't know. I honestly don't think it will help that much." She redirects the conversation to me. "What about you? How are you doing really?"

"Well…" My mind draws a blank. I'm still worried about her. "I'm doing actually pretty well all things considered. I mean, don't get me wrong, it is hard and my energy is all over the place. Like somedays I'm up and somedays I can't even muster the energy to get out of bed. Except I have to work, so I do get out of bed. I really like my therapist a lot. And the medication seems to be working. I don't like that I live back here because the rapist does, too. Every time I go somewhere, I worry about running into him."

She nods. "I can only imagine. He really messed you up."

"Yes he did." My mind wanders back to retreat. "Do you remember that bucket of yuck I made on retreat?"

She makes a face. "Yes, that was disgusting. Remember that one guy even spit in it?"

"It was so gross. I put everything gross in there I could possibly think of. Dirt, rocks, garbage, spit from him and a few others. I stirred in water. Remember, I kept stirring and stirring until something gave away and I sobbed my eyes out. That was so cathartic."

"Yeah, you did a lot of that kind of stuff on retreat." She pulls the blanket around her tighter. "I didn't have the energy for any of that."

"I remember that. We were really worried about you. You spent a lot of time in the small group room."

"Ugh. I don't want to think about that." She returns the focus of the conversation to me. "Remember when you punched that thing and threw the rocks against the wall?"

I giggle. "Yes, that was also super cathartic. I pushed and punched and kicked that big old thing until another piece of the dam inside me broke. Then our counselors sandwiched me, remember? And they made me look them in the eyes and say something good about myself. Like what was it? Something like 'I have courage.' Or was it 'I'm giving that back'? Something like that. And throwing all those rocks against the wall and yelling at the same time. Remember, I threw so many rocks that I cut three of my fingertips open. It felt so good to do all that. All that pain and aggression. That anger." I pause for a moment. "I'm afraid if I see Evan the rapist, all of that rage will come out again, but I won't be in a safe place to express it."

Camille shrugs her shoulders. "Yeah. I'm not sure what to say to that. But it was cool to watch you do all that on the retreat, even though I couldn't do it for myself."

We move on to lighter topics before going to bed. I have to work a half day tomorrow and Camille has to work on a project for a class. Sasha knocks on the door around 2AM. Once she is settled in her room, I fall into a deep sleep.

∞∞∞

The next day, Sasha and Camille are sitting on the balcony soaking in the sun when I pull in the driveway after work. I can hear them giggling as I walk up the steps to the front door.

"What's so funny?" I yell up to the balcony.

Sasha peaks her head over the railing to see me walking to the front door. "Did you see that car parked in the driveway?"

Camille joins her. "Sasha almost killed us today." She giggles.

I drop my bags in the foyer and head upstairs to the balcony.

I hear Sasha exclaim, "Camille, I did not almost kill us! All these drivers out here don't know how to drive."

Camille giggles some more. "No Sasha. I think you don't know how to drive."

They are both laughing when I come outside.

"What happened?" I smile imagining the two of them loose on the town in the VW Bug parked in the driveway.

Sasha starts. "Well, first of all, they didn't have the car I wanted, which was a convertible. So I had to pick that one. My knees go halfway up the steering wheel! So this morning, Camille needed her Diet Dr. Peppers and I wanted to get some snacks."

Camille chimes in. "And Sasha honked at every car, pedestrian, and bike we passed on the way." We all laugh now.

Sasha fakes innocence. "What? They were in the way and I couldn't have you go another second without Diet Dr. Pepper."

"The Bug turned Sasha into a speedy little critter," Camille banters.

"No, I'm like a giraffe in that car. Not a little critter," Sasha counters. "I just need a sunroof to stick my head out."

Our laughter continues.

"Oh how I've missed being with you," I say. "What time does Dusty get in? I think she said around 9 tonight. I wish she could come earlier."

We spend the rest of the day walking on the beach, chatting about life and laughing a lot. We prepare our own dinners because we have different preferences. Sasha cooks Salmon and vegetables. Camille heats a frozen cheese pizza. And I have rotisserie chicken and salad. After dinner we curl up on my bed downstairs to watch a movie. We couldn't figure out how to get the TV working in the living room. We decide to watch The Other Woman starring Cameron Diaz, Leslie Mann and Kate Upton. Something about the movie reminds me of us on retreat. The three main characters form an unlikely friendship to take down a deceitful man and empower each other. Not that we were connected because of a common boyfriend. But we were brought together because of crappy circumstances and formed an unlikely lasting bond that has helped each of us heal.

"Remember when we were all late for group because we were having mini spa in Dusty's and my room?" I reminisce.

"Sasha pulled the cucumbers off her eyes and..." Camille recalls the moment.

Sasha doesn't miss a beat. "...And I yelled 'Shit you guys. We have to go.'"

"We got such evil eyes from the facilitators. I felt bad, but whatever." I shrug my shoulders. "It was an accident. Plus we were doing self-care. Didn't we do family sculpts[34] that night?"

Camille has the best memory. "Yes, you went that night Anna. Your sister was a baby and your parents were putting the contact lens in her eye. You did something with the jump rope around them."

---

34 Family sculpting is a role-playing technique that works on traumatic memories. It was developed by Duhl, Kantor, and Duhl in 1973.

I remember my family sculpt vividly. "Yes. When I was little I put a jump rope, or blankets in a circle around them to protect them when they had to do that. I was only 2. She was an infant. I knew she was born with an eye that couldn't see and the doctor made them do that to her."

Sasha adds, "I just remember you were outside of the jump rope and when it was over, your dad stepped around you and your mom comforted Violet. I'm sure it was overwhelming for them, but I just remember you were out there all by yourself. And you were so little."

"I remember Violet crying a lot." I shudder at the memory. "Then during the family sculpt, the main facilitator asked if he could lightly put his foot on my foot since I had said when watching other family sculpts that I dissociate in crisis. That was so weird. I felt my energy try to escape through my head, but it came zipping back down to the ground. My legs were like jello. It was kind of cool actually."

Camille recalls part of our small group debrief after. "Remember when our counselor pointed out that even though you knew the doctor told your parents to do that, you were only 2 and what you saw was your parents making your sister cry on purpose? That was really interesting to me."

"Yes, I do remember that." My mind takes me back to that small group room with all the pads, cushions and blankets. "My young 2-year-old brain couldn't make sense of all of it. I just wanted to keep them safe in my jump rope and blanket circles."

The doorbell rings and we all jump up, much like we did when we were late for group only this time we weren't flinging cucumbers on the ground as we darted out the door.

Dusty waits on the front porch with a huge grin across her face. A chorus of "yayyyys," "ahhhhhs," and giggles erupt as we hug the last member of our small group. We are complete.

∞∞∞

Saturday is our only full day together. Over breakfast we decide to drive up Highway 1 along the central coast of California. We got ready in no time.

"Dusty, put on that song we all danced to in our room on retreat." I reverse out of the driveway.

"Which one?" she asks.

At the same time Camille giggles. "We listened to a lot of music on retreat Anna."

I put the sun visor down to shade my eyes. "You know…burn burn burn, light light light."

They all laugh at me.

Camille states the obvious, which makes us laugh even more. "O.K. that really doesn't help."

"Wait!" Dusty exclaims. "I think I know which one."

A sound beeps as she scrolls though the music on her iPhone. Soon Ellie Goulding's voice echoes through the car.

"Yes!" I glance in the rear view mirror to make a face at Camille. "Burn burn burn, light light light. Dusty you are good."

"I got you girl," she says with a wink.

Camille giggles again. "Dusty you always say that. That's like your trademark."

"You do Dusty," Sasha confirms. "I like it. It's so you. Always there for us."

Dusty shyly smiles. "Oh you guys. Shhhh."

"You are Dusty," I concur. "You are steady."

I think back to the first time Dusty and I talked. It was so beautiful on that porch in front of our room on retreat. I asked if I could join her and she said yes. Within minutes we started sharing about why we were there. Turned out we were going through divorces and just couldn't seem to clear the fog in our lives. We were instant friends.

We head north on Highway 1 towards Cambria. North of San Luis Obispo, the road travels along the coast again. Sasha and Camille can't believe all the tourists stopping to take pictures at the scenic lookouts.

"Thank God you're driving Anna," Camille says. "If Sasha was driving all these tourists would be dead from fright with all the beeping she does."

We all laugh.

"Camille, I'm not that bad," Sasha retorts.

"No you aren't," Camille agrees. "I'm just being silly."

We finally get to Cambria and park the car. We decide to walk around the town since none of us have been there.

"Do you guys want to find something to eat?" I ask. "Or if there are other shops you want to go in, we can do that, too."

"We passed an art gallery with a lot of sculptures on our way into town." Dusty asks, "Can we stop there?"

"Sounds good to me," I agree. "I need a coffee, too. Let me know if you see anything."

We find a little café that serves soups, salads and sandwiches. They also have an espresso bar. After we finish eating, we take coffees to go and walk towards the gallery Dusty saw on our drive into town. I spot the sculptures before I see the building. I'm struck by how similar the sculptures look to what I felt in my lower stomach on retreat.

"Oh. My. God. You guys that's what my stomach felt like when we were on retreat." I point to large round, black, shiny sculptures in front of the gallery.

"Those are pretty." Camille walks toward them.

Dusty shudders. "They look cold and menacing to me."

Sasha stands next to Camille and reaches her hand out to touch one. "They are silky, almost seductive with no way in or out. Is there a seam anywhere?"

I inspect them and don't see any seams. "There isn't a way out or in. It's a hard shell that is pretty, silky, seductive, cold, and menacing. It's protecting something, but also trapping something."

"Oh that's deep," Camille jokes. "In all seriousness, that's cool that we gotta see this. They do look like what you described."

We browse the gallery and sip coffees. Nothing catches our eye to actually purchase. We decide to head back to the beach house to get ready for dinner at Aunt Tessa's house.

∞∞∞

The traffic on Highway 1 south was heavier, so it took us longer to get home. We took showers and got ready in record time. My hair is still wet on our way to Aunt Tessa's.

"Shit!" I just remember that I want to say the Yom Kippur prayers, but I forgot to look them up.

"What?" Sasha asks from the passenger seat.

"Can you look up Yom Kippur prayers on your phone Sasha?" I signal to turn left. "You guys are being good sports doing this with me. I feel like such a bad Jew. I don't know anyone here in the Jewish community, I'm celebrating a week late, and I'm making you do it with me. Between all of us and my family we have a Baptist, a few Catholics, a Lutheran, a Presbyterian, and a Jew."

"Anna-Gem, you are doing the best you can." Dusty reassures me from the back seat. "I'm sure God knows that. Plus I'm excited to do this with you. It's a new cultural experience for me."

"I don't know that I'd call this cultural. I'm totally winging it!" I frown and shake my head. I think to myself, *I guess it's better than nothing.*

Grandma G and Mom are already at Aunt Tessa's house when we arrive. We instantly settle around the island and begin enjoying appetizers. Aunt Tessa reviews the menu selection with us. She tells us to help ourselves to wine or water. Sasha and Dusty serve us wine.

"Annie, did you start drinking again?" Mom asks with a hint of concern in her voice.

"Well, last night we all talked about it." I gesture towards Camille, Dusty and Sasha. "They agree that the suicide crisis has passed and I'm more stable, so we had a glass of wine on the balcony."

"Oh. O.k.," Mom says simply. I sense her concern, but she doesn't continue.

Grandma G redirects our conversation. "So I know you all met on the retreat, but how did you stay connected?"

"Well, it all started on the shuttle from the airport to the retreat center," I start.

Dusty, Camille, and Sasha say unison, "Ohhhh God."

We all laugh.

"Camille is the first person I saw in the airport," I continue. "She was slumped in a chair with her earphones in. I wondered if she was part of the retreat as I wandered to get my bag, which turned out to be a waste of time because my bag never made it."

"Oh Jeez," Grandma G said.

"Oh yeah, Anna, I forgot about that." Dusty shakes her head and rolls her eyes.

"It sucked donkey balls. Here I was in the middle of nowhere, with a bunch of strangers, mentally fragile and I have no bag." I turn to Sasha. "Do you remember walking to the shuttle with me and when I told you I didn't have a bag, you offered to lend me clothes?"

Sasha nods. "Yes I remember that."

"I was so relieved. You were so nice. Anyway, we finally get on the shuttle. Well, more like pack into the shuttle. I think there were 10 of us in a small van with all our luggage. The further we went from the airport and town, the more I felt like we were headed to the twilight zone. I was smashed between the window and two huge guys in the second to last row. I turned to see what was going on in the last row, and I see Dusty smashed between three women. Her eyes were huge and not really blinking. I remember smiling at her and thinking 'at least I'm not the only one who feels like we are headed to the twilight zone.' She smiled back."

"Sounds like quite a ride," Grandma G remarks. "So, you and Dusty were roommates right? What about you, Sasha and Camille?"

"Ohhhhhhh no!" Camille exclaims. "We weren't that lucky. Sasha and I had different roommates."

Sasha bulks at the memory. "Yeah, I almost left the first night when they couldn't switch me to a single."

"We hung out in our room most of the time anyway," Dusty shares. "Our room was awesome. We totally lucked out with a full kitchen."

"Yeah, and my room had grass growing out of the drain." Sasha makes a disgusted face.

Camille chuckles. "Oh yeah. And Sasha is like the least likely to enjoy roughing it."

"That's mostly true," Sasha confirms. "I'm just so glad we were all in the same group. Who would've thought we were the youngest there and our age difference is almost 20 years?"

"Dinner is ready," Aunt Tessa calls from near the stove. "Grab a plate from the table and bring it over. I think it will be easier to serve from here."

I read the prayers for Yom Kippur before we eat. Everyone appreciates my attempt to share my experience as a recently converted Jew. Dinner is delicious and the conversation is lively. We are sad to say goodbye when it is over.

The next day as we sit drinking coffee looking out at the ocean, we promise to keep keeping in touch.

"I swear if it wasn't for you three, I don't know where I'd be," I say quietly. "I'm sad you are leaving and we have to return to normal life."

"Trust me, I know Anna." Camille looks wistfully at the ocean. "I really don't want to go back to reality."

"Keep texting. I love our group texts." Dusty smiles at each of us.

"I have something for you all." Sasha pulls a bag from behind her. Her eyes twinkle as she hands each of us glow in the dark star wands and gold star stress squeezies. "Now, we can always be connected even if we are busy and can't text. We all have magic star wands and stress balls to squeeze the shit out of whenever we need."

∞∞∞

The following weekend, it is Saturday night. Nothing going on. Next weekend I'm going out to celebrate a high school friend's birthday. This weekend, I'm home alone. I say to myself *I miss the girls and it's only been a week since dinner at Auntie's.* My journal glares at me on my nightstand because I'm supposed to write left handed about my therapy session two weeks ago. I meet with Jennifer tomorrow. *Fine, I'll do it!* I giggle. A voice says, *you really need to get some friends. Now you are talking to yourself and inanimate objects.* I roll my eyes and chuckle some more.

Untitled Journal Entry- Written left-handed

Why I fear love?

I've avoided this for days and tonight for an hour instead of choosing to read about beheadings, rapes, prison deaths, and ISIS hostages and Ricky Martin, JLO, and their kids. Writing left handed hurts my hand. Flo & the Machine Never let me go arms of the ocean I'm not giving up, I'm giving in and the crashes of heaven a sinner released Ornpucrme.

I fear love because I don't trust it. It's confusing. It hurts. I've been controlled by it. Love = Sex = Object = Emotionless = Dirty = Shame. Love must be protected against. Love betrays and deceives. Love lies. Love isn't authentic. Love isn't honest. Love makes me doubt myself. Love makes me question my identity. Writing left handed is for the birds. Can't write fast enough. I'm not lovable because I cry, I get scared, I have needs = too needy. I'm empty on the inside. I'm tarnished.

Love takes faith.

I'm learning faith.

I set my pen down and squeeze the gold star stress ball from Sasha with my left hand. I re-read what I just wrote. A voice says *that doesn't even make sense. What is ornpucrme? Lame.*

151

Reflections ∞ Reactions ∞ Responses

_____

_____

_____

CHAPTER 15

MY SAFETY AND COMFORT
CAN COME FIRST?

As I drive to my meeting with Jennifer, I notice the sun is setting early now and the air is brisk. My anxiety is in high gear and has been all day. I can't figure out why. All I know is I can't catch a deep breath. My heart pounds rapidly like it's about to pole vault out of my chest. I say to myself, *shit heart. You aren't trying out for the Olympics.* A weak smile crosses my face. *At least I have a little humor. That's a good sign.*

I'm grateful I requested a 2 hour session with Jennifer earlier in the week. My anxiety is so intense that I arrive about ten minutes early for our session. I'm usually late. My earbuds play the grounding and centering meditation that helped in the airport after I called Jennifer. I sit at the patio table under the pergola by the front door of our meeting space. I say to myself, *Ugh. I hate this tightness in my chest. And my skin is crawling with jitters.*

"You're here early!" Jennifer and Pansy get out of her car. Pansy pulls Jennifer in my direction from the parking lot.

My eyes well up with tears. She looks at me with concern. Pansy sniffs around my feet and reaches one paw up on my shin as if to say she is concerned, too.

"I just can't catch my breath and I have no idea why." My voice quivers. "It's so frustrating. I just wish I knew what set it off and why it happens so I could stop it. I don't like feeling so out of control."

We arrange the pillows on the ground and settle into them. Pansy wiggles under the pillows and snuggles up to me.

Jennifer inquires, "You haven't had anxiety like this in a month or so, right? Since you called me from the airport?"

"No. Even Pansy can sense it. She doesn't burrow up next to me very often." I pause to pet Pansy. "I don't know if it is work, or what. I haven't talked to Liam. I went for a hike yesterday and did some yoga today. Or at least tried to do yoga. I only had a few drinks this weekend."

Jennifer's eyebrows shoot up. "Oh, you are drinking again? When did that start?"

"When the girls from the retreat were here a few weekends ago." I recall how it came about.

Her alarm is palpable in her voice. "And how has it been?"

"I think it's been O.K. I haven't really noticed a big difference in anything."

"O.K. It's just when doing trauma work, alcohol can make it harder. I just want to make sure you are O.K."

Her words sink in. A voice reminds me, *you were really drunk the night of the rape. Could alcohol be a trigger?* But I don't share that with her because it suddenly dawns on me what may have triggered my anxiety. As soon as I start talking about it, my heart slows down.

"I think I know what triggered this." I take a deep breath. "Last night I went to a birthday party for one of my high school friends. A bunch of girls I grew up with were there and every one was drinking a lot, except me and this one other girl. It was my first night out in a social setting like that since the suicide crisis. I thought I was ready. Elizabeth has been urging me to come out and be social again. It was nice of them to include me. But maybe it was too soon. I felt so out of place. And I looked at all of them, most of them are married with kids enjoying a girl's night out. With great jobs and lives. And here I am, don't even know what to wear, how to carry myself. So self-conscious. Living at my dad's house. I was just uncomfortable. And they are all the same people who went to high school and college parties with Evan. I hate that seeing my friends makes me think of him and how vile he is. And I just…" My hands clinch.

"Do you feel anger?" Jennifer's curious tone directs me to the present.

"I guess its anger." I shrug my shoulders and make a face. "My jaw is clinched now, too. I don't do anger well. It scares me. The first time I confronted my anger was around the time I was working with that EMDR therapist and working in residential life at that university down south. I signed up for a self-defense class[35] put on by the campus police and the Women's Center. It was a whole weekend. The Friday night session was powerful. There were a series of scenarios[36] with a hat and two people. Very little talking. Like 4 or 5

---

35 The self-defense class I took was a Rape Defense Aggression (RAD) Systems course to teach women how to defend themselves if attacked. For more information visit rad-systems.com.
36 The scenarios in this activity demonstrate consent and non-consent. The hat represents sex. The first 4 scenarios show situations when nonconsensual sex occurs, such as through coercion, force, and when someone is asleep. The last scenario shows a situation when consent is not given and respected.

scenarios. In the first scenario, the person who wasn't holding the hat asked the person holding the hat if they could have the hat. When the person with it said no, the person without it grabbed it and there was a tug-off-war for it. The person without it ended up with it. In the next scenario the person with the hat was coerced into giving the hat to the person without it. In the next scenario the person with the hat had it on and was sleeping with their head on the table. The person without the hat walked by and took it from the sleeping person. That's what happened to me. The last scenario showed consent. The person with the hat and the person without the hat ended up sharing the hat after agreeing together. Oh the other scenario was the person without the hat respecting that the person with the hat didn't want to share. Have you done an activity like that before?"

Jennifer shakes her head. "It sounds really powerful like you said."

"Yes, it really was. It was the first time I actually saw what happened to me. I wasn't even asked. I couldn't even struggle. I remember that night when we got in bed after drinking a lot and smoking some pot when we got home, we were lying on our sides facing each other. I remember that we were sort of caressing the sides of our bodies with the hand that was free and I thought to myself 'Uew, I don't want to hook up with him.' And I rolled over on my other side, so I was facing away from him. I think I mumbled that I wanted to go to sleep. The next thing I knew I was suffocating in my pillow. I couldn't breath and that's what woke me up. He had rolled me onto my stomach, pulled my pants and underwear down. By the way I was wearing a big t-shirt, granny panties and gray drawstring pants. He raped me, just like the scenario where the hat was taken off the sleeping person. The next day he wouldn't make eye contact with me when we all went to breakfast. I don't even know why I went to breakfast, but I didn't know what else to do. I was in shock.

"A few months later I was home for a long weekend or Easter or something and was out at one of the local bars with all our friends. He[37] came up to me and said something like 'I'm really sorry we didn't even kiss when we hooked up.' And the worst part about it that I replay often as I cringe deep into the pit of my being is I looked at him and said 'it's O.K.' And walked away. I was so angry I didn't know what to do in that moment. I was so caught off guard by what he said. Didn't even kiss? Yeah, because I was passed out and you raped me, you asshole.

"I've thought of so many responses since then. So many things I could have done differently. The Tuesday after it happened, I told the girl I carpooled to work with that I needed to go to Planned Parenthood on the way home to get the morning after pill. When I told her what happened she gently said 'it sounds like you didn't want that to happen.' I told her I didn't, but what could I do about it? She offered to give me one of her morning after pills. I still wonder if I had gone to Planned Parenthood, how my life would be different. Had I seen a professional right after it happened, well 2 days after it happened. I mean it was in my bed. I can't escape my bed. No matter where I live, I still have a bed that is mine that I sleep in every night."

"It makes sense that being out with all of your friends who used to be included in those parties with Evan triggered your anxiety." Jennifer pauses to let those words sink in. "I wonder if you have anxiety about sleeping in your bed."

"You know, I probably do, but I'm not sure I've ever been aware of it. That would make sense though." My mind wanders to all of the nights I spent hysterically crying in my bed, needing to take sleeping pills or drinking a lot of wine to be able to fall asleep.

---

37 I'm referring to Evan, the friend who raped me. His name is used on a limited basis in this session because I flinched every time I said it. Not being able to say his name without physically reacting is common in trauma recovery work.

Or some combination of the three. "Now that you mention it, yes I think you are on to something. In the months after it happened, I could only fall asleep if I was drunk, on sleeping pills, or from complete exhaustion after being hysterical. Once I called my friend from undergrad just sobbing. She lived on the east coast, so it was like 6:30 in the morning for her. No one I knew near me was awake and the pain was so unbearable. She was like 'Anna, what's wrong?' I couldn't tell her because I didn't understand it. I just kept saying 'I don't know. I'm so afraid. I'm a disappointment. I don't know what's going on. I don't know what I'm doing. I'm so lost.' And she stayed on the phone comforting me as best as she could by reminding me that the transition out of college is a hard one and I will figure out what to do with my life. She didn't know what happened. My roommate at the time one night saw me in hysterics, too. He was like 'Whoa. Anna, what's going on? Let's go for a drive and get some cigarettes.' I told him the same things as my friend from undergrad and he did his best to help me calm down. At that point, he didn't know what happened either. In fact, he was there the night it happened. He was sleeping in the living room with another friend of ours he used to hook up with. That's the whole reason Evan slept in my bed in the first place, so that he and our other friend could have privacy in the living room."

Jennifer's tone is gentle and direct. "Did you feel like you had to let Evan sleep in your room?"

"No, it wasn't like I had to. It's like that's just what happened. If there is an extra place to sleep, like a double bed with only one person sleeping in it, then you let whoever needs a place to sleep have it. Not that that meant hook up. Guy, girl, it didn't matter. Don't make your guests uncomfortable. That's the way it always was at my dad's house. Bend over backwards to accommodate everyone else. Otherwise it's rude. And you don't want anyone to think you are rude." The words pour out of my mouth as if they are trying out for the Olympic pole vault team.

"So it sounds like you were not taught that it is O.K. to accommodate your own needs first." Jennifer's tone continues to be gentle and direct. "Do you know that now? It is O.K. for you to have guests sleep on the couch, even if you have a big bed you could share."

"I've never thought of that. When I stayed at some of my friends' houses or at my cousin's house when I was little, it was always so weird to me when I had to sleep in the guest room or on the couch when they had a big bed to share. I didn't understand that and thought it was rude. I guess what you are saying is that is actually normal to keep your bed to yourself, which makes sense. I've never thought of that before. Like it is O.K. to set boundaries for my safety and comfort." My mind suddenly focuses.

Jennifer's tone becomes tentative. "What does safety look like to you?"

My mind goes fuzzy. After a long pause I whisper, "I have no idea."

"Would you be interested in doing some guided imagery around safe spaces?"

I nod, "Sure." I lie back on the mat and pillows she put out for me.

"Do you want a blanket over you?" She asks.

"Yes, that would be nice. I'm cold."

She begins with a soft voice. "Close your eyes and take some deep, slow breaths. Try to let your thoughts move through your awareness without focusing on them or trying to stop them." She pauses while I settle in. "Now imagine a place where you felt safe when you were little. When you have the image, let me know what it is."

An eternity passes. Tears form at the outside corners of my eyes. I can't conjure up a safe image. "Nothing's coming up."

"That's O.K." She reassures me. "You talked about your grandma's house when you were little. Perhaps you can start there."

I subtly nod and find myself sitting on Grandma's lap eating peaches on a summer morning. "Yes, I can feel her blue velour robe and smell the coffee and peaches. It is calm."

"Good. Thank that image for revealing itself to you. Let me know when you do that."

"O.K. I did." I think to myself, *that's really weird to thank the image, but just go with it.*

Jennifer gently instructs, "Now, see if any other safe place images come up."

After another eternity, I'm at the beach and the sun is setting. I can feel the sand shift through my toes as the warm water flows in and out. All of a sudden I'm riding bareback across a prairie on a beautiful horse. The grasses are vibrant green and sky a crisp blue. The breeze is not too cold and not too hot and the sun is high in the sky.

"What are you seeing now?" Jennifer prompts me to share with her.

"The beach and the prairie. I'm riding bareback on a horse across the prairie. My hair is really long. I'm small at the beach. Like when I was a child."

"Good. Thank those images for revealing themselves to you."

I think to myself, *that is just so weird.* "O.K. I thanked them."

"When you are ready, open your eyes."

I blink a few times and take a deep breath. I turn and look at her. Her face wears a serene expression.

"That was beautiful to watch. Your face got really soft when you spoke of your grandma. And the tears stopped." She pauses to glance at her watch. "It's been about an hour. I need to take Pansy out before our next hour. Do you want to go with me or stay here?"

My internal dialogue rapid fires. *It's so warm in here, do I really want to get up? Do you really want to be by yourself? Not really, but it's getting foggy and dark out there. It will be cold. Yeah, but you will be in this big empty building all by yourself. Fresh air will do you good.*

"I'll go with you." I sigh and fling the blanket to the side and slowly stand up.

∞∞∞

Out the window, I see the fog creeping towards us in a ghost-like fashion. Finally outside, Pansy pulls us across the parking lot behind the building to the golden grassy open space. There aren't a lot of dirt trails, so we walk across the dry hill side. I startle when something swooshes over us. I'd been staring at the ground since we left the building.

Jennifer notices. "Oh this is a Frisbee golf course. Did you not know that? I'm sorry I didn't warn you."

"No I had no idea. That's really cool though." I'm contemplative.

"What are you thinking about?" She asks.

"I didn't finish telling you about being angry and the self-defense class." Pansy barks at a squirrel. "That Saturday, we learned a variety of different moves. I remember in the morning, my mouth was really dry and my palms were cold and clammy. I was really nervous. The trainers from the police department were fantastic. They were so kind and safe. I remember thinking there really are good men out there who want to help and protect women." I wipe a tear trickling down my right cheek. "On Sunday, we got to put it all together. The police guys put the full puffy suits on and those gigantic masks. We did a few scenarios where we had to use the moves they taught us to break away. We had to repeatedly scream NO NO NO as loud as we could. It was really scary at first. I was afraid of my strength and my anger. It was liberating to scream, kick, punch, and poke their eyes out before sprinting away to safety. Such a rush. Like in that moment I had power. I'm really afraid of power, though. I have been for a long, long time. Maybe forever. It is so destructive." I smile at the memory and glance at Jennifer.

"Wow. I can see the liberation in your face right now," Jennifer notes. "It really impacted you."

I glance up. Through the fog emerges a large beautiful barren oak tree with gnarly branches twisting every which way. My voice catches in my throat. I blink a few times to be sure what I am seeing.

"Jennifer." I'm breathless. "That is the tree that lives in my left hip."

She smiles. "That tree is meaningful for a lot of my clients. Let's go to it and rest your left hip on it."

The closer we are to the big beautiful barren, but very much alive oak tree, the shyer I feel. A voice says, *put your hip on the tree. That sounds so weird. What are the Frisbee people going to think while I'm rubbing up against a tree?* A barely there smile appears on my lips. Another voice says, j*ust do it. You have nothing to lose.*

Jennifer offers guidance. "You could start by putting your hand on the tree, or walking around the tree. Whatever you are comfortable with. I will stand over here with Pansy. Oh and pay attention to any thoughts, feelings, images, or sensations that come up."

I gingerly step towards the living manifestation of the barren tree in my hip and rest my right hand on its trunk. I slowly walk around the trunk all the while keeping my right hand on it. When I get to the place I started, I repeat it with my left hand. This time I stop where the lowest branch juts out about at my shoulder length. I take a deep breath and stare at the tree.

I say to myself, *it's almost like extending an arm to put around me. I didn't see that when I walked around with my right hand. Maybe I should rest against it.*

Pretty soon I'm snuggling into the tree with my left hip firmly, yet gently resting against its trunk. My head rests in the nook between the top of the branch and the trunk. I close my eyes and take another deep breath.

I continue talking to myself, *sorry. I'm so sorry it has taken me so long to get here.* I see young me and early twenties me looking at me standing against the tree. I say to my younger selves, *I'm so sorry it has taken me this long and I put you through all of this. I'm so sorry. I love you.*

My eyes dart open as my chest begins to stir. I step away from the tree to where Jennifer stands with Pansy looking west towards the coast blanketed in thick fog.

"Are you ready?" She turns and smiles.

"Yes." I'm pensive again on our walk back to the building.

"So, what was that like?" She gently invites me to share.

"That was different than I thought it would be. I wasn't quite sure what to expect and thought probably it was just a little hocus pocus." We chuckle. "But I'm game for trying things. Anyway, I kept hearing myself tell myself 'sorry for taking so long.'"

"Like sorry that this happened to you?" She is uncertain about what I'm saying.

"Well, yes I'm sorry that I was raped. But this was different. I think I said sorry for all the self-destruction I put myself through since then, for almost ending my life." I feel tears spring up again. "I'm just a weepy machine today."

We get back to the meeting space. Pansy darts for her snacks as soon as the leash unclips.

Jennifer reassures me. "Anna you have done a lot of work in the last few months. You have come a long way. As you heal, it's normal to feel weepy. And angry. And sad. And hopeful. You are really doing good work. And you move fast."

"Well, I think I was really ready this time to do the work. I dabbled before, but I wasn't ready. I think that's another gift from my marriage. I'm not sure I ever would have moved back to this area if it wasn't for Liam. He really liked it here. I wasn't really fond of the idea, but anything was better than where we were. I'm grateful to him for that. I think being here, in a familiar place, even though I could run into the rapist at any time, helped me feel ready to do it this time. To really understand and heal from trauma."

Jennifer observes, "You haven't talked about Liam in a while."

"Yeah, there isn't much more to say. In the end, I know he meant well. He had the best intentions, and so did I. We just weren't right for each other. We both had a lot of growing up to do. I know I did. Well, I still do. I have a lot of un-learning and re-learning to do. I hope he is in a good place."

"It sounds like forgiveness?" She raises her eyebrows.

"Yeah, forgiveness of myself and him. I think acceptance is next. I have a lot of that to do." I'm thoughtful again. "When we were walking towards the tree, you asked what I was thinking. I was also wondering about the prairie and bareback horseback riding I was doing during the safe place visualization. It was like a different time period. And I was actually on the horse, whereas the image of me as a child on the beach...that one I was looking at. In fact,

I was looking at her from behind. We were both staring out to sea. Something about that difference is interesting to me, but I can't put my finger on why."

"It sounds like it could be past life stuff," she suggests.

"Yeah, maybe. I'm going to meditate on it."

She invites me to do a movement. "We've done a lot today and it sounds like your hips were activated. Would you like to do some movement honoring that?"

I'm hesitant. "I was so anxious before and I don't feel anxious at all. I don't want to stir up anxiety again by moving. I guess we could try."

"Of course, and if you start feeling any discomfort or anxiety, we can stop the movement." She stands facing me in the middle of the room. Pansy looks up from her snack to see what we are doing. "We are going to make figure eights with our hips." She demonstrates moving very slow.

"Do we have to do it that slow?" I want to rush through it like I did with the labyrinth on the retreat.

She encourages me to try to move slowly. "If it's O.K. with you, we can link arms by holding each other's forearms." She demonstrates by clasping each of her arms between her elbow and wrist with her hands. "Do you know the sacrum?"

"What?" I'm trying to concentrate on the movement and her question disrupts me.

"The sacrum is the place in your spine that connects with your hip bones in your pelvis. That is what we are attempting to connect with right now," she explains.

"I've honestly never heard of it." I think to myself, *why are we trying to connect to the sacrum? I said the tree lives in my hip.*

Jennifer continues to move. "I'll bring in a diagram of the human body so you can learn about that region. It will be important for you to have an idea of your anatomy."

Another eternity passes of slow figure eights before Jennifer stops the movement. "Can I go in the other room and you can do some of your own movement?"

"O.K.," I say. "What should I do?"

"Whatever you want to honor the work you have done today." She picks up Pansy and heads toward the door.

I take a deep breath and move into Warrior 2, my favorite yoga pose. After a few moments, I swing my arms in big circles. It feels good. I shake my legs out and plant my feet firmly on the ground. I start swinging my arms around the center of my body- right to left to right to left. I think of a video in my child development class where the babies and toddlers move their arms from left to right in sync when they learn new things. My arms swing wider with more assertion. I feel really good. I ask myself, *why did I just think about that class? I'll ask Jennifer.* I look toward the door and think I see her quickly turn around. *Was she watching me? I thought she said she wouldn't.* I slowly decrease the vigor in which I'm swinging my arms around my body until I'm standing in Tree pose. I take a deep breath and whisper, "Thank you."

"O.K., I'm done Jennifer." She comes in with Pansy.

"How was that?" She asks.

"It felt good. Kind of invigorating, yet calming."

"So, are we on for next weekend?" She asks.

"Yes. Our meetings are the highlight of my weekend." My tone is sincere.

She hesitates. "I know you don't love doing homework. But, if you have a moment, try drawing your safe place and also writing left-handed for 10 minutes about why you are afraid of power and what happens when you feel power. Also, maybe go to the ocean and let your feet sink into the sand."

"It's not that I don't like doing homework. It's more that I'm so busy with work and feel so raw and tired most of the time that I don't have it in me to do homework. I'll try though. This stuff, today's learning… it is important." I gather my belongings. "Bye Pansy. See you both next week."

Reflections ∞ Reactions ∞ Responses

_____

_____

_____

CHAPTER 16

MY SAFE PLACE

The next day after work, I settle into my bed and put my favorite new music on, the one Phora played in our second session. I've been looking forward to doing my homework all day, which is weird since I'm reluctant to agree to do homework. I pull out my sketch book that was once my dream journal and begin sketching my safe space.

It's a room with a big window overlooking a beautiful big tree with a swing. A young girl is on the swing facing toward the window. Soft, luscious curtains are draped on either side of the window. Built-ins are on each wall adjacent to the window with all of my books, pictures, rocks, and a flower vase. A picture is on one wall of someone outside in the rain and the words "Dancing in the rain • Not waiting for the storm to pass" are written around the frame. The words and symbol "Live <3 Love" are etched into a piece of repurposed wood hanging on the other wall. Under the window is a sideboard with a whimsical top edge and different sized drawers. More flowers, pictures, and a candle are on top. The round rug is soft and plush marking the middle of the room. An oversized chase lounge chair is kitty corner towards the window.

I pause to look at my drawing. I notice the only living thing in there, besides the flowers, is a little dog in a little doggy bed at the foot of the chair. It looks like Pansy. Interestingly, I'm not in it. If I was in it I'd be curled up with a blanket reading a book. Also interesting, it is sketched in black ball point pen, so there aren't any colors. Yet, the room is warm and cozy.

I think to myself, *the only thing missing is a fireplace. That's probably on the fourth wall that isn't in here.*

A cheeky voice says, *your art is getting better, but it's not that good.*

I grip my pen with the left hand to begin writing about power. I set the alarm on my phone for ten minutes and begin writing.

Untitled Journal Entry- Written Left-Handed

Why do I clinch my jaw?

My power is narcissistic (spl.?). How do I get to where I want? I want to do good for people. But power is bad. I won't be able to show pain if I am in power. And I'm full of pain. And I also feel power. Like I'm here to speak and change things for many people. I'm supposed to do this for ten minutes. What else to say? I want to change hands because this arm and hand hurts. Also because I'm writing about power left handed I'm handicap because I want to write faster.

Pause journal entry. Within a minute, my phone alarm sounds. I exclaim to myself, *oh thank God.* My right hand grabs the pen and I continue writing.

I just avoided the question → this is right handed. How I dissociated:

1. Power poises →alone

Before that Jennifer held my right arm as I figure eighted- "You aren't alone" All I thought was I was alone. That night I was alone. My body was dead. I couldn't breathe. I couldn't say no. I just laid there. Until I couldn't breathe. My toes are curled under. They are grabbing the ground. Yet they only tell one story → I'm in pain and I have to hold on tight or I'm gone from this world. So Jennifer grabs my hand and she is with me. The image in my head is a familiar one. I'm dead- a body outlined on the asphalt. And when I draw it, I'm in my bed. The subconscious is powerful. Maybe that's why I'm afraid of power. Because my subconscious is full of shit. A "shitcom" (instead of "sitcom") as we said tonight. The timer just went off again. I didn't write the steps. My limbs are jittery like earlier today. Why did that fuck me up so bad? Because I didn't want to have sex with him. He intruded my body. Did I lose my marriage because of him? My hand feels not connected. I'm dissociated. Please don't diagnose me with dissociative personality disorder. My hands are numb. I'm thirsty. Maybe I do have that disorder. My feet are tingling. My jaw is clenched. I could never have a child right now. I might as well be one of those magician helpers getting cut in half. Now I taste blood. Something is wrong with me. This can't be normal. I can't be so tingling, so tense, so full of adrenaline, yet want to close my eyes.

2. I'm avoiding my power

3. What I remember

   - I moved into warrior

   - I felt it in my face

   - I wasn't watched

   - My eyes saw Jennifer move out the door

   - My mind thought she saw me, she deliberately looked even though she said she wouldn't

   - My feet tingled

   - I lost my balance

   - I could no longer make eye contact

   - "What's happening?" –Jennifer

   - Jennifer wasn't with me. She wasn't holding my arm. I was alone

   - My jaw clenched

   - My head felt heavy. Her head is cut off and she can't speak.

   - My ears were hollow and echoed.

   - My eyes couldn't focus → "She would see my crazy."

Stay focused. Stay here. Stay grounded

I put the pen and sketch book down. A voice asks, *what was that? It doesn't even make sense.* I feel tired and anxious. I taste blood in my mouth. Reluctantly I climb out of bed to look at my mouth in the mirror. No sign of blood. Back in bed, I focus on the image of my safe place drawing. Somehow, that image helps me fall asleep instead of succumbing to the taste of blood.

Reflections ∞ Reactions ∞ Responses

_____

_____

_____

CHAPTER 17

GUARDIAN ANGELS

"Hi Beautiful." Phora's familiar warm embrace envelopes me. "How have you been?"

I'm instantly calmer and notice the taste of blood is gone for the first time since I did my homework earlier this week.

"Exhausted," I answer. "I've been traveling so much for work. And therapy has gotten to the place where I shared details of what happened to me." I pause and take a deep breath. "One thing I haven't told you yet is I was raped when I was 22. I was on my stomach and woke up as I suffocated in the pillow." My right hand touches the back of my neck. "Where my head meets my neck is like a dull steady ache. I'm really happy to be here. I've been looking forward to seeing you all week." I flash a weak smile.

Phora's eyes show empathy, care and anger all at once. "I'm sorry you went through that Anna. Your body has held that trauma, and other trauma for a long time. It may be that the base of your skull is achy right now because you are talking about it all in greater depth for the first time. The neck, well throat, has held secrets for a long time and now they are coming out. Like a wound that's infected and the infected goo is finally coming out, which makes the opening of the wound more tender. Does that make sense? Your body has held the trauma and is healing now."

"Hmmm," I ponder. "I've never thought of that, but it does make sense. Jennifer, my therapist had me do a movement to connect with my sacrum in our last session. Honestly, I'm not sure what the sacrum is." I recall the figure-8 movement. "You and Jennifer would really get along."

Phora turns and looks up to the human anatomy posters on the wall behind her. "Well, the sacrum is just here." She circles the bone at the base of the spine. "It sits within your pelvis bone and holds your hips in place. It connects your lower skeleton to your upper skeleton." She begins moving her finger up the spine and circles the base of the skull. "Your soreness here makes sense if you were focused on moving energy within your sacrum. You have a lot of pain in there. The good news is, it's moving. Let's see if we can help it along tonight. Let's start on your back. Is that O.K. with you?"

I nod as she moves towards the door. I smell Clarity when I climb on the table and pull the blankets around me. I shiver even though the room is comfortably warm and the heating pad is on.

"Anna, are you ready?" Phora cracks the door.

"Yes." I look up as she comes in. Usually I am face down and can't see what she does at the start of the massage.

She goes to her shelves and opens a cubby. She pulls out a steaming neck pillow. "I'm starting with you facing up and comforting you with the warm neck pillow to honor what happened to you. You did not deserve any of that, nor was any of it your fault. There are bad, evil people out there that prey on others. None of what he gave you is actually yours. Tonight is about honoring what is yours through comfort and love. Please remember to let me know if anything ever makes you uncomfortable or if you want the pressure to be different. This is for you and healing your body." She gently places a tissue and scented eye mask over my eyes.

The coldness I've felt all week begins to leave my body. My eyes close. Phora begins as she always does by placing both hands gently on my feet outside the blankets. She moves up my right leg, torso, arm, shoulder and down my left side.

I fall into a meditative state. Different colors swirl around me. I'm surrounded by stars, floating in outer space. The music drifts in and out of my awareness. My muscles feel as if they are melting off everything toxic and stressful that has ever weighed me down. My attention is pulled back to the present by a sudden cool breeze that gusts through the room from the direction of the door.

"Phora, did you feel that?" I ask with mixed curiosity and fear. "I was seeing my usual light show, but even more vivid and intense than usual. When that breeze came through it went dark."

A voice criticizes, *are you hallucinating now?*

"Yes, that was one powerful gust!" Her voice is hesitant. "This may sound strange, but do you have anyone in your family who died in an accident?"

"Yes, my grandma. My dad's mom. She died in a single car accident. She had been drinking and there was negligence on the part of the responders."

"She is here with us right now. I don't think she is alone either. You have a lot of guardian angels.[38]"

---

38 Phora's massage therapy training and certification does not include counseling and clairvoyance. She asked that readers be informed that her massage therapy practice does not normally include conversations such as the one described in this chapter. Since I initiated it, she engaged in the conversation to help me process this experience. In California, massage therapists must hold a certification through the California Massage Therapy Council. Please visit www.camtc.org for additional information about massage therapists' scope of practice.

Suddenly a 3-d image emerges in my conscious of Aunt Lisa in high school. Aunt Lisa is the middle sister between Dad and Aunt Tessa. She died in 2004.

"Phora, that's so weird because my Aunt Lisa's face just emerged out of the darkness. It was so vivid. Just how she looked in high school. Before she was sick. She was mentally ill and killed herself." I feel excited now, despite the sadness that comes when I think of Aunt Lisa.

"Yes, she is here, too. She wants you to know she isn't sick anymore." Phora pauses all the while continuing to massage my legs. "Is there anyone else who might be with them?"

"Maybe my Grandma Ophelia. My mom's mom. She died from cancer and she was the one in the family who made me make sense…if that makes sense."

"She has a calmer energy, but no less serious." Phora giggles. "They are very loud. Are there any kids? I'm feeling the energy of a lot of young children at your feet."

"Yes, I sense them, too. My Uncle Nick might be there, too. He was married to Aunt Tessa. He died from cancer in 2003. They miscarried a few times I think."

Jovial energy circles around my feet accompanied by the sound of young children playing at a park after school. I see purple fetuses drift through the darkness behind the eye mask. I say to myself, *I saw those fetuses at the mental health retreat during the evening music meditation, too.*

"Yes, they are all together," Phora confirms. "The three women, your aunt and grandmas want me to move to your neck and jaw. They want you to know you are not alone and they are with you. They are always with you, protecting you."

Phora steps away from the table to get a set of tuning forks[39]. "I'm going to try using these tuning forks on your jaw. They vibrate with the energy of your body. For some reason, I'm being called to use them tonight." She snaps them against a rubber mallet to start their vibration. Then she places one on each jaw. After several minutes, Phora exclaims "Wow! I've never seen these hold the vibration for this long."

"Well, whatever it is, it feels great. It feels like it is sucking all the toxic shit out of my body through my jaw. That's so weird."

"Good, that's what it's supposed to do for you." She repeats, "I can't believe how long they are holding the vibration."

"It almost feels like little static shocks. It feels really good." The eye masks remain in place, so I'm still in darkness.

After several more minutes, Phora puts them down and pulls the neck pillow out. She begins to massage my neck. She places her fingers firmly at the base of my skull and applies increasing pressure. "Is that O.K.? Too much?"

"No, keep it coming." That pressure feels even better than the tuning fork vibration. "You could probably pull my head off and it still could go with more pressure."

"I knooown." Phora continues applying pressure to the base of my skull. "I'm holding it as firmly and for as long as I can, but I have to give my hands a break. That also doesn't happen very often." She instructs, "If you can, open your mouth and firmly exhale." I try. "That's good. Do that a few more times."

I feel the dull ache dissipate with each breath and round of pressure from Phora's fingers. That melting sensation I had earlier floods over me again. Colors begin to swirl. "The colors are back. Not as bright, but definitely there."

---

39 Tuning forks are used in sonopuncture, which is an alternative healing method.

When the massage ends, Phora and I do our usual debrief. She seems more tired than usual and isn't making as much eye contact. She blinks a lot.

"Anna, I want to give you some things. Sometimes people give me things that don't necessarily work for me, but I know someday I will come across someone that they are meant for." She hands me a heart-shaped rose quartz[40] that fits perfectly in the palm of my hand. "Rose quartz is for protection of the heart. You are going through some really painful times and your heart is thawing. It needs a lot of protection and comfort right now."

I'm struck by its smooth surface, hard protective shell, and soft swirling shades of pink deep within.

"Thank you Phora." I'm filled with gratitude.

"And these are angel cards." She hands me an unopened deck of Archangel Oracle Cards by Doreen Virtue, Ph.D.[41] "They didn't really speak to me, but for some reason I feel compelled to give them to you."

I look at the pink box with an image of an angel on the top. "I've never seen these before. I will check them out." I look up at her and she is still blinking a lot. "Thank you so much Phora." I hope she can feel the depth of gratitude I feel towards her many gifts. I know she put a lot into my healing tonight.

"Ohhhh. You are so welcome Anna." She looks at me briefly. "You are amazing. You have gifts. You have big things coming your way."

---

40 Crystal healing is an alternative healing method. Several books and resources are available on the topic. One that I read was Healing Crystals and Gemstones from Amethyst to Zircon: A Comprehensive Listing of the Therapeutic Uses and Healing Effects of the Most Important Crystals and Gemstones by Dr. Flor Peschek-BÖhmer and Gisela Schreiber.
41 Angel therapy is another alternative healing method. Please visit www.angeltherapy.com for more information.

That night I open the angel cards and read the guide book. Shuffle the cards, ask a question, and pull out three cards. I wonder to myself, *what question should I ask...Nothing's coming to me.* I sigh and pull out my journal.

Untitled Journal Entry

I believe generations of trauma are trapped in my body. Over the course of the last 4-5 months I've experienced something that I want to be able to share. I just am not sure how to make it make sense. I was touched by God. My cellular being was re-birthed. I wonder if I am many generations rebirthed. I wonder if in this lifetime I was dosed with the right amount of love and brains, plus born in the right era to handle the degree of generational trauma my cells have endured. I'm not sure how to make sense of this. What I know is my body is cellularly altered. My legs are alive. My skin is showing its infections. My hips hurt. My body vibrates. Where before it was numb. I was an It. I was an object. I couldn't even love animals because I saw myself as one- an animal devoid of emotions. How much I've lived out the trauma I've carried with me without even knowing it. I didn't even know I was dying, until I did die a spiritual & cellular death.

And now I'm rebirthing.

Snakes have it figured out. They shed a complete layer of skin with each growth spurt. I'm shedding my first adult skin- where I'm not physically growing. I'm cellularly growing. I'm affectively growing. I'm mentally growing. I'm shedding years, decades & centuries of trauma, of pain, of toxicity, of baggage. My mind is softer and my heart more open. Because I'm letting go of the rock solid outer shell I've lived in for so long. The stone coffin is crumbling.

I want to chart my healing via diagrams of my body. The sensations I get now → I want to capture them w/ a USB stuck in my ear. What is happening to me is real. It is not yet known or expressed to the world. In an era of self-expression through media, we are in need of a conversation such as this.

Early sensations

Dec. 2010→ 1 night/2 days → could not get out of bed, needed safety, needed rest, needed anonymity

2011-ish: Brain sensations → prickling, tingling sensations

2012-2013 Academic Year = insatiable itching along the base of my skull- where the trauma is stored. Do I have lice?

Oct. 2013 → 5 Days couldn't get out of bed, needed comfort, rest, peace, safety

Feb-Mar. 2014 → Black out rage

June to July 2014 → Suicidal; I'm sunburned living in a tanning bed

End of July to Aug 2014 → Feel disassociations, rubbery legs, no more lice, rage erupts from my core, metal box to steaming to block of unsweetened cooking chocolate to melting with rounded corners, sweating profusely, smelling new smells, a river flowing replaced a dried river bed.

Arms ache	Feet tingle
Skin itches	Stomach never stops →searing pain
Hard puss filled zits	Throat burns
Dry skin	Tongue burns
Tingling hamstrings	Nausea
Chills	Black crows spewing
Right brain tingles	I see Dr. Lewis's aura- so bright
Hip aches	I wonder, can he see mine?
Vagina spasms	

I saw images again when I pushed on my legs, my quads just now. Images of horrible men w/ sharp features. I know my hips and legs hold the cellular trauma of many generations. I will release you. My hamstrings are on fire right now. Screaming to be released. I will do this for our family. I do not want to bear children in the cesspool of trauma. Thank you God for letting me bring this gift to my family. I'm scared of those images. I don't want to face them alone. They are dark. People wonder why the rape affected me so much. It unleashed a tremendous amount of toxins, pain, disgust from generations. Someone else w/o the past trauma baggage might not be exposed or affected in the way I am →they have more room to cope.

The physical reconnection is so crucial!! I have to learn about it and write it down more. Body diagrams → get them.

I fall asleep holding my heart rock against my chest and listening to a chakra waterfall meditation on my phone.

∞∞∞∞

The weekend is finally here. I'm sitting under the covers on my bed at Dad and Lindsey's house. They are out at an event this evening. The angel cards are in front of me on my lap. I've thought about them since Phora gave them to me a few days ago. I came up with a question. I review the guidebook. First ask the question. Then shuffle the cards. Then lay out 3 cards from the top of the deck from left to right.

I begin to read the book out loud because it helps me understand. "The card to the left shows the origination of the current situation. The center card describes the truth of the current situation. And the right-hand card shows its resolution or outcome if everyone's thoughts and beliefs stay unchanged."

I dump the cards into my hand and ask out loud "Am I really healing?"

I shuffle the cards and lay the top 3 from left to right. The origination of the current situation is spiritual understanding. The truth of the current situation is sensitivity. The outcome if my thoughts remain unchanged is remember who you are.

I sit back baffled and say out loud "Humph. That actually makes sense." *Spiritual understanding is the origination...well actually lack of spiritual understanding. My current situation has been plagued with a disconnection from my spirit for a long time. My sensitivity to this disconnection is so intense that I wanted to die. And if I don't change my thoughts, I have to remember who I am to survive.* "Humph," I say out loud again. "Am I interpreting this the right way?"

I move the cards off my lap, keeping them in the same order to make room for my journal. I recalled new memories today that seem to be connected to these cards.

Untitled Journal Entry

A thought I haven't had for a long time creeped in my head tonight – when my parents separated I went through a phase of cleaning the house- like deep cleaning it. Only when my mom was gone did I clean it. Babysitters hated doing it. I just remember thinking "this will help my mom. If we just clean the house it will help my mom." I was 8 to 10 years old and already sensitive to the healing that our spirits needed after Dad moved out. Like we needed to cleanse our family and the way I expressed it was to clean our house.

Tonight I also had a thought driving home from the airport. The highway, the roads...some have such embedded memories, all of which have huge emotional ties of fear and deep sadness & loss of love. Every time I drive by or on these roads I'm brought to those moments. So the different thought today was the activation in my body when I drove on one particular stretch of road. My

hip bones activated- as the road curved, my hip bones-
the top where it curves & is exposed were activated. As
if the first love lives in there. Where I would be if I just
let myself love and not seek to achieve more and more.
I'd probably be in a similar place only I'd be wondering
where I'd be if I just let myself see out my dreams. I'm
reconciling my dad's and mom's dreams – he to achieve
a business he believes in and she to have a family. A
breadwinner and a housewife[42]. And neither of them
particularly like the role- or feel good in the role, yet
they love the role.

Spiritual understanding * Sensitivity * Remember who
you are

These were my angel cards tonight. I've seen many
images lately, ever since I invited them to come. The
fetuses, all purple, floating through the darkness- those
are unborn babies from my family. I know it in my
heart. I have only seen their faces since they visited my
feet at the massage room.

I'm not afraid of evil anymore. I still wonder about my
mind...I still feel fragile. I'm beginning to feel the difference between the stone coffin armor and my internal strength & power. One is hollow and heavy and the
other is light and solid. I want solid light more often,
more consistently.

---

42 Mom did not care for the terms "breadwinner" and "housewife" when she read a
draft of this manuscript. She prefers the term "homemaker" because for her housewife
implies ownership. She also inquired if the terms could be switched to "breadhusband"
and "housewinner." She is on to something that I am sure has roots in feminism, women
and gender studies, and sociology to name a few. I decided to leave the terms as they were
written in my journal to maintain integrity.

As I close my journal and put it on the nightstand, I start humming "Shake it off, shake it off off off." I think, *nice a little Taylor Swift feels about right right now.* I sleep soundly for the first time all week.

Reflections ∞ Reactions ∞ Responses

_____

_____

_____

CHAPTER 18

DIAGNOSIS THAT FITS

I'm running late as usual on Sunday. I remembered to bring my journal to show Jennifer the safe place drawing and read some of the entries I've made recently.

Pansy comes screeching around the corner when I knock on the door. Jennifer follows close behind laughing. "Pansy. Pansy. It's Anna. Yes, it's Anna." She smiles and shakes her head at the same time as she scoops Pansy up and opens the door. "Pansy just loves you. She is always so happy to see you." Jennifer closes the door and sets Pansy down. Pansy jumps up to greet me. "Pansy. Pansy. Enough." Jennifer looks at me laughing some more. "I'm sorry about that. I hope it doesn't bother you too much that she jumps on you."

I bend over to pet Pansy. "No it doesn't bother me. Pansy you are the best greeter ever!" We walk by the kitchen and granola bars catch my eye. "Do you think it's O.K. if I have a granola bar? I was helping my dad get dinner ready and I forgot to eat lunch."

Jennifer immediately goes to the counter. "Oh sure. Do you want anything besides a granola bar?"

I feel suddenly shy. I think to myself, *that's weird. Why am I shy? Maybe because she is so immediately caring and didn't look at me like I was needy or a burden.* "No, just the granola bar."

I pull out my journal as we settle on our pillows on the ground. "I've been meaning to ask you about writing left handed. Why am I doing that?"

"Great question." She asks, "Do you have any ideas?"

"Well, I figure it has something to do with doing something different, with using the non-dominate hand, with learning something new. But I'm not sure why or how it fits into therapy."

"You are on to it. It does have to do with all of that. When you write with your non-dominant hand, you can have more access to emotions. If emotions are blocked, it can be a great way to just be raw and also young…Like you get access to your younger parts. Those parts that are more vulnerable."

"It kind of reminds me of neuroplasticity. The rebuilding of, or building for the first time neurological nets in the brain." My psychopharmacology class comes flooding back to me. "The brain regenerates old or generates new pathways to transmit chemical and electronic signals that are responsible for making our bodies function including emotions. So writing with the non-dominant hand is forcing my brain to think differently."

Jennifer nods. "Yes, that, too. So you know about the primitive brain and executive brain, right?" I nod as she holds up her hand. "O.K. When I make a fist, I tuck my thumb inside. My thumb is the primitive brain. My fingers covering my thumb are the executive brain. The executive brain is…"

I finish her sentence. "…where memories are stored, personality exists, and decisions are made."

"Exactly. So you know about trauma memories?" She asks.

"Yes, but refresh my memory," I say with intrigue.

"With trauma memories, they aren't stored in the proper place. The primitive brain is driven by fight, flight, freeze. So when a threat comes our way, the primitive brain takes over and essentially cuts off the executive brain. The primitive brain goes into survival mode, so there isn't any cognitive reasoning, rational processing. It's like when trauma happens, the connections between the primitive and executive brains are severed. The primitive brain stayed with us through evolution because we face many threats every day. Not all threats are traumatic."

I vigorously nod my head. "Yes, I learned about this. Why haven't I thought of applying this to myself? I apply it to my clients."

"That's why we can't be our own therapists!" She exclaims playfully. "Anyway, the purpose of writing with your left hand is to try to access new or old, locked up emotions. Plus, learning builds neurological nets."

"That makes so much sense. So does movement right?" I'm hesitant because I haven't studied dance/movement therapy.

"Yes, that is one of the things movement does. It helps activate different parts of the brain." She smiles thoughtfully. "Do you think that has been working for you?"

"Yes, I do. I can sense differences. Even in my journal entries." I glance down at my journal resting in my lap.

She asks excitedly, "Did you do your homework?"

I nod and begin flipping the pages to the most recent journal entries.

"How was it? Did you notice anything while doing it?" She is curious.

"Yes, it drove me crazy. I couldn't rush through it. I had to write slowly because writing legibly took more concentration. And my hand hurt really badly. It like cramped up pretty fast."

"Interesting." She looks down at the entry. "Wow. Your left handed writing is really legible!"

"I was a switch hitter in softball, so maybe that had something to do with it." I look down suddenly nervous. "You know how I told you about riding through the prairie and maybe it was past lives stuff? Well, I had this experience with Phora, the massage therapist I've been working with. You both really need to meet. You are so much alike. Such healers. Anyway, I think we connected with my guardian angels." I tell her the whole story. "Do you think I'm crazy? I really thought maybe I was hallucinating or something, but it honestly felt so real. But then again, hallucinations also feel like reality. But I wasn't by myself. She felt them, too."

Jennifer's expression is open and believing. "No you are not crazy. Past life stuff and guardian angels are well documented. Did they tell you to do anything?"

"No. They just said I wasn't alone and they were always with me. Oh and my aunt said she wasn't sick anymore." Jennifer's expression is uncertain. "My aunt who died by suicide[43]. I've mentioned her before."

"Oh yes, I remember now." She nods her head slowly. "Not being alone is a big part of your recovery. You said that during your EMDR, right?" Jennifer's tone is inquisitive.

---

43 I intentionally say completed suicide or died by suicide instead of committed suicide to use de-stigmatizing language. The verb "commit" is often used in conjunction with a crime or sin. For instance, you'd likely hear "They committed a crime." Suicide is not a crime or a sin. It is the result of a mental illness, severe pain and suffering, trauma, crisis and terminal illness. I encourage readers to Google these terms to learn more about de-stigmatizing suicide.

"Yes. I've felt alone for so long, but not anymore." I look down again. "O.K., the one I will read to you is about what I think about power and what happens when I dissociate. I didn't get much down with my left hand. It took ten minutes to do one paragraph. I realized I was avoiding talking about power and dissociation. I wrote it after I drew my safe place."

"Oh can I see your safe place, too?" Jennifer adds quickly, "Only if you want to share it."

"O.K." I flip to the previous page. I'm shy again.

She looks closely at the details. "Wow Anna. This is really good. There are so many details. It looks so cozy in there." She points to the little dog. "Is that Pansy? Oh Pansy you made it in Anna's safe place." She chuckles. "This is beautiful really."

My confidence soars. "Thank you. It was really fun drawing it. Many of those things I have. They are in storage right now though."

"I'm sorry. I got us off track. You wanted to read what you wrote about power and dissociation." She leans back as she hands me my journal.

I don't look up while I read it to her. I'm embarrassed by what I write in there. A voice rapid fires questions in my head. *What if she does diagnose you with dissociative personality disorder? What if she thinks you're crazy? What if she is mad by what you wrote about her looking at you even though she said she wasn't going to?* One glance up tells me she is recalling that moment in our last session.

She is thoughtful. "Do you want to talk more about that? I don't remember looking at you because I said I wouldn't, but maybe I did. Either way, I'm sorry that is what happened for you and I startled you, or broke your trust." A hint of eagerness is in her voice. "Are you angry with me?" She reassures, "It is O.K. if you are angry with me."

"No, I'm not angry. Maybe you didn't. I thought I saw you quickly turn around when I looked. I don't know why it bothers me that you would look anyway." I try to dismiss my feelings about that moment.

"Well, one reason is that I told you I wouldn't and then you saw me go against my word. That is a trust breaker, or at least might have damaged your trust in me. There are parallels in terms of others whom you trusted breaking your trust."

My response is too quick. "Yes, good point. But I'm not mad at you. I was startled more than anything. And a little self-conscious. I also don't know why I was self-conscious either."

"A possible reason for that is you have been disconnected from your body for a long time and you are learning to feel it again, and move with it. That can be vulnerable. It is new, too, and that could also make you feel self-conscious." She's thoughtful. "Can I ask you one more thing? Do you think you have dissociative personality disorder?"

"No. I don't," I state matter-of-factly. "But sometimes I'm afraid I do because that happens a lot."

"Do you want my opinion?" I nod. "You have PTSD[44]. You don't have dissociative personality disorder. Or borderline personality disorder. You experienced capital T trauma with the rape. Plus you experienced trauma as a young child and likely into your adolescence. And I don't just mean lower case t trauma. You had that, too. The unpredictability and unsafety from your dad's alcoholism and

---

44 PTSD stands for Post-Traumatic Stress Disorder. The diagnostic criteria may be found at the beginning of this book or in the Trauma- & Stressor-Related Disorders section of the DSM-5. One important piece to making a formal diagnosis is assessment. Standards of practice in the mental health field include the use of batteries of assessments that have been empirically validated to inform diagnosis and treatment. For instance, the Institute on Violence, Abuse and Trauma offer neuropsychological testing and educational assessments. Visit www.ivatcenters.org.

the limited emotional support you received from either parent, those are capital T traumas. There were degrees of abuse and neglect." She pauses. "That doesn't mean your parents are horrible people. They did the best they could given their circumstances. And they showed you and your sister love in the best way they could. Your basic needs were always met. You had a clean home, with food. You had support in doing your schoolwork. You had friends and a neighborhood where you could play safely outside. As the oldest, you took a lot on and were parentified[45] in a lot of ways. And it sounds like you experienced verbal and emotional abuse and neglect."

"So you don't think I have anything other than PTSD?" I heard the rest of what she said through a tidal wave of relief that washed over me.

"At this point, given everything you have shared with avoidance of people and places, flashbacks, dreams, rage, dissociation, hypervigilance… no I don't think you have anything other than PTSD." She looks intently at me. "You seem relieved."

"I'm so relieved. I've always been afraid that I was bipolar like my aunt, or schizoaffective, which they diagnosed her with at the end. Or something else like those other ones you mentioned. For some reason, PTSD seems right. It really fits."

She smiles and lets silence marinate my relief.

"Not that having one or more of the other diagnoses would be a bad thing. They just never felt quite right and I couldn't see how I'd be treated for them if they weren't quite right." I glance down at my journal. "I want to share the other two entries since our last meeting, but I think we are running out of time."

She looks at her watch. "We have about ten minutes."

---

45 Parentified means that a child took on a parental role within the family system.

"O.K. I will pull out the main parts. I wrote a lot about generational trauma, which is also something I have read a lot about and attended several workshops on the topic. I wonder if part of why I was so affected by the rape is because of my early childhood, but also because of the trauma that I believe existed in previous generations in my family."

She nods in agreement. "Yes, there is research on trauma passing from one generation to the next. It's legacy burden[46]. Also, predators, such as your rapist, can just sniff that out in their victims. It's like they have a sixth sense of people predisposed to trauma."

"I'm going to read up on generational trauma again." I flip a few pages in the journal and quickly glance over the entry. "The other main topic was about the importance of the re-connection with my body, like all of my body. My legs, bones, skin. For so long I walked around with my lower half numb. I can tell that movement has made a big difference in terms of my healing.

"There is one part in particular. I was driving home from a work trip and there was this stretch of road that I've driven hundreds of times in my lifetime. This particular time, the top of my hips activated. Like they tingled. As soon as I felt it, I noticed where I was on the road. My first love lived around that area. I'm really so fortunate because he was a great first lover. He was really patient with me and didn't pressure me. My first orgasm was from touching a long time before we had sex. Like vaginal sex. Anyway, something about my hips on that road that night when I was driving home was different than the pain or numbness that I usually feel in my hips. It was like love coming back.

---

46 Epigenetics studies how environmental factors affect genetics. Research supports that external stimuli, such as trauma can alter the body at a cellular level, which changes genetic codes for future generations.

"It also made me remember when I was on retreat and my lower abdomen looked like those sculptures I told you about that I and the retreat girls saw on our drive to Cambria. Well over the course of the retreat, the black metal shiny box without an opening turned into a block of chocolate that started melting." I stop talking as I suddenly realize it's been ten minutes. "I'm sorry, we are right at time."

"That's O.K. Anna," Jennifer reassures. "You are identifying new sensations and new emotions. And remembering important memories that may have been locked up in that metal, chocolate box. This is part of the healing process. Thank you for sharing with me."

I'm calm on my drive home. I notice the vibrant colors in the sky from the setting sun. The highway brings back pleasant memories, which is a change from no memories at all.

Reflections ∞ Reactions ∞ Responses

_____

_____

_____

CHAPTER 19

SPIRITS AND SKELETONS

I dial Aunt Tessa's number to confirm our dinner plans for later this evening. We have a special bond. She was my first babysitter as an infant and the first person I had a slumber party with when I was 2 years old. I was the flower girl in her wedding when I was 5 years old. My sister and cousins were jealous because I got to stay at her reception and they had to go home with a babysitter. I am the oldest and they weren't in the wedding. No matter how much distance is between Aunt Tessa and me, our special bond remains strong.

"Hi hon." Aunt Tessa picks up after a few rings. "Are you still coming for dinner?"

"Hi Auntie. Yes, I was thinking about spending the night if that's O.K."

"Oh sure. Does 6 still work?" She asks. "I have something to show you."

"I can't wait. I have a lot to share, too." I bend down to tie my running shoe. "I'll see you then. Can I bring anything?"

"No nothing. Just yourself." We hang up soon after.

I look at the clock and have just enough time to go for a jog. The sun is bright in the crystal blue sky. I gulp in the crisp December air to find my breath rhythm. Inhale 3 counts. Exhale 3 counts. My mind wanders to high school when I learned how to breathe while running. Our cross country coach said to adjust breath counts like you adjust car gears. One count in one count out for uphill, two in two out for sprints and three in three out for a comfortable pace. I say to myself, *wow I haven't thought of that in a long time.* I recall my coach's instructions to focus on arm pumps for the uphill and leg strides for the downhill. I tell myself, *that's right. Arm muscles are smaller and easier to move, which is good for the uphill.* I smile when I remember his words- the legs will always follow the arms. I say to myself, *our bodies are really remarkable. Like machines.*

My mind wanders to tonight's dinner. I look forward to spending time with Aunt Tessa. We are rebuilding our relationship after several tumultuous encounters since Violet's wedding five years ago. A pain pierces my heart when I recall my mom's tears at the wedding. She seemed so vulnerable and alone. I was angry that Aunt Tessa was not there for Mom that night. A voice says, *then there was the whole incident in Las Vegas with Kate when you called Aunt Tessa some awful names.* I shake my head and take a deep breath despite my pace. The voice continues, *don't forget about living with her earlier this year with Liam when she didn't feel like she could come home if Dad and Lindsey were there.* I shake my head again. I tell myself, *hopefully tonight is a good night with us.* I see the big hill ahead of me. I instruct, *arms get ready. We are almost there.* I focus my mind on adjusting my breath to one in one out and pumping my arms. I say to myself, *this run feels good.*

∞∞∞

My muscles still tingle from my jog. I pull up Aunt Tessa's familiar driveway and say a prayer. *please take the awkwardness away.* The back door light is on and a soft glow comes from inside her home. A brief knock before turning the door knob. I'm met with delicious aromas floating through the air and sizzling sounds from the stove top. She has Spotify playing in the background.

"Hi hon," she calls from the kitchen.

A big smile spreads across her face when she turns to me. Her arms open as we walk toward each other in a familiar greeting. I take a deep breath as she embraces me. A voice says, *just like when you were little.* I feel safe. I'm filled with gratitude that she has forgiven me. In an instant I recall the millions of moments when I called her after Dad left me feeling like I was lower than scum on the bottom of his shoe. A voice says, *you were not alone because Aunt Tessa was always there and always got it.*

I sit at the island and pour myself a glass of wine. It wasn't long ago that I had a glass of wine with Sasha, Camille and Dusty for the first time since the suicide crisis at this same island.

"It smells so good Auntie." I bask in the comfort of her home.

"I hope you like it." She flips the chicken to sear the other side. "So tell me everything. How's it going?"

I take a deep breath. "Well you know I have been working with Jennifer." She nods. "And I've been going to massage therapy, too, with Phora."

"Yeah. Are you still liking it?" She asks.

"Yes. They are both healers. And we've had some really powerful moments with past life stuff and talking with the dead." I pause unsure if I should continue since it involves her deceased mom, sister and husband.

"Ohhhh. I'm so intrigued. And that is so funny because I wanted to show you pictures that I found of Grandpa's family." She continues, "I cleaned out the bonus room the other day and came across all these old family portraits. You can see the mental illness in some of them." She glances at me. "But first, tell me about your experiences."

I tell her about the gust of cool wind that came through Phora's room.

"Auntie, I swear your mom and Aunt Lisa were there in the room. Their presence was so strong. Aunt Lisa's face appeared, but not her face in the years before she died. It was her with long blond hair, looking so youthful." Words tumble out of my mouth now.

She put the tongs down. "My sister was beautiful before mental illness took her. Well all those drugs she was on. They didn't know what they were doing back then. How to treat mental illness. She was so beautiful. So natural. She loved you kids."

"Lisa told me she wasn't sick anymore. She looked so peaceful." I smile at the memory of her image. "I have one other thing to tell you about. It is hard." I pause to see if she objects. She doesn't say anything, so I take a deep breath. "Did you and Uncle Nick miscarry?"

She nods. "We had a hard time getting pregnant again after Kate."

"Well, he was there, too, Auntie. He was with your unborn children. They were all together at my feet."

Sadness and love wash across her face. "I'm sure he was with them. That sounds like Nick. He loved children."

"They were joyful, Auntie. Full of cheer and giggles." I imagine them in Phora's room so clearly. "Is this too hard for you? I debated telling you. But they all seem so good. Phora said they were very loud, well your mom was loud, telling her to tell me that they are always with me and to massage my jaw and neck. Phora said they were insistent. She said Uncle Nick is keeping the children safe until I'm ready to have one." I feel suddenly shy.

"You will have a baby Anna. I can't wait for you to have one." She looks thoughtful. "I'm glad you told me. That sounds just like Nick. He was such a great father to Kate and Bradley. He was so protective and loving with them."

"I always hoped I'd have a relationship like you had with Uncle Nick. He was such a caring, kind, gentle person. So unlike what we have in our family."

"I know. He was so patient. I think about all that we had to go through between my sister's mental illness and Great Grandma's passing away. There were times when I was nutso. And he was so patient." She dishes the salad. "You will find that Anna. Those men are out there."

"Yeah. I hope so." Doubt lingers in my voice.

"Wait until you see these pictures." Aunt Tessa changes the subject. "You seriously won't believe the mental illness. You can see it in the eyes. I mean crazy. Like KA-razy."

She sets my plate down in front of me on the island. "Are you O.K. to sit up here?"

I nod. She grabs her plate and walks over to the stool next to me. I fill up our wine glasses.

"What else?" She asks. "What are you and Jennifer working on?"

I take a bite of chicken.

"Oh. My. God. This is so good Auntie!" I exclaim.

She smiles. "Thanks honey. It's an easy one I've made a million times."

"I love it." I swallow before sharing about my struggle with identifying a safe space, the image of riding through the prairie on horseback, and dissociation. "It's so weird Auntie. Like I leave my body. I can't feel my legs or my feet. In fact, the bottom half of my body has been numb for a really long time. I can't remember when it went numb, but I'm sure it had something to do with the rape."

She nods. "That makes sense hon."

"It's like this whole region." I wave my hand over my lower abdomen. "And down both legs. When I was on retreat, we did this family sculpt and the leader guy gently stepped on my toes. I guess they knew I have a tendency to dissociate. Anyway, he stepped on my toe when it was my turn to watch my family scene play out. It was like an electric current going through my legs. I felt weak and jello-y after. But I remember thinking how cool that was because I hadn't felt it for a long time. I didn't even know that my energy would leave my body."

"Wow that is amazing, Anna." She asks, "So are you feeling it more now?"

"One of the reasons I wanted to do dance/movement therapy was because I want to reconnect with my physical body. I dissociated when I was doing my homework for Jennifer the other night. I do that a lot actually."

I tell her about dissociating in session a few weeks ago and the grounding meditation Jennifer walked me thru.

I take a deep breath before continuing. "The other big news is Jennifer confirmed a diagnosis. I was so afraid I had dissociative personality disorder or bipolar or schizoaffective disorder. But it turns out I have Post Traumatic Stress Disorder. Which totally makes sense given everything."

"Well, yeah it does. You've been through a lot honey." Her smile is soft and full of love.

"So much clicked when she and I talked about it. I mean remember all those rages I would go into. Like with Kate in Las Vegas?" She nods. "I had a flashback that night. I remember I was frantically looking for her and my brain kept flashing to this image of her in a back alley being attacked. The club we were in that night was no longer in focus and I couldn't breathe and I couldn't hear anything, even though the music was blasting. I watched myself and her friend look for her. And when she finally came home, I reacted with such intense anger that scared me. It was too intense for the situation. Now I know why I was so scared. I was gripped in a flashback. I was angry that I couldn't get the image of the back alley out of my mind. I was angry that she didn't tell us where she was going. I mean that was normal to be angry that she left without telling us. But my reaction, screaming at her and calling you names and threatening to leave them in Las Vegas, that was way over the top. I've had so many other moments where that intense anger and rage erupts during or after a flashback."

"Well she shouldn't have left you both like that. She wasn't being safe or smart." Aunt Tessa hesitates. "Have you shared this with her?"

"Not yet. It just all clicked in the last week. I want to tell her. I feel so bad she was on the receiving end of that. It is not the way I want to be towards anyone I care about, even when I have a reason to be angry."

"You should. I know she will really appreciate hearing it." Aunt Tessa begins clearing our dishes.

"Let me help you." I stand up. "I can do these while you get the pictures."

"O.K. Thanks hon. I'll go grab them in the bonus room."

Aunt Tessa and I return to the island after the dishes are done. A box and an album are sitting in front of her. She carefully opens the album. Inside are black and white photos from the 1800s. Portraits of single women and men, and families dressed in attire congruent with those times.

"They were from the South," she starts. "I think it was during the Civil War. Some of the men are in military uniforms." She turns the page. "I mean look at those eyes Anna. Crazy-ness. That is mental illness. I think that was Grandpa's grandpa or uncle."

The man in the photo is dressed in a Confederate Army uniform. His eyes are empty. There is not any life behind them. I shiver. He seems to be looking straight through us.

"Wow," I whisper. "Those eyes remind me of Aunt Lisa's eyes sometimes. When she was not on her medication. There is nothing there but scary unpredictability."

"I know," Aunt Tessa agrees. "Mental illness has been part of our family for a long long time Anna."

"I think when I dissociate, my eyes are like that. From the inside, they get really heavy and I can't focus on anything. It's like they are paralyzed or something and turn into boulders. It's weird. Like I can't feel them anymore, but I do feel them become empty." My breath quickens.

"Is this too hard for you honey?" Aunt Tessa's words are full of concern.

"No, not at all. The opposite actually. It makes a lot of sense. I often wonder why I was so affected by what happened to me. There are so many reasons that some people get PTSD and others don't when they have similar experiences. One has to do with family history. Even though we don't know what he had, knowing the brutality of slavery and the Civil war makes it easy to conclude he was exposed to trauma. And he could've also had another mental illness. There is some really interesting research on intergenerational trauma and the heredity of mental illness." I pause and look back at the picture.

Aunt Tessa sighs. "My sister's eyes looked like that so much of the time. She had a voice that went with those eyes. I could tell when she was having an episode even over the phone."

We turn to the box. More black and white photos are in there. One is framed. None of the people seem happy or joyful.

"I wish I knew which one was Grandpa's dad," Aunt Tessa says. "I'm just not sure."

She points to one man. "I think this one maybe."

At that moment a gust of cold wind sweeps through the room and the lights throughout the entire house flicker. We scream and grab each other, startled by the sudden change.

"Oh my God. Anna, what was that?" Aunt Tessa grips my arm.

"I don't know. That was weird. Let me look at my phone to see if there was a disruption to power in the area." I reach for my phone and search for the utility company website.

"Do you see anything?" A hint of panic in her voice.

I key in her address. "No known outages in this area," I read aloud.

"As of when? Does it say?" She asks insistently.

"As of a few hours ago. I will check back in a little while, maybe the website hasn't been updated yet." I look at her. "This was like what happened in Phora's office."

"Oh my God. The spirits are talking to us. They are here Anna. The spirits." She looks up towards the ceiling with wide eyes. "Hello family."

I squeeze her hand.

She looks at me quizzically. "Did that really just happen? You saw and felt that right? It wasn't just me?"

"It did just happen. I felt it, too. I feel weird now. Like unsettled. Are we safe?" My breath quickens and my chest feels tight.

"Yes, I think we are. I don't think they were here for harm. Even though we were talking about them." Nevertheless, she closes the album. "Let's put these away."

I take a deep breath. "Yeah. O.K."

"Do you want some more wine?" She asks.

"Yes. Please." I push my glass towards her.

"Let's dance. We need some time on the magic carpet. Maybe that will clear the air." She pours two more glasses and walks to the speaker where her phone is plugged in. "What do you want to hear?"

The magic carpet is a small floor rug in the space between the dining room table and living room. We have dance parties on the magic carpet at most family gatherings.

"You know that song that is about home or hearts or something like that?" I am terrible at remembering names.

She laughs. "I'm not sure what you are talking about honey."

I laugh. "You mean my description isn't helpful. Hold on. It will come to me."

I walk over to the magic carpet.

I attempt to sing. "I belong to you. You belong to me. In my heart. Or in my home. Or something like that."

She nods. "I think I know."

Ho Hey by The Lumineers fills the room. We get into a groove of dancing and singing along. I close my eyes and concentrate on my feet, ankles, calf muscles, knees, and thighs. I think the names of each bone and muscle group that I know as I move in rhythm with the music. We take turns picking songs and mimic each other's dance moves. We laugh. We cry. We throw our hands up and move our hips.

I feel myself become more and more present with each song. I forget about PTSD, mental illness, Zoloft, divorce, rape, alcoholism. Suddenly I feel my legs. An image of my pelvis bone springs into my consciousness. I see my femur bones. I see my hip and knee joints. All of them I see moving together to the rhythm of the music. I am moving them. Joy floods my system.

When the song ends, I pause the music. "Auntie I just felt my whole body. I could see my pelvis and hips and legs. They move in the way I want them to. Like a switch just turned on in my brain. My body is connected." My arms gesture down my body. "I can't believe this night."

"Woohoo Honey." Auntie throws her hands up and twirls in a circle.

I throw my arms around Auntie. "Thank you for always being there for me. For making it O.K. to share these things with you without judging me. I can't tell you how much it means to me."

Later in bed, I do a body scan. I am afraid maybe the connection to my body did not last. I say to myself, *there you are legs. I can see all of you. I haven't seen you for so long. Thank you for coming online.*

My eyes bolt open. I grab my phone and open Safari. The utility website is still up. I hit refresh. No known outages in our area. I say to myself, *wow. Can it really be that the spirits were here?*

∞∞∞

Jennifer and I are in our familiar places on the floor surrounded by pillows and blankets. Pansy gnaws on a chew toy in between us. This session is our last one of the year. I recount the details of my time with Aunt Tessa last night.

"Do you think we are crazy?" I inquire. "That we felt and saw the spirits. And then that I saw my skeleton for the first time maybe ever. Now when I feel myself dissociating, I can return to that image of my legs and pelvis dancing. I bet it will help."

"No you are not crazy," she reassures me. "And the imagery you described of your hips and legs moving to the rhythm is really beautiful. You are using it to help yourself stay grounded and in your body. That is really remarkable. You are moving so fast in your healing."

I smile and am pensive for a moment. I ask myself, *am I moving too fast? Am I doing too much? Trying too hard to get through this? Like the labyrinth on retreat.*

"What are you thinking about?" Jennifer's gentle curiosity encourages me to be honest.

"Do you think I am moving too fast? One of the things I have been thinking about is how I plow through things." I pause and gaze out the window. "Like on retreat, my friend Dusty laughed when I told her I didn't have patience to walk through the labyrinth and just wanted to beeline for the center. Why bother with the whole process?"

She replies, "Well, it could be that you are moving too fast. What do you think about that? Are you moving too fast?"

"I'm thinking about what my step-mom said when I was getting ready to leave on retreat. She put her arms out in front of her with her palms facing me and said she wishes I stop pushing through life so hard." I put my arms straight out in front of me with my hands flexed so they face Jennifer. "At the end of retreat I shared this with the group and said one of the things I realized over the ten days is I want to learn how to embrace life and approach life with open arms." I spread my arms as if I'm getting ready to hug someone.

"That imagery is beautiful Anna." Jennifer hesitates before continuing. "Can I share what's coming up for me as you talk?" I nod. "I'm thinking about you in the bathroom. When you said you spent your life hiding in the bathroom. And when I just saw your arms up in front of you, it's almost like when you leave the bathroom you have to push through. Your hands are like shields in front of your chest and your arms are extended straight out creating a mote around your heart. And as long as you plow through with your arms out and hands up, you can get things done." Her soft gaze comforts me. "When you do that movement with your arms, from straight out in front of you to open wide, what comes up for you?"

I'm not sure what she's asking. "You mean like right now what comes up for me?"

"Yes. Do you have any sensations or images that come up that relate to our work and moving too fast?"

"Oh." I take a deep breath and check in with my body. "My chest flutters and my heart feels jittery. Nervous but excited. It's a new way of existing I guess. Maybe I'm afraid if I move too fast through this I am just checking boxes and not really ingraining new ways. Like I'm not really getting better. I'm just fooling you and myself because I'm going through the motions. I'm doing the homework, going along with the imagery and meditations, trying movement, talking to trees, making sculptures, writing with my left hand.

You know, like I'm doing everything you are asking, but am I really doing it with my arms open or are they closed?"

"That is a great question Anna," she replies. "What do you think?"

"To be honest, I am not sure what I think." I crack my knuckles. "On the one hand, I try everything you suggest because at this point why not? I can't get much worse. And everything I try seems to have a positive effect. My brain is firing in new ways. I can feel it. On the other hand, I'm not sure that my arms are all the way open yet. I'm still protecting myself and part of me is just doing everything because you ask and I don't want to let you down."

"Is it possible that both of those things are true and can happen at the same time?"

"Well, yes, I guess that's possible. It doesn't have to be one or the other." I massage my hands. "I can be healing and still guarded. And even if the only reason I do things is because I don't want to let you down, I'm still doing them and they're benefitting me."

"Yes they seem to benefit you. Eventually, I hope the new things you are trying become habits that you do for yourself and not only to not disappoint me." She glances at the clock. "Can we shift gears because I know you are leaving for Europe soon to see your sister over the holidays, which means we will not meet for a while. Is that right?"

"Yes that's right. Thank you for reminding me." I sit up taller. "I'm excited to go. Vi and I have spent every single Christmas holiday together for our entire lives. Plus I didn't want to stay around here. But I'm nervous. I feel fragile. Like so many changes are happening in my body and my mind. I don't want to be stuck over there and have a panic attack and not know what to do. It is so hard sometimes because my family, and some friends, don't understand what happens for me. Like sometimes I just want to stay home and cuddle up in a blanket. And other times I want to go out. But I feel like I am fragile and I'm afraid if I am pushed to do something I don't feel comfortable doing I will go into a rage or panic attack or something."

"What are some of the things you have felt pushed to do in the past?" She asks.

"Well, Franz and Vi have a great group of friends. I've known them since 2002 when she and I first went to Europe. They are super fun. We typically go out to clubs and bars and go dancing. Drinking goes along with that. My sister used to come, too, but now she has the babies so she doesn't come as much. I don't like going without her. I can tell her I need to leave and also trust that she won't leave me. But their friends, I don't know that they would understand why I need to leave." I notice my breath quickening.

Jennifer asks pointedly, "Weren't you at a club dancing and drinking with a group of friends the night you were raped?" I nod and look down at my hands. "Well it makes sense that the thought of being out with friends dancing and drinking could be a trigger for you."

"Ugh." Tears well up in my eyes. "I just want to be able to function like a normal person. It's like everything I used to enjoy triggers me now."

She smiles empathically. "I know. It is hard. This work. It takes time. You are noticing important things about yourself and your environment. Knowing potential triggers can help you navigate them. For instance, can you share with your sister about your concerns about going out to clubs?"

I'm annoyed. "Yes, I guess. But I have to tell her that it is connected to the rape. They have to be getting tired of hearing about it. I am tired of hearing about it. Like 'there Anna goes again…can't even go out and have fun without bringing it up.' I feel like I am obsessed with it sometimes."

"It can feel that way Anna," she reassures. "There are so many layers that have to be teased out. That is the nature of trauma. It buries into you and hides in places and sneaks up on you. It takes time. You are doing incredible work. It is also incredibly painful."

"I guess I can tell my sister. One time when I was there, I think she was pregnant with Leah or Leah was just born, and everyone was going out. She couldn't go. I didn't want to go, but she kept insisting and reassured me that her sister-in-law wouldn't leave me. I felt pressured to go and I went, but I was anxious and on edge the entire time. I couldn't have fun. I didn't know where we were, or how to get home. We were in an industrial area, so there weren't cabs readily available. It was cold. I put on the calm-cool-collected mask and smoked a lot of cigarettes. But I was really miserable. I know Vi meant well, but I really just wanted to stay home with her." I haven't thought about that in a long time.

Jennifer asks, "Could you tell her that?"

"Tell her what? That I felt pressured to go out and had a miserable time?"

"Well, yeah that, but I was thinking maybe you could tell her that if you say you want to stay home, not to pressure you."

"Oh. Yes, I could tell her that."

"What else might be helpful for her to know? Or maybe is there something she could do if you start feeling anxious?"

I gently bite my cheek. *What could she do to help me if I'm feeling anxious?* "Well, I guess I could tell her I need a hug or to put her hand on my shoulder. That helps to ground me. I could also tell her that it's O.K. for her to ask me if something is wrong. Like if she senses something, it would be helpful for her to reach out to me and tell me she notices something."

Jennifer's eyes twinkle and her head nods. "Those are great Anna. Can you tell her that before you go?"

"Sure, I don't see why not."

"So I will see you in January?" She sets her notebook down. "You can always call me or text if something comes up."

Reflections ∞ Reactions ∞ Responses

_____

_____

_____

CHAPTER 20

HAPPY NEW YEAR FAMILY

I arrived in Europe ten days ago. We celebrated Christmas with Violet's in-laws. The sounds around the holiday dinner table include children now, which brings a different joy to Christmas. I celebrated Hanukkah before I left with Elizabeth and her family. Her young nieces' excitement had the same impact. The holidays have been more enjoyable this year than in recent years.

I stare at myself in the mirror of the only bathroom in Vi and Franz's apartment. They live in a 4-story walk up. Even though it is small for the four of them and me, I feel comfortable and safe here. We are getting ready to go to their friend's house for New Year's Eve.

The mascara brush is in my hand midair. I look myself in the eye and take a deep breath. A voice half pep-talks and half criticizes, *what is going on? You've been good since you've been here. You don't need to be anxious. You are fine. You are just going to Violet and Franz's friend's house. They have kids, too. It will be mellow and safe. Why are you going there?* My eyes implore my mind to get it under control. A new voice chimes in, *just finish getting ready.*

You will be fine. You are comfortable in your dress and boots. You look pretty. Violet let you borrow jewelry to complete your outfit. I put mascara on my top lashes. *It is O.K. that you don't have kids and you are getting divorced. They don't judge you.* I shake my head to try to stop this inner dialogue. I remind the voices, *I do want kids and now I never will have them. My life wasn't supposed to be this way. I wasn't supposed to be alone here this year. I was supposed to be growing a family.*

Violet comes around the corner holding Max, her youngest child. I hurriedly return to applying my mascara. Concern flashes across her face. Leah calls out to her for help getting dressed in the other room.

"Here, let me take Max." I put the mascara brush away and reach for him. He smiles and reaches out to me. My heart calms. We make faces in the mirror at each other. He giggles.

Violet comes back to the bathroom. "Hey, I know you said if I notice something it's O.K. for me to say something." She takes a deep breath. "Are you O.K.? You've been really quiet for the last hour."

Tears gather in the corners of my eyes and my cheeks flush. "I will be O.K. Thank you for noticing." I look down.

She reaches out her hand and gently squeezes on my shoulder. "You can tell me more if you want."

"Not yet, but I will." I concentrate on taking deep controlled breaths. "I really want to have fun tonight and I don't want to bring you down."

"You aren't bringing me down." Her tone is sincere. "Do you want to not go?"

"No," I answer faster and with more force than I intend. "Sorry that was a lot. No, I want to go. I'm just having a moment."

Franz peeks his head in the crowded bathroom. "Are you ladies ready to go?" He smiles.

Violet answers before I can say anything. "Why don't you and Leah go now and Anna, Max and I will leave in a few minutes?"

Franz notices my tears and nods. He and Leah put on their jackets, scarves, hats, and gloves before leaving the apartment.

A few minutes later, I meet Violet in the foyer to put our layers on so we aren't too cold on the walk to their friend's apartment.

"I'm sorry Vi. This is all so weird and new to me. I'm just feeling a little sad right now. I'm so glad we aren't doing a big party thing like in years past. And being with you guys and all the babies reminds me that I am not there yet in my life. It makes me sad. And angry. Mostly sad."

She reaches her arms around me in a tight embrace. "You are O.K. Anna. I can only imagine that being with all of us reminds you of what you don't have. You will one day though. I know you will. I'm glad you told me."

"I'm glad you asked, Vi. I don't think I would've told you had you not asked. Like 'hey poor me my life sucks. I can't even figure out how to stay married let alone have kids.'" Sarcasm drips from my words.

"No, A. You made a really hard decision to get divorced. Remember how hard it was for us when we were little and mom and dad got divorced? You aren't doing the same thing to your kids. And your life does suck right now. You are going through a lot. It's O.K. for you to be sad."

I'm filled with relief and gratitude. "You always know what to say, Vi. What would I do without you?"

We pass happy people on the walk to their friend's house. The celebratory mood helps lighten my mood. The kids play in their pajamas after dinner. Of course they do not want to go to sleep and miss the fireworks at midnight. We decide to walk home before midnight so Leah and Max can fall asleep right after the fireworks. We enter the apartment at 11:55PM. Quickly we take off our layers and gather at the dining room window overlooking the street. Violet holds Max and I hold Leah. Franz puts his arms around all of us. The fireworks start at midnight to mark the beginning of 2015.

He squeezes our shoulders. "Happy New Year, family."

My eyes well up again. I realize I do have a family. I am not alone. I am right where I need to be.

∞∞∞

The next day, Violet and I pack my clothes while Leah and Max sleep. As usual, my pending departure leaves me unsettled. Violet is the person whose life is most similar to mine because we moved between Dad's and Mom's houses together. Her presence makes me feel safe. I hear my voice, *wow that word. Safe. I've never intentionally thought of this word so frequently.*

"What are you thinking about?" Violet eyes me with curiosity.

"How much I love being here with you and your family. How much I don't want to go home. I mean I live with Dad. Did you ever think I would utter those words?" I exaggerate the question.

She giggles. "No, honestly I didn't. I lived with Dad in high school. After you left for college, I spent a lot more time with him and Lindsey was gone most of the week working. He really tried hard. I mean he made me breakfast every day."

"I know. He really is a good person. I mean I think I am so driven because of him. But Violet, you were there for all of our knock down drag outs. We are so alike in so many ways but with completely different motivations. That Gulden family rage plagues us both. You have it but only when you drink. And you just get sassy more than anything. It's like the mom in you subdues the dad in you." I wrap the picture frame of all of us on Christmas Eve that Franz's mom gave me as a going away gift.

"The Gulden family rage is no joke. I remember those times. It was and still is really hard." She is thoughtful for a moment. "How long do you think you will stay with Dad and Lindsey?"

"Honestly, I don't know. I feel like it is getting close to moving out time. I've been there since July. And now that I am drinking again, Dad and I stay up drinking more than I care to admit and Lindsey doesn't like it."

Violet's eyes glaze over. She refocuses on me after a moment. "Anna, you know how hard Dad's drinking was on Mom. Remember how he was? You never knew if he was going to be the nice, fun guy or the angry, scary guy. Lindsey has to deal with that now. We aren't there. We drink with him and she has to deal with the aftermath."

"That's true. I never thought of it like that. But she drinks with him, too. I mean he was sober for the first 6 years of their relationship." The dynamic confuses me.

"Yeah, but do you think she really knew he could be that mean? I mean do you think she knew when he started drinking that the Gulden family rage was so terrible?" She makes a great point.

"I never thought of it all in that way before, Vi. Mom has said she feels for Lindsey because she also experienced that rage. Lindsey met Dad sober." I put the last pile of clothes in my suitcase. "Back to your original question. I think it is time for me to move out. It has been six months. I'm on Zoloft. I have a steady job. My counselor and clinical supervisor are amazing. But I'm really scared. What if I fall back into my old thinking habits again? I don't know that the voice that said 'put the phone down and tell your family tomorrow' is strong enough to come out again. And if I live alone, I mean there is no telling what my brain might do." I sigh and look away because I don't want to see her worry.

"A, that voice is strong enough because that voice is you. It is scary. Getting that picture of the contract thing was the scariest moment of my life. I mean you've called before sobbing hysterically. Many times. But that was the scariest moment. Franz was like 'do you need to go there?' He was ready for me to fly over and Max and Leah were so young."

"I'm glad you have faith in my voice." I can't make eye contact. "I'm just not sure. I feel so fragile. Like it is the right time because it has been six months, but also, what if it's too soon. What if I am really not ready?"

"I remember when you told me that night after the produce convention when you had been with Dad and Lindsey…you said that you just wanted the pain to bleed out. You didn't want to die." She continues with conviction. "You are dealing with the pain now, Annie. You are facing it. Whenever the time comes for you to move out you will be O.K."

"I hope you are right." I raise my eyes to look at her. "I've battled those thoughts for a long time. I mean, I told my EMDR therapist that I had those thoughts back in like 2006 or 2007, but didn't want to be admitted to the psych ward because of what happened to Aunt Lisa. During those ten days, Violet, nothing helped me. Leah and Max were always my go-tos. Facetiming with you every day or every other day, even seeing their little happy faces for a brief moment. I mean, even seeing their crying faces for a brief moment gave me hope. But in those ten days, even they didn't help. It was a fucked up time, Vi. I'm really scared of going back to that place."

"Do you think staying with Dad and Lindsey will help you stay away from that place?" Her tone is serious. "I mean you have said you are so grateful for them taking you in and paying for the retreat. But I also know that you don't do well with Dad for an extended period. And you have been there a long time."

"That is a great question. And you are right. A world war breaks out eventually. Dad has been surprisingly great. Did I tell you about when we sculpted together?"

She shakes her head and chokes on her sip of water. "Uh no. What do you mean sculpted?"

We both start laughing.

"Like with this clay stuff I bought at Michaels. On retreat I realized how much I loved to do sculpting and art. So when I got back and I was on my first work trip I went to Michaels and bought a journal and some quick drying clay."

Her eyebrows raise. "And Dad did it with you?" She's incredulous.

"Well yes." I start laughing again. "The first thing he made was a dog peeing on a fire hydrant."

We deep belly laugh holding our stomachs until happy tears stream down our faces.

I take a deep breath and calm down. "But then he rolled it up and made this beautiful rose. Like it was full of individual pedals that he affixed to the stem. And he gave it to me and said something like 'this is what I think of you. You are a rose, Annie. Beautiful, strong, kind. You need to be treated like a rose.'"

Violet's face registers surprise.

"I know." I nod. "I was surprised, too. It was deep for him. And really meaningful. Thoughtful. Heartfelt. I think that is who he really is, but he has all kinds of messages working inside his brain, too, from his childhood."

She nods in agreement. "Yeah, you're probably right. I think you will be fine if you move out." After a pause, she points out the obvious. "I mean, you can always move back in if you need to, right?"

"True." I shake my head and take another deep breath. "My stomach hurts. That was a good belly laugh. I love that we laugh-cry together."

Reflections ∞ Reactions ∞ Responses

_____

_____

_____

CHAPTER 21

SEXISM AT THE DINNER TABLE
& MOVING OUT

I've been back from Europe for a few weeks. As usual, work has been hectic after a long vacation. It is finally the weekend. I sit across the dinner table from Dad and Lindsey's best friend Jason. His wife, Kayla is to my right. Lindsey is across from Kayla. Dad is at the head of the table to my left. Jason and I are locked in a lively conversation about ways in which education and business could partner to expand opportunities for young adults to enter the work-force beyond after-school internships.

"At our company, we do internship programs with the local high schools," Jason explains. "What your students need are internships."

I shake my head. "We aren't at the internship phase yet. Our students need to learn about the agriculture industry and that there are careers available outside of picking lettuce." I jump in my seat. "Ouch! Dad why are you kicking me under the table?"

He growls, "Anna, you weren't supposed to say that out loud." He looks embarrassed and angry. "You aren't letting Jason finish."

"Yes, I am," I retort. "Jason's internship suggestion is a good one for our students once they have a better idea of the type of jobs that are out there, and they learn important skills, like punctuality and communication." I turn back to Jason. "I'm sorry. I didn't mean to talk over you or cut you off. Our students are non-traditionally aged high school students with an average reading level of 6th grade. For many of them, the prospect of working in agriculture equals working in the fields. We are trying to expand that view. So we need to think creatively about exposing them to the diverse careers available in the industry."

Dad kicks me again. I give him the evil eye.

"What?" I snap at Dad.

"Well, let the man talk." Dad glowers at me.

I sigh and suggest we change the subject.

Jason and Kayla leave shortly after dinner. Lindsey moves to Jason's seat, which puts Dad at the head of the table between us.

"What was going on Dad?" I ask genuinely confused.

"You weren't letting him talk, Anna. You can't interrupt someone when they are trying to help." His tone is short.

I turn to Lindsey to ask her perspective on my conversation with Jason. "Was I interrupting him? I don't think I was. He was engaged and animated and so was I. But if you saw that, too, then I missed something."

"I didn't think you interrupted him any more than he interrupted you." Lindsey confirms my conclusion.

I look Dad squarely in the eye. "So, Dad did you kick Jason under the table when he interrupted me?"

He looks exasperated. "Of course not."

"Well, why not?" I fire back at him.

"He's our guest."

"Yeah, but you've said a million times that they are family. You invite them to Christmas and every other family function. You go to their house for family functions. He is hardly a guest in that sense."

"Anna, you just get on a roll and you wouldn't hear him."

"What didn't I hear?" I genuinely want to know what I missed.

"He was trying to help you with the internship idea. He is a CEO. You don't interrupt a CEO and you don't jettison their ideas." His tone condescends and patronizes me.

"Oh really? In what decade?" Now I am on a roll...a pissed off roll. "Last time I checked we were two people having a conversation about how to serve underprivileged youth through a partnership. I didn't jettison his idea. I simply said our students aren't ready for internships right away and we need to also think about exposure to different jobs." I take a quick breath. "I think you kicked me under the table because I'm a woman and women need to listen and not speak when men are speaking."

"Oh here you go again." He rolls his eyes. "You always go here. Like I wanted sons and got stuck with daughters."

"Well why not just say 'Anna, Jason is trying to finish his point. Please listen.' Or 'Jason, do you think Anna is interrupting you too much?' I mean you really didn't need to kick me under the table. In fact, don't ever kick me under the table again. It is demeaning and rude."

"Charlie, Anna has a point," Lindsey softly chimes in.

He explodes on her. "YOU DO NOT INTERRUPT US. THIS IS BETWEEN US."

My body stands between them before I could figure out what was happening. Lindsey is stunned. I square my body to Dad with my hands on my hips. A voice in the distance echoes, *you've been here before here before here before. You aren't safe aren't safe aren't safe.*

I stand as tall as I can. "Dad, you can be angry all you want. But you CANNOT speak to any of us that way. That is violent and rage-filled." I gesture towards Lindsey. "She doesn't deserve that. We ALL are having a conversation. I asked for her input. She is family. You are being an ass." My tone is calm, yet firm. "Go cool off. Like I said, anger is O.K. Rage is not. We are going in the other room."

He looks dumbfounded. Silence fills the space.

I grab my glass of wine across the table and turn on my heel. "Lindsey let's go."

We walk to the living room, which is adjacent to the dining room. The lights are dim in there. Lindsey and I sit facing each other on the couch. I'm between her and the entry way to the room.

"I haven't seen the rage come out in a while," I say softly.

"Yeah, me either," she replies. "One time I had to lock myself in the bathroom and call Kayla to come over because he was so out of control."

Sadness fills my expression. "I've been there...literally." I reach out to hold her hand. "My first memory of locking myself in the bathroom was when my parents were still married. I was like 5 or 6 and Vi was 3 or 4. It is really scary. I'm glad you had Kayla to call. And I'm sad you have to deal with this. I wish he would deal with his anger."

I recall my conversation with Violet a few weeks ago when she pointed out that Lindsey now takes the brunt of Dad's alcoholism. He walks by the entry way with his shoulders slumped on the way to their bedroom.

"Goodnight, Dad," I call. "I love you and hope we can talk about this tomorrow."

His head gestures yes as he turns the opposite way from us down the hall to their bedroom.

"Do you want to sleep in my room tonight?" I ask Lindsey.

She smiles. "No, he is fine now. He looked remorseful and guilty just then. He will sleep it off. Thank you, though."

The following day I recount the story to Jennifer. I'm excited about the outcome because we did not have a huge family blowout, which used to happen in the past when sexism and alcoholism reared their ugly heads during family time.

"Jennifer, I was so strong in my resolve. I know he kicked me under the table because I'm a woman, and younger than Jason. I didn't get all caught up in Dad's denial of that. I didn't engage in his rage. I stood up, said what I needed to say calmly and firmly, and removed myself from the situation. In the past that would have been fodder for another world war."

She smiles. "You are disengaging from the negative family dynamics with your dad. That's great. What happened the next day?"

"As soon as I saw him in the morning, I asked him about what happened for him. I let him know that it was a really scary outburst and that he didn't need to express his anger in that way. I told him that it wasn't fun for any of us to see him so angry and be on the receiving end of it, especially when he is drinking. I reiterated that there is another way to say 'I'm embarrassed because Anna keeps interrupting you Jason,' without kicking me under the table. And certainly Lindsey did not deserve the response she got. He was receptive. He apologized. I called Kayla, too and asked her to apologize to Jason if he felt I was interrupting him. She said she didn't see that happening and reiterated that it was simply a lively conversation and we both talked over each other a few times. She said there was nothing to worry about."

"It sounds like you really handled it well, as an adult in charge of herself and her emotions." She pauses to let that sink in. "I want to shift gears a little bit. You are planning to move out soon, right? How does your dad feel about you moving out?"

"Yes, right. I am planning to move out soon. Vi and I talked about it when I was in Europe. Dad says he is really happy for me. I wonder if he is also sad. This is the closest we've ever been. I mean I haven't lived with him since I was 8, so 25-plus years. And when I did live with him, we certainly didn't have a great relationship."

"How do you feel about moving out?" She asks.

"I'm O.K. Some moments I'm freaking out because what if it's too soon? What if I can't handle it? And other moments I'm super excited. I'm looking forward to having my own space and going through my things in storage."

She shifts back to the interaction with Dad's rage. "How do you feel about the way your dad treated you and Lindsey?"

I look at her with furrowed brows. "I don't know. Surprised because I haven't seen the rage in a long time. Sad because it doesn't have to be that way."

"What about angry? It is O.K. for you to also feel angry?" She shares, "I feel angry at the way you were treated."

"You know how I am with anger. It is hard for me to express it. I guess I am angry, too, but also exhausted. It is a reminder of how women are oppressed and how I am oppressed because I am a woman. It is infuriating. And also…like…what does anger really do? It is just exhausting."

"Is there a form of movement we could do to express anger?"

I avoid her question. "You know I think confusion is another feeling. It was so out of left field. Actually his response wasn't even in the ball park that I was sitting in. It is so confusing." I pause to ponder her question about expressing anger. "Well, I just thought of the time on retreat when I threw rocks against a wall as hard as I could. It felt sooooooooooooooooooooooo good to get the aggression out."

"Well, let's go do it," she suggests. "We can go out back and throw rocks against the wall of the building."

I feel a sudden rush of adrenaline and jump up. "Yes, let's do it. It feels so good. I never thought of this before but I played softball growing up. It was a similar feeling. Hitting the ball, throwing it really hard. I bet softball played a part in me controlling my anger when I was younger."

"Probably," she says as we head out the door.

First, we gather rocks into a small pile. I pick one up and heave it as hard as I can at the wall. It shatters on impact. I take a deep breath. A voice instructs, *pick up another one.* My chest pounds with anticipation. The next thing I know I am heaving them one after another at the wall. I pause long enough to see Jennifer scurry to gather more.

She suggests, "Next time let out a noise."

I think annoyed, *I like the physical exertion. I don't want to yell.* "O.K.," I say out loud.

She hurriedly says, "Only if you want to. You don't have to."

The next pile of rocks I heave at the wall with grunts and yells. I think with less annoyance, *well, that does feel good. Plus, I think I'm throwing them harder.* My mind wanders to my high school pitching lessons when my coach, who happens to now be my step-dad, made me grunt upon release of the ball. *It certainly worked back then to increase the speed. Plus it was a distraction for the batters.* I smile at that memory.

Jennifer calls out, "Maybe say something next time."

My breath catches in my chest. My eyes drop. The wind is out of my sails. A different voice is doubtful. *What will you say? What should you say?* Another one criticizes, *whatever you say will be dumb. You will sound ridiculous.*

"O.K.," I say softly.

She looks up from where she is collecting rocks. "Only if you want to, Anna." She notices my change.

I look down at the few that are left. Begrudgingly, I pick them both up. I force myself to take a deep breath and bring my arm back. The critical voice says, *you're really going to do this? You will sound so stupid.*

"I hate you," I say softly as I throw one rock. My cheeks grow hot and tears well up. "I HATE YOU," I scream when I let the last one go. I turn to Jennifer. "I'm ready to go inside now."

Jennifer drops the rocks she collected where she stands and walks towards me. "That was beautiful to watch, Anna." Her tone is reassuring and kind. "I can tell it brought something up."

"I'm so confused." I open the door to go back inside the building. "I just don't know why I can't express anger. Why it is so hard for me. Why it is so full of shame. Like I'm not supposed to be angry. I feel guilty for feeling hatred. It is so ugly. I am angry that I have hatred in me."

My tears stop as the words tumble from my mouth. We stand in the middle of the room.

"Anger is a hard one for so many reasons," she says gently. "Historically, women weren't allowed to be angry. Or to express anger. That programming may be operating in the background. Plus for you, you saw how ugly and violent anger can be. Both in growing up with an alcoholic parent and in your sexual assault. It is a scary emotion. Go easy on yourself. What you just did out there opened something up. You released something. That is powerful and takes courage. Do you know what I mean?"

"I guess so." I feel tired. "I just wish it was over. I want this healing to happen already. I don't want it to be so hard."

Jennifer smiles knowingly. "I know. All my trauma clients, or clients who have experienced trauma and are doing the work like you say the same thing. What you are doing is really hard. It takes so much time and commitment to work through everything. Can we do a movement to close out today?"

"O.K. What do you have in mind?" I ask. "Nothing too strenuous I hope. I'm tired."

"I was thinking something to show compassion to yourself and honor what you just did." Her gaze seeks my permission.

"O.K." I barely nod.

"Start with opening your arms as wide as you want." She brings her arms out to her sides like she is preparing to give a hug. "Then wrap them as tight as you can around yourself and slowly lower yourself to the ground. Then I will put pillows and blankets over you. Does that sound O.K.?"

The voice ridicules, *seriously now you are going to hug yourself. Is this 4th grade camp? This lady is whacked. This is so cheesy.* I ignore this ridicule. I take a deep breath as my chest flutters. I drop my shoulders and open my arms wide. I slowly wrap them around myself. I inhale slowly. I close my eyes and exhale as I lower myself to the ground.

"Great breath work, Anna."

My inner critic is quiet. I smile. "Thanks," I mumble.

I lie cocooned in blankets and pillows with my eyes closed for several minutes. Inhale to a count of 4. Exhale to a count of 5. The critic snaps, *well that didn't work. You can't breathe like that when you are riled up.* I try again. This time I inhale 4 and exhale 8. And again. And again.

Jennifer suggests, "If you can, either silently or out loud, say thank you to yourself for your incredible work today."

I say to myself, *thank you for doing this. Thank you for fighting through the inner critic and giving this work a chance. Thank you for trusting Jennifer.*

"When you are done, open your eyes." She sits in her usual spot on the floor across from me. "That was really beautiful to watch. Whatever you said to yourself. Your face softened." She reiterates, "You did great work today, Anna."

Her genuine kindness and encouragement sink in more deeply than before. My inner critic is silent.

I look at her with gratitude and sadness. "Last weekend was the anniversary of the rape. It just dawned on me."

Her eyes widen with surprise. "I'm sorry I did not remember that. Did you do anything symbolic?"

I shake my head. "One year when I lived on the east coast two friends, who are also counselors, came over and we did an art project and wrote letters to ourselves. It was a nice ritual. But mostly the anniversary sneaks up on me and I dread it. I'm more sensitive than usual. I get angry at myself that it has been so long since the rape and I'm still affected by it. The anniversary usually sucks." I roll on my side and push myself up to get my checkbook.

"Maybe this week you can do what we just did at the end each day." She gestures to the pillows and blankets. "Show yourself compassion and comfort for this year's anniversary."

"Yeah, I'll try. That's a good idea," I say softly. I hand her a check. We hug good bye. I pat Pansy's head and turn towards the door. An exhaustion settles in my body that I haven't felt in a long time. I think, *sadness has settled in your bones.* I sigh a long, exasperated and defeated breath.

Reflections ∞ Reactions ∞ Responses

_____

_____

_____

ON MY OWN AGAIN

"Health and healing are possible." - California Coalition Against Sexual Assault, 2017.

"Recovering from sexual assault or abuse is a process, and that process looks different for everyone." - RAINN, 2018

CHAPTER 22

PANIC ATTACK NUMBER 87 THOUSAND

I'm driving home from a work trip. Catherine left me a voicemail yesterday. I put my earbuds in my ears and click "play" next to her name in my voicemail list.

"Annie Bananie. I was thinking the other day that I miss you and want to see you soon. I just had a birthday and you have one coming up soon. We can eat birthday cake. Ohhhh and we can drink wine. Ohhhh and don't forget about catching up on celebrity gossip. Let me know if you want to come up or I can come down. Or whatever. We can FaceTime. I just miss my friend. Sooooo in other news, my kids are busy in school. Being a parent is busy! I like my new job. I actually have a student situation that I want to run by you. Call me about that, too. O.K. well I think I've rambled enough. I miss you. Yeah. Like I said before. See ya' later alligator."

My heart constricts because I miss her, too. But I can't be bubbly and happy and helpful and fun to be around right now. I'm tired, stressed and overwhelmed. I know it is time to move out of Dad and Lindsey's house. *When will I feel normal again?* A wave of nostalgia washes over me for the days Catherine and I were in school together having fun at our favorite bar or the beach or our living rooms. We even had fun coming up with group activities for workshops. We actually published a few of those together in a peer-reviewed activity workbook. *I miss you, too my friend.* I sigh.

Next, I call Mom. She picks up after several rings. I'm traveling a lot for work and can't find time to look at apartments during the week. Mom offered to preview apartments while I'm away so on weekends I can visit the ones she thinks would be best for me.

"Hi, Momma." I smile when I hear her voice. "Any luck?"

"Hi, Annie." I hear her smile. "I think we found the place for you. Aunt Tessa and I both saw it and it is really cute. It is a condo by the community college. Two bedrooms like you wanted, so you will have a space for your office. I think one room is big enough to have a bed and desk in it and the second room can also have a bed. You can have the guest room, your room, and an office space like you wanted."

"That's awesome." I switch lanes to go around a slow truck. "And it is obviously in my price range. Can I check it out?"

"Yes, they are willing to show you this weekend when you get back. Aunt Tessa and I want to come, too, if that is O.K. with you."

"Of course, I want you both there. You found it after all. Did you find it on Craigslist?"

"Yes, I did." She giggles. "I know you said only call the places with pictures and this place didn't have pictures, but the price was right and the location was good. We saw some places that were gross that had pictures. So anyway, I called. They are grey-haireds like us. They don't know how to use technology, so they didn't put up pictures. You really shouldn't ignore the ones without pictures."

"Gray-haireds. That's funny, Momma," I say out loud while thinking to myself, *I'm more worried about the serial murderers and rapists. Grey-haireds without technology savviness didn't cross my mind. I wonder if my automatic thought is because of my rape?* "Thanks, Momma. I can't wait to see it."

That weekend, I sign the lease. It begins in ten days.

∞∞∞

Dad, Lindsey and I sit at the patio table at their house after another grueling week of work travel. The outdoor heaters are on and Dad made a fire. We just finished a great meal. One of the last ones since I'm moving out in a few days.

"Annie, how are you feeling about your move?" Dad sips his martini.

I take a sip of wine and stare at the mountain line in the distance. The vultures don't hunt there anymore like when Samantha visited last September. I think about the selfies we took that day we sat out here on the patio. Her words come back to me, too. She said, *I don't know what I would do if you died.*

"Honestly, I'm mixed. It is exciting. I am looking forward to having my own things out of storage. I like the condo I rented. But I'm scared. What if it is too soon?"

Lindsey leans forward in her chair. "Honey, we will have Tony go over and secure the place for you. It is a really safe area. You will be fine."

Tony manages Dad and Lindsey's properties. He is reliable and kind. I know he will secure my new condo.

"How are you feeling Dad?" I eye him over our wine glasses.

"About your move?" He raises his eyebrows.

"Yeah."

"Well, I'm happy for you, but I've really enjoyed having you here. It has been really nice to reconnect." He reaches his hand towards mine across the table.

"I will definitely miss sitting out here for dinner. It is so peaceful and serene." I reach my hand towards his outstretched hand and give it a squeeze.

"When are you clearing out of the office in town?" Lindsey changes the subject. I've been working out of an office in one of their companies since I moved in with them.

I let go of Dad's hand and take a sip of wine before answering her. "My mom is going to help me on Friday move the rest of the books. My new landlords said I could start moving stuff in on Friday, even though the lease doesn't officially start until Sunday."

"Oh that's nice," she says. "And when do you move your stuff out of storage?"

"I scheduled the movers for Saturday." I shift in my seat. "Dad, you can still help me right? I'm not comfortable being by myself in the storage facility with two strange men. And Mom is going out of town." I'm uncomfortable asking for his help after they've allowed me to live with them rent-free for so long.

An involuntary image flashes through my mind of myself trapped in my storage unit by these two men. They tie me up and put tape over my mouth. A voice commands, *stop thinking this.* I can't stop the thoughts. They wheel me down the hall to the loading dock stuffed between furniture and put me in the moving van. I shake my head slightly and shiver.

"Yeah yeah, I can help. I will be there." He turns to Lindsey. "We don't have anything Saturday right?"

She takes a deep breath and holds it. "Well, you don't have anything, but I have stuff." She exhales a blast of air. "There is the one thing you were going to meet me at in the afternoon, but you don't have to come."

I cringe internally because I sense I am disrupting their lives. "The movers are coming in the morning so we should be done by the afternoon." I want to say don't worry about coming, but the image of me tied up stops me from declining his help. "I really appreciate you being there. I don't have anyone else I could ask who is in town. Even Elizabeth is going to be out of town."

"No, no. I can be there," he reiterates. "Are you cold, A? I thought I saw you shiver a moment ago. I can add another log to the fire."

The voices are loud. I'm not sure how many are present. *They will think you are crazy if you tell them what you were just thinking. Well, what if I'm not safe? That happens all the time to people. And it's not like movers have the best backgrounds. You are so stereotypical. Don't be ridiculous. You aren't going to get raped on Saturday. Or kidnapped. You don't know that. I could. It is possible. Those halls are long and my unit is far away from the office.*

"No, I'm not cold," I lie. "Just got a little chill. We are going inside soon anyway, right?"

Lindsey stands up. "Yes, I have to get up early tomorrow." She begins stacking our dinner plates.

"I can get those, Lindsey," I insist. "You cooked. Dad and I can pick up."

"Yeah, yeah," Dad agrees. "A and I will do it."

I finish the bottle of wine that was open for dinner and he has another martini while doing the dishes and closing down the patio. Before going to bed, Dad reassures me that I will be fine. He confirms that he will be there on Saturday.

I try to take deep breaths as I walk towards the bathroom. Ever since the image of being kidnapped and raped by the movers, I've felt a panic attack lingering in the shadows. The voices continue to chatter in my mind. *Breathe. You will be fine. Stop thinking that. Stop seeing that. You will not be raped. What if I will be raped? You will not be raped. You think all men will rape you. No I don't. Yes, you do.* An image of me on the night of the rape pops into my conscience. Evan's face looms in front of me. I hear his words. *I'm sorry we didn't even kiss when we hooked up.* I shake my head and look at myself in the bathroom mirror.

I say out loud to his face in my mind, "We didn't kiss because I was suffocating in the pillow and we didn't hook up because I didn't want to have sex with you. I told you I was tired and rolled over to go to sleep. I never liked you like that. You asshole."

No matter how many times I count my breaths and scan my body, I feel panic rising in my blood. Once I lie down in bed, it washes through me like a tidal wave. My ears fill with static, I can't breathe, sobs heave tears down my cheeks, my legs float away, my jaw clenches, my back and shoulders contract. The voices grow louder and more urgent. *Oh, no. Why does this happen? You aren't ready to move out. What if this happens all the time when you are alone? You are safe here. You shouldn't move alone. You can't take care of yourself. You will be a target. You will not be safe there. You are ridiculous. Get yourself under control.* My chest constricts. I hyperventilate. *Go get Dad. Maybe he is still up.*

I force my legs over the side of the bed. I give myself instructions to try to calm down. *Step. Step. Step. Touch the door knob. Turn the light on. Step. Step. Step. Turn right. Go up the steps. Turn the light on. Breathe. Oh no, I still can't breathe. Be quiet. Don't wake up Lindsey. Turn right. Go down steps. Silent. Their TV is on. Turn left.* I stop in my tracks when their bed comes into view. Lindsey is sitting up with a look of shear anger across her face. Dad is curled up asleep facing away from her.

"I'm really sorry," I whisper. "I wanted to see if Dad was still up. I'm having a panic attack."

Her faces softens. "Oh no. Sit down."

I sit on the chair near her side of the bed.

"I'm so afraid, Lindsey." I try to keep from sobbing. "And I feel so helpless when these happen."

"You are going to be fine," she tries to reassure me. "And don't worry about waking your dad up. He just woke me up. He's so loud when he comes to bed drunk. How much more did you guys drink?"

I shake my head. *Really, this is what you want to talk about?* Internally, I roll my eyes. I reply, "We finished the bottle of wine from dinner. I think he had vodka or scotch. One of those. I'm really sorry." I feel responsible for his drinking and remember my conversation with Vi. "And I'm sorry that I am keeping you up. I really didn't mean to do that." I stand to go back to my room. A voice commands, *make a pillow fort. You will be O.K.*

"You don't have to leave, honey," she whispers. "I'm sorry you are having a panic attack. You are going to be O.K. The condo is safe and we are going to have Tony come over. You will see. And you can always come back."

"Thanks." I turn back towards her and see a look of concern and sadness cross her exhausted face. "I'm sorry again, Lindsey." I focus on directions back to my room.

My breath slows as I return to my room. I can feel my legs again. My thoughts are calm. I gather all the pillows off the bed in the next room. I line each of them around my body with one under my head and two on top of my body. I pull the covers tightly over me. A meditation fills the room. The waterfall chakra meditation.

I like that one because it includes seeing colors aligned with each chakra. I think, *swirling colors remind me of Phora. Massages with Phora are relaxing.* Eventually I fall asleep.

∞∞∞

The move went surprisingly well. Today is Sunday and I lost track of time to leave for my session with Jennifer. I text Jennifer that I am going to be late while running to my car parked in my new space. I think, *shit, I must make extra time to walk to my car now.* I hit every red light on my way there. Of course today there aren't any parking spaces left. By the time I actually enter the building, I'm fifteen minutes late.

"I'm so sorry, Jennifer." I reach down to pet Pansy.

Her tone is understanding. "That's O.K., Anna. You moved today, right?"

We settle into our usual spots on the ground.

"Yes, I was unpacking boxes and time got away from me." I brush pieces of hair away from my face. "I haven't showered or brushed my hair. My dad came through and went with me yesterday morning to meet the movers at the storage unit. Then he surprised me and came with me to my new condo while they moved me in. I wasn't expecting that."

She smiles and nods.

I take a deep breath. "I had a panic attack earlier this week. It was a big one. I haven't had one like that in a long time."

Her eyebrows furrow with concern. "Oh. Do you know what set it off?"

"You know, I've wracked my brain about what actually triggered it. It being the thought I had of the movers kidnapping and raping me in the storage facility. And my dad bailing on me at the last minute. And living alone again. And being afraid I'm moving out too soon. What if the suicidal thoughts come back? It was all of those things. But I don't know what triggered the initial image of the movers attacking me. I mean they were really good guys. I hate that all men become villains in the blink of an eye. It is so irrational and involuntary." I describe the physical changes that took place over the course of the panic attack.

I pause and focus on Jennifer. She is poised with her pen not moving across her note pad. Pansy chews on her toy in between us. I'm struck by how easy it is to share these experiences with Jennifer.

"Is there something more?" she asks.

"A sidebar. I was just thinking that I am so glad I have this space to share about these experiences now. I don't have to do them by myself. I'm not left wondering if I'm crazy or questioning if that just happened or chastising myself for allowing them to happen. It is just really nice. I guess what I am trying to say is I don't feel alone in this craziness anymore. That just dawned on me." I smile and take a deep breath.

Jennifer grins widely. "Thank you. That really says a lot. You aren't crazy. Panic attacks happen with trauma. I'm struck that you are able to verbalize the images you had of the movers, the physical changes you felt, and that these are irrational and involuntary. You've come a long way, Anna. Before, you couldn't describe them with such detail. Even though they continue to happen, you are much more aware of them. That awareness is tied to new pathways in your brain. Neuroplasticity. That's good."

"Yeah. Thanks." I look down.

"You still wish you didn't have them anymore and that the work was over." Her matter of fact tone matches my wishes.

"Yep, you guessed it." I smile at her. "I know we are doing the hard work. I know it has gotten better already in so many ways. I just want the involuntary irrational stuff to stop. It is so not who I am. I'm not a fearful person. I believe in the inherent good nature of people. But when these happen, it's like my brain is invaded by something that turns all men into perpetrators. It's so…wild."

Her tone reassures me that my experiences are normal. "Anna, you went through an attack by a perpetrator. You were a victim of a crime. Prosecuted or not, you were passed out when he raped you. The involuntary irrational stuff is left over from that. Trauma work deals with the left over stuff and it takes time. You are doing incredible work. We aren't doing the hard work, you are."

"I know. You remind me of all that a lot. Anna-before-the-rape was not consumed with panic attacks despite the traumatic moments I had as a child. I thought about moving home after the rape happened, like in my twenties. I did not move home on purpose because I did not want to live in a place where I could see Evan potentially any time I went to the grocery or out to dinner." An image of me fighting back tears at my ten year high school reunion appears in my mind.

"I mean at my ten year high school reunion, I really didn't want to go because I had a feeling we would run into him. My friends convinced me and promised they would leave with me if we saw him. I caved and of course we saw him. In the middle of the bar, the crowd stopped moving and went silent, except for him. He moved in slow motion. I burst into tears. My friends left with me like they promised." The flashback haunts my memory.

"But honestly, it is embarrassing. I don't want to be that girl who cries at the bar all the time. That is not me. I am social. I like to talk and dance and laugh and have fun. I mean I've avoided coming home because of that fear. In 2003 I opted to move in with my grandpa instead of come home when I was applying to graduate programs. I remember my cousin was like 'wow you must really not like your family if you opt to live with grandpa.' I did not know how to respond to that back then, but I remember that moment like it was yesterday. Because I actually do like my family despite all of our challenges and moments where we caused pain to each other. We have always been there when worse comes to worse. Or when best comes to best. We have always been there. We forgive, we talk, we do things together, we enjoy each other. I didn't come home then because the rapist was living here." I take a breath. "Wow, where did all that come from?"

"That is an important revelation. Active avoidance is part of PTSD." Jennifer nods and smiles. "I want to ask you about your support system. So shifting gears a little bit. Is that O.K. with you?"

"Sure." I settle back on my cushion.

"I'm sure you are familiar with collateral sessions[47]?" She raises her eyebrows to inquire.

"Yes, when family and friends come to counseling with the client. Or meet separately with the therapist about how to help the client."

"Right," she confirms. "You've talked a lot about your mom helping you. And today about your dad helping you. You've talked about panic attacks that occur with your family and friends around. You've talked about friends that help you, like the retreat women and your one friend you called the night before you left your ex-husband."

"Yes, Samantha." I remind her of my best friend from my doctoral program.

---

47 Collateral session is clinical jargon for sessions with a client's support system, such as with family and friends. These sessions may include family counseling and psychoeducation to help a client's support system learn how to better support the client.

"Well, it might be really helpful to have some sessions, or one session, with your family. I could share with them about PTSD and how it presents for you. You could tell them ways they can help you. Like you did with your sister over the holiday. It seems like you have enough awareness now that sharing with them may help them help you." She raises her eyebrows again. "Think about it and we can do it if you want."

A sarcastic voice says, *oh lordy...mom and dad and I back in therapy.* "Like in high school when I'd meet with my mom and dad and the therapist." My flat tone has hints of sarcasm, too.

She giggles. "Yes, only we will have a plan together. You won't draw up a list of all the things they have done wrong and share it with them as the final piece to the work. There was no closure or healthy resolution there for you when your other therapist did that in high school."

"Well, would we meet with everyone all at once?" My tone shifts to uncertainty.

"Not necessarily," she says. "We could. Or we could have a couple sessions with different groups."

"Hmmm. Would you be open to using FaceTime so my sister and brother-in-law could join? We'd also have to meet earlier in the day because of the time change."

"Yes, that is fine with me. As long as you know how to do it." Her expression shows encouragement.

"O.K. Maybe what we can do is my mom, step-dad, and Aunt Tessa. We can FaceTime in Violet and Franz. Then we can do my dad and Lindsey and FaceTime in Violet and Franz again." I pause to think about the order of the sessions. "Also, I think we do my mom's group first. Then my dad's."

"Sure. Whatever you think is best. You let me know. We don't have to decide today," she reiterates. "I'm going to shift to another topic. How do you feel about sleeping in your condo tonight? Or did you stay there last night?"

I respond too quickly. "At my place. I feel O.K. about it."

"Are you sure? I'm sensing that you aren't all the way O.K.," she gently probes.

I take a deep breath. "Well my nerves are a little on edge. I have enjoyed going through all my things and setting up my home. My mom, aunt and grandma are coming over later this week for my birthday, so I am motivated to get through the boxes. I have to work tomorrow, too. Luckily, I'm not traveling this week."

"What are your nerves on edge about?" she asks.

"Just sleeping alone there." My forehead wrinkles with worry. "My condo is on the first floor. And I'm fighting off the image of someone breaking in and raping me."

"Have you had that image in other places you've lived?" she asks.

"Well, to be honest, that rape happened in my bed. So I have that image a lot when I go to bed." I shudder. "But this image is pretty detailed and specific. The window in my bedroom opens and the blinds clank. A hand thrusts the curtains aside. I think about my escape route. I would have to run out my bedroom door to the front door. I'd scream for help I guess. I don't know anyone there. In fact, the place right next door is vacant. And my unit is the end unit, so there isn't anyone else on the other side. There are only two stories and each unit's balcony in my building faces the balconies in the units across the walkway. I mean who would actually help me? So, yeah, I am just O.K. about sleeping by myself."

"I didn't realize that image or one like it happens every time you go to bed." Jennifer is sincere. "I'm really sorry about that. We could've started working on creating a safe space in your bedroom."

"How could we create a safe space there?" I recall the session she asked me if sleeping in my bed was a trigger. "I haven't thought about that possibility since that session. I assumed that image was a byproduct of the rape and it would always be with me."

"Well, you could book-end your sleep. You could also do an exposure technique as you get ready for bed. Do you have a bedtime routine?" she inquires.

"You mean like every night I wash my face, brush my teeth, put Chapstick on, take my Zoloft, put a bottle of water on my night-stand, and plug in my phone." I raise a finger to count each activity. "I also put on pajamas, obviously."

"Yes, that's what I meant by bedtime routine," she affirms. "With book ending, once you are in bed the last thing you do before you fall asleep is a soothing or sacred activity. It is a form of sleep hygiene. It is meant to calm you, not activate you, and sets the stage for peaceful sleep. One way to think of book ending is that you are setting an intention for calm or peace between two activities, one right before you go to sleep and one when you wake up."

"I'm not sure what you mean? Like what activities would I do?" My mind works hard to conjure up an image of something that might make sleep peaceful.

"Well, you could set an intention that you will sleep peace-fully by saying to yourself or aloud 'sleep will be peaceful tonight' and perhaps give yourself a hug. Then when you wake up the first thing you could do would be to say to yourself or aloud 'thank you for keeping me safe in my sleep' and give yourself another hug."

"Could I use the heart rose quartz that Phora gave me?" I imagine myself holding it against my heart.

"Yes, that's a great idea, Anna."

"I'll try that. I sleep with it most nights anyway, but I don't set an intention." My brows furrow. "What did you mean with an exposure activity or technique?"

"Yes, thank you for bringing us back to that. Leading up to going to bed, you could start by concentrating on your breathing and talking yourself through your bedtime routine. You could say, 'you are safe' after each activity. Like as you get your glass of water, you would say 'I am safe.' Then after you brush your teeth, wash your face and do the other bedtime routine activities, you'd say 'I am safe.' You could also say those words with each step you take towards your bed. So, as you walk towards your bed, you focus on your breathing. When you feel unsafe, like when the image comes up, you stop where you are and breathe while saying 'you are safe.' Once you feel the image dissipate, continue walking towards your room. It may make your bedtime routine a little longer. Or maybe you have another idea? You could try something this week and let me know how it goes next week?"

I shrug. "Sure why not?" A voice quips, *sounds like more hocus pocus to me.* Another voice chides, *she won't figure out a ritual, don't worry. It won't happen.*

She laughs as if she heard the conversation between the voices. "If it doesn't work, we will try something else."

"O.K." I laugh, too. "You sense my doubt."

"Yes." Her laughter becomes a sincere smile.

My mind wanders to my new bedroom furniture that will be delivered tomorrow.

She notices my distant gaze. "Is there anything else?"

"I was just thinking about my new bed." I feel suddenly shy. "It is really feminine and pretty. The headboard and bed frame are like a soft light grey with rivets along the edges. The comforter is melon. It is linen. I got this beautiful cream satin quilt for the blanket and three decorative pillows. I figure this might be the last time I get to buy bedding based only on my taste. I also got a new duvet cover and shams for the guest bed. It is grey with a simple stitch pattern through the middle. It is all so beautiful. I still want to get a vanity and jewelry armoire. All I wanted during my marriage was a place to put out my jewelry, but I couldn't because of the cat. And my ex-husband didn't really make enough space for me to have my things out. I allowed that, too, so I'm not solely blaming him. But that cat was the reason my jewelry stayed boxed up."

"Wow. The way you described your bed sounds almost palatial. And also soft and safe and beautiful." She adds as an afterthought, "In a way like the womb."

"Yeah, I guess you are right. I feel like I am in a re-birthing process."

We laugh a pleasant, content laugh.

I think about book ending on my drive home. There are several items from the retreat I might be able to use including the rose quartz. The facilitators actually had jump ropes available and they gave me one to bring home. We also were given a stuffed animal. Mine was small and white with silver glitter in its fur. I named her Glitter Bear. I have t angel cards from Phora, too. I decide to find those items and put them around my bed.

Reflections ∞ Reactions ∞ Responses

CHAPTER 23

GLITTER ANNA

That night, I'm so tired from moving that I fall asleep without any trouble. The rest of the week flies by. My bedroom furniture was delivered without incident. I put the jump rope under my bed in a circle like I used to do around Vi, Mom and Dad when we were younger. My heart rock, Glitter Bear and angel cards are on my night stand. I've slept holding my heart rock and Glitter Bear each night this week. I realize I've actually not had any trouble falling asleep this week.

Today is my birthday. Mom, Grandma G, and Aunt Tessa bring me lunch to celebrate. We greet each other with hugs. I give them a tour of my small condo.

Grandma G reaches down to feel the quilt on my new bed. "Wow, this is really a beautiful bed. I mean everything is so pretty."

I feel my face flush. "Thanks. I had fun picking everything out. I wanted my room to be really soft and beautiful."

"Well, that it is." She flashes a warm smile. "Where are your clothes? Will you get a dresser?" She notices I don't have a dresser in there.

"No." I open one side of the closet. "Tony built these shelves for me, so all my folded clothes are here. Plus there are two additional closets in the hallway and other room." I show them the bathroom, laundry, hall closet, and guest room that doubles as my home office. "I don't have anything up on the walls yet. And my couch is on order and won't be here for another month. It is also very beautiful. I've never purchased custom made furniture before. I'm going to look at Pier One for the vanity and jewelry armoire this weekend. I may also look at Macy's for a dining room table. They are having a sale."

Aunt Tessa observes, "You seem really good here, Anna."

I smile. That same shy feeling sweeps over me. I wonder silently, *what is that shyness about?*

"Thanks," I respond. "I feel good so far. There is still a lot I want to do. Like I want to also do my patio. I'm thinking of doing a couch and outdoor carpet. I just really want the spaces in my home to be comfortable and reflect me."

"You really scored here Anna!" Grandma G exclaims. "I can't believe you have all this storage, great sized rooms, laundry, a patio and a fireplace. Yet it doesn't feel too big. This is just a perfect place for you right now."

"Yeah, that's how I feel." I turn to Mom. "And it is thanks to Mom and Aunt Tessa for scoping it out."

"I had a feeling when I saw it online," Mom says. "And then when we saw it in person, we knew this was the one you would like the best. It is a really nice location, too. Easy access to the freeway when you need to travel for work. And it feels really safe to me, too."

We sit at the card table where my dining table will be one day.

Auntie reaches for the salad they brought over. "How is everything going Anna? Are you feeling O.K. here so far?"

"Yes, so far so good. I have been working every day and unpacking every night, or shopping for house stuff, so I haven't had a chance to be anything but tired." I savor the first bite of salad. "Grandma, I'm not sure if you know, but part of why I moved in with my dad and Lindsey was because I was having a mental health crisis. I started taking Zoloft and working with a therapist." I smile to show I'm doing well.

Grandma G's tone expresses empathy. "Going through a divorce is not easy. How are you now?"

"I'm good. I feel like I am right where I'm meant to be. I have a great support system in place between all of you, Phora, Jennifer, and my friends. And unexpectedly living in a familiar town has been really soothing." I feel relief. "When I left at 18, I swore I would never move home. Then I actively avoided home for so long. Now I am grateful this is home. I never thought I'd say this, but I'm really happy to be growing roots here."

Auntie asks, "What about your condo down South? Do you think you will ever move back there? That is such a great place."

"You know, I've thought a lot about that." I pause for another bite of salad. "I'm just not interested in living in a big city anymore. I loved it down there. It was a great place to be a young professional. But I'm just not into that lifestyle anymore. I want a slower pace and quality time with family and friends. I mean I have great friends down there, too. And oh, how I miss my wax lady and my dentist." Everyone giggles. "But I'm good up here. I have tenants in the condo right now. Once their lease is up, I will likely sell it."

Mom jumps into the conversation. "Speaking of growing roots here, you mentioned maybe starting to date again?"

I grin. "Yes, but I don't know. If I do, it won't be for serious. It will just be to date for the sake of dating. I've never really done that."

Auntie asks, "Have you talked with Jennifer about it?"

Mom follows her question immediately. "Yeah, what does she say?"

I can tell they have talked about this and have some reservations. "Do you think it is too soon?" I ask pointedly.

"Maybe, hon," Auntie nods her head.

"YES," Mom exclaims at the same time.

We all chuckle again.

"I haven't talked to Jennifer, but I will before I do anything," I reassure. "Right now I just want to get settled here."

"Well, let's snap a picture of you, Anna. Maybe you can use it for your dating page whenever you get it up and going." Grandma G holds her iPhone up in the air.

Aunt Tessa retrieves the cake from the refrigerator. It is an angel food cake with fresh berries and cream. She places it in front of me on the table and puts long skinny candles on top. I put my elbows on the table and rest my head on my hands. I smile for the camera.

"Here, see if you like it." Grandma G hands me her iPhone.

"Wow, I look genuinely happy." Sadness sweeps through me. A voice asks, *why are you feeling sad now? You just said you look happy.*

I give Grandma G her phone. They pack up lunch and let themselves out. I return to work, which passes quickly.

That night, I write in my journal.

I looked happy for the first time in a long time. Like genuinely happy. Content. A twinkle in my eyes was back.
When I saw that, sadness swept through me. That was
the Anna before. The twinkle. It has been so long since
I saw her. Maybe on the day I passed my defense did I
feel genuinely happy. But otherwise, I don't remember
the last time I felt that way. Present, grounded, in my
body. I'm sad she has been gone for so long. I'm sad
I've had to walk around pretending to be o.k. for so
long. That's it. It wasn't pretend in that picture. I wasn't
faking happiness. My eyes were alive.

I look up from my journal and see Glitter Bear sitting on my
nightstand. I think about the art I did on retreat. Glitter was in every
piece. I return to my journal.

Glitter on retreat. I had Glitter Bear. The ashtray I
sculpted at the beginning had a pile of glitter as the ash.
The feather girl I sculpted at the end had glitter all over
it. Honestly, on retreat I just needed something beautiful on that ashtray. I didn't even know why. Because I
named that piece the Baron Sea. But now I know. I saw
that glitter in my eyes today. That glitter was me. Shiny,
sparkly, fun, containable yet explosive, celebratory, creative. Happy.

I close my journal. Contentment settles over me. I turn off the
light and snuggle into bed with Glitter Bear and my heart rock.

∞∞∞

I haven't seen Phora since before my birthday. I think about last
time I saw her in January. She did grounding work to help with the

rape anniversary and pending move. Today is my birthday gift massage that she gives all clients. As usual she greets me with a big hug.

"How are you, my dear?" Her voice is bright.

"Well, a lot of changes in my life. I moved. I turned 36. I'm on my new path." I feel a wave of nostalgia for Glitter Anna.

"Tell me where you are feeling all of it in your body." She crafts each session around my response to this prompt.

Shyness washes over me. I take a deep breath. "I'm feeling very shy lately. You know how we have worked on the masculine-feminine flow? Well, I brought out the feminine in my condo. Decorating it was like a palette for femininity. I absolutely love it. It's soft and warm with a lot of natural colors. My palm tree pictures are up. And my Dancing Spirits painting is above my bed. Everything is so pretty. Glitter Bear sits on my bed. It feels right. I can't figure out why I keep feeling shy. So, that doesn't necessarily answer your question about where in my body I am feeling it. I guess I feel like I need a big, warm hug."

"Well, that is what you will get today, then." She smiles. "Letting your feminine side out has been difficult. It was associated with weakness and shame for a long time. Now it sounds like you are embracing your femininity as a source of strength and beauty. Your house is a reflection of you. That is vulnerable and so I understand the shyness. Start on your stomach today."

She steps out while I undress and climb under the covers. The massage table is heated and the blankets are just the right weight. The temperature is comfortably warm and the lighting is low. The room feels like it envelops me. I zone out during the massage. Phora skillfully comforts my feminine side and softens my masculine side. I see a beautiful array of colors and shapes throughout the 90 minutes. When Phora is done, she instructs me to take my time climbing off the table. She steps out again. I am on my back at the end of the massage.

I lay there for a moment letting the embrace of the last 90 minutes soak into my body. I breathe slowly and deeply. I feel light and strong. I reach my arms over head. Alternating right and left side, I extend my arms and legs away from my core like in one of the early sessions with Jennifer. I stretch out as I inhale and shift to the other side as I exhale. Tears form in the corners of my eye. I say to myself, *I feel you, my body. I feel my energy. I am not ashamed of any part of myself. Wow it has been a long time since I felt balanced like I do right now.* I pull my body up to a seated position and fold my body forward. My hands reach out to my knees. Instinctively my legs bend so my arms can reach my ankles. I realize I am curled into a seated fetal position embracing my body like my sister was in that dream I shared at the dream retreat in 2011. I say silently, *thank you for coming back to me. Thank you for staying alive.* Those words gently enter my consciousness. I breathe in and out one more time while firmly rubbing my hands down my calves to the top of my feet. I open my eyes and hop off the table. I quickly dress and open my water bottle as I open the door.

"How was that?" Phora asks. Her eye contact is jumpy again and I know she gave a lot during that session.

"I feel my body, Phora. It is amazing. I really never understood the true power of massage therapy until this moment. To think about where I was when I came to you in September. And how far I have come in six months. I'm whole. It feels fragile, but so good. Thank you for all you do for me. You are a miracle worker."

"You know, I've been thinking about possibly referring you to a cranial-sacral massage therapist[48]. They are trained in moving the energy in your body and I really think you would benefit from that in your healing process. Would you be interested?" she asks tentatively. "Not that I want you to stop working with me. I am not trained in that area and I don't want to do any damage."

"Sure, Phora. I am definitely open to try new things."

"O.K. I will put my feelers out there for a referral. The person I know is not one I think will be a good fit for you. Is there anything else I can help you with?" Her tone is filled with interest.

"Well, I am considering joining a meditation group. I think it will be really helpful to participate in a group. At this point, I only do meditations on my phone using YouTube or podcasts or whatever. I don't really know what I am doing."

"I'll think about that one, too. When we meet next I will have resources for you."

She and I stand to move toward the door. We hug goodbye. When I get in my car, I see Phora standing at the door of the building. She waves and smiles. I return the gestures. I say to myself, *thank you for bringing Phora into my life. What a gem. She is another person I feel safe with.* Her sessions are predictable and reliable. She focuses on comfort and takes great care to craft each session to meet my needs. I mental note, *another safe place to add to my list.*

---

48 Craniosacral massage uses gentle touch to regulate the flow of cerebrospinal fluid. It was developed in the 1970's by Paul Upledger, D. O. The goal is to release stress and pain in the head, spinal column, and sacrum.

Reflections ∞ Reactions ∞ Responses

_____

_____

_____

GOING INSIDE

"The Internal Family Systems (IFS) Model…gets you to focus inside. By 'focus inside,' I mean to turn your attention toward your thoughts, emotions, fantasies, images, and sensations – your inner experience." – Dr. Richard C. Schwartz, 2001, p. 2

Internal Family Systems Therapy is listed on the National Registry for Evidence-based Programs and Practices maintained by the Substance Abuse & Mental Health Services Administration of the United States. It promotes general function and well-being and shows promise in treating anxiety disorders and symptoms, physical health conditions and symptoms, self-concept and depression and depressive symptoms. (https://self-leadership.org/evidence-based-practice.html)

CHAPTER 24

PARTS MAP

Jennifer and I meet at her individual counseling office, which is in a different location this week. Her office is near the softball field where I was awarded MVP on my first all-star team in the early 90's. I see my 12 year-old athlete self...*I was on fire then* I think. I park on the street.

Immediately I'm greeted by the fresh eucalyptus tree scent in the cool air. The sun shines bright and the brisk air swirls around my face as I walk to Jennifer's office. Pansy waits at the door for my arrival. She jumps up when she sees me.

"I still can't believe how much she loves you, Anna." Jennifer chuckles. "Thank you for meeting me here today. The regular group space is being used for a training this weekend."

"No problem." I reassure her. "I like coming over this way." I tell her about my all-star team when I was 12. "That tournament was probably my best ever. My offense and defense were on fire that weekend. I still remember how alive and good I felt. I haven't thought about that in years. Maybe decades."

"You were athletic when you were little?" she asks.

"Yes, I played softball, basketball, soccer, tennis, volleyball, and ran cross country." I reminisce. "Oh and once I was on a diving team. That didn't really last though. I was only in 4th grade." I tick off my fingers as I name each sport.

"And what about now?" she inquires.

"Honestly, as soon as I left for college I stopped playing team sports. I played on a co-ed softball team my senior year in college. And I've filled in on some softball teams since then. But I really hated the politics of team sports. It got so ugly, especially on travel ball. The favoritism was disgusting." I pause as a memory comes to me. "My dad always asks me why I stopped playing. He wonders if he and my mom pushed me too hard in that direction because I must not have liked it that much since I didn't continue after I left home. But I did like it. I think playing sports helped me grow my leadership skills and confidence. I learned from an early age the importance of being part of a team that worked well together. Everyone played a role that was essential to the success of the team. I was a pitcher in softball and setter in volleyball, so I had the ball almost every play. And I was the first or second batter usually. But I was only successful in those lead roles when my teammates played well. To this day, I don't do well working under dictator-y leaders who don't understand the importance of cultivating strong teams. And I don't like people who talk down to administrative support or who won't do tasks that are below their paygrade. I think that is a bullshit, elitist approach to life. When people feel valued, they want to do well and when they want to do well, goals are achieved." I take a breath. "Anyway, that was a tangent. You asked about sports now. I don't play anything. I used to run, but I honestly work so much now that I don't even have time for that."

"You do work a lot. Your job is very demanding." Her tone is matter of fact.

"Yes, it really is. I have a few years in me at this pace, but it definitely isn't sustainable."

She asks, "Have you always worked a lot?"

"Hmmmm." I stop to think. "You know, yes. I have always worked really hard and long hours. If I'm not working, then I'm in school. I've never really thought about it, but I'm sure work has been a way to keep myself busy. When I'm busy, I don't have time to think about things that make me anxious. Maybe it has been a way of coping."

Jennifer looks over her notes. She seems to be contemplating something. She looks up and smiles.

"You are very observant," she says. "I'm noticing a change today. You have talked about several positive qualities and characteristics that you see in yourself. You haven't done much of that in previous sessions."

I slowly nod. "Yeah, I can see that."

"I'm contemplative because there is a technique that I've been waiting to introduce and I think now is the time." She deliberates. "But last time, or was it the time before last, we talked about collaterals and book-ending your day. I don't want to overload you with another new thing."

"You aren't overloading me," I reassure her. "I have thought more about the collaterals. I'm just not sure about it. I like the idea of them, but the dynamic with my family...which group would go first? My Aunt Tessa is my dad's sister by blood, yet she is closer with my mom. So does she go with my mom's group or my dad's? Then do I have my sister and brother-in-law in both sessions? That's a lot for them. And how would they attend? Using FaceTime? So, I'm intrigued, but I'm just not sure I am ready for it."

"O.K. I understand those concerns. We can sort them out together if you'd like. There's no rush." She is thoughtful. "Would you be interested in hearing about the new technique?"

"Sure," I say. "I didn't do the book-ending anyway, so there is nothing to talk about there. I was too tired and I haven't had any panicky feelings at bed time since I moved into my new place."

"That's great to hear. You can try book-ending when you need it and we will talk about it then." She takes a deep breath. "There is a therapeutic tool called a Parts Map[49]. Have you heard of it?"

I shake my head. "I don't think so, unless I know it as something else."

"O.K., I'll explain a little about it." She inhales deeply before continuing. "The idea is that we are made up of Parts that each play a role in who we are. There are no bad Parts. They are simply parts with functions that help us survive and sometimes thrive. The behaviors Parts have us do can be self-destructive, but they have a protective function so we don't think of them as bad. In the past, trauma work used to look at some parts as needing to get rid of. Like they were bad and needed to be dispelled. That thinking was very damaging. People would come feeling bad because they were suffering and due to the self-destructive behaviors we would create shame. Like they were somehow bad, and the people who had them were bad if they couldn't get rid of them. Does that make sense? This practice could be damaging."

I nod in agreement.

"A Parts Map gives you a chance to map out your Parts. You can position them wherever you want and show relationships in any way that reflects your inner world. There are no bad parts that we will dispel. Instead, we will work to understand their role in helping

---

49 Parts Maps are created by clients engaged in IFS with their therapist to help see internal parts and the parts' relationships with each other.

you survive to this point and we will work to upgrade their role." She looks at me. "You look confused. It will make sense once we start."

"I am confused. So is it like a geno-gram[50]?" I grapple with how to understand the Parts Map.

Her eyes light up. "Yes, in a way it is like a geno-gram. Only instead of putting your family members on the page and showing relationships between people, you're putting your internal parts on the page and showing the relationships between them. Geno-grams are a helpful way to think of it. Do you want to try?"

"I mean, I'm game for pretty much anything, so yeah I will try." I feel nervous.

You won't do it right. My inner critic is activated. *You're a therapist and have never heard of this. She will see that and see you as a fraud.*

She must sense my hesitance. "I will help you. And it can change. Actually it most likely will change. This is a rough sketch."

She reaches into a closet and pulls out an array of art supplies.

"I know my office is small, but this works well if we can sit on the ground and do it together. Would it be alright with you if we sit here?" She gestures to a small space by the door.

"Yes, that's fine with me."

"Let's start with the layout of the page." She places a large blank piece of construction paper in front of us. "We can make it large, small, horizontal, vertical."

This is so silly. As if you are a child. I wish my inner critic would be quiet. "I think horizontal." I move the paper to the landscape layout.

---

50 A geno-gram is like a family tree that also includes information about relationships and characteristics of each person that relate to the client. They are used in different settings, such as addiction counseling and genetic counseling.

She nods. "It can be in human form. It can be the space inside your head. It can be abstract. Whatever feels right to you, Anna."

My mind feels garbled. "I'm still not sure I am getting it."

"That's O.K.," she reassures. "Do you want to start with a Part?[51] Use any color marker you want and write down the Part that comes to mind anywhere on the page that makes sense."

I tentatively take a blue marker.

"My mind is blank for some reason," I say. "I'm not really sure what you're asking me to do."

My inner critic raises his voice. *You are so dumb. Just make something up so you don't look like an idiot.*

She looks toward the ceiling to think about how to explain it. "Let me see how else I can explain this. I haven't done a great job. A Part is anything that is driving the car. So earlier you talked about being a leader in overdrive. Overdrive Leader could be one Part. You've also shared about panic attacks. Panic Attacks could be another Part. Or maybe Anxiety. I'm not saying you have to use these if you don't see them as Parts of you. Those are examples of things you've talked about."

I nod slowly. "Ohhhhh. I think I get it. Like the Inner Critic is one part? And the Work-A-Holic is another part?"

She exclaims, "Yes! So start with those."

I focus my attention on the paper. A thought dawns on me. *This is like on retreat. Like Travis is one part.* I look up from the still blank page.

---

51 Jennifer says she would've also asked if I wanted to start with Self and described Self at this point in the session. She would've said something like "Self refers to the Vedic philosophical notion of a core of light and love that all human beings share. When we are Parts-driven, we lose access to that core of Self and a sense of who we truly are." I don't remember discussing Self until later in the session. I decided to leave our dialogue as I wrote it in the original narrative based on my memory.

"I'm thinking about the retreat. We did something similar, only we had six pre-assigned parts. I can't remember all of them. One was the critic, another was the inner child. I think there was an adult self and self-doubt. I had a protector named Travis." I smile and feel my shoulders tighten. "I think I've told you about Travis?"

"Remind me again."

"Travis was the masculine side of me. The shield and armor that protected me for so long. But Travis became so good at protecting me that I never took the armor off and it got too heavy."

"Yes, that is a part," she confirms.

"So I can write Travis on the page?" My hand moves toward the markers again.

"Yes, you can pick a color and shape and size for Travis and put Travis wherever you want." She nods encouragement.

I release the blue marker and pick up the gray marker. Travis is gray because of the metal armor that he wears. I put him in big, block letters across the middle of the page. I feel my back between my shoulders tingling. I continue adding my parts with symbolic colors all around the page. Anxiety is orange encircled in thick jagged lines. Worker Bee is black and yellow. Rage is black outlined in red. Heart is purple. Femininity is the colors of the rainbow. Shyness is yellow. Shame is light red and pink.

Inner Critic chastises. *You aren't doing this right because there is no rhyme or reason to the parts. They aren't even in a pattern.*

The last part I write is Inner Critic. I write it in red at the top of the page. I pause and study my Parts Map.

"This is really good, Anna," Jennifer says. "Are you finished?"

"For now, I am." I look up.

Inner critic keeps at it. *She is going to tell you you did it all wrong.*

"Where can we put core Self? Or your adult Self?" She reviews the words on the page. "Sometimes it's called the wise Self. Or you could name it what you want."

I look at her quizzically. "I'm not sure what you mean."

"Well, that is your voice today. Your 36-year-old core Self. It's your heart, your wisdom, your true self, what you call your identity and what Eastern philosophy calls light and love." She must notice the defeat that I feel. "We will get there," she reassures.

After a moment I think I know what she means. "Oh, you mean like the voice who told me to put my phone down and tell my family I was suicidal?" I ask tentatively.

"Yes, that could be your core Self. Where would you put Self on the page?"

I write Core Self in small purple letters with yellow squiggles around it to signify a glow at the bottom of the page. I look up knowing what this placement and size means.

"I've lost my voice. It has been squished by the Inner Critic and Travis." Sadness washes over me.

"Until now," she reminds me. "Inner Critic and Travis have played important roles in your survival." Her smile is sincere. "It is hard to see your Core Self down there. I am struck by the colors of your Core Self."

"Purple is my favorite color. And the yellow around it is supposed to be a glow. Like it is illuminated." I look at Core Self again. "You know, it actually reminds me of Rafiki's drawing of Simba's face in the Lion King when Simba was born. Remember that part of the movie?"

Her eyes light up. "Yes! He drew an outline of a lion face encircled in a mane that does look much like the glow around your Core Self."

I'm still and quiet. I'm also smiling calmly.

"I didn't really include any relationship symbols between the parts. Like other than Travis, Inner Critic and Core Self, everything else was randomly placed. I picked the colors because they made the most sense given the part. It all seems disorganized to me…like I am shattered."

"Shattered is an interesting word. Is that how you feel?" She inquires with gentle curiosity.

"Like I'm shattered?" I ask to buy time.

Inner Critic chimes in again. *You are shattered. But you can't actually tell her that. She won't take you seriously as a professional. Don't tell her that.*

"Well, yes. Another word is broken. Do you feel broken or shattered?" Jennifer continues to gently probe.

My eyes well up in tears. "Honestly, I'm really sad I didn't even think to put my Core Self on there. I'm lost. When that rape happened, I left my body. I wrote in my journal the other night about glitter." I pause to wipe tears now streaming down my face. "I know it sounds stupid, but on retreat we did a lot of art. I always had glitter in some way incorporated into my art, no matter what the purpose was. I realized that the glitter was me. The Me that was shattered that night. She is gone. And it makes me really sad. I feel like I get glimpses of her and I spend a lot of effort trying to be her so that no one knows how much I'm in pain. But the effort is exhausting. Being Me wasn't that tiring before. And everything else on that Parts Map is so all over. So confusing. Like they are flying about without any pilots. I don't like feeling so out of control. Like at any time they can de-bunk the Inner Critic to take the top spot."

"Anna, I know this work is really hard." She takes a deep breath. "When people, kids, experience trauma, they can become fractured out. Ego structures fracture into parts to keep us running, to survive what happened. Does that make sense?" I nod. "The work we are doing is meant to gain access to your Core Self so she can drive the car as much as possible. That glittery version of yourself, your Core Self, is not a fraud. You had so much shame and yuckyness dumped on you that the Core Self had to go somewhere. She is still genuine. She is not a fraud. I see her here." She points to Core Self. "She is glowing."

Silence lingers. I am tired and have run out of words.

"Can I share another thought about glitter?" Jennifer asks.

"Yes," I say softly.

"Glitter also scatters, or in a way shatters. All of its beautiful pieces are tiny. There is something about your description of glitter and the words scattered and shattered."

A slight smile forms on my lips. "That is nice imagery. And it sparkles and shines and brings brightness to the world."

"Do you want me to hold onto your map? Or do you want to take it home?" Jennifer glances at the clock.

"You can keep it," I whisper.

She raises her eyebrows. "Are you sure?"

"Yes, I'm not sure what I will do with it." I prepare to leave.

"O.K." She takes it and begins rolling it up. "Your parts map will change," she reassures me again.

Later that night I text Jennifer to ask if she will bring the Parts Map to the next session. I realize I want to keep it.

Reflections ∞ Reactions ∞ Responses

_____

_____

_____

CHAPTER 25

PANIC ATTACK NUMBER
88 THOUSAND

I'm in a bathroom stall at an all-day work meeting. Phora text messaged me earlier in the day to ask for my email address. These days, toilet texting is the only way I communicate with anyone outside of work during the week.

A voice exclaims, *so gross...there are so many germs.*

I send it to her and ask why she needs it. At the next bathroom break I learn she is sending me a few resources for meditation groups and a surprise.

That evening, I lie in bed.

I wonder, *why am I so restless?* I roll over on my left side.

A voice says, *you haven't been restless since you left Dad and Lindsey's house. Hmmm...maybe try deep breathing.*

I roll my eyes as my familiar can't-sleep routine begins. Inhale for 2, exhale for 4, inhale for 3, exhale for 6, inhale for 4, exhale for 8. I try to inhale for 5 and exhale for 10, but don't make it. I start again. After three rounds, I begin a body scan.

I think, *maybe this will help.* I start at the crown of my head.

My mind wanders, *remember when Dad told you to do this? They were still married.*

Another voice answers, *yeah, he would stand at the door in his boxers and tell us to count backwards from 100.*

I think, *I wonder if Violet could even count that high starting with 1. Sidebar. Crown of my head.*

My eyes bolt open. *Phora!*

I reach for my phone and open my email app. Three forwards from her await me. Two are for meditation groups and one is for a free seminar on the healing properties of crystals. She offers to go with me to the seminar and one of the meditation groups. The second meditation group is a six week class and she can't commit.

A voice says, *these could be cool.*

I reply that I am definitely in for those we can attend together. They happen to fall on days I am not traveling in the next few weeks.

Another voice concurs. *Yay. These will be fun. Plus you have to get your car serviced.*

I say, *thanks for the reminder. My car is due for a service.*

My work travel schedule makes scheduling things like a car service difficult. I sigh. How long will this inner dialogue last? I set my phone on the nightstand. To my surprise, sleep drifts over me in minutes.

∞∞∞

The following Thursday I wake up early to drop my car off at the dealership service department. I climb in the second row of the courtesy van for a ride home. Two passengers are in the van already. The driver closes the sliding door behind me. He asks me for my address and writes it on the clipboard. I notice he asks the other passengers for their addresses, but does not write them on his clipboard.

I think to myself, *that's weird. Why did he only write mine down?* I take a deep breath.

A voice answers, *maybe he is going to come back and torture you tonight, so he needs to remember your address.*

I slightly shake my head and sigh in exasperation. *Seriously, don't start this up.*

The voice responds haughtily. *Why? He is definitely creepy. He is probably going to come after you tonight.*

Another voice says, *no he is not. He is the courtesy van driver. He probably picked the others up already, so he knows where they live. It is 8AM. How could he have picked them up already?*

The first voice is more forceful. *He is definitely targeting you. Make small talk and eye contact. Here we go.*

I tune into the conversation between the driver and the passenger in the front seat. They're talking sports. The driver looks in his rear view at the passenger next to me and informs us she will be dropped off first. The air seems sucked from my lungs.

I start a mantra. *Steady. Breathe. You can do this. You are O.K.* I smile at the woman next to me. *I wish I was her.*

A voice says, *I bet you do.*

The first voice warns, *this guy is going to get you. He will know where you live and get you when you least expect it. I mean look at him. He is probably planning a route that drops you off last so he can be alone with you.*

I silently yell, *STOP please just stop.* I look out the window at the familiar surroundings. I can't focus on anything. Buildings rush by us. I can't make sense of where we are despite having driven on this road for 36 years.

I say to the voices, *maybe he will drop the guy off last. He seems normal.*

The voices become jumbled. *Yeah, no. What if he is also a rapist? What if they're in cahoots together? What if they're both going to come after me? Oh no, they will both know where I live. Fuck. I am really not safe now. Maybe you should move again. I mean, you really need a secure building with locked common entry. Yeah, you were so dumb not to get that. Pretend you are O.K. Plaster the I'm O.K. smile on your face. Don't show him your panic. He will sense it and pounce. Why am I having these thoughts? This is so not helpful.*

He turns the van away from the direction of my house. My heart falls to the pavement. *See I told you. He wants you alone. He is definitely going to torture you.* I shake my head. *Please stop. Please just let me get home. Be normal.* He drops the other passenger off at a coffee shop about 3 miles from my house. *Jump out and say you will walk from here. No don't do that. He already has your address, you dummy. Even if you walk, he can still find you. Just don't bring him into the entrance that leads to your building. Oh, that's a good idea. Turn into the other side. Yay, I will do that.* He begins making small talk. *I so don't want to talk with him right now. Get me out of this car.*

He looks in the rearview mirror. "So what do you do, Anna?"

My inner parts continue to talk over each other. *I don't want to talk to him. Be nice. Don't be rude. You have to answer him.*

"I work in mental health in educational settings." I keep it as brief as possible. I maintain eye contact to show that I am not afraid.

He glances in the rearview mirror and sees me looking straight at him. "I have a question."

I brace myself. I've been here before where people seek free advice not understanding that mental health counseling does not include advice giving.

"Why can't kids who are sexually molested just get over it and see that it's really the perpetrator's problem?" A twisted smile turns up on his lips.

I stifle a gasp. It's hard to breathe. An icy freeze settles over my body. *Fuck am I giving off that I am a victim?* Jennifer's words float through my mind. *Perpetrators have a sixth sense for sniffing out victims. Breathe.*

"That is an interesting question." I attempt to sound uninterested. "And there are many reasons for that. Many more than can be discussed in the next few minutes."

I turn my head to gaze out the window with the hope of indicating I don't want to talk anymore.

He misses or ignores my cue. "Well, perpetrators are sick. They have this thing that takes over them and they have to sexually molest children to feed that thing. I mean it isn't about the kids at all."

Red flag alerts flash throughout my body. Several voices chime in at once. *Either this guy is a victim or he is a perpetrator. Probably he is both. Get yourself safely home and lock the doors. Lock the windows. This guy is sick. You can do this. Get home.* Nausea brews in my stomach. *Breathe.*

I remain silent.

"What do you think? You're in the field," he demands.

"I think these are great questions you might consider asking your own therapist. Check with your insurance provider to find out who in this area is in your network." I attempt a matter of fact tone. *Breathe.*

He turns up my street. I direct him to the first drive way and ask to be dropped off by the mailboxes. Before he stops the van, my hand is on the sliding door handle. I'm ready to jump out as soon as the van is going slow enough to not get hurt.

"Here is fine," I say near the mailboxes. "I have to stop by the front office."

He slows the van. I open the door.

"I'm sorry if I scared you." He puts it in park.

I am already out of the van.

"Have a good day." I begin to close the slider door.

"I'll be back here to pick you up when your car is ready."

"Oh, I have a ride this afternoon. It was just this morning that I didn't have a ride. So I won't need to be picked up." I spit the words out as quickly as possible and close the slider door shut.

I turn and run-walk to the office door, which is around the corner out of his view. A voice instructs me. *Get behind the building. You will be safe. Wait until he drives away. Then run to your place. Look for him coming up the other drive. Don't let him see your unit.* I slump against the wall out of his view. My legs feel weak. My chest flutters with anxiety. *Breathe.* I try to take deep slow breaths, counting as I inhale and exhale. *Look around you. You are safe.* I focus on the intricate fern leaves swaying in the gentle morning breeze. I hear the gardeners blowing leaves from the sidewalks.

My Inner Critic starts in. *Seriously that was harmless. That guy was a twerp. You didn't have to get so worked up. You wimp.*

My eyes well up with tears. *Please don't bash me right now.* I plead with the Inner Critic. *I just can't take any more right now. I have to get myself together for work. I have to find someone to take me this afternoon. Should I turn that guy in? Should I tell someone at the dealership? What if he finds out it was me and he goes postal on me? He is someone who definitely is capable of that. He was nuts.* I shake my head trying to quiet this inner dialogue. *Whoa! A lot of Parts are activated right now. This is what Jennifer was talking about.* I push myself off the wall and peek around the corner. The van is gone. I turn slowly and walk up the sidewalk to my condo. Safely inside, I take a shower before logging in to my computer for work.

∞∞∞

Finally, the end of the day. I look up from my computer. The sun is setting. It is time to log off.

I say to myself, *I'm so tired for some reason. I wonder why?*

The ride home with the creepy van driver is a distant memory after a busy day.

A voice says, *probably has something to do with the anxiety you felt this morning. Good thing Mom could take you this afternoon to pick up your car.*

Inner Critic repeats himself. *You are a wimp. That guy was harmless. A creep, but harmless.* I shake my head and say out loud, "Please don't start again. I really want to sleep."

Comfort food may help. I heat up soup from Whole Foods for dinner and make toast with butter. I turn on my fireplace and make a pillow fort on the floor in front of it. I catch up on my Thursday night T.V. shows. The blood and guts on Grey's Anatomy and suspense on Scandal do not help my racing thoughts.

I think, *you used to love these shows. They helped you zone out.*

At 11PM, I slowly peel myself off the floor and begin the dreadful walk to my bed. Every noise inside and outside ricochets off my chest. I startle at each one of them. I prepare for battle with my parts. As expected, the inner dialogue is on full blast. I can't decipher the parts.

He is going to get you tonight. Shut up. Please just stop. You aren't safe. You are a victim. He knows you will be easy to take. I don't want to go through this.

My breath shortens. I look at my reflection as I brush my teeth.

What did Jennifer say? You are safe. You are safe. You are safe.

My breath accelerates with each statement. My eyes plead with my body. *I know I'm having an attack. Please don't. I am alone. I don't have anyone here to help me.* I look down at my hands. They feel numb.

I hear Inner Critic. *You suck at this. You can't get it under control. Your work is all worthless. What good is it doing for you now? You can't even feel your hands.*

A shrill voice jeers out of the darkness. *Hahahaha. You are crazy just like you said. I don't know why you don't just end this.* My eyes shoot up to my reflection in the mirror.

A firm voice says *NO, do not go down that route. You will NOT go down that path.*

The shrill voice taunts. *Oh really? Watch me. You know you don't like feeling crazy, so just end this.*

I hurriedly climb in bed and pull the covers tightly around my body. I no longer breathe. I cry heavy deep sobs. Numbness starts at my toes and climbs up my legs. Within seconds I can't feel my legs.

I hear my own voice. *NOOOOO. I can't be trapped. I'm having the worst panic attack. Text the retreat girls.*

I reach for my phone. I text "Help. Anxiety attack overload. I don't know what to do." I can't focus on anything in my room. Instead, everything seems to become part of a swirling light show around me. Not like the lightshows when I get massages with Phora. This one is frantic and chaotic. I'm hyperventilating.

You have to breathe. You have to get yourself back under control. This will pass. This will pass. This will pass. This will pass. My mind repeats that mantra over and over.

My phone beeps several times. Dusty, Sasha and Camille all respond to my text within minutes.

"You are not alone."

"I'm sorry A, you will get through this."

"Oh no. Breathe. We are here. Call if you need."

I feel my breath slow. I begin to time my breath with the words This Will Pass. My legs begin to tingle. I look down at my hands. They are not detached from my body anymore. I wiggle my fingers and toes. I look at my tear streaked face in my vanity mirror at the foot of my bed. My eyes are red and my skin is blotchy. *It is passing.* I smile a weak smile. *I am safe. I am going to be O.K.* I bend my knees and wrap my arms around a pillow. I pull two other pillows around the sides of my body. I nestle into my pillow cocoon and continue to breathe. *This will pass. This will pass.* I reach for my phone. I text "Thanks. It is passing." I leave all the lights on that night. I put on a YouTube meditation. I'm not sure when I fall asleep. I do not dream. I wake up the next morning exhausted.

∞∞∞

Sunday is finally here. I've been plagued with anxiety the last three days since the encounter with the creepy van driver. Jennifer text messaged earlier in the week with a new location for our sessions moving forward. The new location is actually a yoga studio. The parking lot is across the street, but the entrance to the office is on a different street around a corner. I can't figure out where that entrance is located. My anxiety gets the best of me. I decide to park on the street directly across from the new location and pay the parking meter.

Jennifer and Pansy greet me at the door, just like in the former location. The floors are a light sandy color. One wall is all mirrors. There is a small waiting area with chairs, a coffee table, and water dispenser to the right of the entrance. The wall facing the street is all glass windows. There are several movable partitions and large potted plants across the windows to increase privacy. Opposite the waiting area is a space with exercise balls and Pilate's equipment. The ceiling has exposed pipes and cement beams. I notice Jennifer set up a space on the floor in front of the mirrors with mats, blankets and bolsters.

I think to myself, *what a welcome sign. A new space, with a similar feel.* Relief floods over me. I set my bag down on one of the chairs in the waiting area and kick off my shoes. My movements are deliberate and forced because I am trying to appear like I am O.K. Jennifer knows me too well.

As soon as we are settled on the floor she asks, "What is going on? You seem out of balance."

My eyes glaze over as I recount the details of my interaction with the courtesy van driver, panic attack, and subsequent multiple days of high anxiety.

"I think I need a grounding meditation today." My gaze remains unfocused.

"Anna, I need to tell you something that I really want you to hear," Jennifer says firmly. "Can you look at me? Or is that too much right now?"

I look up at her. She comes into focus for a brief moment. That brief contact is all I can handle. My eyes dart away again.

"Next time, tell the van driver to pull over and get out of the car." Her instructions are firm yet simple.

I furrow my brows in confusion.

"You do not have to worry about hurting anyone's feelings or appearing rude when you feel unsafe. You do not have to subject yourself to being in the presence of anyone who feels unsafe." She pauses to see if her message registers with me.

I hear her words from a distance. A voice says, *you've been dissociated for the last three days.* Her words seem closer and she comes into sharper focus.

"You have my permission to stop the car and get out. You have my permission to keep yourself safe." Her tone is firm and caring.

I blink several times. I think, *what does she mean? What is she saying?*

Out loud I muse, "How would I get home then?"

She gently offers several suggestions. "You could call a cab. You could walk. You could call your mom."

Her voice is in front of me now. My vision clicks into focus. I say to myself, *I am back under control.*

"Yeah, I guess you're right." I take a deep breath. "I never thought of that. I could just get out. In that moment I felt trapped. Like how would I get home? Would he think I was rude? I don't want to be rude. I never thought I could actually get out of the car." Another deep breath.

Inner Critic doesn't miss an opportunity to bash me. *Yeah, you idiot. You could've just gotten out and avoided this whole mess.*

"Your safety is always the top priority, Anna. A lot of times children who grow up with an alcoholic parent don't learn that. They learn to cope with unsafe, unpredictable environments. To tolerate unsafe behavior. Children can't leave those situations because they are children. They don't have internal resources or freedom yet to leave. It seems you responded to the van driver in a similar fashion. I don't mean that to belittle you. I think you did the best you could in the situation given that you didn't think you could remove yourself from it. Does any of this make sense?" Her tone continues to be firm and caring.

I nod. "Yes, it makes perfect sense. I'm trapped in a response I probably used throughout my childhood. I froze and did what I could to get out of it, then coped with the anxiety built up later on my own."

"Yes, that sounds right." She nods. "Would you like to try something that goes along with the Parts Map?"

"What is it?" I ask.

"Internal Family Systems[52]. Have you heard of this before?" She continues when I shake my head. "IFS applies family systems theory to the internal Parts that make us who we are. It looks at each Part as a family member that interacts with other Parts and makes up a family system inside of us. The Parts Map you did before is a beginning guide to your internal family system."

"That sounds intriguing. How do we work with that?" No longer am I dazed and unfocused. Instead, I'm genuinely interested, even curious.

"Well, I'll guide you through that. It is kind of like a meditation. But I'll ask you to share what is going on along the way. You only have to share if you want to share. There are 3 types of Parts...

---

52 For more information, read Introduction to the Internal Family System Model by founder Dr. Richard C. Schwartz and visit https://www.selfleadership.org/.

Managers, Firefighters, and Exiles. The idea is that all came to be so that they could protect you and help you survive. There are different managers, firefighters and exiles."

A voice says, *this sounds familiar.*

I ask, "Did we do something like this before? Where I had to imagine talking to myself and tell you what I said to myself?"

"Yes," she smiles. "We did do it before. A mini version. I think you are ready to use IFS more deeply now."

"O.K., I'm game to try." Sarcasm bounces around my head. *Oh lordy...here you go again.* Out loud I ask, "What do I do now?"

Jennifer instructs me to get comfortable either lying on the floor or sitting in a chair[53]. I may keep my eyes open or close them.

"I'll lie here on the floor." I roll over onto my back.

"Do you need any pillows?" she asks. "Or blankets?"

I quickly scan my body. "A blanket would be good."

She spreads a blanket over me. I close my eyes. Inhale 3, exhale 6. I hear her sit back down. Pansy snuggles up to my side.

Jennifer giggles. "Pansy, what are you doing?" She asks me, "Is that alright? Or do you want me to move her?"

"No, she is fine. She can stay there." I close my eyes.

"O.K. Start by taking some deep breaths. I can see you already have done a few of those."

I take more deep breaths.

She continues, "Notice what's happening internally. Notice energy, sensations, visual images..."

---

53 Jennifer does not usually have people lie down for IFS, but since we were already sitting on the floor lying down was an option. I actually prefer to do IFS lying down with my eyes closed. I find this positioning helps me access my inner world.

My mind goes black. I ask silently, *are you in there? Come out come out wherever you are,* I say in a sing-song voice. After several seconds I see myself. I raise my hand.

Jennifer says, "Great. What Part is there?"

I say out loud, "A younger me."

Jennifer instructs, "Thank her for showing herself."[54]

Thank you for coming out.

"Did you thank her?"

I nod.

"O.K. Ask her how old she is?"

How old are you?

Jennifer follows up, "Let me know when she tells you."

Younger Me begins to fade.

"She is kind of fuzzy," I say out loud. "Like when I asked that, she started fading in and out, like when using rabbit ears for a T.V. antenna."

"That's O.K." Jennifer reassures. "It sounds like there is a Part protecting her. Can you ask the Part which one it is?"

Which Part are you?

"It says it is the Protector[55]," I tell Jennifer with my eyes still closed.

---

54 Typically in IFS, Jennifer wouldn't start with an Exile, which is a younger, vulnerable version of self who may have been traumatized and has been hidden or repressed. Often the first experience is with a protector part, like a Manager or Firefighter. I remember this exchange being the first with a Part, so I decided to leave it.

55 At this point, IFS would direct us to interact with the Protector Part to build a relationship with it before asking its permission to talk with the Exile that it protects. I decided to leave it written as is to reflect my memory.

"O.K.," Jennifer says. "Ask the Protector to wait in the waiting room. Let the Protector know that you don't need to be protected right now and that you will call on it when you do need to be protected."

"What do you mean by waiting room?" I ask.

"Oh, I forgot to tell you that." She sounds apologetic. "In IFS, the waiting room is where we keep parts until we need them. Until now, the parts haven't had a place to wait, so they run around."

"O.K.," I say out loud. Silently, I instruct, *Protector please wait in the waiting room. The waiting room is right over there.*

I imagine a sterile doctor's office waiting room. I see the Protector's shoulders slump as he sulks to the door that now has a neon sign that reads "Waiting Room."

"Is the Protector in the waiting room?" Jennifer asks.

I nod.

"O.K.," she continues. "Do you see yourself again?"

There I am. No longer fuzzy. A solid image of myself.

I nod.

"Can you ask her again how old she is? Tell her that she is safe and that you aren't here to hurt her."

I'm sorry if I scared you before. I am not going to hurt you. Can you tell me how old you are? To my surprise she holds up four fingers.

"She is four," I whisper.

"Four, great." Jennifer's tone is sincere. "Thank her for sharing her age with you."

Thank you for sharing with me that you are four.

"Did you thank her?"

I nod.

"Did she say or do anything in response?" Jennifer asks.

"No," I say.

"That's O.K.," Jennifer says.[56] "Can you see her surroundings?"

I nod.

"What are they?"

"Like a prison. Or an institution. Cement walls. They're painted a very light beige. There are no windows. The Waiting Room is behind a metal door. It's cold in there."

"What can you tell me about her?"

"She's holding a teddy bear by its arm down at her side. She's wearing shorts and red and white striped shirt. She looks clean. She is sad. She is alone."

"How far away is she from you?"

"Not far. Just across the room."

My eyes remain closed. I'm watching my four year-old self.

"What do you want to tell her?" Jennifer asks me. "You can tell her directly or you can say it out loud to me."

I'm really sorry you have been in here for so long. You are not alone. You have done so well keeping yourself safe.

"O.K.," I say out loud.

"Did you tell her?" Jennifer asks.

---

56 Jennifer and I separately read this manuscript several times. At our final read through, we each noted that at some point during this, and every future, IFS session she would have asked "How do you feel towards (Part)?" This question is a key component of IFS. I am sure she did ask that question and likely it would have been at this point in the session. Interestingly, I did not recall her asking how I feel towards my Parts until later. I decided to leave the narrative as I originally wrote it to reflect my memory. Perhaps my recall of feelings, or lack thereof, towards my parts is an important indicator of my recovery.

I nod.

"Can you tell me what you told her?" Jennifer asks.

"I told her she wasn't alone and that she has done a good job of keeping herself safe," I whisper.

"Good," Jennifer says. "What did she do?"

I see her look up at me. Her eyes search mine to see if I'm telling the truth or if I'm making fun of her.

I am telling you the truth. You have done a really good job and I am here now.

"She looked up at me."

"Good," Jennifer says.[57] "Ask her what she would like to do."

What would you like to do now?

Her voice is sweet and innocent. Her eyes fill with hope. "I want to go outside. I want to see the sun."

At this moment, tears form at the outside corners of my eyes. My heart fills with emotion.

"What did she say?" Jennifer asks.

"She said she wants to see the sun."

"Great," Jennifer says. "Ask her if you can take her outside."

Can I take you outside? I see her nod and smile. She stands taller. I reach out my hand. She reaches back. We take steps towards each other.

Tears roll down my temples in the present time.

"What is happening now?" Jennifer asks.

---

57 Another key IFS question for Parts is "What do you want me to know?" Jennifer likely directed me to ask this question around this point in the session. I decided to leave the session as is because it accurately reflects my memory.

"We are holding hands walking down a corridor. It's sterile. Made of cinder block. No windows. There's a door we are walking toward. It's metal."

"Good, let me know when you're outside," Jennifer instructs.

"O.K. we're there," I whisper.

"What are you feeling towards her?" Jennifer asks.

My heart stirs again. "Sadness. Sorrow. Pride. Joy to be with her. Love."

"Let her know that and anything else you want to tell her," Jennifer instructs.

I love you. I am happy to be with you. I am proud that you have survived on your own for so long. I am sorry that you had to do that all alone and that you haven't seen the sunshine. I am sad that you had to live in a locked up prison like that for so long. You are not alone now. I won't leave you again.

"O.K.," I say out loud.

"O.K. you told her? Or O.K. you will tell her?" Jennifer asks.

"I told her," I say.

"Good," Jennifer says. "Now let her know you are going to take her to a safe place where she can see the sunshine. Think of a safe place where you spent time when you were four, or you can make up a place. Let her know you'll check on her until we can do this again."

I'm going to take you to Grandma Ophelia's house. You can play in the living room. The sun is bright and she always has yummy food. I will check on you from time to time. You will be safe here. You can stay here as long as you need. I will be back again.

She looks up at me with fear in her eyes. She asks if she can keep her teddy bear.

"She just asked if she can keep her teddy bear," I tell Jennifer.

"Tell her of course she can. Does she need anything else to feel safe? It is O.K. to feel afraid. Reassure her that you will be back and that she is not alone," Jennifer instructs.

"O.K. all set," I say out loud. "She is with her teddy bear."

"Great," Jennifer says. "Thank her for her great work today. She did a lot."

Thank you for trusting me. Thank you for your great work today.

"O.K. I told her," I say.

"How do you feel towards her now?" Jennifer asks.

I don't immediately answer. My chest stirs. I ask myself, *what is that feeling in my chest?* The letters L-O-V-E emerge behind my forehead.

"I feel love," I say softly.

"Let her know you feel love towards her. Also let her know you will visit her and she will be safe. Take your time coming back," Jennifer says.

I take several deep breaths. I sense the blanket over me and the floor mat under me. I am back in the room with Jennifer. I open my eyes.

Jennifer's voice is soft. "Anna, that was beautiful to witness."

I smile.

She explains, "In IFS terms, we just did a rescue of your 4 year-old self. She did not know that you are grown up now. The Protector was operating to keep your 4 year-old self safe, which back then was an excellent coping strategy. Parts need to learn that you are old enough now to be in charge. And that you are trust-worthy and will be safe for them. Does that make sense?"

I nod, "Yes, it does. That was really powerful for me. It was so vivid."

Inner Critic jeers, *are you going to tell Jennifer that you also feel like a hypocrite because you just told the little girl you wouldn't leave her and then in the very next breath you left her? And you left her at a picnic table, not in your grandma's living room. Are you going to tell Jennifer that? That will hurt her feelings if you do. Her little technique didn't work like it was supposed to. You are a good liar.*

I do my best to ignore the Critic.

Jennifer asks, "Do you have any questions for me about IFS or what we just did?"

"The Protector. It used like…an invisibility cloak. I couldn't actually see it. And I didn't write Protector on the Parts Map." I pause. "That wasn't really a question."

"Great insight," Jennifer responds. "It is O.K. that you didn't write Protector on the map. You did write Travis, so maybe Protector is another name for Travis. Or maybe it is a separate part since Travis had armor and the Protector had an invisibility cloak. We can visit the Protector next time if you want."

"O.K., that would be fun," I say with a smile.

She studies my face. "Are you being sarcastic?"

"No, I find this incredibly fun. Weird and different, but fun," I reassure.

She smiles. "O.K. good. We can do more of it."

"Great." I remember my Parts Map. "I did want to add Doubt to the Parts Map. Did you bring it with you?"

She stops smiling. "You know what? I totally forgot. I'm so sorry. With switching locations, it just slipped my mind. I'll bring it next time. What do you think of this new space?"

"No worries at all about the Parts Map." I look around the new space. "You know, I really like it here. The natural light, mirrors, plants, light colored floor...it is comfortable. And the space is really versatile."

"It feels private enough?" Her uptick at the end of her sentence turns it into a question.

I nod. "Yes, I think the partitions and plants by the windows are good. I also like the idea of taking counseling out of the counseling office. It is less secret[58]. I like it."

I feel light and solid on the drive home. The sun sets and the leaves rustle from a light breeze. My voice is hopeful. *I am going to be O.K.*

Reflections ∞ Reactions ∞ Responses

_____

_____

_____

---

58 Privacy is crucial in terms of building and maintaining trust and confidentiality in a counseling setting. A byproduct of privacy and confidentiality is secrecy, which could be experienced by a client as shame-bound and add to stigma related to counseling. For me, many of the secrets I processed with Jennifer were shame-bound. I liked meeting in untraditional spaces that felt private, yet not completely closed off from the rest of the world. It didn't seem as shameful and secretive.

CHAPTER 26

MEDITATION PROVOKED ANXIETY PART

I text Phora to confirm our meeting time and place as I prepare to leave my condo. We are going to try a Wednesday night meditation group. The leaders are Buddhist and the meditation group is based on Buddhist philosophy.

I arrive 15 minutes early. The building is located in a high end part of town on a very poorly lit street. Gigantic trees tower ominously over the building and car lined street. I am afraid.

A voice points out the obvious. *There are so many places a creeper can hide and jump out.*

Usually I walk in the middle of the street when faced with this situation. The streets are narrow and this one happens to be divided by a green belt. I think to myself, *fuck. What am I going to do?* I look at my phone to see if it is too late to cancel on Phora. I think with dread, *nope. Can't cancel. Don't have service. Double fuck.* I grip the steering wheel.

A voice says, *you can do this Anna. Take a deep breath. Hold your head up. Stay focused on your breath and the building. It is just down the block in your line of sight. You can do this.*

I inhale 3, exhale 5. I can't quite get to 6 on the exhale, which is my intended count. I think, *shit my anxiety is up already.*

Critic responds, *good thing you are going to meditation dummy. Isn't that what meditation is for?*

I shake my head and say out loud, "Stop. You aren't helping." I open the door, step out, close the door, and keep my back to the car.

A voice instructs, *hit the lock button twice.*

Beep beep. The car doors lock. I look in all directions. No cars. No people.

A voice screeches, *run to the building.*

Critic responds with disgust, *no don't run you will look like a lunatic.*

I roll my eyes. I beeline for the front of the building at a fast walk pace. When I get there, I see it is not the front of the building. It is a dimly lit gate. The sign on the gate says the meditation group is in the back building. The packed dirt path turns to tiny stones that crinkle under my feet with each step. I wonder, *where is everyone else? Am I even in the right place?* I begin to panic. I walk faster along the path. I try to reassure myself, *the sign said so. This path better lead to the fucking door.* I turn a corner. More dimly lit path appears ahead of me. The door to the back building is open. A few people linger in the entry. *Breathe.* I try to slow my breath. I smile at the people gathered near the front door. They smile back. *Friendly. Phew.*

I ask softly, "Is this the Wednesday night meditation group?"

A few nod and one reassures, "Yes, you are in the right place."

"Great thanks." Relief sweeps through me. A voice instructs, *make sure Phora walks you to your car.*

I hang out by myself apart from the group at the entrance to the back building. I don't want to talk. My voice might quiver. I focus on controlling my breath. By the time the group begins entering the building, I can inhale 3 and exhale 6. My heartbeat is slower. My feet feel the ground. Phora is not there when I enter.

I worry to myself, *is she standing me up? She was coming from work. Maybe she got caught up. I wouldn't know since I don't have service. I will be O.K. I can do this. It is a meditation group for fuck sake.*

The entry room is lit by a shrine with a lot of candles. A woman stands near the shrine greeting everyone who comes in with a silent nod and smile. I notice some people dropping money into a jar before either turning right or left.

A voice chastises, *great...you didn't bring any cash.*

Another voice notes, *Phora said it was free. And so did the email she sent you. No one has a purse either.*

The chastising voice asks, *well where do they put their keys and phone?*

Critic answers, *they don't bring a phone you dummy...there is no service remember.*

*Shhhhhh...*I silently plead. Only one more person in front of me.

Another voice chimes in, *fuck what way are you going to turn? You have to act like you know what you are doing.*

I smile at the woman. Several voices talk over each other. *Left. No Right. No Left.* I turn left.

A large room extends behind the entry way shrine. In the center of the large room is a two-way fireplace. Chairs, mats and pillows outline the exterior wall. I don't notice until I get closer to the chairs that they are all facing the exterior wall, too.

I exclaim to myself, *fuck me in the goat ass. I HATE having my back to the entry way.* Every hair on the back of my neck stands up. The muscles in my upper back between my shoulder blades contract. I say, *Hello Travis.* I realize Travis put his armor on us.

I shake my head instinctually at the voices chattering over each other. *This meditation is going to suck. You should just leave. No don't be rude. Maybe it will be good. You won't know until you try.* I sit down in a chair near a light. I try to return to my 3-6 breath. Two-4 is the best I can do. The dim lights flicker.

A female voice interrupts the silence in the room. "Welcome. We will begin with om. Then we will do a walking meditation. Then we will close. For those who wish to stay, I will give a talk on…"

I stop paying attention. I think, *what the fuck? Om. Walking meditation. Am I the only new person here? This is not what I had in mind.*

"OMMMMMMMMMMMMM." The room fills with a single sound made from everyone present.

The chatter in my head pauses for a moment. I say to myself, *that sounds kind of cool.* I inhale to participate in the next one. My ommmm is not long or steady enough to keep up with the group.

Critic jeers, *great…now everyone knows you aren't supposed to be here. You suck at this.*

My third ommmm is steadier, but not as long as the group. I shoot back, *take that Inner Critic…I can improve.* I smile at my bantering Parts. I feel fondness towards them, even though they drive me nuts.

At some point the female voice instructs us to stand. I turn to my right since everyone around me turns that way. The walking meditation portion begins slowly. I keep my eyes down except for the occasional glance up to see if Phora is here. With each step I feel less steady. I think, *this pace is so slow. I mean seriously what is the point of this?* My irritation is palpable by the time I circle the other side of the fireplace. I ask myself, *when is this going to be over? And where is Phora?* I consider slowly stepping out the door when I near the entry shrine.

A voice instructs, *no, just finish. This is almost over.*

Everyone stops. Another voice huffs, *finally.*

I realize I am back where I started. I sit like everyone else does. I note, *wait, are the chairs facing the inside now? Am I losing my mind?* I look around the room without moving my head. The chairs, mats and pillows face inside the room.

The female voice says, "May this day and week be filled with light and love. Namaste."

"Namaste," everyone replies in unison.

People begin to move quickly towards the female voice. I look in that direction. Phora sits near the leader. She catches my eye and points to the door. I nod quickly and jump up. I'm at the door in three strides. The cool night air envelops me. I exclaim to myself, *wow, I didn't even notice how hot that room was!* I breathe deeply and slowly. The air cleanses my discomfort.

Phora joins me. We walk towards the gate. The female voice fades behind us.

"I'm so sorry about that, Anna," Phora says immediately after we exit the gate.

"That was weird. But not your fault at all. I know you've never been either. It was interesting to try." I reassure her that I'm O.K.

"It was definitely not what I had in mind," she says.

We walk in the direction of my car. "Me, either. But now we can say we did it and we know that is not the place for us." I point out the silver lining. "I mean what was that? I felt like we were in a cult."

"I know!" Phora exclaims.

"And at the end most people flocked to that leader lady. Like eager beaver followers. That all just felt so weird to me." I shake my head.

Phora giggles. "We won't do that again. What are you thinking about the crystal talk? I promise it won't be like that. It is during daylight and we can meet for a quick bite to eat first."

I smile and reach for my keys. "Yes, that sounds good. Do you mind if I invite my friend, Elizabeth? She is into gems and crystals. She always wanted to be a jewelry designer, but went into her family business instead."

"Oh sure." Phora's tone is enthusiastic. "Will she join for dinner, too?"

"I'm not sure," I say. "I'll ask her and get back to you. It's next Thursday right?"

Phora corrects, "No, it's in 2 Thursdays."

"O.K., I will plan my work week accordingly. I can travel early that week for work if I have to travel." I click my keys to unlock my car. "Where did you park, Phora?"

"Down the street the other direction."

"Do you want a ride to your car? It is really far and dark." My eyebrows furrow with concern.

"No, that is alright. I need to walk. I've been working all day." She smiles again.

"O.K. Well, thank you for meeting me here and sharing this experience. I really appreciate you." I reach out to give her a hug.

She hugs back. "You are welcome, Anna. I just wish it was a little more along the lines of what we wanted. But, oh well."

"Yes, oh well. I will see you in a few weeks." I open the car door and throw my purse over to the passenger seat. "Thank you, Phora."

I immediately hit the lock button when my door clicks shut. Simultaneously, I turn on the car and a split second later turn on the headlights. I watch Phora fade into the night. I reverse and then pull out of my parking spot. My breath becomes involuntary for the first time tonight. My back muscles soften when I reach the highway.

I think to myself, *I wonder if Phora is afraid of walking alone at night. She didn't seem like she was. Is that normal? Will I ever feel not afraid like I felt tonight when faced with a dark street? Or walking alone at night? I mean rapists are everywhere.* I shake my head. *It sure would be less exhausting to not feel afraid every night since I now walk alone from my car to my condo every night.*

I pull into my parking space and notice the bright lights throughout the complex. I think, *thank god for these lights.* I walk quickly around the building to my front door with the key in hand. I unlock the door, step inside, close the door and fall against it. I listen for intruders. I exhale. Silence. I turn on the hall light. I drop my bag. A voice instructs, *get in bed. Do a meditation on your phone. You are O.K. You made it.*

∞∞∞

I start the next session with Jennifer that weekend the moment I walk through the door. I don't even greet Pansy.

"I tried a meditation group." I kick off my shoes.

Jennifer smiles. "Oh, good. How was it?" Her head vigorously shakes by the time I finish my story. "Anna, no. That is not how meditation groups are supposed to feel. You have to be really careful with meditation groups because they can be led by people who suck other people's energy. I'm so sorry that was your experience." She continues to shake her head.

"Well, I'm glad I'm not crazy. Because it honestly didn't feel right. I mean maybe I went on a bad night. But everyone flocked to the leader at the end. It was like kindergarteners who want to sit closest to the teacher during story time. It was really weird." Now I shake my head.

"Your instinct was on point. Part of what we are doing is helping to build trust in your instincts again."

I smile. I think, *that feels good. To know my instincts were right.*

"Last time we talked about the creepy van driver and how you can get out of the van next time." Jennifer asks, "Was this a time you didn't get out of the van when you needed to?"

I pause. I ask myself, *did I push myself too hard?* "Honestly, no. It felt more like a potential episode of True Blood." Her expression tells me she does not know what I am talking about. "You know, with Soki and the vampires?"

She laughs. "So creepy van driver was worse than vampires?"

I laugh with her. "Creepy van driver was like Anthony Hopkins in Silence of the Lambs. True Blood was like a community and most were not bad. They were all on the same team. Well, they ended up mostly on the same team."

"So your fear instinct was different?" She is serious now.

Again, I pause. I ask myself, *was it different? What was different?* "Yes, it was. My chest didn't stir. And I knew Phora would be there, so I wasn't alone."

"O.K.," she says. "Do you want to do some IFS with the parts that were activated at the meditation group?"

"Yeah, that would be good." I roll onto my back.

"Do you want a pillow or blanket?" She asks.

"No, I'm good today," I say. "Where is Pansy?"

"She is over by the water dispenser with her chew toy."

"O.K., just want to know where she might come in from." I giggle.

Jennifer giggles, too. "Do you want me to hold her so she doesn't bother you?"

"No, I like when Pansy comes over or interrupts. She is always on point."

"O.K., we'll start the same way as last time," Jennifer instructs.

I close my eyes and take deep breaths.

Jennifer's voice is soft. "Good. What parts are present? Let me know when you sense one."

I whisper, "Anxiety."

"O.K. What does Anxiety look like?"

I ask, *what do you look like Anxiety?*

Anxiety answers, *I look like this. Why do you want to know?*

I see a Cousin-It style Muppet with long periwinkle yarn hair wildly sticking out as if he stuck his Muppet white gloved finger in an electrical socket. His eyes, nose and mouth are stuck on his hair. He is the shape of an M&M. His stick legs end with Doc Martin tan boots on his feet.

"He looks like a periwinkle M&M with yarn-like dreadlocks, white gloves and Doc Martin boots," I whisper. "Is that weird?" The image makes me smile

"No, not weird," she says quickly. "Thank him for revealing himself."

I say, *thanks for coming out.*

Anxiety says, *well the waiting room sucks. It is supposed to be sterile, but it is like a prison in there. And no one ever cleans. And we are all trapped in there. It is too close for comfort. Travis is big and Inner Critic is an asshole.*

I say, *I'm sorry about that.*

"Did you thank him?" Jennifer asks.

"Yes."

"O.K. good." She instructs, "Now ask him when he first started being with you."

I ask, *when did you appear?*

Anxiety states, *I've always been here.*

"He says he has always been here." I raise my eyebrows with uncertainty.

"O.K.," she says. "Can he be a little more specific?"

I say, *thank you for that information. Can you be a little more specific about when you first started being with me?*

Anxiety refines his first answer. *Actually I've been here since you lived in your first apartment after college.*

My eyebrows furrow. "He says he has actually been here since I lived down South."

"Very good. Thank him for that. Does he know how old you were then?"

How old was I in that apartment after college?

Anxiety's hair puffs up with a sharp inhale. He exclaims, *I don't know! Probably 22-ish. You were there.*

"He seems a little annoyed," I share. "He said maybe I was 22-ish."

Jennifer instructs, "Thank him for sharing your age. Then ask him why he started being with you."

I ask, *why did you start being with me?* Before Anxiety can answer, I say *also thanks for clarifying. I sense you are annoyed by my questions.*

Anxiety hair seems to deflate and fall around his face. Anxiety simply states, *to let you know when you are in danger.*

"He says his purpose is to let me know when I am in danger," I say flatly.

"Thank him for sharing that information. That is a lot to reveal," Jennifer says.

I raise my hand.

"You thanked him?" She asks.

"Yes," I whisper.

Critic's voice bellows out of the waiting room. *What the fuck is the point of this?*

Jennifer instructs, "Now ask him how old he thinks you are."

I ignore Critic and ask Anxiety, *how old am I now?*

Anxiety's tone is mildly irritated and his hair puffs up again. *Duh, you are 22. Maybe 23. You had a birthday recently. I just told you a minute ago.*

"He thinks I am still 22 or 23. He said I had a birthday recently," I say aloud. To myself I think, *he thinks I am the age I was when I was raped.*

"That is really great information. Thank him for that and let him know you are 36 now."

I share, *thank you for telling me how old you think I am. I really appreciate you being honest. I am actually 36 now. I am a lot older than when I was raped.*

ANXIETY asks, *really? Is that what happened?*

I report to Jennifer, "I thanked him and told him I am a lot older than when I was raped. He said 'really?' And he didn't know that is what happened."

"Can you ask him to share what he remembers?" Jennifer asks.[59]

I ask, *what do you remember from that night?*

ANXIETY responds quickly. *You went from being really calm to being really stressed. Like we didn't have any time to respond. It was instant. I was in overdrive from that point on.*

I share with Jennifer. "Thank him for that information. How do you feel towards him?"

I take a deep breath to be present with my feelings. "I feel grateful that he has been working in overdrive since then. He has been my warning system."

"Good. Please tell him that," she encourages.

ANXIETY, thank you for sharing what you remember. I'm grateful for you working in overdrive all these years. I thought I was alone that night. But you were there and have been here since.

---

59 Jennifer and I reconstructed this next bit of IFS after she read a draft of the manuscript. The dialogue in the original version read "let him know he does not need to know the details. Ask him what he would rather be doing now." That did not ring true for either of us. I reflected on why I might have written it that way. The image of me sitting at a coffee shop writing this chapter came up along with a thought that I didn't feel like hashing out the details of the rape at that moment in the coffee shop, so I avoided it by telling ANXIETY he didn't need to know the details. Perhaps I experienced a new part in the coffee shop that day. Jennifer and I agree that we did IFS with this Part at this point in therapy. We also know that ANXIETY became Mini Monster and retired in the way described next. I made the decision to revise this dialogue to reflect the essence of how Jennifer and I work with Parts.

"O.K., I told him that I'm grateful and that I thought I was alone that night, but that he was there and has been there ever since working hard." I feel a sense of peace settling around me

"How do you feel now?" Jennifer must sense another shift in my expression.

My face softens, and my muscles relax. "I feel more peaceful. Like knowing he was there with me that night makes me feel like I wasn't alone. And I still feel a lot of gratitude. Like deeper, more sincere gratitude. Maybe love, but I don't know. More like we went through battle together and kept each other alive."

"Yes." I sense her smiling and imagine her nodding her head. "Can you let him know that?"

I see ANXIETY stop moving. His body settles on his feet firmly, yet softly planted on the ground. He looks at me with a calm expression. He nods knowingly when I tell him how I feel towards him.

I raise my hand. Jennifer asks, "Did you tell him?"

"Yes."

"Did he say or do anything?"

"He stopped moving, relaxed and nodded. His expression was calm."

"Good. Ask him what he would rather be doing now," she instructs[60].

I ask, *what do you want to do now?*

---

60 Jennifer noted in her edits that she's not sure we moved this fast with negotiating ANXIETY's new role. My memory is that we did re-purpose ANXIETY at this point. I left this dialogue as it appeared in the original draft.

I see Anxiety's hair calm down. It falls around his face. He pulls a sombrero from behind his back. A hammock appears and he jumps in it.

I tell Jennifer, "He didn't say anything. His hair calmed, he put on a sun hat and jumped on a hammock."

ANXIETY looks up from the hammock. *You didn't give me a chance to say anything. I want to retire on the beach. I have a lot of reading to catch up on.*

Out of nowhere in my mind, a beach appears around the hammock with palm trees, seashells, aqua clear water, bright sunshine and a light breeze.

I shake my head incredulously. I ask myself, *is this really happening?*

I report to Jennifer, "He just said he wants to retire to the beach and catch up on reading."

Jennifer says, "That is great. Is he on a beach?"

"Yes, out of nowhere, a beach, palm trees and hammock appeared, and he jumped right in. He is lying there with his little legs crossed and a book in hand."

I hear Jennifer smile. "So, he is relaxing?"

I nod and smile. "Oh, yes. He is definitely relaxing."

"Can you ask him another question? Or would that disrupt him?"

"I think I can ask him another question." Anxiety rests his book on his chest and looks at me out of the corner of his eye without turning his head. His eyebrow is slightly raised.

"O.K., ask him how he wants to help you in this new role?"

I stand on a stone path near the hammock. *Can I ask you is it O.K. to call you Mini Monster? Also how do you want to help me in this new role?*

Anxiety lies on the hammock with a sombrero tipped over his face, perhaps to think about his answer. He pulls the sombrero down and looks at me for a moment. *I'll spend my energy helping you relax. You don't do that enough. And maybe being your cheerleader because I have a lot of energy. And, yes, Mini Monster is O.K. I'm not really a Monster though.*

I clarify, *no you aren't a scary monster. You remind me of one of the good monsters from that movie Monsters Inc.*

He smiles and pulls the sombrero over his eyes.

"He said he will help me relax because I don't do that enough and be my cheerleader because he has a lot of energy." I'm not sure why I don't tell Jennifer that his name is Mini Monster.

She giggles knowingly. "Thank him for that."

I raise my hand.

"Now ask him if he will be available to come out of retirement if you are ever in real danger. Let him know his services may still be needed but that you are 36 now and will be in charge of getting him out of retirement."

I tap Mini Monster on the shoulder. *Look, I am 36 and in charge. But I will still be in danger sometimes. Will you be there to help me if I ask for your help?*

Mini Monster holds the sombrero up and looks me in the eye. *Yes, I will be there. But you will have to ask because I like this hammock. And the temperature is much better here than that damn waiting room. And the air is cleaner.*

I report to Jennifer, "He said O.K. and really likes his new place on the hammock."

"Great," she says. "Let him know you will call on him when you need him. Then when you are ready, wiggle your toes and fingers and open your eyes."

I do as Jennifer instructs. I'm light and solid.

"That was really great," she says.

"Yes, it was." I feel calm. "What a character he was. I wish I was better at drawing because he was like a mascot. And then at the end he put on a sombrero and put it over his eyes while he reclined on the hammock. He was stoked to be retired." I chuckle thinking of that image.

She chuckles, too. "How do you feel right now?"

"Honestly, I feel light. I feel grounded. I feel happy. Is that possible?" My expression is uncertain. "Like it is almost too good to be true."

"Yes, that is possible. Happy in what way?" she probes.

"Like I have a reference point for anxiety. I have a place I can put anxiety. I have a new role for anxiety so it's not in over-drive all the time. I'm like giddy happy. Like I didn't know it would be possible to manage anxiety."

"That is one of the great things about IFS," Jennifer affirms. "We used to think of some parts as needing to be disowned. I told you that before. But we can't disown parts. It's just like we can't decide we no longer want our right arm. IFS helps reassign parts to new jobs so that they can fill their intended role more accurately. In IFS, this stage is called negotiation. Does that make sense?" I nod. "Can I return to your meditation experience?"

I nod. The image of Mini Monster in the hammock fades.

Her tone is sincere. "I'm sorry that was your experience and I hope you don't give up on it. I do think if you find the right group it will be great for you."

"Do you know of any?" I ask.

"Well, I have one I go to, but that would be a conflict of interest[61]. I'm sorry I can't tell you about mine." She looks away. "But if you keep looking you will find a good one."

I look away, too. I think to myself, *I'm so annoyed and I totally understand the ethical boundaries. Still...just give me some clues.* "It's O.K. I know about our ethical boundaries and I totally appreciate you respecting those." I look at her and smile.

"You do?" A look of doubt appears on her face.

"Yes, I get it. I wish it was different, but I get it." I smile again.

We move towards the door. "Thank you for understanding." Her tone is apologetic.

We hug. I look down and say goodbye to Pansy. I reach for the door handle, but turn around quickly. "Wait, I forgot one thing. I want to do the collateral sessions. Let's talk about setting those up next time."

Her eyes widen with surprise. "O.K. great. We will do that." She smiles and nods.

---

61 Relationship boundaries are very important in mental health work. Therapists maintain appropriate relationship boundaries with clients based on ethical codes of conduct from professional associations, such as the American Counseling Association and the American Psychological Association.

Reflections ∞ Reactions ∞ Responses

_____

_____

_____

CHAPTER 27

RESCUE LITTLE ANNA

The week flies by. The sun is out and birds are chirping. Jennifer and Pansy are waiting at the door for me. We greet each other as usual and settle on the floor. Jennifer rests her back against the mirrored wall. I face her and my reflection. Pansy sniffs around the outer edge of the room.

Jennifer starts with a simple question. "How was your week?"

"It was a good week actually." I smile. "It flew by. I went with Phora to this workshop on the healing properties of stones and crystals. It was really informative and interesting. We got to reach in a bag and pull out a stone at the end as a take away. I drew out a rose quartz. Those are meant to heal the heart chakra and keep you safe. I thought it was fitting since we are doing IFS now. I actually sleep with it and the heart shaped rose quartz that Phora gave me a while back. It seems to calm me down and help me sleep. Whether it's real or perceived, it makes me feel safe."

"That sounds great." Jennifer smiles. "I would have really enjoyed that. And it was free?"

"Yeah, that was the best part. There was a jar for donations, but it was otherwise totally free. Phora and I had a nice dinner, too. She is so grounding and calming. I'm really grateful for her."

"I still need to contact her[62]." Jennifer frowns. "I know I've said that before and I haven't done it yet."

"That's O.K. I don't think I gave you her contact info anyway," I reassure her. "So, I want to do the collateral sessions. I've been thinking more and more about it. It would be really helpful if my family learned about PTSD and how to help me through it. And doubly helpful if I don't have to teach them myself. I've been thinking more about the family groups. For myself, I think doing one session with everyone would be great so I don't have to do the same one more than once. And for Violet and Franz, too, because they've got to coordinate childcare, so one session would be easier than two. But for my parents, I think doing two sessions would be best. That way each set may feel more comfortable. We can FaceTime Violet and Franz into the sessions. What do you think?"

She pauses to reflect. "I think you know best. Another consideration. Even though you might hear similar information from me, their responses will be different. And your experiences with each group are different, so the information I share may lead to different ways they can support you."

"That's true." I slowly nod. "O.K., let's do two sessions. Where will we do them? And when?"

---

62 Jennifer continues to say this because she and Phora still haven't communicated. One challenge in healthcare, including mental healthcare is integrating service providers and support people across professions. The burden often falls on clients to coordinate treatment and supports. Healthcare professionals may not be able to bill for time spent communicating across professions and support people. HIPAA, while necessary, complicates communication across professions. When integration does not happen, risks include disjointed treatment and, in some cases, could cause harm.

"We could use the group room at my other office. And we can do them whenever you want." She hesitates. "Usually when I do family sessions, I like to talk with each family member. But I am not sure I will have time to do that and I don't know that it is necessary. What do you think?"

"I don't think you need to. This is more of psychoeducation[63] versus full on family counseling. Plus if they have follow up questions or comments after, they can always contact you right?"

"Yes, of course," she says eagerly. "That's right. O.K. we can do it whenever."

"Let's do the session with my mom, step-dad, aunt, Violet and Franz next time we are scheduled to meet. Will that work?"

"Oh, that's soon." Jennifer's eyebrows furrow. "Like next weekend? I'll need to check to see if the group room is available. I can check tomorrow and let you know."

"O.K., perfect. I'll let everyone know to hold the time. Also, can we do it at noon so that Violet and Franz can join from Europe? There is an 8 or 9 hour time difference."

"Yes, we can do that." Jennifer looks over her notes. "I want to check in about what we did last time. Has Anxiety stayed on the hammock?"

The image of my dreadlocked Mini Monster sitting on a hammock on a tropical beach sipping a piña colada floats into my mind. I smile.

"Yes, he stayed put. It seems retirement suits him well," I chuckle.

---

63 Psychoeducation intends to share information and resources about mental health related topics. It often occurs in group settings with a facilitator presenting information. Reflection, activities and group process may be included to support information sharing. Jennifer's intention was to do psychoeducation and family counseling, just in case both were needed.

The image in my mind now includes a sombrero on his head and a newspaper. He pulls the newspaper down enough to show his eyes and winks at me. He says, *thank you.*

"That's great." Jennifer chuckles, too. "That really is quite an image. What about Little Anna? Should we check in with her?"

"Yes, that would be a good idea." I hesitate before sharing more about Little Anna. "I tried doing that a few times this week. She wasn't in my grandma's living room. She was sitting outside the building we exited on the picnic table. She seemed lonely. She was waiting for something. The sun was setting and there weren't any animals or people or other parts around her."

"Well, let's start there," Jennifer says. "Do you remember how we started last time?"

I nod and lie back. I close my eyes.

"Start by taking a few deep breaths."

Inhale 3. Exhale 6.

"Good. Let me know when you see her."

I raise my hand.

"Where is she?"

"She is sitting at the picnic bench."

"What else can you tell me about where she is?"

I whisper as if I don't want to disturb Little Anna. "The building is behind her. There is a cement sidewalk leading to the door. The picnic table is on the right side of the sidewalk. The grass is patchy. There are dirt spots and gopher holes in the grass."

"Where are you in relation to her?"

"I am standing at the fence entry way. There is a fence around the area where she is sitting. It is cinder block on the bottom like the building and has metal bars at the top. It is taller than me. There is an opening, like an entry way. There isn't a door there. It is just open. I am standing there looking at her sitting on the bench."

"How far away is that?"

"Not far. Like maybe 10-ish feet or maybe 15."

"O.K. Ask her if you can join her at the table."

In my mind I see her stare off in the distance longingly.

I ask her, *can I join you?* I smile at her. The air is cool. She shifts her gaze in my direction. Her eyes focus on me.

She whispers, *O.K.*

"She said O.K.," I report to Jennifer.

"Ask her how she has been?"

I walk from the entry way to sit on the picnic bench across from her.

I ask, *how have you been?*

She looks down at her hands. She continues to whisper, *O.K. I'm here all alone.*

"She said she is alone," I report to Jennifer.

"How do you feel toward her?" Jennifer asks.

"I'm sad and sorry she is alone," I say without hesitation.

"Let her know you are sorry she is alone. Ask her if there is anything you can do to help her."

I fight the urge to reach out for her hand. I tell her, *I'm really sorry you have been alone. Can I do anything?"*

My question is met with silence.

I begin to worry. "She isn't saying anything," I tell Jennifer. "She is looking down at her hands."

"That's O.K.," Jennifer reassures. "Ask her how she's feeling?"

I ask, *how are you feeling? Are you afraid of something?*

She looks at me with big round eyes. Tears puddle in her lower lids. I hold her gaze and hope my expression shows care and concern. I wait silently for her to respond.

After some time, she responds, *yes. I'm scared you will leave me again.*

"She says she's afraid I will leave her again."

"How do you feel towards her?" Jennifer asks.

My eyes remain closed and my head turns slightly in Jennifer's direction. *How do I feel?* "I feel…nervous and sad that I've left her in the past."

"What do you feel nervous about?" Jennifer probes.

"That she is right that I will leave her again." My bad habits flash through my mind. I see myself sitting at my desk for 8 hours straight, barely taking a break to eat or go to the bathroom.

"Are there other parts present, Anna?" Jennifer must notice a shift in my expression.

"I think so…maybe," I say hesitantly. "I just had a vision of myself working all day without eating or taking a break to go to the bathroom."

"Can you ask that part to wait in the waiting room for now because you are talking to Little Anna?" Jennifer clarifies, "Tell that other part that you will be able to talk to it later."

Can you wait in the waiting room please? I'm not working right now. Right now, I am talking with Little Anna. The vision dissipates. I see Little Anna again. Her big round eyes look at me with urgency, almost as if she is waiting to see if I leave her again. I smile at her.

Jennifer says, "Is the other part in the waiting room?" I nod. "O.K. Where is Little Anna?"

I report, "She's looking at me with big urgent eyes. They seem to be waiting to see if I leave her again."

"Thank her for waiting for you and for sharing that she's scared you will leave her again. Can you share with her how you are feeling towards her?"

I tell Little Anna, *thank you for waiting while I directed that other part to go back to the waiting room. Also, thank you for telling me you are scared that I will leave you again. To be honest, I am nervous about that, too, which is why I think that other part came out. I'm sad I've left you in the past. I will do my best not to leave you again.*

She looks down at her hands and whispers, *I don't know if I believe you.*

"She doesn't know if she believes that I won't leave her again." The edginess in my voice is palpable.

"What is happening for you right now?" Jennifer asks.

"I'm starting to panic. What if she is right?" My chest constricts and breath becomes shallow.

"Check in with the parts," Jennifer instructs. "Ask which part is coming out right now."

I scan my body. Mini Monster is still in the hammock. The newspaper is resting on his lap and he is intensely watching Little Anna and me.

I instruct Mini Monster, *stay there in your hammock.*

He nods and continues to watch.

315

A new part says, *I'm here. Doubt. What if she is right and you aren't safe? You might leave her. Don't make promises you can't keep.* I don't see an image of Doubt, only hear a voice.

I tell Jennifer, "It's Doubt. Doubting if I can keep my promise of not leaving her. Like I won't be able to be safe all the time."

Jennifer guides me. "Can you ask Doubt to wait in the waiting room? Let Doubt know that you are talking with Little Anna right now."

I direct my question to Doubt. *Can you wait in the waiting room?*

Doubt is disbelieving. *Really?*

My tone is firmer. *Go to the waiting room Doubt. I am talking with her right now.*

I notice the sun shines brighter on the picnic table. I think to myself, *maybe Doubt was a cloud?*

I raise my hand.

"Is Doubt in the waiting room?" Jennifer asks.

"Yes," I whisper.

"Good. Thank Doubt for going there."

I look towards the sky. *Thank you Doubt. I know you don't want to be in the waiting room.*

I sense Doubt sulking in the waiting room.

I raise my hand.

"O.K. Ask her what she needs from you to feel safe," Jennifer instructs.

I turn my gaze back to Little Anna across the picnic table. *What do you need from me to feel safe?*

Tears spill down her cheeks. She asks, *can I hold your hand?*

I report to Jennifer, "She asked if she can hold my hand."

"Tell her yes and hold her hand. Also tell her you are 36 now and you are learning how to take care of both of you."

I take her hand across the table. It is small and familiar. It fits inside my hand perfectly. I gently squeeze her hand.

I tell her, *of course I will hold your hand. I want you to know that I am sorry I haven't been there for you. I am 36 now and I'm learning how to take better care of us. I can promise you that I will keep learning and trying to keep us safe. But I may make mistakes along the way.*

She stares at me with big, wide innocent eyes and listens intently. Her little hand squeezes mine back. She asks, *can we make pillow forts? That is fun.*

I nod and smile. *Sure. We can make a lot of pillow forts.*

"O.K. I told her."

Jennifer instructs, "Ask her what she would like to do now?"

I ask Little Anna, *what do you want to do now?*

She looks hopeful and shy. *Can I sit on your lap?*

"She asked if she can sit on my lap."

"Good. Let me know when she is on your lap."

I move to her side of the picnic table. I reach my arms around her as she climbs on my lap. She rests her head on my shoulder and drapes her arms around my neck. Her teddy bear dangles down my back. The air is warm around us. We rock gently from side to side.

Tears begin rolling down the sides of my face in the counseling session.

Jennifer notices my tears. "What do you feel towards her Anna?"

Without hesitation I whisper, "Love."

"Good. Tell her that," Jennifer instructs.

I look down and whisper in Little Anna's ear, *I love you.*

"O.K. I told her."

"What else are you feeling?"

"Remorse." After a moment, I add, "And pride."

"Tell her that, too."

I hold her tight and tell her, *I feel sad that you have been alone for so long. I'm so proud of you that you have stayed safe and kept your teddy bear with you. You are a brave, strong girl.*

"I told her."

"Good. Ask her if she wants to leave there with you."

I ask, *do you want to leave here with me? We could go together.*

She pulls her head back to look in my eyes. Her expression questions me.

I reassure, *I won't leave you again.*

She smiles shyly and whispers, *O.K. we can go.*

Little Anna jumps down. She looks a lot taller than when she was sitting on the picnic bench. Her teddy bear dangles down to her knee. I stand next to her. She reaches her hand out to me. I take it. We walk through the fence opening. The sun sets in front of us over rolling green hills.

I raise my hand.

Jennifer instructs, "O.K. let her know we have to wrap up today. Can you take her back to your grandma's living room?"

I look down at her. *Little Anna I'm going to take you back to grandma's house. We can make a pillow fort there now and then I will go and check in on you throughout the week. It will be O.K. I won't leave you again.*

She nods. *Can I keep teddy bear?*

I smile at her. *Of course you can keep teddy bear.*

We are in grandma's living room in a pillow fort. The air is warm and the sun is bright. Blocks, books, crayons, and paper are in the fort.

Jennifer says, "When you are ready, open your eyes."

I say goodbye to Little Anna and teddy bear, focus on my breath and slowly wiggle my fingers and toes. I feel warm, like the temperature of grandma's living room. I don't want to lose that image. I open my eyes.

"That was beautiful," Jennifer says. "You really do remarkable work, Anna."

"Thank you," I smile. "That was powerful. I think I felt love towards myself for the first time. Like real love. Like I can take care of myself. I can be safe. I have a new purpose for being safe. Does that make sense?"

Jennifer's eyes seem to twinkle with delight. "Yes, it does. That is one of the great things of IFS. You get to connect with and rescue yourself at different points in your life. It is really powerful."

I'm excited. "I feel invigorated. Like something important just clicked in my brain about how to live a healthy life."

"That's great Anna. You really do work fast. Usually that takes several sessions, but you rescued her in 2 sessions." Jennifer continues, "It seems IFS really works for you."

"Yes, it does. I am really enjoying it. It is helping me sort out everything I think and feel and get overwhelmed by." I look at her with gratitude. "Thank you really. I mean it. Thank you."

∞∞∞

I ask myself, *where is she?*

It is Saturday morning. One week after Little Anna's rescue. I fold laundry. Last night I bought a pack of cigarettes. I felt scared at the thought of standing outside on my patio, so I crawled out instead and sat on the ground with my back against the fence.

I say to myself, *I know smoking is bad. I was stressed. It helps me unwind.* I begin to feel frantic. All week I tried to check in with my younger self. All week Little Anna alluded me. I felt her with me, but she was hanging on with her eyes closed.

I say to her, *it was a stressful week. I know I worked long hours and didn't eat right. I will try to do better. Please just come out.* Silence.

"Fuck," I say out loud. "I didn't even make it one week." I shake my head.

I tell her, *O.K., let's make a pillow fort and listen to the inner child meditation.*

I set my laundry aside. I arrange 14 pillows on the ground in front of the fireplace so that I will be surrounded by them. I pull three throw blankets from behind the chair in the living room to put on top of me. I turn on the fireplace, grab my phone and nestle in. The inner child meditation is 45 minutes. I usually fall asleep.

I tell her, *I will try not to though. I am doing this for you. Please come out when you feel ready.*

Silence.

After 45 minutes, I am noticeably calmer. But Little Anna remains unseen. I start the inner child meditation again. Finally, with 10 minutes left in the meditation she peeks out of a curtain of darkness. Her eyes are wide and she looks unsure.

I smile at her. *There you are. I am sorry. I know I didn't take care of us this week. I know I worked too hard, ate and slept too little, smoked, was outside in the dark and was generally stressed out. That is not a safe environment.*

She continues to stare at me with uncertainty.

I tell her, *you hung on this week though. You didn't give up on me.*

She nods and with the honesty of a young child says frankly, *you messed up my house this week. I couldn't breathe good and I didn't have enough to eat.*

I look down with regret. *Yeah, I know. I messed up. I will try again to not let work take over my life.*

She encourages me. *You can do it. Like you are now. You made us a pillow fort just like you said you would.*

She is lying next to me now with teddy bear.

I smile at her. *Yes. It was fun. Thank you for asking me to do this.*

She asks, *can we do it more often?*

I nod. *Yes, of course.*

Reflections ∞ Reactions ∞ Responses

_____

_____

_____

REACHING OUT

"It's not always easy to know what to say when someone tells you they've been sexually assaulted, especially when that person is a family member, friend, or loved one." RAINN, 2018

Learn about how to help someone after sexual trauma.

https://www.rainn.org/articles/
help-someone-you-care-about

https://www.rainn.org/articles/
tips-talking-survivors-sexual-assault

CHAPTER 28

COLLATERAL SESSION & MATCH.COM PREP

After Little Anna came out, I drove to Mom's house. We made plans to go for a hike. I want to tell her about the collateral sessions and get her input about inviting Aunt Tessa and Ben, my step-dad. Jennifer and I decided to do it next weekend because the group room isn't available tomorrow. Mom and I grab the water bottles she put on the table in the foyer of her house. I open the front door.

"Ben, we are going for a hike," Mom yells down the hallway from the foyer.

We walk down the front steps to the street. I think about the hike when I told her about the rape. We were on the same trail as we are hiking today. She was stunned. She seemed to dissociate. Her reaction was not what I expected. But I'm not a mother, so I don't know what hearing something like that from your child would do. We haven't really talked about my rape or that interaction between us since then.

The day is bright with a cool breeze. We walk to the trail head on the street in which I grew up. Memories flash through my mind of childhood fun. Football games on the Navarro's lawn across the street from Mom's house, pretend surfing the Big Cowabunga from Down Unda' on our skate boards, climbing trees, trick-or-treating, running through sprinklers, riding bikes. I say to myself, *we had a lot of fun on these streets.*

Mom and I enter the trailhead. I look to my left and see my Dad's parents' old house. I recall to myself, *Remember swimming in the pool there? That was fun, too.* We cross a dry river bed. *Remember cross country training in high school? These hills kicked our ass.* My skin tingles with delight as these memories flood my conscious.

"We had such fun growing up here, Mom." A hint of nostalgia lingers in my voice. "It has been a long time since I thought about all of it. What fun."

I see her smile out of the corner of my eye. "Yes, it was fun. We had quite the neighborhood crew running around with all you kids. It's hard to believe I am one of the old ones in the neighborhood now. I remember when your dad and I bought this place in the seventies. We were just starting out. It's neat to see all the young families like yours and your sister's ages coming in now."

I take a deep breath. "Mom, I have to ask you something." I begin slowly. "You know how I have been working with Jennifer?"

She stares at a dried up pond to our left. She nods slightly. I know this topic is hard for her. A bird caws in the distance.

I take another deep breath. "Well, we think it would be really helpful to have you and the rest of the family to a session to learn about PTSD and how to help me. It would be for 1 or 2 hours on a Sunday. I want to have Violet and Franz join via FaceTime. I also want Ben and Aunt Tessa to come. What do you think? Would you be interested?"

To my surprise, her response is enthusiastic. "Absolutely, yes. I would love that. I've been wanting to ask you if there is anything I can read to learn about how to help you. But I didn't know how to bring it up."

My chest opens, and relief fills my body. "Awesome. We are thinking maybe next weekend. Would that work for you and Ben?"

"I don't see why not," she says. "I will make sure Ben doesn't schedule work then. Are you sure you want him there?"

Ben works out of Mom's house. Our relationship has been strained with periods of calm over their decades-long relationship.

"I thought you might ask that," I reply. "I've thought about it a lot. I do want him there. It is important to me that those closest to me know what happened and how to help. Plus, I think him knowing will be good for you, too. I also thought about Aunt Tessa and which session she should come to. I decided I want her to come to your session and not Dad's. You and she are so close and when you are together it gives me strength. Hopefully Dad is O.K. with that."

The dirt path crunches under our feet for a few steps. I wonder what she contemplates.

"I think that sounds like a great plan," she smiles. "I look forward to it."

She does not share anything else. I think to myself, *Mom is hard to read sometimes. At least she is willing and excited to come.*

"I'll ask Jennifer about some books. I am reading Facing Shame right now." I suggest, "You could read that one."

Ben is working when we return to the house. We hug good-bye. She re-confirms that she will ask Ben to clear his schedule.

"This will be good, Annie," she calls from the porch before I close my car door.

I call Aunt Tessa on my drive home. I know she will be on board to come as long as she is free.

"Hi, hon," she answers.

"Hi, Auntie," I reply. "What are you doing?"

"Just having my afternoon iced coffee." I hear the ice clink in her glass. "What about you?"

"Mom and I just went for a hike and I'm driving home."

"It is a nice day for a hike." She takes a sip.

"Yes, it is. I also want to ask you about something." I don't wait for a response. "I talked with Mom about this, too. Jennifer, my therapist, and I want to have family to a session to learn about PTSD and how to help me. I would really like for you to be there. You have always been such a strong support for me. I will never forget when you called a few months after I told you about the rape and said if I ever want to talk more about it you were there for me but that you didn't want to ask too many questions because you didn't want to be nosey or bring up hard memories. That was such a brilliant and profound moment. No one had ever said that to me. It was a relief. I don't want to burden anyone with it, so I never feel like I can talk about it. Even though we haven't talked about it much since, knowing I can call you is such a huge help. Anyway, I want you to come to the session with my mom instead of my dad because I think you and she can support each other. I think this will be hard on her."

Without skipping a beat, she emphatically agrees to come. "Oh I'm so excited, Anna. I want to be there for you and for your mom. I think you are right. It is hard for her. It is hard for any mom when their child suffers. Plus I love the psychology of it all, so I look forward to learning."

"Awesome, Auntie. I knew you would be on board." I explain, "I'm going to have Dad and Lindsey go to a separate one. The dynamic with them is different. Is that O.K. with you that you will only come to the session with Mom? Also Ben will be there and Violet and Franz via FaceTime."

"Oh sure, hon. Whatever you think is best is fine with me."

We chit chat a little longer before hanging up. Next I call Violet even though it is late in Europe. She and Franz want to come, too, as long as their children fall asleep in time for the session. I text Jennifer when I arrive home that everyone is a go.

I feel light and solid. I exclaim to myself, *I won't have to do this alone anymore!*

Next I call Dad and Lindsey. Their schedule will dictate when their session will be.

"Dr. AAAAAAA." Dad answers with his usual enthusiasm. "How you doin', baby?"

"Hi, Anna," Lindsey says in the background.

"Hi guys," I reply. "I'm doing good. Mom and I hiked today. It was beautiful and felt so good to be out there."

"Great, honey," Dad says. "So what can we do for you today?"

"Well, I want to invite you to a session with Jennifer."

Silence.

"Not a session to do family counseling," I explain. "But a session to learn about PTSD and how you can help me."

Dad speaks first. "Well, O.K. honey. If it will help you, we will be there. When is it?"

"That depends on your schedule. Jennifer and I are pretty flexible on Sundays. Is there a Sunday in the next couple of months that work for you?"

Lindsey's voice is louder. "Hold on let me check our calendars. Charlie, pull up your calendar."

Dad mumbles, "Shit, what button did I hit? I hate these computers. I can never get it to work right."

Lindsey commands, "Charlie, just click that button on the bottom."

He's exasperated. "What button? There are like 50 buttons down here."

Lindsey's annoyed. "Charlie, you know which one. Take a second to look at them."

I chime in. "Dad, it's the one that looks like the envelope. Go to your email and then click the calendar button. Remember? We've all showed you."

After a pause he says, "Ohhhhhhhh, that button right in front of my face."

"Good Dad! I knew you could figure it out," I encourage and roll my eyes. I feel for both Dad and Lindsey.

"Anna," Lindsey calls out. "It looks like we can do the third Sunday in April or the second Sunday in May."

"O.K.," I say. "Can you pencil in both and I will check with Jennifer about which one?"

"Sure, what time?" Lindsey asks.

"Pencil in 12 to 2. We will FaceTime in Violet and Franz."

"Done!" Lindsey exclaims.

"Is there anything else, honey?" Dad asks.

"Nothing in particular. Anything else with you?" I ask.

"Are you dating yet?" Dad asks.

"CHARLIEEEE!" Lindsey's tone indicates he shouldn't have asked about that topic.

"It's O.K.," I interject. "Dad, I'm still thinking about online dating. I have to make a profile though and I haven't quite gotten there yet."

"Cool," Dad says simply. "Well, nothing much else is going on here."

We say goodbye and hang up.

I think to myself, *maybe I will do my profile. What will it say? Ugh. Something really simple. I don't want a relationship. I only want friends and a social life.*

A voice says, *probably no one will like that.*

When I get home, I settle on my couch with my computer and open Match.com. I ask myself, *do I really want to do this again? Should I try those other ones?*

A different voice answers, *no, just stick to Match. You've used that one before.*

Several hours pass. I review my profile. I think to myself, *pictures are good. Not risqué. Simple. Happy. Profile is short, sweet and to the point. Honestly answered all the questions, even the controversial ones like does he want kids, his income and my smoking status. I'm not wasting time with people who don't want kids, make less than $75,000 and have a problem with my occasional cigarette.* I enter my credit card information for a 6 month subscription. I reaffirm to myself, *casual dating and finding friends. That's it. No relationships.* I double check that I set my search filter area for all of California. I remind myself, *no need to limit to here since I travel all* *the time. Plus, do I really want to meet someone here? I mean I'm better off meeting people in the places I travel so I can have a social life during the week.* I click submit. I feel excitement fluttering in my chest. *This will be fun.*

Reflections ∞ Reactions ∞ Responses

_____

_____

_____

CHAPTER 29

MOM'S COLLATERAL SESSION

I wake with a start. A voice asks, *what time is it?* A glance at my phone shows it is 8:30AM. The voice says, *phew.*

Today is the first collateral session with my family and Jennifer. I want to eat a hearty breakfast, charge my iPad and get there a little early. I have 3.5 hours to complete those things.

The voice points out, *well, you also want to shower.*

Duh, yes I do. I throw the blankets off my body. I stick my legs up in the air and flex and point my foot. My arms instinctively stretch above my head. A smile forms on my face. I think to myself, *today I will not be alone anymore.* My legs swing over the side of the bed. I stand up and raise my arms above my head. Inhale 4 Exhale 4. I notice, *a balanced breath today.*

I brush my teeth and wash my face. My reflection in the bathroom mirror looks less worried than usual.

I tell my reflection, *that's because I'm not alone anymore. I will have help.*

I walk joyfully to the kitchen opening window blinds on the way. Morning sunshine warms the living and dining rooms. I open the slider. Fresh air waltzes in. I set up the drip coffee and turn on the kettle. I open the refrigerator and pull out the eggs and almond milk. I open the pantry for the English muffins. I begin to fry an egg over medium and toast an English muffin.

My giddiness continues while I shower and dress for the day. My steps are light and solid on the way to my car. The colors of the landscape in my complex seem more vibrant. The air smells fresher. The birds sound more beautiful. I hit only a few red lights. Some of my favorite songs play on the radio. I notice, *the world is brighter today. How interesting!*

I park on the street outside Jennifer's individual counseling office. We are meeting in the family room that is next door to her individual office. I have not yet been in there. I wait in my car with the windows down half way for my family to arrive. Jennifer pulls up first. She parks in the office complex parking lot. Pansy is not with her. I climb out of my car and walk to where she parked.

"Hi, Anna." She greets me warmly. "What a great day!"

"Yes, it is. I am just in the best mood," I say cheerfully.

"Oh, good," she replies. "I'm hopeful for today."

"Me, too. I think it will be really good."

"I'm still a little worried that I haven't talked with anyone. Do you think that will be a problem?" she asks.

I shake my head. "No, they are all looking forward to being here and learning how to help me. I think it is going to go really well."

"O.K. I blocked 2 hours, but if we only go an hour and half or whatever, that is O.K. We can take the time we need."

I see Mom and Ben pull up. They park across the street.

Jennifer notices my recognition. "Is that your mom and step-dad?" I nod. "Great. I will go open the family room and meet you back here in a minute once everyone arrives. Does that sound O.K.?"

"Yes, that works." Cheerfulness emanates from my core.

I walk across the street to greet them. Ben has his walker. While they gather the rest of their belongings from their car, Aunt Tessa pulls up. She parks in front of them. I smile and wave. She waves back. As soon as she opens her car door she greets us cheerfully. We walk back to the parking lot and wait by Jennifer's car.

Auntie looks around. "This is a really pretty place."

Mom agrees. "Yes, all the eucalyptus trees are pretty. Do you remember playing softball up there Anna?" She points in the direction of the softball field where I played my best tournament.

"Yes," I smile. "Many games. That is a nice field. And we'd all go get pizza after at that one place. That was such a treat"

"That margherita pizza from there is the best," Mom recalls.

Jennifer approaches us. "Hello, everyone," she says warmly.

We turn towards her. I introduce everyone.

"Let's go inside and get started." Jennifer turns towards me. "Anna, will you do the FaceTime thing for your sister?"

"Yes," I say. "I brought my hotspot and iPad, so I will get that set up. It won't take long."

The family room is inside a small hut-like structure in the middle of the complex where Jennifer's individual counseling office is located. It is octagonal. Jennifer set up chairs and mats in a circle. Aunt Tessa sits on my left, and Mom and Ben sit on my right. Jennifer is between Aunt Tessa and Ben. Ben's walker is next to his chair. He rests his arm on it and taps his fingers to a tune in his mind. Mom and Aunt Tessa put their purses down and settle into their chairs. We decide to place the iPad on another chair between Mom and me. Violet answers after a few rings.

"Hi," Violet greets us. "The kids aren't falling asleep, so Franz is with them. He will join once they fall asleep. I think they knew something was up."

"No worries Vi," I say into the camera. "We are going to put you on the chair next to me so you can see Jennifer. Let us know if you can't hear or something goes wrong."

"O.K." As soon as I place the iPad on the chair, Violet greets Jennifer. "Hi, Jennifer. It is so nice to finally meet you. I know Anna speaks highly of her work with you."

Jennifer smiles brightly. "Hi, Violet. Thank you. Wow you 3 look so much alike!" She points to Mom, Violet and me.

Everyone in the room nods in agreement.

"We get that a lot when we are together," Mom confirms.

Jennifer asks, "Shall we get started?"

"Yes," I say.

"O.K." Jennifer intentionally looks at each person. "Thank you all for coming. I want to explain a little bit about therapy first and what we are going to do today. Anna and I have been working together since last September. One of the things we are doing together is identifying and building her support system. All of you being here today is part of that. I am going to explain about what Anna is going through and hopefully you all have questions that we can talk about. Anna knows if anything gets too difficult all she has to do is say so and I will stop us. All of you can say so, too. As for confidentiality, that means we don't talk about what is said in here outside of here with anyone other than who is in this room. That helps maintain a safe space to share openly. Does that sound good to everyone?" Everyone nods. "Great. Are there any questions before we start?"

Ben timidly raises his hand. "I have a question. I'm sorry to ask this. But what are we all doing here? I'm really not sure. Your Mom just said we need to go do this thing for Anna next week."

Jennifer looks from Ben to me. "That is a great place to start. Thank you Ben. Anna, do you want to share with the group why we are here today?"

I take a deep breath. "O.K."

A voice says, *ugh, sharing again. What a burden.*

My stomach begins to knot. "So, in 2002 I was raped by someone who was supposedly a friend. I'd known him for six years and never felt remotely attracted to him or any romantic feelings towards him. He was like an older brother."

Ben's eyebrows shoot up. "I had no idea. Why didn't anyone tell me?"

My mom starts to answer. "I…"

I interrupt. "Well, I didn't even tell anyone in the family for 5 years. And then, you know how Mom is. She doesn't like to talk about anything bad."

Ben nods in agreement. "That is true. I'm sorry I didn't know. I would kick his ass. I have friends, you know."

Jennifer intervenes. "Let me stop you for a moment, Ben. I understand our anger, but as a therapist, I have a responsibility to do what is called Duty to Warn[64], which means I have to warn someone when a threat of harm is made against them no matter who they are. I have to legally break confidentiality for that. I say that now

---

64 Duty to Warn is a legal obligation for a therapist to break confidentiality and warn someone outside of therapy whose safety is threatened in a counseling session. This legal obligation arose from the Tarasoff vs. Regents of University of California case in 1976.

because I'm sure your words are an expression of your anger and not serious. But if they are serious you need to know what I am obligated to do."

Ben nods. "O.k. I mean I wouldn't actually do anything. But I am pissed." He clutches his walker until his knuckles turn white. "That is terrible. Did you press charges, Anna?"

I shake my head. "No. I did not. It is one of my biggest regrets in the situation. After it happened, I was going to go to Planned Parenthood for the morning after pill. But a friend of mine had one, so I didn't end up going. I still to this day wonder had I gone to see a professional right away what would have happened differently. I mean there is no way to know. But he is from Santa Maria and at the time I just didn't want to drag our family through the mud. Dad is so connected here with the business and everything. I just didn't want to do that to all of us. I was afraid." My hands are clammy and cold.

Ben slightly raises his hand again. "Can I ask one more question?"

"Sure," Jennifer says at the same time that I say, "O.K."

"Can you tell us what happened?" He says softly.

Jennifer turns to me to check in. "Anna, do you want to do that? You don't have to, though. Only if you want to."

"I'm O.K. to share." I glance at Aunt Tessa and turn back towards Mom and Ben. "Once Aunt Tessa called me and invited me to share whenever and if ever I wanted to. I have wanted to, but I haven't known how to bring it up or when. Like, 'Hi, Auntie I was thinking today I'll tell you how I was raped.' That just sounds so nonchalant for something that is so serious and painful."

Everyone chuckles to ease the heaviness of the moment.

"True," Aunt Tessa agrees.

I grasp my fingers tight in my lap and take a deep breath. "It happened when I lived down south after college. I was out that night with a big group of friends from home who mostly lived down there. It was Martin Luther King weekend. He was visiting because he had recently moved back to Santa Maria. There were like 8 or 9 of us out. My roommate was out of town that weekend. Half of the group was ready to go home around 1AM. Evan, the rapist, and two of our other friends didn't want to go yet. I offered that they could stay at my house. I got really drunk and threw up in the bathroom, which was unusual. Not the really drunk part, but the throwing up in the bathroom at the club part. I don't usually get so drunk that I barf. Anyway, we took a cab back to my apartment. It was the one-bedroom apartment, remember?" I pause briefly. "The two other friends that were there had hooked up on and off since high school. To give them space for that, I said they could sleep in the living room and Evan could sleep in my room. Not at all thinking anything would happen. Evan and I had slept in the same bed before with other friends and nothing sexual had happened. I made a bed with blankets and pillows on the living room floor for the other two friends. We smoked pot. I took one hit and was like 'no thank you.' I brushed my teeth and washed my face. I put on gray drawstring pants and a big t-shirt. I got water and climbed in bed. Evan, too. I faced away from him on my left side and passed out. Next thing I know, I am face down in the pillow and can't breathe. I turn my head to the right and say, 'what the fuck.' My pants were down. He was raping me. Vaginally. All of a sudden it was morning. My pants were up, but the drawstring was not tied. He didn't make eye contact with me all morning. We all went to breakfast. I don't know why I went to breakfast. I was in shock I think. I didn't know what else to do."

I take a deep breath and look at Jennifer. Her eyes are warm and compassionate. Her expression is soft and caring.

"Thank you, Anna," Jennifer says. "Have any of you heard the story before?"

Mom, Ben and Aunt Tessa softly declare, "No."

Violet confirms, "I have heard versions of the story. Bits and pieces. But not entirely, like that."

"How was that sharing for you, Anna?" Jennifer asks me.

"It wasn't easy. I don't want to be a burden. Plus there are parts of me that worry that I will be seen as a slut or somehow in the wrong because I was drunk and stoned and invited him to sleep in my bed. But also, it felt and feels good. Like almost relieving because now everyone here knows the details from me. There isn't a need to worry about how to bring it up anymore. And I don't have to carry it alone. It is out in the universe." A weak smile forms on my lips.

Jennifer looks at everyone else. "Do any of you have any other questions or want to respond to what Anna went through?"

"I am pissed. I want to do something…" Ben's fingers rapidly tap on his walker. "But I won't say it here. I'm sorry, Anna. I'm so pissed. I could've helped sooner if I knew. But that's O.K." He is sincere.

"Wow, Anna." Aunt Tessa opens and closes her mouth a few times. "I'm not really sure what to say. I'm so sorry, too. You didn't deserve or ask for any of that no matter what you did."

"Yeah, Anna." Violet's voice reassures through the iPad. "No matter how drunk or stoned you were, or that you invited him to sleep in your bed. You didn't even have a chance to say no because you were passed out. That is sick."

Jennifer looks at Mom. "Mom, do you want to say anything?" she asks gently.

Mom's voice quivers. "I'm just so sorry. I'm feeling a lot of things right now. I'm mad, sad, guilty. I'm mostly just sad that my daughter went through that. As a mother, you never want your child to suffer."

"I know, Mom," Violet says. "I can totally relate. If something like that happened to Leah, or Max for that matter, I don't know what I would do."

Jennifer's gaze settles on me. "Anna, what is it like hearing from them?"

"I mean, you all expressed many of the feelings and things I say to myself about it all. It feels good to not be alone with it." I wish I had something more profound to say, like something that would make it all O.K., especially for Mom.

"Shall I explain what happens post trauma?" Jennifer asks me.

"Yes, I think now is a good time for that." I'm relieved the focus will be off me for a while.

"O.K." Jennifer looks around. "Violet, I'm going to draw something, so you might not be able to see it. But we can hold it up when I am done." She draws a triangle on her notepad. "Anna has Post Traumatic Stress Disorder. The external situation that she went through, the trauma, gets internalized. One way to understand what happens when someone goes through a trauma is with what we call Karpman's Triangle[65]." She points with her pen to the top corner of the triangle and writes Perpetrator. "Someone who goes through trauma gets trapped inside Karpman's Triangle, like the Bermuda Triangle. They bounce between three roles- the top here is Perpetrator. They internally or externally bully and perpetrate. They might beat themselves up verbally or get really aggressive with others, verbally or physically. Next is the Victim." She points to the

65 Karpman's Drama Triangle was developed by Stephen B. Karpman, M.D. in 1968. For more information, visit https://www.karpmandramatriangle.com/.

bottom right corner of the triangle. "They also take on the role of victim. They might say things like 'I'm weak. I'm ugly. Something's wrong with me.' They don't take action where they might usually take action. They are passive." She moves her pen to the lower left corner. "Finally, there is Rescuer or sometimes it's called Bystander. Here they relate to and take on the role of someone who could have intervened. They become hypervigilant about safety and may take on the role of rescuing people in the group. They may bounce between Perp, Victim, and Bystander in one sitting." Her pen moves around the triangle. "Does this make sense?"

The group slowly nods.

Violet speaks first. "So like Anna has called me before crying uncontrollably saying that she doesn't feel like she is worth anything." She stops sharing about those phone calls. "Annie, is it O.K. for me to share this?"

"Yes, that's O.K., Violet," I confirm.

"So, is she in the victim role then?" Violet continues uncertainly, "I mean, it is out of character and usually happens after a night of partying."

Jennifer smiles. "Yes, that is a great example of how Anna portrays victim, Violet. Thank you for that. Would it be helpful to hear other examples?"

"Yes," Auntie and Mom say simultaneously.

Ben asks, "Remember when you helped me set up my jewelry display, Anna?" I nod. "The other guy working that day was talking to us. He was being flirty-ish with you and I didn't like it. He put his arm around you. You didn't really do anything, so I thought maybe you were O.K. with it. I didn't want to say anything if you were O.K. with it. But I didn't like it."

"I remember that vividly." I nod emphatically. "I was soooooo uncomfortable, but I didn't know how to get out of the situation. So I froze. I just thought if I stand really still and smile, it will pass. He was totally creepy. I'm not good at getting myself out of unsafe situations. I didn't want to hurt his feelings. Next time, please say something if you don't like it. That will really help me. I don't always respond the way I want to."

"Anna, do you think you were in the victim role there or the bystander?" Jennifer asks. "Like you knew the interaction wasn't right, but you didn't know how to intervene. That is bystander. Or like you felt weak or undeserving and like this always happens to you, so you didn't stop it. That is victim."

"Bystander." I am certain. "I actually left my body. When I think about that interaction, I am watching it from above."

"Thanks for that example, Ben." Jennifer nods in his direction.

"I have a question," Auntie chimes in. "Anna remember how we are working on seeing men look at you? You don't see men look at you as inviting or validating. We talked about seeing men notice you. You are such a beautiful person, inside and out."

Jennifer interjects. "That might be something else. Let me explain triggers. Triggers are when Anna is exposed to something in the environment that remind her of her trauma. When she is triggered, she may enter Karpman's Triangle, or, for Anna, she dissociates, or has panic attacks. People respond differently when they are triggered. Those are some ways that Anna responds to triggers. Tessa, it sounds like seeing men look at her may be a trigger for her."

"Yes," I agree. "It is a trigger. I don't trust that they aren't rapists. I think they see me as a piece of meat. Like in Madagascar the movie, when the lion sees his friends as steaks when he is hungry. I don't see men noticing me in friendly ways. To be honest,

I don't know that I believe there are men who look at women as anything but sexual objects. That is one of the things I am working on in here."

"I see." Auntie slowly nods her head.

"Anna's right," Ben confirms. "Men are men. They like to look at women's bodies. It's just what we do."

Jennifer interrupts before Ben can continue. "I'm going to stop the conversation for a moment because I want to see if it is triggering Anna." She turns to me. "Anna, is this hard for you to hear?"

I body scan. My forehead feels like it is bigger than it is. "Yes, I am starting to dissociate."

Jennifer says gently, "I thought so." She turns back to Ben. "So for Anna, she has grown up in this environment in Santa Maria with the produce industry that she describes that reaffirms over and over that women are objects for sexual pleasure for men. Women are not human. Her trauma reinforced that." She pauses to let her words sink in. "But, there really are men out there who do not subscribe to that behavior. Who do not objectify women in that way. The feminist movement is all about not objectifying women." She pauses again. "Ben, do you think you can agree for now that that behavior in men isn't just the way men are and can actually change?"

"I never thought of it like that," Ben says thoughtfully. "Yes, I can agree with that. It's just been all I've ever known, but that doesn't make it right."

Jennifer smiles widely. "Wow, great. Ben, thank you for being open to seeing something differently." She turns back to the group. "So, for Anna, being an object is something that developed perhaps over time from her childhood but was exacerbated with her rape. Her brain sees all men looking at her as objectifying her, which is a threat. She goes into fight, flight, freeze mode. Tessa, you are talking about the looks men give that are friendly. Like when a man or woman smiles at you when you walk past them. Or something like that, right?"

"Yes," Auntie says. "That, and also flirty. Like not objectifying, but flirty. Innocent flirting."

"I don't think Anna is there yet. Anna what do you think?" Jennifer asks me.

I nod in agreement. "Yes, I am not there yet. I want to be there. I don't know how to tell when someone is being creepy like the guy from the jewelry shop and when someone is being friendly and maybe flirty in a fun, innocent way. It's like my intuition or my instinct is silent. Or maybe it's that I don't hear it right now or I don't trust it. I'm working on all that, though."

"There is also something called re-enactment[66]," Jennifer explains. "When someone reenacts, they put themselves in the same or similar situations and try to make a different outcome. Research supports this concept. People who are raped are more likely to be raped again than people who have never been sexually assaulted[67]. Triggers and re-enactments are common in trauma survivors. You may see Anna put herself in unsafe situations in the future, or maybe in the past. She may be in reenactment. Does that make sense?"

"Wow," Violet says. "Yes, that makes complete sense."

"So, you've seen her do that?" Jennifer asks.

---

66 Sigmund Freud described repetition compulsion as the human tendency to repeat the past. Freud connected trauma to repetition compulsion. Since the 1970s, researchers and practitioners have used the term "re-enactment" to describe this phenomena that largely operates at a subconscious level. It addresses the question traumatized people often face- Why do I keep doing the same thing when I know it doesn't work?

67 Researchers using various research designs over at least 4 decades confirm that victims of sexual violence are more likely to experience future sexual assaults compared to those who never experienced sexual violence.

"Well, yes," Violet confirms. "I mean, I don't want to share details because I don't think it is my place. But there have been times when she does stuff that I'm like, why in the world would you do that? Even when she is drinking or whatever, she usually makes really smart decisions. But sometimes it's like she clicks into a mode and pushes the envelope and is really unsafe."

"That is often how people describe reenactment. She likely was in reenactments then, Violet." Jennifer nods towards the iPad.

"Vi, you'll have to tell me about them sometime, because I have a hard time seeing reenactments," I say. "That would be helpful."

"Nice segue, Anna," Jennifer says. "Let's spend the rest of our time together talking about ways you can help Anna knowing what you now know." Everyone nods. "Anna, what are some ways they can help you?"

My mind goes blank.

A sharp voice says, i*f I knew I would have asked a long time ago.*

Another voice commands, b*reathe. You know some things. Just tell them.*

"Hmmm." I buy time. "One thing that would be really helpful is letting me know if you notice that I am behaving differently. Like when I am in one of the Karpman's Triangle roles. When I am in that triangle, I don't really know it."

I look around. Everyone stares at me. I can't get a read of their expressions. It makes me uncomfortable.

Jennifer jumps in. "So, when they notice that you are not quite yourself, you want them to say to you something like 'Anna is everything O.K.? You seem a bit off.'"

"Yes," I nod. "Or say something even more specific like 'you seem like you are being extra aggressive or extra fearful or whatever. Did something happen to trigger you?' Saying those things will be helpful because I don't always know when I am triggered. It will help me learn how to be aware of when I am in a trauma response."

Jennifer looks around the group. "Does that make sense? What Anna is asking from you?"

Everyone nods and says "uh-huh" or "yes."

"What else, Anna?" Jennifer asks.

"It will also be helpful if I can say to you 'I think I am triggered' or 'I think I'm having a trauma response' or 'I'm not sure if I am responding to this situation appropriately, can you tell me what you would do?' So basically when I need to bounce something off you to reality check it. Reality check is more of a clinical term. Do you know what I mean?"

"Like when you want to get another perspective on a situation to compare your perspective to see if you are approaching it reasonably or not." Mom's description is on point. "Is that what you mean?"

"Yes," Jennifer and I say in unison.

"It is also helpful if on MLK weekend or leading up to MLK weekend you reach out and say something like 'I know this weekend is hard for you.' Or like 'I'm thinking of you and I'm here if you want to talk.' That weekend and the weeks before and after tend to be wonky for me. Sometimes I'm more irritable and other times more down. It just depends on what exactly I am not sure. But it is a hard time." I pause and look around.

Jennifer reinforces the difficulty of that time of year. "Anniversaries of trauma are really difficult for survivors. Anna, that's great that you are giving them specific ways they can help. Is there anything else?"

"Well, there is one more thing." I look down. "Any talk that objectifies women really triggers me. If possible, I need that talk to be limited around me. Well to not happen around me."

"Is it too much to ask that this talk not happen at all around Anna?" Jennifer gently challenges the group and me.

Mom's voice is fierce. "No, not at all. I don't like it either. We can definitely do that."

"Great." Jennifer smiles. "Does anyone have any questions?"

"I do." Aunt Tessa leans toward the group. "I'm a little unclear on the reenactments. How do you know if you are reenacting? Like how can we help point out to Anna if we think she is reenacting?"

"Yes, great question Tessa," Jennifer encourages. "Anna, do you want to answer that?"

I shake my head. "No, because honestly I am not sure how to know when I am reenacting either."

Jennifer chuckles. "O.K. So for Anna a reenactment may include inviting a male friend to stay over and sleep in her bed without intentions of being intimate. Or it may involve partying hard and making unsafe decisions about who comes back to her house or where she goes. If you see her doing that or hear her talk about doing something like that, it could be that she is reenacting the event to try for a different ending. Another reenactment could be the types of men she chooses to be in relationship with. Do they have similar unhealthy, perp-like characteristics as those who perpetrated against her? Almost always reenactments re-traumatize because they do not take away the original trauma and have potential to repeat it."

Aunt Tessa nods. "O.K., so if we see Anna doing something unsafe then it's O.K. to say, 'you seem like you are reenacting something right now' or 'that guy doesn't seem like a good guy?'"

"Yes!" Excitement and gratitude flow through my body. "Also, the more specific you can be the better for me. Like 'that guy doesn't seem like a good guy because he drinks a lot' or 'seems to objectify women' or whatever. I haven't yet told you all that I made my online dating profile. So your help in this area is so important to me. I clearly don't know how to pick guys that treat me well, so I am serious that I want your input this time around in the dating department."

The group nods.

"Great." Jennifer smiles at me. "I knew you were thinking about dating, Anna. Good for you for asking everyone to help you with that. Are there any other questions?"

Violet speaks up from the iPad. "I have one that may be dumb. But I have known a long time that MLK weekend is when it happened and I never want to bring it up because I don't want to remind her of a bad time. Like I don't want to re-traumatize her. That's a new word for me. How do I know I won't do that?"

Jennifer exclaims, "Another great question!" She peers closer at the iPad. "Franz, are you there?"

"Hello." Franz's voice comes through the speaker. "I'm sorry I was late. The kids would not fall asleep. Violet will catch me up. I've been listening."

"Not a problem at all," Jennifer says. "Do you have any questions about what you've heard so far?"

"No, maybe I will later and I will ask then," Franz responds.

"O.K.," Jennifer says. "Let us know if you do. And like I said to everyone in the beginning, or at least I think I said this, I am available after this via phone or email if other questions come up. So, back to Violet's question. Anna, do you want to respond to that one?"

"Sure," I say. "It all depends on the way you approach me, I think. So on MLK weekend or around it, you might say 'Hey, I know this weekend is tough. I'm here for you.' Versus saying 'Hey, I know you were raped this weekend. That sucks.' Do you see the difference?"

"Yes," Violet confirms. "So it won't re-traumatize you if we bring it up without you bringing it up first?"

Jennifer interjects. "Well, honestly you can't ever be 100% sure. But Anna is right. It is all about the approach. I'd also like to suggest that Anna, if you feel you are being triggered, then you can say something like 'I'm feeling triggered, can we change the subject?' And whomever she is talking to would understand without taking it personally. Would that be O.K. if Anna said something like that?"

The group nods. Violet says, "Yes, for sure."

"Anna, would you be willing to do that?" Jennifer asks me.

"To say I'm triggered right now?" I continue when she nods. "Definitely, if I am aware of it. Like earlier today when Ben was saying that men will be men and gawk at women, and Jennifer you noticed that I was triggered. I could feel myself dissociating, but I didn't have the wherewithal to say 'I'm triggered.' But maybe now I will since before now we haven't talked about this stuff. And now everyone here knows what 'triggered' means, so we have a common language to refer to. That is all so helpful."

Mom tentatively says, "Anna works a lot. She has always been a really hard worker. But I've noticed in the last several years, she is like on work overdrive." She turns to me. "You, like, don't stop. And I really worry about you overdoing it. Because you don't sleep or eat good and you are so stressed. Is this behavior part of what we are talking about here? Like keeping busy helps you avoid thinking about your trauma? Or maybe being stressed all the time is somehow connected to your trauma?"

Jennifer's tone is encouraging. "That's a great observation, Mom. And you approached Anna with it in a non-threatening and non-judgmental way. What do you think about your mom's question, Anna?"

I'm recall the vision I had during IFS with Little Anna. "I think you are on to something, Mom. I need more time to mull it over though because I haven't thought that deeply about working in that way. I can say work is a treadmill that I can't get off of very easily. In fact, it is to the point that I don't even notice the treadmill anymore. It is just the way it is and it is very unhealthy. I wish I could turn it off."

"You all have done such great work today," Jennifer reflects. "I feel very honored to be a part of this. I can see so much love and care between all of you. I am encouraged. Anna, you and I talked about doing this as part of a way to build your support system so you don't have to manage all of it alone. How has this been for you?"

"Honestly, I woke up today so elated. Like really joyful and cheerful." I reflect on my morning. "Then I got really nervous when we first started. Like maybe this will be too much or I will be disappointed. But now I feel relieved. And joyful. And a little more free. Like I don't have to walk around with this burden hidden inside me anymore. At least with all of you, I know I don't have to pretend. And even if I feel like I need to pretend, you will call me out. I feel like I have a safety net." I smile and feel tears forming in my eyes.

Jennifer asks gently, "What are your tears saying?"

I pause for a moment to listen to my tears. "They are saying thank you. They are grateful. I am grateful. I am also hopeful. Maybe I am turning a real corner in the healing process."

Jennifer reiterates that she is available any time after this session. We end the session. I write a check for Jennifer. Mom ends FaceTime with Violet and Franz. We walk out. The colors are still vibrant. Inhale 5. Exhale 10. A voice says, *wow. That is the deepest breath you have ever taken.*

∞∞∞

Aunt Tessa calls a few hours later.

"Hello," I answer.

"Hi, hon. I just have to say thank you. That was one of the most interesting things I have ever been a part of. You are just doing so great. I really learned a lot. And Jennifer is wonderful. I can see why you like her so much."

I smile brightly. "Thank you, Auntie. It meant a lot to me that you were there. I learned a lot, too. It is just so relieving that we are in this together now."

"Oh I bet, honey," she affirms. "You have carried that all by yourself for such a long time. I'm just glad you trust all of us enough to let us help you."

"Yeah. I feel very lucky that you all are willing to help. I'm not sure how people do it without a support system." I change the subject. "Have you talked to Mom? I was worried about her."

"Yes, your mom and I talked after," Auntie confirms. "She is doing good with everything. I mean it is hard for her. Anytime your child suffers it hits you like ten times worse. You will see one day when you have a baby. She is good, though. She found it helpful."

"Oh good. I was surprised by how open-minded Ben was. Especially when Jennifer stopped him when he insinuated that men will be men." I am smiling again.

"I know!" she exclaims. "I saw a side to Ben that I haven't seen. It was nice to see him be so thoughtful."

We chit chat about dinner and the week before hanging up. I talk with everyone else who participated in the group throughout that week. Everyone had a similar experience. My hopefulness grows.

∞∞∞

I've looked forward to seeing Phora tonight all week. I think, s*he is going to be so happy about my family session last weekend.* I remain genuinely happy and hopeful since the family session three days ago. I park in my usual spot, which is the 15 minute visitor space and say a quick prayer that I won't get towed since it is after hours. In the building, I am greeted with a familiar aroma as I round the corner to her office. The door is cracked and a dim streak of light lets me know she is ready for me. I softly knock as I push the door open.

"Hi Phora." I see her facing the towel warmers.

"Hi there!" She turns to look at me. "Wow, you are different. In a good way. What's going on?"

"I knew you would notice," I say joyfully. "I am different. I feel different. I feel hopeful. Like the crud is finally moving out of my body. My brain feels different. We had a family session with Jennifer. My mom, step-dad, aunt, Violet and Franz were there. Well Vi and Franz joined via FaceTime. It was so powerful, Phora. For the first time ever, I feel like I can actually talk with them about what happened and they will help me get my bearings back. If that makes sense. Like there is only so much I can do on my own because I am in it. But now they know the signs to look for when I am having a trauma response and we have ways that they can approach me. It is like such a huge relief not to be doing this alone anymore."

"Oh, Anna." Phora's expression exudes joy. "That is what you need. I am so happy to hear that they were all open to ways they can help you. What about your dad and Lindsey?"

"We are doing a session with them next month. Vi and Franz will FaceTime in for that one, too."

"That is so great. You really have a very supportive family." Phora smiles warmly. "Now for today. Where are you feeling everything?"

"Honestly, I don't really have any hot spots. I mean the usual soreness from being in the car and sitting at my desk for long hours. Mostly tonight I am just happy and hopeful and don't want any of this to end."

She nods. "Tonight we will work on massaging these feelings into your body. How does that sound?"

"Love it." I begin to take my sweater off. "Face down?"

"Yes, I'll be right out here until you are ready." Phora closes the door behind her.

I notice a framed picture of horses on her wall. I think, *those horses are beautiful. So strong and graceful.* I pull my shirt over my head.

A voice says, *horses are beautiful? You don't notice animals very often and never are you taken by their beauty.*

I smile and whisper out loud. "Yes, I know. But something is different." I place the last article of clothing on a chair and climb on the table. It is heated to a comfortable temperature. The sheet is soft against my body.

Another voice asks, *has it always been this soft and cozy?*

I nod and whisper "Yep, you just didn't notice before." Then I say silently to my parts, *I think I am finally getting better. Like lasting healing.*

Phora knocks softly and cracks the door open. "Are you ready for me, Anna?"

"Yes." My voice is muffled by the face cradle.

I hear Phora come in and close the door behind her. She starts like she always does by placing her hands around my body on top of the sheet covering me. She opens and closes the towel warmer and shuffles something else around on her work shelf. She starts massaging my feet.

"You don't start there very often," I observe. "In fact I'm not sure you have ever started at my feet."

"No, I don't usually start down here unless someone requests it," she confirms. "But I want to ground those feelings of hope and joy so I am starting down here. I will blend the energy into your feet, which are closest to the ground, and continue to knead that energy as I move up your body. Does that make sense?"

"Absolutely does." I take a slow deep breath. "You have different music on. It is piano. Kind of light and cheerful."

"Yes, you sure are observant." She chuckles. "I had an intuition today before you came in and this music matched my intuition."

"Well, it was right on. It is dancing through my body. A joyful jig." I giggle at my cheesiness.

"So, I found another meditation resource for you. I haven't been to this woman in a long time but I have clients who have worked with her. She is doing a group for beginners on Tuesday nights starting in a few weeks. Are you interested? I can email you the information."

"Cool," I mumble. "Yes, I am definitely interested. Please send it to me."

"I'm still contemplating the cranial-sacral therapist. The one I was thinking of I talked with and didn't get a good vibe for you. So I put it back out to the universe. I just think that will be really helpful for you. And don't worry if you decide to stop coming to see me. You know that. Never any hard feelings. I am one piece of your journey."

"Phora are you trying to break up with me?" I smile into the face cradle.

She laughs. "No, not at all. I just want to make sure you know that I am O.K. if your healing process includes leaving me to do something else for a while or forever."

"I doubt it will be forever Phora," I say sincerely. "You are stuck with me forever whether you like it or not." I chuckle.

"Well, that's good because I enjoy working with you." She sounds equally sincere.

The 90 minutes pass too quickly. I feel grounded in solid light. My feet connect to the ground more firmly than I've ever remembered. My legs feel strong and stable. My hips and spine are aligned. My neck and arms gently connect and move with my body. I say to myself, *wow, I think I am actually free of stress.* I sleep soundly that night and wake to the memory of pleasant dreams.

Reflections ∞ Reactions ∞ Responses

_____

_____

_____

CHAPTER 30

TRAVIS, MY KNIGHT
IN SHINING ARMOR PART

I have so much to share with Jennifer from the last few weeks. The Sunday afternoon sun is bright. A cool breeze blows in from the west. Pansy waits at the door when I walk up. Jennifer opens it. We greet each other with a hug. I begin while I take off my shoes.

"I have so much I want to share today. The week before the session with my mom and everyone, I had a really stressful week. I didn't do a good job taking care of my little self. So that Saturday I made a pillow fort by the fireplace, closed the blinds and put on an inner child meditation. It took listening to the meditation twice and almost 2 hours, but I found her. Or rather she came out. I was so guilty and anxious that I failed that first week and I wouldn't be able to find her. Or she wouldn't trust me enough to come out again. I'm really starting to have a better understanding of what it means to be trustworthy. I mean when I'm a maniac work-aholic who doesn't sleep good, drinks wine and smokes cigarettes, that is not trustworthy behavior. I always thought of trust as something that goes into relationships with others, not as part of my relationship with myself. Anyway, then when Mom asked the question last week about how much I work and push myself as part of my coping with trauma I was like 'ding ding.' A light bulb flickered. So anyway, I want to talk about that. And I also want to tell you about Match. I made my online dating profile. And I want to talk about the family session."

"Those are things I wanted to check in about, too," Jennifer nods. "Also, I wanted to follow up on the book-ending and coping card."

"O.K.," I say. "Let's start with checking in about last week. It was so awesome. For me, it was amazing to watch my family engage in helping me heal. And their questions and observations were so insightful. Thank you so much for introducing the idea of a collateral session to me and facilitating it so skillfully."

"You're welcome." Jennifer smiles warmly and nods her head. "It was really a pleasure. You have such a supportive family. Were you surprised by your step-dad? I was really impressed with his open-mindedness about not all men gawk at women. A lot of times men, especially men from his generation, are not as receptive to those ideas."

"I know!" I exclaim. "It was an awesome moment. His wheels were definitely spinning. And my mom, aunt and Violet asked such great questions. I'm just so glad we were all there together."

"Has anything in particular stood out to you this week?" she asks.

I pause to collect my thoughts. "Well, a few things. Like I said in the beginning of our session, the whole work-aholic thing. I mean, not just with my current job. I have been an overachiever for a really long time. During my master's degree I worked two or three part-time jobs and was a fulltime student. Then I took jobs that required on-call and long, late hours. When I had a day job only, I took a teaching job at night. And the same in my doc program. I mean, I absolutely see a connection between keeping busy as a way of distracting myself from trauma responses. I'm exhausted all the time. Like if I just go go go, then hit the wall, I have no choice but to sleep."

Jennifer offers insight. "I wonder if your anxiety around going to bed also factors in to this way of going until you hit the wall. Book-ending might help with that."

I pause again to mull that insight over. "Yes, maybe it is my brain's way of avoiding the panic I feel about getting in my bed and going to sleep. Interesting. I will have to think about that. Another thing I thought about this week is what Aunt Tessa talked about. I want to be able to tell the difference between a friendly glance, smile with a flirty glance and creepy gawking smile. Right now, I can't tell and inevitably all looks or smiles or small talk means they are creepy. It is exhausting being in public sometimes because I am constantly having to guard against invasive looks and interactions with men. But really most of the time those happen it is from an innocent, friendly place. It's like my creep-odometer needs to be recalibrated."

"I wonder if doing some IFS might help with these areas." She looks questioningly at me.

I shrug my shoulders. "Sure, it can't hurt."

I settle into my normal IFS position on the floor and close my eyes. I begin to take deep breaths and scan my body.

"Good," Jennifer says. "Let me know when a part surfaces."

Travis emerges out of darkness. He is wearing his knight armor complete with a sword and shield.

Travis's voice is deep and stoic. *Here I am. You are looking for me.*

I say to Jennifer, "Travis came out."

"Great. Thank Travis for coming out and ask if he is willing to talk with you."

I say, *thanks Travis for coming out. Can we talk for a bit about your role?*

Travis nods. *Sure, I'm at your service.*

"He says he is at my service," I tell Jennifer.

"Good. Ask him what his purpose is?"

I ask, *what is your purpose Travis?*

Travis's eyes are kind. *I keep you safe. I protect you from your anxiety and panic.*

"He says he protects me from my anxiety and panic."

"Thank him for that insight," Jennifer guides me. "Ask him how he does that."

I ask, *how do you protect me?*

Travis's tone is patient. *I make you tough and give you drive so you can perform in a man's world.*

Mini monster appears in the hammock. His hat is on the sand next to him and he sits up. He seems annoyed. He tells Travis, *you think you are so tough. But I always find a way around you.*

I share with Jennifer, "Anxiety just popped in when Travis was telling me how he protects me."

Jennifer instructs, "Ask Anxiety to wait in the waiting room or stay on his hammock. Let him know you are talking with Travis right now."

I direct Mini Monster. *Thank you for chiming in, but right now I am talking with Travis. Please stay on your hammock.*

Mini Monster huffs, reaches for his sombrero and lies back down.

"O.K.," I say out loud to Jennifer.

"O.K. Anxiety is in the waiting room?" Jennifer asks.

"Yes, he went back to lying on his hammock," I confirm.

"Go back to Travis and ask Travis how he protects you," Jennifer instructs.

"He already told me. He says he makes me tough and gives me drive to perform in a man's world," I report.

"O.K. great," Jennifer says. "Thank him for sharing that."

I say, *thank you Travis for sharing that you make me tough and give me drive to perform in a man's world.*

Travis nods and smiles kindly. *Anytime. I'm at your service.*

I raise my hand to indicate to Jennifer I thanked him.

"Did you tell him?" Jennifer asks.

"Yes," I say.

"Did he say anything back?" She asks.

"That he is at my service."

"Good," she says. "Thank him for being at your service. Ask him if there is any other way he would like to be at your service."

Travis, thank you for helping me be tough and driven. Is there any other way you want to be at my service?

Silence. Travis disappears.

"He went dark," I report to Jennifer.

"Oh," Jennifer says. "That's O.K. Reassure Travis that you don't want to get rid of him and you appreciate how he has helped you up to now. Ask him how long he has been in your service."

I clarify, *Travis I'm sorry if I made it seem like I wanted to banish you. I don't. I really appreciate how you've helped me stay tough.*

Travis reappears. Stoic and thoughtful. Almost statue like.

I ask, *how long have you been in my service?*

Travis replies, *since you were 22.*

"Since I was 22," I say softly.

"Thank Travis for sharing that information," Jennifer says.

Thank you Travis. I know that was a tough year. It makes sense that I needed to be tough.

Travis nods with surprise. *Yes, ma'am.*

I raise my hand.

"O.K.," Jennifer says. "Let Travis know you are 36 now. Tell him you don't need him to be on all the time anymore. Ask him if there is something else he wants to do."

I look directly at Travis. *Travis, I am 36 now and don't need you to be on all the time anymore. Is there anything else you want to do?*

Travis answers quickly. *I'd love to sit down. This armor is heavy.*

"He says he wants to sit down because the armor is heavy," I report to Jennifer.

"Great," Jennifer says. "Ask him if there is a place he wants to sit down and let him know he can sit down."

I encourage, *you can sit down Travis. Is there anywhere in particular you want to sit down?*

Travis clarifies, *well, I want a stand to place my armor next to a lazy boy recliner.*

"He wants an armor stand and a lazy boy recliner," I giggle.

Jennifer giggles, too. "Let him know you can arrange that. Ask him if he is willing to be at your service when you ask him to be, but only when you ask him."

I say, *O.K., Travis. Here is your armor stand and Lazy Boy recliner.*

A sturdy wooden stand appears next to a dark brown leather oversized Lazy Boy recliner.

Travis's tone includes surprise and gratitude. *Thank you. Can I sit down now?*

I nod. *Yes, go ahead.*

Travis takes off his armor and places it on the stand carefully. He is an older man with gray hair and a twinkle in his eye.

Travis seems relieved. *Phew. That was getting heavy.*

I smile. *I may still need your help, Travis. I will let you know though. Is that O.K? You don't have to put the armor on unless I ask you to.*

Travis nods and smiles back at me. *Sure. I am at your service when you ask for me.*

I say to Jennifer, "Travis is settled into his recliner. He is an older man with gray hair and kind eyes. He says he is available if I ask for him."

"Great." Jennifer instructs, "Say goodbye to Travis and make your way back here."

I do as she instructs. When I open my eyes, I feel relieved and happy.

"That was great." Jennifer smiles when I look at her.

"Yes, it really was," I say. "Each of these parts are such characters."

She chuckles. "Yes, they are. You are really in tune with the details."

I smile, but don't say anything. I'm thinking about my parts and how fond I am of Travis and Mini Monster.

Jennifer interrupts my thoughts. "We are out of time. I know you wanted to share about the inner child meditation."

"It's O.K. I said it all at the beginning. I'm proud of myself that I took the initiative to do that. It felt really good even though it took over 2 hours."

Jennifer nods with encouragement. "Have we talked about coping cards yet?"

"No, but I know what they are. I use them in my practice when I am the counselor."

"The inner child meditation, book-ending, breathing, reaching out to your family, making pillow forts…All those activities are new ways of coping when your trauma is activated." She pauses to let that list of healthy changes sink in. "As you know, the coping card is a great way to help you when you are in a trauma response to not let the parts take over. You only have to remember to look at your card and do each of the activities until the trauma response passes. Do you think this week you have time to make one?"

"I can try. I have a super busy week with work. But I will try."

"O.K.," she nods encouragingly. "Did we decide about next week?"

I raise my eyebrows. "Hmmm…"

"I have in my calendar the first collateral session with your dad's group. Do you think you are ready for that?" She waits patiently while I mull that over.

"You know…," I start tentatively. "I'm almost thinking it would be better to meet with only Dad. I'm hesitant about that because I don't want to get into dad bashing again like in high school. But it just seems like we have a lot of unresolved stuff. What do you think?"

"That makes sense to me," Jennifer agrees. "I will help in making sure we don't go into a bashing zone. That's one of the important roles of a therapist in a family session."

I nod. "Yes, you are correct."

She chuckles. "You, of course, you already knew that."

I nod again. "I'll let Dad know. I'm sure he will be O.K. with it as long as I tell him we won't be bashing each other."

I think about the upcoming week as I drive home. I say to myself, *shoot I forgot to tell Jennifer about the meditation group.* Phora emailed me earlier in the week about a group for introductory meditation. It starts tomorrow, Monday and not Tuesday like Phora told me.

Reflections ∞ Reactions ∞ Responses

_____

_____

_____

CHAPTER 31

MEDITATION THYME

I ask, *when did you creep in here Mini Monster?* I shake my head in hopes Mini Monster and any other parts will go away.

The sun is setting and I needed to leave five minutes ago for the first meditation class. My breath is shallow. My mouth is dry. *That's a new one- dry mouth.* I close my laptop and push the desk chair back to stand and walk toward the front door. I grab a granola bar and water bottle to have in the car. My keys drop when I try to lock the front door. *I'm not supposed to be so anxious and stressed going to meditation.*

I focus on my breath while I drive a few miles to the class. It is in a house converted to offices. The property for the class has two buildings.

Critic rudely interjects, *great, which one is it? It is probably in your email. If you only took 30 seconds to read it and get ready for it. You aren't doing this very well.*

I shake my head again. The front house looks closed, so I decide to try the back house. The door opens to a small foyer with low ceilings. It smells musty. There are two internal doors partially closed. The second one looks like a bathroom. I tentatively peek my head around the first door and seven faces turn toward me. I think loudly, *Shit I'm really late.*

"Hello, I'm Meredith." The woman sitting in the chair closest to the door smiles kindly.

"I'm sorry…" I begin.

Meredith interrupts. "It is O.K. We just started. Have a seat on the couch over there." She points to the only seat left in the room.

I smile shyly at other group members as I walk as quickly as possible to my seat. I notice I'm the only one with a big purse.

I wonder, *where do they keep their keys, wallets, and cell phones? Shit my cell phone is on.*

I attempt to quietly wrestle through my purse without looking to silence my phone. A few people shuffle in their seat.

I chastise myself, *great. I'm THAT girl.* I look around and smile apologetically to anyone who makes eye contact.

All eyes return to Meredith. "So are there any questions before we get started with group introductions?" Silence. "O.K., let's start with you." Meredith gestures to the person closest to her on the left.

I think loudly, *great I missed the instructions.*

A voice says, *just listen and you will figure out what you are supposed to say.*

I do my best to tune into other people's introductions. I say to myself and my parts, *it seems like name, previous experience with meditation and what I want to get out of this class.*

My breath noticeably slows for the first time since I left my house. I listen to everyone's introductions and am struck by the age range and prevalence of anxiety.

"My name is Anna Gulden," I begin. "My past experience with meditation is really just searching for guided meditations on YouTube or iTunes and listening to them by myself. Mostly I use them to fall asleep. But recently I started using them during the day. Well, I only did that once on my own. I intend to do them during the day thought." I'm relieved when a few others nod and chuckle knowingly. "I'm working with a therapist and we do some guided imagery work, too. Anyway, I hope to learn about meditation so that I can be more informed and intentional in my practice. So yeah, that's it. And I'm sorry about being late."

Two remaining people to my left introduce themselves.

Meredith calmly and slowly looks around the round. I hear a few others shift in their seats. I think, *this silence is a little unnerving.*

Meredith's annunciation is deliberate and slow during her introduction of group meditation. "So there seems to be a lot of anxiety in the room today. One of the benefits of group meditation is getting to work on a shared focus. That shared focus often comes up organically when the group is together. Usually in the first class of the introductory course I start with a guided meditation inside this room. But today I am going to do something different. The energy from this group is bubbling up and I'm feeling like we need to be outside to release some of it. As I mentioned in the beginning, we will use this space in here and also the space on the side of this building in our practice together. We may also have a guest facilitator lead us in meditation using sound."

She pauses and looks slowly around the room again. I think to myself, *it's almost as if she is taking our energy temperature or something.* Meredith takes a steady deep breath and calmly instructs us to find a space outside with at least an arm's length apart.

I quickly walk outside because I want to make sure to get a spot in the back. I realize in that moment that ever since the rape,

I've been vigilant about limiting exposure to people behind me. It reminds me too much of being attacked from behind. I secure a space in the back corner. To my left is a tall, thick hedge with a sweet piney scent. Behind me are flowers, bushes and a small tree. The tree is fairly bare and the little branches are strong and pliable in the gentle breeze. I reminisce, *those branches remind me of Violet's little arms around me all those nights ago down south.* I instinctively feel calmer. I know she is with me in spirit from Europe.

Meredith stands facing us with her back to the side of the building we started in. "We are going to do movement[68] together to help dissolve some of the anxiety and ground us. There is not a right or wrong way to do these movements. We do not judge anyone for the way they move. If a movement ever feels too much or uncomfortable in any way, simply stop the movement and stand with your feet firmly on the ground and your arms resting by your side- or you could wrap your arms around you for a hug- and concentrate on your breath. Are there any questions before we begin?"

Everyone stands tense and stiff. No one says anything. A few slightly shake their heads.

Meredith nods. "O.K. let's start by focusing on our breath. As you inhale, I want you to feel your feet on the ground. Notice if one foot is more firmly planted or one part of your feet, like your heels. As you exhale, feel your toes. If you can, gently wiggle them." She is deliberate in looking at each person. "Good. Now adjust if you need to so that your weight is evenly distributed across both feet and try to stand on both feet so the whole foot is firmly planted on the ground. Continue to breathe. Now soften your knees so they

---

68 Meredith is a board certified Advanced Practice Psychiatric Mental Health Nurse Practitioner, certified Hakomi psychotherapist and trained in Mindfulness Based Stress Reduction, which inform her facilitation of meditation groups. For more information, please visit https://hakomica.org/ and https://www.umassmed.edu/cfm/mindfulness-based-programs/mbsr-courses/about-mbsr/

aren't locked. They are comfortably supporting your body. Great. Continue to focus on your breath. Good. Now, on your next exhale drop your shoulders gently down and feel your arms comfortably dangling from your body. They are soft and engaged in your movement. Stay here with your breath for a moment."

I fight the urge to look around to see if I am doing it right. I instruct myself, *breath in 1-2-3-4 and out 1-2-3-4-5-6-7-8.* I'm relieved that my breath is so calm. The sun's rays tingle against my skin. I say to myself, *like Grandma Ophelia's fingers rubbing my back.* A slight smile comes with the memory of the many nights she drew pictures on my back to help me fall asleep.

Meredith speaks again. "So now we are going to begin moving the anxious energy up and out of our body. This I call Dropping Leaves[69]. I'll demonstrate first and then we will do it together." She turns around so she faces the same direction as us. Over her shoulder she describes her movements as she does them.

"First, keep your feet planted like we did a moment ago. Turn your torso to the left and reach down with your arms to pick up a tree. Raise your arms as high as you can and then release your arms down with a burst of energy, like you are dropping the old dead leaves off the tree. Then turn towards the right and do the same movement." She demonstrates one more time. "As you drop the leaves, push the breath out of your mouth and if you want make a noise with it." She demonstrates the movement with a sharp exhale and gasp. She turns to face us again. "O.K. let's begin. We will start together but we do not have to do the movement at the same pace. Do it at your own pace and only go as high and low as you are comfortable going. Does that make sense? This is not about pushing yourself."

---

69 The names of these movements are based on my memory. They may not be exactly accurate. The descriptions of the actual movements are accurate. I practice these movements regularly and refer to them by the names in this chapter.

I inhale and twist towards the hedge. I imagine bending over to pick up a tree at the base of the trunk. I lift my arms up over my head. My voice says, *this tree is heavy. Is it supposed to be heavy?* I realize I'm holding my breath when my arms are extended as high as they can extend over my head. I let my breath out with a burst as I throw my arms down.

I continue to talk to myself throughout the movement. *Like am I really supposed to throw the whole tree? It feels like that's what I'm doing. But I thought I was supposed to just get rid of the dead leaves.* I turn towards my right to begin again. *O.K., this time it's more like I'm bending down to grab the tree and then shake it, so the dead leaves come off.* A small grunt escapes my lips as I collapse down. *O.K., maybe it's not about the damn tree and leaves. Because you don't shake a tree by collapsing around it.* I turn left again. *It's a large sprig of thyme. I start at the root and run my hands up with the leaves.* Slowly I inhale through my nose and my movement glides down and then up in a fluid motion. *And now pinch the sprig to go against the grain to release the ripe leaves.*

Continuing the fluid motion, I exhale sharply and drop my arms at the same time that my torso and knees release. My feet remain firmly on the ground. My movements continue in a fluid motion. I'm not sure how many thyme sprigs I cleared before Meredith instructs us to slow our movement and return to the initial standing pose.

"The next movement we will do is called Clearing The Clouds From The Chest." Meredith remains facing us. "For this movement, start by reaching one hand across the chest and opposite shoulder with palms open. When you reach as far past the shoulder as you are comfortable, close your fingers and sweep your arm back across your chest rolling your arm open so it extends out beyond your body. Turn your palm down and open your hand." She demonstrates continuously while she talks. "It's almost like you are pulling a curtain open across your chest. That is you grabbing the clouds around your Heart Chakra[70]. And then when you pull it as far from your body as possible, you offer it to the earth by releasing your fist so your heart can shine as the sun shines when the clouds part. Does that make sense?" I and a few others barely nod. "Good.

"O.K. like with the other movement, we will start together, but we don't have to go at the same pace. Go at your own pace and extend your movements as much as you are comfortable." She smiles. "I forgot the breath. As you move your arm across your body and grab the curtain you inhale. When you start pulling the curtain open, you begin to exhale and then when you open your palm to the earth you sharply exhale whatever breath is left. Work up towards that breath-movement coordination. O.K.? Let's begin."

My right arm reaches across my body toward my left shoulder. My palm turns towards my body. My inhale is too slow because my arm has to pause at my left shoulder to wait for the exhale to start before clearing the clouds away from my chest. My exhale is not long enough for my right arm to extend out from my body to release the clouds to the earth.

I wonder, *that's weird...the clouds going to the earth. Maybe it's supposed to be the rain from the clouds watering the earth.* Another voice questions, *maybe it isn't meant to be literal?* A small grin acknowledges the question. *Yes, my analytic mind is on.*

---

70 Chakra translates to wheel or disk in Sanskrit. The chakra system is historically connected to yoga, Ayurveda, Hinduism, Buddhism and other Eastern traditions. The number of chakras range from five to twelve depending on the tradition. Meredith's meditation practice was based on seven chakras, which is most common today. The seven chakras begin at the base of the spine and end at the top of the head. The first chakra relates to basic needs; second to creativity and sexuality; third to personal power; fourth to love and connection; fifth to verbal expression of our truth; sixth to our intuition or "third eye"; and seventh to enlightenment and spiritual connection. For more information, visit www. sacredcenters.com and https://chopra.com.

I begin the movement again with my left arm reaching across my chest to my right shoulder. My inhale matches the pace of my arm. I imagine gently pulling the soft fluffy clouds across my chest and away from my body. As I sharply exhale when my palm opens down, I imagine a burst of rain exiting my body. I observe, *interesting, my heart is stirring.* I smile at my heart as I begin the movement again.

My awareness startles when Meredith instructs us to slow our movement and return to standing pose. I say to myself, *I like that one. I feel lighter.*

"The next movement we are going to do is called Clearing The Rocks From The River." She begins to bend her arms at her elbows and extend her forearm and hands toward us. "You start by bending your arms like this. Do not raise your arms higher than your waist because we are clearing the rocks from around your waist and lower abdomen. Move your arms slowly out in front of your waist and then scoop your hands away from you almost like you are doing the breast stroke in a swimming pool." She demonstrates turning her hands away from each other and circling them in opposite directions around her body. "Once your arms are behind you as far as they can go, cup your hands and bring them forward near your waist to return to starting with your arms bent at your elbows."

She demonstrates the full movement again with her eyes closed. Her forearms face up and her hands are clinched in a fist. She slowly moves them in front of her as if she is pushing something away from her body. She turns her arms and cups her hands pushing them away from each other as they circle her lower torso. She returns to the starting position and opens her eyes.

Meredith smiles. "I forgot the breath again. This movement is slower and evenly paced. The breath mimics that pace. You inhale as you bring your forearms up and push your hands out in front of your body and you exhale as you circle your hands around your body and back to the starting position. If you are comfortable, try this one with your eyes closed. Also, pause your breath and the movement after each circle is complete. OK? Let's begin."

I close my eyes. I notice to myself, *wow such calm in my body.* I deliberately slow my arm movements to match the calm inhale of my breath. I describe the imagery that appears in my conscious. *The river water is cool and the rocks are smooth and round. Not too big, not too small.* My exhale naturally follows my cupped hands as I push the river rocks away from my torso and allow the cool water to surround me.

I exclaim, *ohhhhh! This one feels good!!! Like the creek at the cabin.* An image of Violet and me swimming in the creek around the island our dad constructed for us dances in my awareness. I tell myself, *I haven't thought of that in a long time.* Despite the cool water in my imaginary river, my body feels warm and safe.

These words suddenly pierce my mind: *It's cleansed and pure.* My eyebrows furrow and I involuntarily shake my head. I know my parts are activated.

A voice asks, *what's cleansed and pure? My body?*

My lower abdomen, near my reproductive organs tingles. I say to myself in awe, *wow. When was the last time I felt that part of my body?* I pause to take a full inhale and exhale in the starting position before starting the movement again. I wonder, *that voice- it's cleansed and pure- where does that voice come from? It is the same one that told me to put my phone down and tell my family about wanting to die.*

Meredith's gentle voice nudges me back to the present. "Begin to slow down and return to standing pose." She deliberately gazes at us from left to right. I am the last person on the right. She looks intently at me and smiles a reassuring smile.

I ask myself, *does she know what just happened?* I feel suddenly self-conscious and quickly look away.

"O.K. We are going to end our movement portion with a walking meditation. For those who have never done a walking meditation before, the idea is to walk slowly and with each step intentionally connect with the earth. So you want to feel the soles of your feet touch the ground with each step. Let your breath happen naturally. Let your gaze soften so you aren't focusing on any one thing. We will walk in a counterclockwise circle. When you get back to your original place, we have completed one circle and the person over there may begin leading the group back inside." She turns her gaze to the last person on the right in the front row directly opposite me.

I yell silently, *FUCK. I have to walk in 1.5 circles. Great. Slow walking never works for me. Remember the maze on the retreat?*

A voice corrects, *it's not a maze. It's a labyrinth.* I shake my head at the activated parts.

Mini Monster stands next to his hammock. He calls, *So much for being calm.*

I command, *pipe down you guys.* I turn towards my right and begin the walking meditation. I think, *this pace is so painfully slow.* I stumble to the right. I cuss, *shit. Now I'm losing my balance.* My gaze falls on pink flowers.

A shy voice observes, *those are pretty.*

I start instructing myself. Inhale. Step. Heel. Arch. Toe. Exhale. Step. Heel. Arch. Toe. I encourage, *O.K. I can do this.* Inhale. Step. Heel. Arch. Toe. Exhale. Step. Heel. Arch. Toe. I judge, *I'm going too fast. Hurry up person in front of me.* I pause to allow space between me and the person in front of me. I feel the person behind me abruptly stop. I cuss again. *Shit I'm fucking this up for everyone.* Inhale. Step. Heel. Arch. Toe. Exhale. Smaller step. Heel. Arch. Toe. Inhale. Small step. Heel. Arch. Toe.

A voice cheers, *it's working. Yay. Now one more lap to go.*

Mini Monster slumps down in exasperation. *That all happened in only half a lap. If only you could turn towards the building and go in now.*

I realize I am crossing the place where Meredith instructed the group member to go inside.

I whine to myself, *why-o-why did I have to pick being so far from the building?*

Travis appears sitting in his recliner with a newspaper on his lap. He gently commands, *just breathe. You will be fine. Stop being so dramatic. Be quiet all of you.*

Somehow I manage to breathe and step in pace with the group with only one more stumble. As soon as I reach the place to turn toward the building entrance, I increase my pace and step length. I exhale a sigh of relief. My spot on the couch seems to call my name. It envelops me as I settle in the corner of the armrest and back.

Mini Monster settles back on his hammock. *Thank God that's over.*

Meredith addresses the group after everyone sits down. "How was that?"

The question sits in the middle of the group. Meredith patiently waits for someone to talk.

My voice is urgent. *I will not fill the silence because I'm uncomfortable. Do not talk. Do not talk.*

A woman with light gray shoulder length hair sitting in a chair to my right begins to talk. "It was interesting. I haven't done that type of meditation before."

"What was interesting about it?" Meredith probes.

The woman replies, "I knew you'd ask me that." We chuckle. "I'm not sure. I felt like there was a lot going on. The movement, the breath, the environment, the group. There were moments when I felt like I got in a groove. But most of the time I could only concentrate on one thing, like my arms and then I'd forget the breathing part."

Several people giggle and nod.

Meredith smiles knowingly. "It seems you are not the only one who had that experience. And I can tell you from past groups, your description is very common when people first start out.

"I'd like to do a short, seated meditation in here before we wrap up. Please close your eyes. Or if you aren't comfortable closing your eyes, or you are afraid you will fall asleep, soften your gaze to a place on the floor a few feet in front of you." She looks slowly around the room. I quickly shut my eyes before she gets to me. "Good. Now focus on the breath. Inhale through your nose and exhale gently through your mouth. There are four parts to the breath because there are pauses between the inhale and exhale and again between the exhale and inhale. Simply notice those pauses without doing anything to them." After a few breaths she continues. "Feel the chair or couch that you are sitting in. Pay attention to where it touches you and doesn't touch you. Pay attention to how firmly it touches you in different places. If you can, on your next exhale, sink further into the couch or chair to really feel it supporting you." She pauses to give space for us to feel whatever we are sitting on. "Good. Now stay here focusing on your natural breath pattern. I will use the bell to let you know when to open your eyes."

I scan my body with my next inhale to see where tension lies. I note, *of course in the shoulders.* My shoulders drop a little lower with my exhale. I respond to myself, *oh that feels good. Why don't I do this more regularly throughout the day?*

I refocus on my breath. My inner voices fade. Colors begin to swirl behind my eyes. Infinite darkness surrounds the peripheral. I am floating. My head nods forward before jerking up. I hear myself, *shit did I just fall asleep? I wonder if she saw me.* I refocus on my breath. Again colors swirl behind my eyes. I am not sure how much time passes. I'm not sure if I actually did fall asleep. I hear the bell. The sound gets closer. Meredith's voice instructs us to open our eyes when the sound stops. The sound fades. I open my eyes. My vision is blurry. I feel calm.

Meredith's voice is soft and breathy, unlike when we began. "How wonderful was that? The energy in the room has changed. Do you feel it?" She slowly exhales and gazes around the room. A few group members nod. A gentle smile dances on Meredith's lips. "Great. What happened for you?"

A few shuffle in their seats and avoid eye contact. The same woman who started our last share out says, "I'll start again if that's O.K. I don't want to take over air time if anyone else wants to start." Every head shakes. "I was thinking it would be easier than the movements. But I was wrong. I had a hard time focusing in here. It was…almost like it was too quiet and I heard every single noise. Then I'd forget the breath. Overall I was distracted." She looked uncomfortable while she shared her experience.

I observe, *interesting that she almost looks opposite the way Meredith described our calm energy.*

Meredith makes a similar observation. "So you aren't as calm as I felt in the energy? That's O.K. What happened for others?"

I raise my right arm slightly.

Meredith turns to me. "Do you want to share?"

"Sure." My voice is timid.

Inner Critic's sharp voice appears in my mind. *Where is that timid voice coming from? You always share in groups.*

I clear my throat and sit up taller. "The walking meditation was really hard for me. I kept falling out of balance and it seemed to take forever. The other movements took a minute to get settled, but I feel like I found a flow. Like the other movements and the one in here. I see a lot of colors when I meditate. So I got a light show in here. It was pretty." My gaze settles on Meredith.

Her eyes narrow on mine ever so slightly before turning to the group, almost as if she attempts to see in my soul. I ask myself, *am I reading into her interactions?*

Meredith's breathy voice responds to my description. "So you've done some meditating before and you see colors. The walking meditation can be hard. Especially if everything in your life is fast paced." My head nods before I can stop it. "Yeah, that is common for busy people. You might practice walking at a slower pace throughout your day. And also focusing on your steps and feet connecting with the ground when you walk. Like when you are at the grocery store."

My head nods again.

Inner Critic criticizes, *damn, why are you confirming her statements? She wants you to do that so she can feel good.* I smile at Meredith. *Hopefully she can't read your mind because she will know you are judging her.*

I yell, *be quiet all of you!*

377

A few other group members share about feeling calmer. One shares about struggling with perfection. I can't concentrate on anything other than my desire to leave that small packed room.

A voice observes, *it has been over an hour.*

I can't stop looking at the clock next to Meredith. Finally she says we are done and confirms who plans to attend next week. I say I'll be there even as the excuses for missing the class pop in my thoughts.

I hurriedly grab my big purse and wrap my sweater tight around me. Everyone seems to be chitchatting. With my head down, I beeline for the door. As soon as the cool air hits me, a calm wave washes over me. I think of the thyme sprigs, clearing clouds, river rocks, the color show and stumbles. By the time I reach my car, I want to try the group again.

I tell myself, *maybe I read into Meredith's stare. She wasn't trying to impose herself in my soul.* I turn my car on and begin to pull away from the curb. Two group members chat in front of the house. They wave to me. I observe, *so friendly. I will come back.*

My drive home is uneventful. I pull into my parking space in the carport. I tell myself, *O.K. I will try to walk meditate to my front door.* Instead of racing to my front door, I focus on my breath. I walk slower than normal, but not slow. I feel the ground under my feet. I hear the leaves of the ivy wrestling in the breeze. I ask myself, *why don't I do this more often? Look at the purple flowers. So pretty.*

I manage to keep the slower pace until I'm half way to my front door. A car door slams. My shoulders shoot up and the hair on my neck bristles.

I see Mini Monster jumping up and down next to his hammock. *What if someone is coming to get you? You won't be able to defend yourself walking this slowly.*

My breath quickens. My heart rate increases.

Travis stands tall and looks at me intently. *Get to your front door.*

I clutch my purse tighter. My stride widens. Next thing I know I'm inside my apartment.

Mini Monster slumps back on his hammock. *Thank God you made it inside. Whoever slammed that car door did so with such conviction. They were maybe going to come after you.*

My hand finds the door knob and lock.

Travis reassures, *yes, you locked the door.*

I slowly walk into the living room. I turn the fireplace on. My shoulders begin to settle down. The hair on the back of my neck calms down. My breath and heart rate return to normal. I say to myself, *phew, that felt like a panic attack coming on.* I arrange my pillows and blankets on the floor in front of the fireplace. I settle into my pillow fort and watch the fire dance with the shadows. At some point I fall into a peaceful sleep.

Reflections ∞ Reactions ∞ Responses

_____

_____

_____

CHAPTER 32

COLLATERAL SESSION
WITH DAD PART 1

The following Sunday, my phone buzzes. The notification reads Dad iMessage.

Dad: Dr. A, what time are we meeting Jen today? Do you want to meet there? Where is there?

I smile and shake my head. I say out loud, "Oh Charlie…we went over this yesterday."

I text back the information he requested. He responds with the thumbs up emoji.

I look at the clock. I say to myself, *hmmm it is 11. I have just enough time to go for a jog, get ready, eat and go. Do I really want to jog?* I haven't gone for a jog in a long time. I started having anxiety when I jog.

The sun filters through the blinds into my living room. I open the blinds and slider. Warmth hits my face. My body tingles. I want so badly to go for a jog like I used to. Hurriedly I change from my pajamas to my running clothes. I grab my phone and earbuds. Music starts playing as I begin running down the parking lot to the street.

I wonder, *which direction should I go?* I look right towards the community college then left towards the nursing home.

A voice instructs, *run uphill first.*

I take a deep breath and turn left up the hill toward the nursing home. My gaze softens and the music fills my body. I focus on counting my breath. In-2-3. Out-2-3. After 20 yards running uphill my breath count increases to In-2. Out-2. I repeat, *two in. Two out.*

A voice asks, *when was the last time you ran?* I can't remember.

I notice, *my legs are burning. My chest feels on fire.*

Mini Monster chimes in, *maybe you should stop?*

I look up to see the top of the hill.

Travis commands, *no, don't stop. You've made it up this hill before. You can do it. Breathe.*

My jaw clenches. My fists tighten. I think of the little engine that could. I repeat the words that helped get the little caboose up the hill in the popular children's book. *I think I can I think I can. Chug Chug. Get up the hill. Step Step Step Step. Breathe 1-2. Breathe 1-2. Go. Go. Go.*

Somehow I make it to the top. My lungs feel like they are about to explode. My mind floods with images of my rape, past panic attacks, my dead body outline on the cement. In rapid succession I am drawn down a rabbit hole of horrible images.

My voice and my parts' voices mix together. *Where did all this come from? Get it together. You like running. You've done this a million times. Seriously. Look at the trees. Feel the air. See the sunshine.* I let my legs carry me down the hill. *Remember the mattress on the street down there? That was scary. There are so many woods. If you are taken no one will hear you scream.*

I shake my head and increase my pace. I turn right up another small hill.

Travis flickers through my mind. *Get to the top of the hill and you will be saved.* The hill is a back entrance to the community college. *Then you can cut through by the track and get back home.*

I'm not sure how much time passed when I turn the lock on my front door. The door closes harder than I intend and the walls shake. I say, *sorry neighbors.*

I quickly get water and lie on the floor in front of the slider. The sun's warmth dances on my skin. My heart rate slows. I close my eyes. My hands are on my stomach. I feel its rise and fall with each breath. I ask myself, *where did that come from?* The same images that flooded my mind at the start of my jog, filter through again only slower this time. I question with urgency, *why am I having flashbacks? Running used to be a calming tool for me. It helped me.*

I sigh and say out loud, "Not anymore."

Sadness fills my heart. My eyes are heavy with tiredness. I peel myself off the floor to get ready for the session with Jennifer and Dad. I force myself to take a quick shower even though I want to crawl into bed. I say to myself, *I wish I was meeting alone with Jennifer.*

I drive on autopilot to our session. I recall my conversation with Lindsey explaining why I'm meeting with dad first and not both of them. Dad worried that she would feel left out.

I wonder to myself, *we are always doing things, apologizing for things that aren't necessary. Like why do I have to apologize for needing to spend time with just my dad?* Anger begins brewing under my sadness. I begin to ruminate. *It has always been that way.*

I need XYZ, but XYZ doesn't put everyone else first, so it is wrong. It is bad. Why can't he just be O.K. with putting our need to spend time with him first? I know Lindsey gets it. She wasn't mad. I shake my head. I tell my thoughts, *stop. You can talk about it all with Jennifer.*

I pull into the parking lot and drive to the end. I don't see Dad's car there yet.

I think, *maybe he is late. Good I can talk to Jennifer first.*

As soon as I open my car door, I hear Dad's voice in the distance shout "Dr. A." I look around. Dad waves both arms in the air as if he is directing an airplane into a gate. I wave back. He is on the upper lot.

I think, *no wonder I didn't see his car. So much for talking with Jennifer first.*

He walks towards the steps to come down to the same parking level. I fight the urge to turn and run into Jennifer's office to get a few moments alone with her.

"Hi, Dad," I shout. "What are you doing up there?"

"I couldn't figure out how to get to this level," he shouts back.

I smile at him even though he is too far to see it. "Ohhh. Yeah the entrance is over there." I point to the left. I see him nod.

Once he reaches me, we walk together down the stairs to street level.

He asks, "How's your day so far honey?"

"It's pretty good," I lie. "How is yours?"

"Oh good." He continues with a chipper voice. "The usual. Woke up. Had my lemon water. Took a dump. Ate breakfast. Got ready and came here."

"Sounds about right." I try to mimic his chipper voice. "How was the drive over?"

"Oh fine," he responds. "No traffic. It is Sunday."

We cross the street. I point to the sign above the door to the space where we meet. "She works out of there. It is a yoga space. Well, workout space."

"That's different." He sounds skeptical.

Pansy paws the glass at the door.

I turn quickly towards Dad. "I forgot to tell you about Pansy. I hope it's O.K. that she is here."

"You've mentioned Pansy before. It is no problem. I just won't touch her." Dad makes a face.

I giggle. "Yes, I know germs aren't for you. Remember when we were going to get you a dog at your old house? So you could have a buddy while you walked around the deck in your blue robe each morning."

"Oh yes!" he exclaims. "That would have been not a good idea. I can't stand germs."

Jennifer unlocks the door. She greets us warmly.

"Dad, you can take your shoes off if you want and leave them here." I kick my flip flops off under the chair where I set my purse.

"Ahhhh," he grunts as he sits down. "O.K. I just have to untie them."

I notice how labored he is while untying his shoes. I say to myself, *that's weird. I've never noticed that before. He's getting older.*

Jennifer gestures towards the middle of the room. "I put down blankets and pillows. We usually sit on the ground. I could get you a chair if you prefer."

Dad looks up to scope out the seating arrangement. "Uhhhhh. Yeah, actually I'll take you up on that. Here we can bring this chair over." He stands and turns around to pick up the chair he was sitting on.

Jennifer steps towards him hurriedly. "I can grab it if you want."

"No, I have it. It is pretty light." He begins walking towards the blankets and pillows that Jennifer set up.

I sit down on the floor and kick my feet over a bolster. I adjust it so it is under my knees. Dad sits down.

Jennifer asks, "Do you want a bolster for your feet, Charlie?"

"Ummm," Dad ponders her question. "Yes, that would actually be really nice."

I give him my bolster from under my knees.

Jennifer turns to me. "Are you O.K. with that? Do you want a different bolster?"

I shake my head no. "It wasn't that comfortable actually."

"Oh, O.K." Her gaze zeros in on me for a brief moment. "Are you sure?"

"Yes," I confirm. "I'll take another blanket though."

She hands me a blanket that is next to her. I fold it twice so it is higher and put it under my knees.

I look at her and smile. "That's better. It isn't so high."

"O.K.," she says. "Let's begin shall we?" Dad and I nod. "Great. Thank you both for being here. Charlie, is it O.K. that I call you by your first name?"

Jennifer looks up to where he is sitting. I fight the urge to roll my eyes. She hasn't asked that of anyone else. Must be a tool she uses with fathers to give them a sense of power.

I say to myself with mild repulsion, *patriarchy. And he is sitting in his chair, as if it is a throne and we are on the floor. Typical.*

"You know, thanks for asking," he responds. "Charlie is fine."

"O.K. great. I always ask fathers because you never know in families how they want to be called." She looks at me and raises her eyebrows. "Do you want to share a little about why we decided to have him come in first?"

My mind goes blank. "To be honest, I can't really remember. Can you?"

A puzzled expression briefly crosses her face.

I say to myself, *she can tell I'm off.* I flash my best calm-cool-collected smile.

"Anna is there anything you want to talk about before we get started? Do you want to meet with just me for a moment? Your dad can wait outside."

A voice says, *damn, she is good.*

"No, I'm ready to start with Dad."

She pauses as if to say silently "are you sure?"

I nod. "Really. I'm O.K."

She turns towards Dad. "O.K. So Charlie, we thought it would be good for you to come by yourself without Lindsey because there are some things from Anna's childhood that happened before Lindsey came into your lives that are important to discuss."

"Yeah yeah. That is all fine and good," Dad interrupts.

"O.K.," Jennifer says. "Anna, do you want to talk about those things?"

"Well, yes." I begin slowly. "I think the biggest one is that I want us to find a way to connect that doesn't involve drinking and your friends, like when we sculpted together and you made me a flower after making the dog peeing on the fire hydrant." He chuckles and nods. "Growing up was so unpredictable. You were drunk and high and your mood changed. It was like walking on egg shells. And you really objectified women in front of me and Violet. I got a lot of mixed signals about what it means to be a woman in this society. Be independent. Don't be needy. Take care of yourself. Look hot. Be sexy. Let the man be in charge. It was all so confusing.

"And then there were really great times where I felt very connected to you. Like when you came to help me with the furniture for my condo. We had so much fun driving down the freeway with the double chair strapped to the roof. But that side of you only consistently comes out when you are alone. The problem is you don't ever want to do things with just me and Violet. You always feel like you are leaving everyone else out. Like your friends and Lindsey. And then there is the whole you have a family business and excluded family from it. Violet and I weren't ever considered since we have vaginas. But you let Lindsey in. I mean what is that all about?"

Jennifer interrupts me. "May I stop you for a moment, Anna?" I nod. "You summarized nicely all of the points we talked about. I want to make sure your Dad gets why he is here. Like how all that fits into your treatment for PTSD. Is that O.K.?"

Dad seems perturbed. "Yes, that would be great!" he exclaims. "I mean, Anna and I went to a counselor when she was in high school. It was basically bash dad sessions. I think it helped her, but I'm not sure it helped overall. I want to help Anna with whatever she is going through now."

Jennifer nods. "Yes, I thought you were hearing 'bash dad' as Anna talked." She turns to me, "Not that that was what you were doing, Anna. You were summarizing why we wanted time with just your dad and you before meeting with Lindsey."

I nod in agreement.

Jennifer turns to Dad. "O.K., so, Charlie, as you may or may not know, Anna has experienced what we call capital T traumas in her life both as an adult and in her childhood. Do you know what I mean by capital T trauma?"

He shakes his head. "No I haven't heard that before."

"O.K., that's O.K.," Jennifer reassures. "Capital T traumas are those significant big traumas that leave a lasting mark on someone. For instance, witnessing violence, fighting in a war, fearing for one's life like in a category 4 or 5 hurricane. Lowercase t traumas are those that are more common. For instance, when you were little and fell off your bike when you were trying to learn how to ride it. You probably scraped your knee, and maybe even broke a bone. But most of the time, that type of trauma is normalized and is not life threatening. Does that make sense?"

"Yes." He focuses his gaze on her. "Let me see if I can say it back to you. When I was little, Anna's heard this story before, when I was little, I was scooting along on my skateboard and hit a crack in the side walk. The skateboard stopped and I kept going until my chin stopped me on the pavement. I have a scar from the stitches I got from that." He rubs under his chin. "That would be a lowercase

t. My dad, on the other hand, he fought in World War II. He didn't talk about it much, but at the end of his life I got this life coach interviewer lady who recorded him talking about his life. He opened up to her that he stepped on a landmine and it didn't blow up until a few guys behind him because it was frozen. It blew up guys in his crew. He actually teared up when he was telling her. I'd never seen him cry before. Even when Mom died. He just holed up in his room. In fact, I had to handle everything related to Mom's death."

"Wow," Jennifer says. "Yes, you understand the different types of traumas. When did your mom die?"

I chime in. "November, 1979. I was an infant. The only grandchild she ever knew."

"Yes, right, Anna," Dad affirms. "My dad was hunting. I had to call all of the hospitals in the area because she didn't come home the night before. I finally found her at a hospital we never went to. We still don't know why she went there. I had to go identify the body. Dad was out of range. The sheriff had to drive into the hunting club to get him. I was sitting on the front porch with my sisters when he got home. He didn't say a word. He just stepped over us and went to his bedroom. He didn't say I'm sorry, or thank you. I had to organize the funeral services. He was absent. Silent. Which was typical. I don't remember a lot from that time. Anna was just a baby. It was a hard time." Dad stares off into space.

"So, Charlie, you have experienced capital T traumas," Jennifer states matter-of-factly. "The loss of a parent. Her death was sudden and unexpected. And you saw her body."

"Yes," Dad says. "As the first born and only son, it was my job I guess. Especially in my dad's absence. Who else would do it?"

"How do you think that impacted your ability to be a father, a parent, to Anna?" Jennifer redirects the conversation to me.

He pauses and looks directly at Jennifer again. "That is a good question, Jennifer. I wasn't around much. I mean with my business, I had a new business that took me on the road six months a year. Dealing with Mom's death. Honestly, I buried it once it was all over. I buried it in work. Anna and her sister Violet were never shy to tell me I was a work-a-holic. They were right. Shoot. They are still right. I've been trying to retire for years now. And I just can't seem to unwind from everything."

"You were also drinking and doing drugs." My voice is flat. "When did you start using cocaine? Wasn't it around that time?"

He shifts in his seat to look at me. "Yes, it was around that time." He turns back towards Jennifer. "In our industry, we all started making big money at the same time. It was the 80s. Cocaine was big. I remember having lunch meetings and doing lines to seal the deal." He turns back towards me. "One time, it was your mom's birthday, I was down the valley in a wine cellar all afternoon. Your mom was home with you and your sister. We were hootin' and hollerin'. All your mom wanted was to go out to dinner with me. She was stuck home with you girls all day and night. And I was so fucked up that I couldn't get home, so I radioed my field manager and asked him to pick up a bouquet of flowers and take it to her. Back in those days, we had 2-way radios. That's just like what we did." He shrugs his shoulders. "Looking back, it wasn't right."

"So, Charlie," Jennifer begins gingerly. "I have to share some information about children growing up in homes with drugs and alcohol. Is that O.K. if I pause and do that for a moment?"

"Sure," he says. "But before you do, let me just say that I know it is really bad. Melanie, Anna's mom, did an intervention with some of our family and friends way back then. There was a counselor there. I did an outpatient program and AA. I took a self-esteem class. We were involved in a retreat program that focused on healthy relationships and feeling good about yourself. I was involved in the leadership of it."

"Oh, O.K.," she hesitates. "So, you understand that growing up in unpredictable environments where drugs and alcohol are present is difficult for children. That is also considered a capital T trauma."

Silence descends on the room. I look up at dad. His eyebrows are raised, almost like a deer caught in headlights.

"Oh," he says quietly. "I never saw it that way. Like my dad being in World War II?"

Jennifer continues gently. "Yes. Like instead of an actual landmine, Anna and her sister and Melanie never new when you would be triggered or what mood you would be in. Children who grow up in those environments are also trapped. They don't have the maturity or resources to get out of those situations. Further, parents are in charge of them and are supposed to keep them safe. So when one parent is drunk and high and the other parent is trying to keep it together, the children are often trapped in a confusing and unsafe environment that they can't escape. Does that make sense?"

Silence settles around us again.

Jennifer turns to me. "How is it hearing this right now? I know you know this from your training, but how is it hearing it about yourself?"

I take a deep breath. "Honestly, it is validating. The overwhelming feeling associated with my childhood for me is fear. I remember hiding in the bathroom, distracting Violet, crying under the covers. I had a recurring dream that rescue guys in helicopters, like on ladders, came to get me and Violet out of our bedroom window at night. I remember the night my cousin's head was cracked open. I remember Dad telling me he was going to leave and never come back because I told Mom and my aunt that my cousin was bleeding. I remember Dad sitting on the fireplace in the corner near the heater in a light blue polo and pastel plaid shorts looking ashamed and exhausted. I remember Dad stepping over me after putting Violet's contact lens in. I remember Mom pouring orange juice into our Cheerios because she was absent from her body. I was scared and confused most of the time. And I couldn't leave. Well, I ran away to the corner a lot."

"To the corner?" Jennifer raises her eyebrows.

"Yes, there was a cul-da-sac a few driveways down from ours and I would pack my jelly bag with a blanket and stuffed animals and go sit on the corner."

"So you tried to run away?" she asks.

"I guess you could say that," I say. "I'm not sure I ever really thought I'd run away. I just wanted to leave."

She turns her attention to Dad. "What is it like for you to hear this?"

He takes a deep breath and starts to talk, but closes his mouth before words come out. He shifts in his seat. He looks at me. "Honey, I am sorry. I guess I never saw it from this perspective. My parents were always drinking. I didn't really see anything wrong with it. But you are right Jennifer, it was very unsafe. I couldn't be counted on and Melanie did her best with the situation."

Jennifer continues to describe capital T traumas in relation to me. "So, for Anna, she experienced capital T traumas in childhood and in early adulthood with her rape. She also experienced lower case t traumas. We call this complex trauma. It actually changed her brain. Her flight-fight-freeze response was activated so much that it became her normal. Does that make sense?"

Dad nods. "Fight or flight. I've heard that. But what is freeze?"

"Good question." Jennifer smiles in affirmation. "So, our primitive brain, which is located back here." She places her hand on the back of her head. "This is where we deal with threats to our survival. Fight and flight are most commonly known. You either fight your threat or run from your threat. Freeze is like the opossum who plays dead. You freeze, almost like temporary paralysis."

"Oh, O.K. I get it now," Dad says.

"O.K., good." Jennifer encourages, "Please stop me to ask any questions. That is really good. So back to Anna. She and I have been working on re-wiring her brain so that her executive brain is in charge. The executive brain is up here." Jennifer places her hand on her forehead. "It is the place where we think, problem solve, our rational brain. When fight-flight-freeze kicks on, the executive brain automatically shuts down. Think about if a bear was attacking you and you were like 'wait bear, I have to figure out the best way to solve this problem' the bear would get you before you had time to finish the sentence. So this on-off switch serves an important purpose to our survival. But the problem for Anna is that she can't tell what a real threat to her life is and what is not. To over simplify, everything and everyone are threats. She didn't learn how to decipher real and perceived threats. So she didn't learn how to keep herself safe. We are working on those things in her. I've just said a lot."

She stops talking. Silence settles in once again. A wave of relief washes over me. I'm speechless. Her description so clearly connected safety, my brain, my childhood, addiction, the rape.

I take a deep breath before sharing what is happening for me at this moment. As soon as I begin to talk, tears collect in my lower lids. "Wow. I've never heard it so succinctly put Jennifer. I'm not sure what to say. Thank you. I learned something just now. Well, not something new about how all of it connects. I knew that from my school and professional work. But I am aware of how I have been impacted by it. I always felt a connection between everything, but honestly wasn't aware of what the connection was."

"Oh, honey." Dad points out, "You're welling up. What's going on with the tears?"

Jennifer jumps in before I can answer. "Do you want to share about where your tears are coming from?"

"They are in my chest and shoulders," I describe. "I'm sorry Dad. I hope it doesn't hurt you. But it feels so relieving and so good to hear Jennifer normalize my experiences. I've been so confused for so long about how it all fits together. But as a child I couldn't escape it. I was trapped. Then as a victim I couldn't escape it either. I mean I was raped when I was passed out. I was trapped. It was unpredictable. There are many connections to the feelings. Not that you are responsible or to blame for my rape. That was only one person's fault. But maybe knowing I was pre-disposed to fight-flight-freeze helps to understand why that night shot my survival brain into overdrive."

"That's O.K., honey," Dad says calmly. "You don't have to apologize. I don't feel like you are blaming me. It has been good learning today for me, too. I'm sorry I didn't realize any of this sooner."

Jennifer glances at her watch. "Unfortunately, we are at the end of our time. We covered a lot today. It seems there are still topics to go into. Would you both be interested in doing another session with the 2 of you before we bring Lindsey in?"

"Sure," I say. "I agree there is still more to do. Maybe next time we can do one and a half hours or two? What do you think Dad?"

"Yeah, O.K." Dad pauses for a moment. "I think one hour is good for me, though. I don't really have a good attention span."

"O.K., Sure," Jennifer and I say simultaneously.

We stand and walk over to our shoes. I slip on my flip flops while pulling out my check book.

"I think we went over a little bit. Is it still $125?" I ask Jennifer.

"Actually, it is $150 for collateral sessions, remember?" she clarifies. "And, no, don't worry about the little time we went over."

Dad watches me write her a check. He shifts uncomfortably in his seat and grunts as he lifts his foot onto his knee to tie his shoe.

"Honey," he says between grunts. "Let me know if you want me to pitch in for these sessions. I'm happy to do it."

"Thanks Dad, but no. I have it covered." I sign the check, tear it off and hand it to Jennifer. "So does next Sunday work for both of you?"

Jennifer nods. "Same time?"

Dad pulls out his phone. "Uh, let me see." He scrolls to his calendar. "Yes, it looks like we are in town. Let's plan on it, but I have to check with Lindsey. She is the keeper of our schedule."

I fight another eye roll. "Yes, same time. If Dad can't come, I will still come. Does that work?"

She nods. Pansy comes out from under a chair with her chew toy.

"Hi, Pansy." I bend down to pet her. "You've been quiet this session." I pet her back briefly before she saunters away.

We say goodbye to Jennifer.

"So what are you doing the rest of the day?" Dad asks once we cross the street.

"Nothing. Just getting ready for the week. I am traveling this week." I pause to decide if I want to tell him about online dating.

"You know I joined Match? The dating website. I'll probably do something with that."

"No, I didn't know that. Good for you, honey."

"Yeah. It has been fun. I'm not looking for anything serious. Just looking for a social life. In fact I'm talking with guys across the state. I figure I travel so much for work, that maybe I can make friends in the places I go most frequently."

"That sounds great." We stop by my car. "Thanks for this honey. Let me know if I can help pay for it."

"I will." I look at him. I am struck by how young and old he looks at the same time. "Thank you for coming. I know it isn't easy. And I mean what I said. I don't blame you for any of it. We all did the best we could, you included. I really appreciate you helping me now."

He gives me a hug. "Of course, honey. Anything I can do."

I watch him walk towards the stairs up to his parking level. I say to myself, *he looks so young and fragile, yet old and tired all at once. I wonder if any of that stuff Jennifer said will sink in and stick.* I drive home feeling hopeful.

Reflections ∞ Reactions ∞ Responses

_____

_____

_____

CHAPTER 33

EDUCATED GUESS, GOLETA
& GREY'S ANATOMY

I ask myself, *what day is it?* I am driving home from a work trip in northern California.

Critic's voice pierces my conscious. *Duh, it's Thursday.*

The setting sun blinds me as I drive west.

I respond, *oh, yeah! Grey's Anatomy is on tonight. And Scandal. That Shonda Rhimes. Love my Thursdays with Shonda. I wonder if Camille is going to watch Grey's.* Camille is my friend from the mental health retreat. We share an affinity for Shonda Rhimes and especially Grey's Anatomy. Shonda's leads are strong women and she explores love, relationships, sexism and dismantling systems of oppression in addition to simply providing drama entertainment. Camille and I have watched every single episode of Grey's Anatomy and Scandal. During graduate school, Catherine and I watched it every week. It was our beacon of escape from schoolwork.

My mind wanders to other topics. *Maybe I'll check in on Match. Maybe I'll take tomorrow off.*

The closer I am to home, the deeper the exhaustion settles into my bones from a heavily scheduled work trip. The last 45 minutes of my drive flies by. Next thing I know I am inside my apartment. I open the refrigerator. Not sure what I expect to see in here because it is empty. I pull out leftovers from last weekend that have a subtle putrid scent wafting out the lid.

Mini Monster looks up from the hammock with alarm. *Gross.*

I grab my keys and head back to my car. Whole Foods is my kitchen away from kitchen. Per usual the parking lot is a cluster fuck. I park several rows away from the entrance to avoid angry, tired drivers fighting over closer parking spots. Once inside, I wander through the prepared foods section.

I think to myself, *hmmm...do I want pizza? A salad? Burrito?* Nothing sounds good. I walk by the hot foods section. I read the buffet signs to myself, *bar-b-que chicken, mashed potatoes, steamed veggies.* I could get my mind around that.

A voice asks, *what about those yummy meatballs in the chilled section? You could make a meatball sub with the single served rolls and pair it with a salad.*

I like that idea. I grab the meatballs from the refrigerated section, make a salad, and select the perfect roll.

I think, *hmmmm...maybe some wine tonight?* I turn towards the wine section. *Red to go with the meatballs.*

Usually I select Chardonnay or Pinot Noir. Tonight I look at the Cabernet Sauvignons. There are so many to choose from. My eyes scan the second to bottom shelf, which is my usual price point. I notice sale tags hanging on the shelf under most bottles. They must be having a wine sale. My eyes travel up to the top two shelves.

I think to myself with slight annoyance, *ugh. I've never heard of any of these wines.* I continue to scan the bottles.

Educated Guess almost jumps off the shelf. I exclaim to myself, *that's perfect! All I ever do is make an educated guess on which bottle to choose.*

I reach for the bottle and turn towards check out. The 10-items-or-less line moves fast. Fortunately there is a lull in cars exiting the parking lot.

I am home in pajamas on my couch 15 minutes later. The fireplace is on even though it is May. Grey's Anatomy's episode before the season finale will start soon.

I say to myself, *I think Derek dies in this one.*

The meatballs are warming on the stove and the bread roll is toasting under the broiler. I turn on my computer and take a bite of salad while it boots up. The timer beeps for the meatballs and bread. I set my salad box on the coffee table. The ABC announcer's voice booms from the television, "Grey's Anatomy starts now."

I pause the TV and think, *thank God for DVR.*

I decide to call Catherine even though I doubt she will be able to answer because it is a school and work night for her and her family. Her voicemail picks up. "Hi Catherine. So, I'm watching Grey's. Yes, I know it has been forever since the days when we mimicked Cristina and Meredith dancing it out with tequila. Oh, those days. And yes, you are still my person. I miss you and I'm sorry I haven't been able to connect. Anyway, call me back. Love you and your kids and hubs."

I assemble my meatball sub, open the Educated Guess bottle and pour a hearty glass. I curse as I struggle to pull a paper towel off the roll with one hand. Three pieces come off the roll. I roll my eyes and say out loud "Whatever."

I set the plate and glass on the coffee table and sit back down on the couch. I enter my password to access the home screen on my computer and hit play on the remote. Meredith Grey's voice fills my living room. The meatballs are steaming. I take a sip of wine. I exclaim to myself, *Wow! That's really good. Educated Guess pays off. Thank you, sale!*

Derek is dead. My inner commentary continues. *Oh man. I forgot this was happening tonight.* I see Meredith wandering through the hospital, a blank stare plastered on her face. She walks outside and screams. Tears begin to pour down my cheeks. I take a bite of my meatball sub and wash it down with another sip of Educated Guess. Catherine and Richard are planning their wedding at Meredith and Derek's house. I think about everything Meredith and Derek have gone through. They really fought for love. They matured together. They worked through the tough times and got to this point. *I can't believe he's dead.* I forget my computer and Match. I feel nostalgic for Catherine, my grad school friend who watched Grey's religiously with me from 2003 to 2005. Back then Meredith and Cristina were each other's person. Any issue they were confronted with, they danced it out with tequila. *Life was so much simpler back then for me and for Meredith.*

After Grey's Anatomy ends, I turn my attention to my computer. As it wakes up from sleep mode, I put my plate in the sink, throw away the salad box, and pour a third glass of wine. I say to myself, *this wine is seriously so good.*

I grab a bottle of water on my way back to the couch. The fireplace is still on. Scandal started on TV while I was in the kitchen. I enter my password and click on Google Chrome. I click on my bookmarks and scroll to Match Log-in. I enter my username and password and take a sip of wine while my account loads. I have a handful of messages from potentials in Southern California, Silicon Valley and San Francisco. SexyBigGuy69 messaged again. I note to myself, *I'm not sure why since I never opened the first message.* The guy from Goleta responded to my last message. He wants to talk on the phone. I wonder to myself, *hmmm. Am I ready for that?* I open another message from a different guy in San Jose. I say to myself, *he seems really sweet.* He asks if I want to meet for dinner some time. I ask myself with uncertainty, *whoa...am I ready for that?* The guy from the Inland Empire wrote a flirty message and let me know he will be out of town this weekend in case I write back and he doesn't respond. I pause. My gaze lands on the fire. I take a sip of wine. I ask myself, *am I ready to begin meeting people?* The flames dance and change colors. There must be a draft coming through the house.

I decide to smoke a cigarette. My smoking fleece is in my room. I put it on and grab a lighter out of my purse. I top off my wine glass. Outside the air is cool. Most of my neighbors' blinds are closed with the lights out. I sit on the patio couch and light my cigarette.

I continue to talk to myself about Match. *I guess I could meet people. They all seem nice and friendly.*

A voice asks, *but are you ready? Do you really want to do this?*

I inhale deeply and lie back on the couch. The smoke swirls are back lit by the parking lot lamp. I watch it disappear.

Another voice answers, *fuck it. Just do it. If something doesn't feel right you can just leave or stop talking or whatever. It's not like you are going to marry any of these people. It is just for fun.*

I finish my cigarette and put it out in the ashtray I keep under the patio couch. I don't want Mom, or anyone in the family for that matter, knowing that I'm smoking again.

Back inside, I top off my wine glass again and sit in front of my computer. I agree to meet San Jose guy for dinner and suggest next Thursday since I will be up that way for work. I message Goleta my phone number. I wish Inland Empire a safe and fun trip this weekend.

A few new guys winked at me. I review their profiles using my carefully designed protocol. First I review their pictures. If I get a good vibe from those, I scroll down to review their education, income, desire for kids and marital status. If they have at least a bachelor's degree, make the same amount as me or more, want kids and are anything but separated for relationship status, I read their entire profile. If I find it interesting, I wink back. If I find it interesting and am curious about something, I write a message. Tonight none made it past the second step. A few don't want kids and one is separated.

I sigh and finish the wine in my glass. I feel a slight buzz. I think, *perfect time for sleep. Maybe I can do the book ending thing Jennifer suggested. Or I could do my coping card.*

I pour the remaining wine into my glass and walk to my home office. A stack of pink, green, blue and yellow index cards are in the top drawer of my desk. I pick pink and reach for a pen. I need to pee. I set my wine glass, pink index card and pen on the bathroom counter. The night light lets off a dim soft hue. I decide not to turn on the overhead light.

I turn on the water to wash my hands and look at myself in the mirror. Eye contact is easier now.

A voice observes, *you still seem sad and tired. But so much better than before.*

The voice startles me. I sigh again and dry my hands. I tell the voice, *I'm lonely.*

I collect the items from the counter and walk back to the living room. I turn off the TV and spread a blanket on the ground in front of the fireplace. I settle in on my stomach and begin to write. The ink won't come out.

I say to myself, *ugh I need something hard to write on.* I crawl over to the coffee table. *Ugh again. No magazines.* I get up and walk to the shelf behind my dining room table. The Giada cookbook will do.

My phone buzzes. The notification shows a new phone number. A voice says, *well that was fast.* I open the message from Goleta.

He writes, "Hi, Anna. Thanks for giving me your number. I hope it isn't too late to text. How's your evening?"

I hit the power button to blacken my phone.

A voice instructs, *do at least some of the coping card before texting.*

I begin to write ideas on the index card.

- Call Aunt Tessa
- Ask for a hug
- Make vegetable beef soup
- Lie in a pillow fort
- Get a massage
- Play a meditation
- Listen to music
- Look at pictures of the babies

I take a sip of wine and review the list.

I say to the voice, *that's good enough for now. What should I write back?*

I activate my phone and open the message from Goleta. I type my response, "Hi. You're welcome. Not too late. My evening is good. I just got back from a work trip. How is your evening?"

I stare at the fire. My mind zones out. Exhaustion I felt earlier settles back in.

I sigh and say to myself, *time for bed for reals.* I push myself up to sitting. *Should I have one more cigarette?* I shake my head no.

A voice says, *you are so tired. Just go to bed.*

I stand up and bend over to collect the book, index card, pen, phone, and wine glass. As I walk to the kitchen I take the last sip of wine. I rinse the glass out with a little water and set it on the counter. There is a little left in the bottle. I wonder, *should I finish it?* Again I shake my head no.

The voice instructs again, *just go to bed. You are exhausted.*

I put the cookbook back on the shelf. For a split second I consider picking up the pillows and blankets in front of the fireplace.

The voice says, *no, those can wait until tomorrow.*

I turn the fireplace and lights off and walk back to the bathroom. I say to myself, *shit, I forgot to grab a water.*

I put toothpaste on my brush, wet it and turn it on. In the 2 minute toothbrush cycle, I walk to the kitchen for a water bottle, check that the doors are locked, put the water on the nightstand, plug my phone in to charge, and pull out my pajamas. The toothbrush beeps and stops vibrating. I turn on warm water, spit out toothpaste and wash my face.

Back in my room, I see my phone light up. Goleta responded. "My evening is good. I had dinner and some drinks with friends and now I'm texting with you. What are you doing this weekend?"

I settle into bed before typing my response. "I'm relaxing. Will probably get my nails done and go for a run. You?" I click on the iTunes app to start a meditation.

He responds in less than 30 seconds. "We should get together. I could come up there."

Without a pause, I respond. "O.K. Let's get a pedicure and then go for a walk on Saturday."

An incredulous voice asks, *where did that come from? A pedicure? He isn't going to want to do that.*

I laugh out loud. Then I respond to the voice. *Maybe not, but it will be a good test to see how comfortable he is in his own skin. Pedicures feel good for anyone and he doesn't have to get polish.* I think about my male cousins and nephews who enjoy pedicures. *Maybe he will be open.*

I send a second message. "Let me know tomorrow. I'm going to sleep now. Have a nice evening."

I start the chakra waterfall meditation and settle into my pillows. The meditation guide instructs me to take deep breaths. I follow along. A few thoughts about Goleta and pedicures cross my mind. I let them pass. The guide instructs me to walk into the waterfall. The waterfall changes colors to correspond to each chakra. The last color I remember is yellow before I settle into a deep sleep.

∞∞∞

BEEP BEEP BEEP.

What the fuck is that? I think before opening my eyes. *Oh my alarm.* I reach for my phone to hit snooze. *Did Goleta write back?*

To my surprise, he did. "Hmmm I've never gotten a pedicure before. I'd be open to that. Let me know what time and where on Saturday. Sleep well."

I say to myself and my parts, *well, what do you know? A man who isn't afraid to try something new and something on the feminine side. That's cool.*

I get up before snooze ends. My head begs for coffee. I walk to the kitchen.

With mild annoyance I say to myself, *ugh the living room is a mess.*

Little gnats circle the open wine bottle. With more annoyance I tell myself, *shit, I forgot to rinse out the bottle last night.*

I start the coffee. While it brews, I tidy up the kitchen and living room. The sun shines bright, lighting up the room as soon as I open the blinds. I notice, *not a cloud in the sky.* I open the slider. *No May gray today.*

My mind returns to the idea of calling in sick. A voice instructs, *no, just take it easy today. Get through emails and organize your office. Take a break for lunch and end at 5.*

The coffee maker beeps indicating the brew cycle is complete. I pour a cup of coffee and add almond milk.

My annoyance continues, *damn, why didn't I get something for breakfast at Whole Foods last night?*

I open the pantry. A large Quaker Oats canister greets me. I say with relief, *perfect. I'll make some oatmeal.* I fill a small pot with a cup of water, put it on the stove and turn the heat on high.

My phone lights up. A notification shows Goleta texted again. He writes, "Good morning. How'd you sleep? Let me know about tomorrow."

I smile. A voice jeers, *he is eager.* I respond, "Good morning. I slept really well. What about you? I'm glad you want to get pedicures with me. Let's do 1:00 on Saturday. Does that work? If so, I'll make appointments."

He responds immediately. "1 works. I slept ok. I'm not a great sleeper. Send me the location and I'll meet you there."

I reply, "Sorry to hear you aren't a great sleeper. I can relate. Sleep is hit or miss for me. I'll send the address in a moment. Have a great day and see you tomorrow."

I search for the address of my favorite nail salon and forward it to him.

He writes back, "O.K. sounds good. See you then."

The water boils. I pour ½ cup of oats into the saucepan, stir with a wooden spoon and reduce the heat. I lay the spoon across the top of the saucepan to stop the water from boiling over. I recall, *my first roommate back east taught me that trick.* I set my phone timer for 5 minutes. While the oats cook, I brush my teeth, wash my face and change into workout clothes.

My phone lights up with Catherine's name. I say silently to her, *I can't talk now my friend.* I send her call to voicemail.

The timer beeps. My oats are done. I walk to my office and turn on my computer so it can boot up before returning to the kitchen. I add honey, cinnamon and almond milk to the oatmeal and bring it and the coffee to the office. My computer screen asks for my password. The oatmeal steams. I take a bite and wait for my email to open. I say with dread, *237 messages. Ugh.*

The next time I look at the clock, it says 3:54. I say apologetically to myself, *whoops. I didn't take a lunch break.* I decide to close down my computer at 4:30 to compensate for working through lunch.

I check my phone. Goleta texted at 2:00. He asked, "How's your day?"

A voice instructs, *go for a run first. Then text him. Well, first throw in a load of laundry.*

I don't go for a very long run because I'm tired, hungry and felt anxious again. I remember Catherine's voicemail. Her messages bring me out of my head. I tap play and speaker phone on my voice-mail. Her happy, familiar voice fills my living room while I stretch.

"Dude, you are still watching Grey's? I totally didn't even know it is still on. I watch family shows now. Either way, you are still my person, too. Let's dance it out soon. I miss you. Gotta run. Dropping my little bean off at school. Love ya."

Her message makes me smile and reminisce about those days when I felt more normal. Next, I text Goleta back.

"It was good. I got consumed with my inbox and forgot lunch. How was your day?"

He responds, "It was good, too. Busy, but made the day pass faster. What are you doing tonight?"

"Laundry. What about you?"

"Really? You won't go out? I'm meeting some friends for din-ner, which will probably turn into drinks."

"I know it sounds boring. I'm tired from the week and don't have clean socks and underwear. Hehehe"

"I get it. Can't go around with dirty underwear and smelly socks."

"Exactly."

I set my phone down to change the laundry from the washer to dryer and take a shower.

A voice says, *another boring night.*

I respond, *maybe I should look for potential matches in this area. I mean I don't want to travel on the weekends, too, to see someone.*

I put on yoga pants and a comfortable shirt. I ask myself, *what should I have for dinner?* Back to Whole Foods I go.

A few hours later, I sit with my back in front of the fireplace and stare at the mound of clean clothes that need folding. My phone lights up. It's Goleta.

He asks, "So do you want to talk on the phone before we meet tomorrow?"

Surprise flickers across my face, followed quickly by uncertainty. Several voices chime in at once. *Hmmm...what would be the benefit? Maybe he is deciding if he really wants to drive down here. Should it be a surprise? I mean that could be a romantic story... meet at the nail salon without ever talking before, fall instantly in love over OPI's Taupe Less Beach and live happily ever after.* I shake my head. The voices continue, *what are you thinking? This isn't supposed to be that serious.*

I confirm, *yes, it isn't. I'm not looking for The One.*

My phone lights up again. Goleta texts, "We don't have to. We can wait until we meet tomorrow."

I say to myself, *ahh. What should I say?* Panic sweeps over my brain.

A voice reasons, *you could not say anything at all and pretend like you didn't get the message until way later.*

I feel calmer. I say to the voice of reason, *true. Good point.* I set the phone down with a sigh, crawl from the fireplace a few feet to the coffee table and reach for the remote.

I roll my eyes and think, *of course nothing good is on. Why do I even pay for cable?* I turn on the spa music station.

A voice says, *just text the poor guy back. What do you have to lose?*

I pick up my phone and re-read his messages. I respond, "Sure we can chat tonight. I'm folding a mountain of laundry now." I snap a photo of it and hit send before I realize that is probably lame.

My phone lights up within minutes.

Critic arrives to my mind, *oh, great. He is already calling you. What are you going to say? Don't sound lame. You shouldn't have sent him that laundry pic.*

My stomach knots and chest tightens.

Another voice says, *take a deep breath. You will be fine.*

"Hello," I answer.

"Hi. Is this Anna?" An unfamiliar male voice sounds in my ear. "This is Paul."

"Hi Paul. Yes, this is me." My nerves spike. "I mean this is Anna."

"Hi." His tone is kind. "How's the laundry going?"

I chuckle. "It's not. I really don't like folding laundry. How is your night?"

"It is good. I'm having dinner at some friends' house. I just stepped outside."

A voice says, *he left his friends to talk with you? That's kind of weird, right?*

A frown forms on my face. "We can talk later. I don't want to interrupt your dinner party."

He laughs. "Oh, no. We do this every Friday. You were a great excuse to leave for a little while. My friends will just make me drink more." He laughs again. "So what do you do?"

An unimpressed voice says, *and so it begins...the get-to-know-you questions.* I begin folding my laundry.

Our conversation lasts about 15 minutes. Paul is an IT consultant who manages a team of techs in internet security. He works from home. He has a close knit family with two brothers and one sister. Two siblings are married with children. He likes the community he lives in because he knows everyone. He frequents several bars, pizza joints, and restaurants that he wants to show me someday. He asks about my interests. I tell him about the 10K race my brother-in-law and I are running on Mother's Day. It raises money for foster care in the county, a cause that is important to me. He asks if I am a 'do-gooder type' and I roll my eyes as I say 'yes, you could say that.' We confirm the place and time for our pedicure date tomorrow and hang up.

My laundry piles are neat and organized. I stare at the fire. I say to myself and my parts, *well, that was…interesting, I guess.*

In my mind, Travis appears in his recliner. He pulls his newspaper down and looks at me. He says in his matter of fact tone, *no, it was boring. You were bored with that conversation.*

I agree with Travis. *I guess you could say that. I was bored. He had some redeeming qualities.*

Travis looks skeptical. *Not really. He seemed like a perpetual party guy who used to work out and now has a beer belly. The lost child in his family. Do you really want that? You don't have to fix people. Remember, Jennifer says that. You can see people for who they are and not feel bad about it. It doesn't mean they are bad people. It just means they aren't for you. Do you really want to be bored all your life?*

I am slightly annoyed. *Whoa why are you going to the forever thing again? This is just for fun. Besides it might be fun to meet some people who like to have dinner parties and go to fun bars and restaurants.*

Mini Monster appears. He swings his legs off the hammock. *Yeah, if you were in your 20s again and living in the city.*

Travis nods in Mini Monster's direction. *You don't want that anymore.*

Anxiety Mini Monster's eyes widen. *He probably lives in a grimy bachelor pad.*

Travis remains calm. *Project. He sounds like a project.*

Mini Monster jumps up and down in front of the hammock. *RUN! RUN the other way! His apartment is probably crawling with germs.*

A Big Loud Voice commands, *STOP. All of you. Just stop. This guy is what Anna is used to. You know you are Anna. You will go after it like you did all the others. And that's what you should do. You are only good for your body anyway, so just get it over with.*

I ask, *is that another part?*

Travis stands protectively. *Go away, Brute. Your criticisms aren't needed here.*

I shake my head. This conversation is too heated for me. I focus on the fire and my breath. I sigh. I say to myself, *time to put away the laundry.* I decide to get ready for bed after the clothes are in their proper places.

∞∞∞

I wake up around 9AM. My phone screen shows a text message notification from Goleta. He writes, "I'm not going to be able to make it today. Maybe another time. Sorry about that. I have to help my brother with a project for my sister-in-law."

I roll my eyes. The new part that Travis called Brute says, *he must have been bored, too. Plus, he is a guy. They don't do manicures and pedicures. That is way too girly.*

I wonder, *is that another part?*

Travis opens his eyes. *It is for the better. He wasn't the one.*

I am annoyed again. *Travis I am not looking for the one. Stop bringing that into it.*

Travis returns to his newspaper unfazed.

I start the coffee. I will have a lot to share with Jennifer tomorrow. I put bread in the toaster. I curse to myself, *shit, no. Tomorrow is a session with Dad.*

Brute sounds certain. *Your dad will side with Paul. Manicures and pedicures are girly. And being girly is weak.*

Reflections ∞ Reactions ∞ Responses

_____

_____

_____

CHAPTER 34

COLLATERAL SESSION WITH DAD PART 2

My phone buzzes on the way to Jennifer's office. Dad's calling.

I answer on speaker phone. "Hi, Dad."

His voice bellows through the phone. "Doc-TOR Aaaaaaaaaaaaaa. It's your dad. I'm here I think. Are you here?"

"I'm almost there. Do you want to wait in the parking lot and we can go in together?"

"Sure honey. That sounds good."

"I'm turning into the parking lot right now. Do you see my car?"

"Hmmmmm." He seems to be searching the parking lot. "Oh, crap. You are down there in the next level. I couldn't figure out how to get down there again. I'll start walking now and meet you at your car."

"O.K. Good plan. I'll show you the entrance to this level. It is confusing."

"Thanks, honey." He hangs up.

I see him put his dark glasses case in his pocket and close his car door. I say to myself with a sigh, *here goes nothing. Please let this be productive.*

I put my cell phone in my purse and grab my water bottle. In my rearview mirror I see Dad waiting by the trunk of my car. Inhale-a-Quick 4. Exhale 2. I say to myself with exasperation, *whoops, that isn't very deep breathing.* I try again and smile when my inhale and exhale match each other at 3. I encourage silently, *better than nothing.* I open the car door.

I force my tone to be chipper. "Hi, Dad. Thanks for coming again."

He reaches out to give me a hug. "Oh, sure, honey. I'm glad we could make this work. Our schedule has been so packed as usual."

We walk towards the stairs that take us to street level.

He stops to look across the parking lot behind us. "Oh this is why you park way over here. I couldn't figure it out because I thought we had to walk across the bridge back over there. I didn't see these stairs." He gestures behind us to the walk bridge that leads to the second floor of the building that houses Jennifer's office space.

I look at him quizzically and say to myself, *he was here last week. Doesn't he remember?*

"I took that bridge the first time I came here." I explain, "There isn't a direct way to get to her office from the second floor. You have to walk all the way over to the side of the building, go down the elevator and then walk all the way back down this way, exit the building and walk down the street to enter. Her office doesn't have an entrance from inside the building. It is quicker to go this way, cross the street and enter the office directly from outside. It is confusing, though."

We walk down the stairs in silence. I notice the sunlight through the tree leaves and feel the cool spring air on my cheeks.

"How have you been, Dad?"

He responds in his usual way. "Oh, good, honey. Busy as usual. I can never seem to get untangled from everything the way I want. I try, but it just doesn't work. New opportunities come up that interest me and I can't say no. You know how your big ole' dad is."

A knowing smile crosses my face. "Yes, I know. I hope you can at least slow down because the stress of it all has to take a toll on your body."

He pats his belly. "You mean this?" He laughs. "I know. Lindsey says the same thing."

We walk up the two steps to Jennifer's office. Pansy greets us at the door. Jennifer reaches down to hold Pansy so she doesn't run outside when the door opens.

Jennifer smiles brightly as she opens the door. "Hi, Charlie. It is really good to see you again. I set up the blankets, pillows and a chair for you like last time."

I set my purse on the chair and kick my shoes off. I grab my water and turn towards the space Jennifer set up for us. Dad does the same thing.

"Thank you for the chair, Jennifer," he says. "This fat ole' body of mine doesn't sit well on the floor anymore."

"Sure, Charlie," Jennifer responds. "It is important for everyone to feel comfortable in here." She pauses while we settle into our spots. "So, how was last week's session for you?"

Dad chimes in first. "It was really helpful. Good. A really good session. The capital and lower case trauma was helpful."

Jennifer smiles at him. "Great, Charlie. I'm glad to know what stuck with you. And for you Anna, how was it?"

My mind goes blank again. I think in a flash, *what is up with that? This happened last time, too, right at the beginning.* I stammer, "It was a good session."

Jennifer looks quizzically at me. "Is everything O.K.?"

I nod. "Yes. It is just so weird. This happened last session, too. My mind goes blank right at the beginning. Like the curtain gets pulled and I can't think of what to say. It is so weird."

Jennifer's expression shows empathy. "Like your executive functioning brain goes dark? Perhaps you are nervous about being here and saying the right and wrong thing? We can look at that Part at our next session if you want."

Relief washes over me. "That would be great. I think I found another new part yesterday, too, that I want to tell you about."

She looks at Dad. "You must be confused. Are you wondering what parts we are referring to?"

Dad smiles and nods. "Yes, but I don't need to know either."

She asks me, "Is it a good time for me to explain IFS to your dad?"

I nod. "Sure."

"O.K. Anna and I have been using a tool called IFS, which stands for Internal Family Systems. I will try not to get too technical on you, Charlie. Let me know if I do. IFS was developed by a man named Richard Schwartz, whom I've trained with. Basically his idea was that just like families consist of different people interacting, inside each of us are different parts that interact and make us who we are. Parts could be like the different internal voices you hear during the day. The idea with IFS is that we identify the parts, learn their purpose, and then help them get along better with the Core Self."

Skepticism settles on Dad's face. "O.K. that sounds a little woowoo to me. But if it works great."

Jennifer smiles and raises her eyebrows. "Woowoo? I haven't heard that before from you."

Dad smiles back. "Well, basically woowoo is when stuff is just a little too out there for me to grasp, but that's O.K. I don't need to grasp it. If it is working for Anna, that's what matters."

"Oh, O.K.," Jennifer says. "Let me know if you have questions like last time we met. Where do you want to start today?"

I chime in. "I was thinking this week about the dad bashing sessions. I don't want to bash you, Dad. But we do have some difficult things to discuss, so I don't know how to do that without running the risk of sounding like I'm bashing you."

Jennifer smiles again. "That's how I can help facilitate this conversation so it doesn't get into the bashing zone. Maybe we can come up with a word that I can say or you can say if the conversation is getting to a bashing place?"

"How about Pansy?" Dad suggests.

We both look at him with confusion. Pansy is chewing on a snack by our shoes.

I ask, "What about Pansy?"

He clarifies. "No, I mean the word could be 'Pansy.'"

Jennifer giggles. "Oh that's cute. Does that work for you both?"

We nod. I say, "Yes, for sure. I love Pansy."

Jennifer segues to decide what topic we will focus on today. "Now that we have that sorted out, do you have an idea of what you want to start with today?"

Dad and Jennifer turn towards me. Silence descends again. My brain goes dark. Then in the distance a small voice whispers, *family business.*

I take a deep breath. My stomach drops like it does on a roller coaster. "Let's talk about the family business that isn't really a family business."

Dad jumps in before Jennifer can respond. "You mean you are still hung up on me treating you and Violet differently because you are girls. You just have to get over that. It is not true."

Jennifer sees my jaw clench. "I'm not following. Can you explain what you mean, Charlie?"

He rolls his eyes. "Yes," he snaps. "Anna and Violet have this belief that if they were sons, I would have included them in the family business. But since they are girls, I did not. When really it is that they didn't have an interest in the business."

My face scrunches in disbelief. "What?" I am incredulous. "I've never heard you say that before. Of course we didn't have an interest. You were not welcoming. You did not include us. We were treated like greedy vultures. There was not space for us to have an interest."

He spits words out. "What do you mean? I gave you a job in high school and you walked out. You WALKED OUT. You wanted nothing to do with it. You went off and got another job. That was the last of it. You wanted nothing to do with it."

The wind knocks out of my stomach. I feel like I've been slapped. I shake my head. My eyes fill with tears.

"Well obviously I hit a nerve because you are crying now," he jeers. "That is how it happened isn't it?"

Jennifer's soothing voice floats through the air. "Anna, where are you feeling this? Take your time."

I don't want to speak. My body wants to curl into the fetal position. I remember the teenager who tried so hard to please him and make him proud. I remember sitting at the conference table as he berated me for something I said or did that gave him the impression that I was a greedy vulture. I see myself walking out of the office building as tears stream down my face and my chest heaves with shallow breaths. I watch my teenage self sitting with Lindsey who met me for lunch as I sobbed and asked why he treated me that way. She looked at me with empathy, compassion and sorrow.

A voice urges, *you must tell this story today.*

I take a deep breath and turn to face Dad. "I was a child then. I didn't walk out and close that door forever. Working for you was the most challenging job I've ever had. You treated me like I was an invader. Like I was somehow in there trying to take advantage of you. You said repeatedly that I was acting like a greedy vulture. You and Mom made me start working. I didn't have a choice in the matter. I did what you asked. I showed up every day. I filed returned bank checks out in that freezing storage room. I answered the phones. I helped the payroll lady with her administrative tasks. I worked on the sales desk that one week. And other than that one week, you did not expose me to anything other than receptionist, secretary-type tasks. Which I might add are all female-typical roles.

"You did not take on the task of teaching me the family business. You missed the opportunity. And instead you picked at me all day. What I wore. When I came and went. You never noticed when I got there early, stayed late or took a short lunch. You always noticed when I was 3 minutes late or wore shorts that were too short. You berated me in front of the controller because I asked if I could go to lunch, at lunch time, instead of listening to a conversation that I didn't understand. You told me how rude and disrespectful I was and how much of a greedy vulture I was. When really I was just hungry. You never made me feel like I was more than lowly administrative support. I was raked through the coals weekly that Summer. Would you want to work in that environment with that kind of boss? No.

"And now I learn that because I 'walked out,' I closed the door of being included in the family business. You were the adult, Dad. You never stopped to think about what that experience was like for me. It was horrible. I wanted to be included. I wanted to make you proud. But that was impossible."

I feel stronger. My breaths deepen. My head is clearer.

Mini Monster appears in my mind jumping up and down and shouting, *yay!!! Way to go. You said it.* Travis's normally stoic face appears wearing a smile and his eyes twinkle.

Jennifer looks at me with encouragement. "You aren't tearing up anymore. What are you feeling now?"

Words tumble out of my mouth. "Honestly, I feel really angry. Like I am fucking pissed." I turn back towards Dad. "As for the girl versus boy discussion, do you honestly expect me to believe you would have had a son filing and answering phones? No, he would have been learning about operations or spent more time at the sales desk. Your company was staffed in traditional gender roles. There is no way your son would be doing what I was doing. Whether you want to ever admit that to yourself or not doesn't matter to me. It is my truth and I know to my core that you treated Violet and me differently because we are girls."

My inhale is full and deep and even. My shoulders relax. A calm settles over me. Sadness creeps into my chest. I feel tired.

Jennifer turns towards Dad. "I want to check in with you, Charlie. Anna just shared a lot about what her experience was like working in high school. You did not say 'Pansy' so I am assuming you did not feel like you were being bashed. Is my assumption correct?"

Dad's eyes are wild with fury. It is subtle. I wonder if Jennifer picks up on it. His rage is boiling under the surface. I feel myself shudder and the urge to curl into a tiny ball returns.

The faraway voice whispers again. *Hide. Get away. He's coming after you.*

Dad's voice pierces the air between us. "None. Of. That. Is. True. It is simply not true. You were spoiled. How many kids get a job because their dad owns the company? Not many. You took that opportunity and you threw it in the gutter. As far as the sons versus daughters thing, also simply not true."

I fight the urge to actually curl up in the fetal position. I want to be strong and tough, like Travis when he wears his armor. I want to show Dad he can't hurt me. I begin to cry again. I realize Travis was born to protect me from my dad, even though he said he came to be the year I was raped.

Jennifer's tone is firm. She squarely faces Dad. "Charlie, I need to ask you to take a few deep breaths. If you need to get up and walk around, that's O.K. This is a time when saying 'Pansy' is needed."

His face softens. "No, no. I don't need to step back. I'm fine. I have it under control."

Jennifer looks doubtful. "Are you sure? You seem pretty angry right now. And my observation of Anna right now is that she is crying and clearly in pain. Do you see that?"

He shifts his gaze to me. I think he sees me for the first time. His face softens even more and I detect guilt fluttering across his face.

"Besides, you don't want to be in the produce business," he says nonchalantly. "It is a shit industry to be in. You have to travel all the time. Constantly on the go. You can't settle down. It doesn't work for family. You don't want that kind of life. I don't want that kind of life for you."

Jennifer redirects Dad. "Charlie, you did not answer my question. Do you see what Anna is feeling right now?"

Silence. He looks at me with curiosity. Uncertainty crosses his face. "I'm not good with that whole naming feelings. It's woowoo."

Jennifer does not let him off the hook. "You don't have to be good at it. I'm asking what you see in Anna right now?"

"I see tears," he finally acknowledges.

"Yes," Jennifer encourages. "And do you presume those tears are happy tears, sad tears, or angry tears? Or maybe something else?"

"Definitely not happy tears," he says softly.

"Yes, they are not happy tears." Her tone is soft to match his. "You see a lot for not being into the woowoo. Anna, what are you feeling?"

I answer without missing a beat. "These are sad tears. I'm really sad, Dad. I wonder sometimes what my life would be like had the opportunity been there to really learn from you. Would I have ended up down south for nine years? Would I have been raped? Again, I am not saying the rape is your fault and I really hope you aren't hearing me bash you. I just think what happened in high school when I worked for you that Summer had a profound impact on the direction of my life and on our relationship. I'm sad about that. I have felt disconnected from you for a long time with few exceptions. And all I want is to feel connected. To have a place to grow roots. I've been running for so long. Chasing something. Running from something. I'm not sure which. Maybe both. I'm sad that you don't believe me when I talk about my experience. I can see how you would take my leaving as a sign that I didn't want to be involved. And back then it was a sign of that. But I'm sad that you gave up on me forever. I'm just sad."

Kindness and compassion spread across Jennifer's face. She smiles gently and nods. Her expression and gesture seem to say 'well done. I know that was hard.'

She turns her gaze towards Dad. He stares at the floor. His shoulders slouch. His expression is blank. He seems defeated.

"Charlie, I sense by your posture that something struck a chord in you when Anna was talking about her sad tears," she says empathically.

He looks up at her and shifts in his seat. "Yes, I obviously don't like to see Anna sad. No parent wants their child to be sad." He hesitates before turning towards me. "Anna, I'm sorry you feel like I don't believe you. I simply don't remember it like you do. Neither of us are right or wrong."

Jennifer jumps in before I have time to respond. "Charlie, it is important for you to acknowledge that you see Anna's sadness, regardless of how you remember that time. Can you try to address her sadness?"

Dad haughtily retorts, "I thought I just did. I told you I don't like to see Anna sad."

Jennifer does not break eye contact with him. "Yes, you told me that you see her sadness. You did not tell her. Try telling Anna that you can see her sadness and let her know how you feel when you see her sadness."

My head bounces from Jennifer to Dad throughout this exchange. I silently cheer, *she is holding him accountable. Go, Jennifer, go.*

Dad's tone softens. "Oh," he says simply. "I guess you are right."

He looks uncomfortable as he shifts in his seat to face my direction again. His gaze jumps from me to the ground to the ceiling to Jennifer and back. I hold my breath.

He seems to force his eyes to stay on my face. "Anna, I am sorry you have so much sadness about that time. I did not realize I made your work experience so bad. I'm also sorry that we never talked about it. I should've talked about it with you again at some point since I was the adult and the parent in the situation." He turns his head towards Jennifer seeking validation. "How was that?" He asks with a hint of shyness in his voice.

Her gaze softens to match his shy tone. "That was great, Charlie. You acknowledged Anna's sadness and how you could've done something differently. Could you try and tell her what you feel when you see her sadness? I know that can sometimes be harder for people, especially for dads because there is pressure to be strong and not show emotion."

Dad smiles. "You are good, Jen. Can I call you Jen? I shorten everyone's name."

She smiles back at him. "Yes, of course you can call me Jen. Most people eventually get to that."

He nods. "You are good because you are helping me break through some of my own programming without me even knowing that I need that." Tears begin to form in the corners of his eyes. "As you can both see, I have some emotion here." His voice cracks. "Anna," he whispers. "Whew, clearly there is something here for me." He pauses again. "Anna," he says clearer. "When you said something to the effect of wanting to feel more connected, it hit me. I, too, want to feel more connected. I felt that way when I was younger in my family with my dad, too. I tried for so long to do everything to connect with him. We used to connect over hunting and fishing. And, of course over drinking. At the end, he couldn't do anything but sit in his wheelchair and move from his bedroom to the living room and occasionally the deck outside. That's when I started drinking again. We only really had that in common. Your sadness reminds me of my own sadness."

Jennifer's tone comforts. "Charlie, that was really beautifully said. I can see that you carry some old wounds from your relationship with your dad that help you relate to Anna's sadness. Anna, what is it like for you to hear this from your dad?"

A wave of relief washes over me. "Honestly, I didn't know any of that. Dad, I always thought you and grandpa were really close through business and money and all the other things you mentioned. I didn't realize you felt disconnected, too. I'd really like to work on connecting with you more. Like doing things together that don't involve alcohol and maybe even doing things together without anyone else. Like just the two of us or maybe when Violet is here, just the three of us. Nothing against Lindsey. I know you are protective of her. We really like her and hanging out with her. But sometimes I'd also like to hang out with just you. Like when you and I went up to the cabin that one time when I was little. Remember, we saw a fox on the way up. And you told me about some business problem. I was little, like 7-ish. I remember another time when I was like 10 and we were driving in your Porsche in the grocery store parking lot listening to Don Henley. Or like I said last week when we sculpted together when I lived with you. I guess I miss those times."

Dad nods again. "I'd really like that, too. Now, if I may, I need to bring up Lindsey."

Jennifer interjects. "Hold on for a moment, Charlie. I'd like for us to look at what just happened before we move on to a related, but different topic. Is that O.K.?"

"Yes," he agrees. "But you have to help me remember. I'm really bad at remembering things, which is why I always interrupt. When the girls were little they called me Mr. Talkable because I had to get my point across when I thought of it otherwise I'd forget it."

"O.K." She points to her notebook. "I wrote 'Lindsey' right here on my notes. Will that do?"

He nods. "Yes, and can you also write 'the girls being open to her' to help me remember what I wanted to focus on."

Jennifer writes those words and shows the notebook page to Dad. "Is this O.K.?"

"Yes, yes," he says quickly. "Thank you. I just don't have a good memory."

Jennifer rests the notebook on her lap. "What I just saw happen between the two of you was really beautiful. You both seemed to take some risks in opening up. You talked about something really painful from your past, each shared and acknowledged feelings, and even moved towards talking about how things could be different in the future. I don't usually see conflict resolution happen so quickly and sincerely in a family. What was that like for each of you?"

Dad and I look at each other. We nod in agreement. We open our mouths to talk at the same time.

"Go ahead, honey. You go first." Dad nods and smiles. His tears are dried up, but his eyes are still red.

I take a deep breath. "My heart feels more open and full. I felt the weight of that Summer without really knowing it this entire time. It feels good now to have some understanding and closure. I am hopeful. I guess that's the feeling."

Dad nods in agreement. "Yes, I didn't realize how much was left over from that Summer either. I'm really glad we got to hash it out. And I didn't feel bashed. Jennifer, that is a testament to your skill. You are really good at what you do."

Jennifer smiles at his compliment. "Thank you, Charlie. I've felt very fortunate to work with Anna and more recently with her family. I see a lot of love for each other in your family." Jennifer looks at her watch before continuing. "I know you want to talk about Lindsey. We are out of time for the one hour session. I could stay longer if you want. I remember, Charlie, you said last week that your attention span is really only good for one hour. So we could also meet again next week."

"Unfortunately, I can't stay longer today," Dad quickly adds. "We have some dinner function tonight. Let me check my schedule for next weekend." He pulls out his phone. "Ahhhh, dee-da-dee," he hums while he scrolls. "I just can't figure these smart phones out very quickly."

"It's O.K.," Jennifer smiles knowingly. "Take your time. I feel the same way. I think it's a generational thing."

He looks up and flashes a knowing smile back to her. "You are right about that. I'd guess you and I are in the same generation." They chuckle in agreement. "O.K., yes, it looks like we are in town next weekend, too. Let's put it in the calendar and like last time I'll check with Lindsey. If something else is scheduled I'll let you know, but otherwise, let's count on next week." He turns to where I was sitting. "Uh, Anna where'd you go?"

I wrestle through my bag for my checkbook. "I'm over here already."

"I didn't even see you get up," Dad says.

"I know. You were zeroed in on your phone. No worries. I obviously am free next weekend, so even if Dad can't come, I will be here." I begin filling in a check to pay Jennifer for this session.

Dad stands and picks up his chair. "Where does this go?"

Jennifer says, "Oh don't worry about that. I will put everything back."

Dad doesn't set the chair down. "No that's O.K. I am walking over there anyway. Where does it go?"

Jennifer concedes. "Well, thank you. It goes by the window." She points to the empty space amongst the waiting area chairs.

I rip the check from the checkbook and set it on Jennifer's bag. "The check is on your bag, Jennifer."

"Honey, I know I said this last week," Dad reiterates. "I am happy to help pay for this. Just let me know."

I smile. "I know Dad. Thank you. I've got this covered."

I put my purse on my shoulder. Jennifer walks by with a stack of blankets in hand. I set my purse back down and return to where we sat during the session. I pick up the bolsters and walk them to the closet.

"Oh you are both too kind," Jennifer says. "You don't have to do that. But thank you."

"I know," I confirm. "But I want to help."

We walk to the door where Dad is waiting to say goodbye.

"I'm sorry I have to run," he says. "We have that dinner function. Thank you again Jennifer. Annie, let's talk this week about grabbing lunch or something. Do I need to wait for someone to grab Pansy to open the door?"

"Yes, sounds great, Dad." I look around the room for Pansy.

"No worries, Charlie," Jennifer says. "See you next week. I'll watch for Pansy. She is content in the other room, so you should be O.K."

Dad gives us each a quick hug and leaves.

Jennifer and I turn towards each other. Her expression is incredulous. Mine is relief.

"Wow!" Jennifer exclaims. "That went really well, I think. Your dad seemed to really open up."

My relief shifts to guarded optimism. "Yes, he did. I'm cautiously optimistic that we will actually get together for lunch or whatever. He and I have had similar conversations in the past with little actual change. But this seemed different. So, I'm hopeful."

Her eyebrows furrow slightly. "Hmm. Really, you've had this conversation before?"

"Well, not this specific one," I clarify. "But we've talked about wanting to connect before. I've asked him to do things without Lindsey and without alcohol. But we just never seem to make it happen. We don't have a lot in common as far as our interests go. We will talk more about all that next week, though. Thank you again, Jennifer. He is right. You are really good at what you do."

Her smile shows appreciation. "Thank you. Let me know if anything comes up during the week. You can always email or text me. Or call."

"I know," I confirm. "I really appreciate your availability to me."

On the drive home I wonder, *why didn't I stay longer with her? I have so much to tell her about, like Match, the new part, and anxiety when running. It's like since Dad couldn't, I didn't even consider it.*

Reflections ∞ Reactions ∞ Responses

_____

_____

_____

CHAPTER 35

A FRANK EDUCATED GUESS

My computer sits on my lap. I mindlessly stare at the television in my hotel room. This week's meetings and deadlines leave me feeling depleted.

I think, *I wonder what's going on with Match.* I focus on my computer screen. I give myself instructions in a sing-song voice. *Save this report. X out of it. Click on Safari. Wait for it to load. Ugh it is so slow.* My gaze blankly stares at the television. Travis's voice sounds in my mind before the image of him in his recliner appears.

Travis suggests, *maybe you should look for profiles near Santa Maria. That way you won't be so tired and will actually have the energy to meet people on the weekends.*

I say out loud, "O.K. I'll do that." I sigh and smile to myself.

That new part's voice instructs, *don't be too forward, though. You don't want to seem desperate and needy. Like a hussy looking for a man to rescue you.*

My brows furrow. I shake my head. *Who are you?*

Travis answers, *don't worry about that right now. Ignore her. Just get back to those profiles.*

I type www.mat and before I finish the web address, the link to the homepage automatically populates in the search bar. I enter my password. A few new messages are in my inbox. A quick glance through leaves much to be desired. I go to the search page and refine my filters to only show profiles from the Santa Maria area. I start scrolling through profiles using my screening method.

One profile name catches my eye- Educated Guess. I ask myself, *I wonder if he has had that wine?* His profile indicates that he has a bachelor's degree and makes the same income range as me. I hesitate, *he doesn't say if he wants kids or not. Hmmm...should I continue?*

Travis points out, *he has never been married. He meets that criterion. Keep looking.*

I click on his pictures. They show him on a boat, a beach, hiking with friends, and in the snow.

Travis nods with encouragement. *He seems good so far. He travels and has friends.*

The last picture shows a man with twinkling eyes and a wide grin. He leans back in a chair as if he just finished a delicious meal. My breath catches and butterflies flutter through my stomach.

Travis seems to stand over my shoulder now looking at the computer screen. *Now that's the face of a jolly and happy man.*

I giggle and say to Travis, *I know. Good thing he seems a little younger than Santa Claus.*

Travis chuckles. *And in better shape.*

I glance at Mini Monster, who just appeared.

I tell Travis, *well that's surprising. Mini is snoozing in his hammock.*

A calm smile spreads across Travis's face. He points out, *you aren't anxious when you look at that face.*

I feel light and peaceful. I look up and notice the bathroom mirror in front of me for the first time since I checked in. I say to myself, *yep, I look like I feel.* My reflection is innocent and at ease. I take a deep breath and return to his profile. It is simple and straight forward. He doesn't describe a fairytale partner. He likes to read, travel, hike and spend time with friends. We seem to have a lot in common.

I say aloud, "O.K., now what should I write?"

New part commands, *don't seem too interested. Be non-chalant. A little flirty. Don't seem too smart or well-travelled. You don't want to be a show off. Men don't like when women are smarter or more worldly or make more money than they do.*

Travis snaps at her. *Be quiet! She can be herself.*

I click on new message and quickly hammer out a message:

Hi Educated Guess,

I like your profile name. Have you had that wine? It is really good. We live in the same area and have a lot in common. Hope to hear from you.

Cheers,

Return2SunnyCA

New Part offers unsolicited opinions. *Way too nonchalant. And you sound like an alcoholic. That isn't very lady-like.*

Travis looks up. His tone is firm and protective. *Seriously, shut up. She isn't done yet.*

I get up to pee before clicking send. I lean in to stare in my eyes while washing my hands. My eyes implore my reflection. I say to my reflection, *you can do this. You want this. If he doesn't reply he's not right for you and that's good to know. You can do this.*

I dry my hands. The evening news anchor chatters in the background. I find the television noise suddenly annoying. I sit back in bed and reach for the remote on the nightstand. I click the power button. The television does not respond. I exclaim to myself, *these fuckin' remotes suck! Why don't they change the batteries when they turn over a room? Or at least once a week.* I laboriously climb back out of bed to turn the television off manually. Silence fills the room.

Travis sits in his recliner. *Now stop distracting yourself. You can be yourself. Like you said, you aren't looking for the one. Just a friend.*

I climb back in bed and pull the laptop on my lap. I re-read my first message. I say to my Parts, *O.K., it is a start.* I hit delete and begin again.

Hi Educated Guess,

I really like your pictures...

New Part interrupts, *now you seem superficial. Like all you care about is what he looks like.*

I delete the sentence and start again.

I enjoyed looking through your profile. We seem to have some things in common, like reading, traveling, hiking and hanging out with friends. I'd like to hear about your favorite books and where you travel and hike. Also, have you ever had the wine Educated Guess? It is really good. I had it last week for the first time. Anyway, I look forward to hearing from you.

Cheers,
Return2SunnyCA

Travis asks, *do you want to sign with your actual name?*

New Part answers, *do. It's good to be mysterious and a little coy.*

Travis snaps, *no, it is not. It is good to be transparent and authentic. No games.*

Mini Monster stands in front of his hammock. *Yes, but you don't want to give him information about yourself without knowing him. He could be a serial murderer for all we know.*

Travis rolls his eyes from his recliner. *Seriously, he likely is not a serial murderer. Just do your first name.*

I delete Return2SunnyCA and type my first name.

I am amused by my parts. *O.K., Travis and gang. Does this look good to you?*

They all answer at the same time.

New Part appears for the first time. Her arms are crossed. She says haughtily, *he won't write you back. You're too confident.*

Mini Monster's hair looks disheveled. *He is going to track you down and kill you.*

Travis remains calm in his recliner. *Don't listen to them. It is just fine.*

I click send and power down my computer. The silence in the room now suffocates me. I reach for the remote to turn it on again. I cuss to myself, *mother fucker. This damn remote.* I aim straight at the television and push as hard as possible on the power button. The television turns on! I exclaim, *yessssss! It's a sign.* I do the same thing with the channel button. It works every other click. I say annoyed, *LAME. I have to remember to tell them at check out.*

I settle in to watch a Law and Order re-run. I fight the urge to check for new messages on my phone's Match app at every commercial. I consider turning on Match message notifications and decide not to. I ask myself, *could you imagine sitting in a board meeting and getting a Match message notification? No way.* I push my phone under my pillow.

Law and Order's dong-dong brings the episode to a close. I'm grateful it was an episode new to me that held my attention. I get up to brush my teeth and wash my face. I click the television off manually on my way back to bed. I pull my phone out from under the pillow to plug it in. My finger taps the Match app. I chastise, *damn finger has a mind of its own.*

To my surprise there is a new message from Educated Guess. My heartbeat quickens.

New Part rolls her eyes. *Loser. He wrote back way too soon. He probably has small balls.*

Travis snaps at her. *You aren't helping. Just stop.*

Travis returns to his newspaper. I click on the message.

Hi Anna,

Thanks for writing. We do seem to have a lot in common. I was hiking Garrapata in the pic on my profile. It's a state park north of here. Have you ever done that? It is really hard, but beautiful and worth it. I've travelled to a lot of places, too. What about you? As for Educated Guess, I was drinking a glass when I made my profile and found inspiration by the name. I figured all you do in online dating is make educated guesses. Plus I really like the wine. Where are you back from? Your profile name indicates you returned from somewhere? I look forward to hearing back from you, too.

Frank

I laugh out loud and shake my head. *Holy shit. Of all the possible names, his is almost the same as my brother-in-law's. Now I've dated all of my uncles' and my dad's names.*

Travis pipes in from behind his newspaper: *I thought you weren't looking for the one and here you are already dating this guy?*

I respond, *you're right. But be quiet.*

I start writing back to Frank.

New Part continues to be opinionated. *DES-peration!!! Don't you remember rule number 1- don't seem too desperate. That means don't write back right away.*

Mini Monster's eyes begin popping out. *The more you share the more he has to find you and kill you.*

I firmly tell the activated parts, *quiet, all of you. I got this.*

I begin typing and notice the smile plastered on my face. I realize, *I'm having fun.*

Dear Frank,

I've never hiked Garrapata. Isn't that the one that is straight uphill for a long time? Good for you. I bet the view from the top is beautiful. I was living in the South most recently for the last four years. Before that I was in southern California and Washington DC. As for traveling, I've been to Europe several times because my sister lives there. I've also been to Australia because we have family living there. I also studied abroad there. Traveling is super fun! Well, when traveling for pleasure. I also travel a lot for work, which is not as fun. I'm off to sleep now. Have an early meeting and then long drive back home tomorrow.

Cheers,
Anna

I plug my phone in, turn off the light and start my sleep meditation podcast. My giddy excitement keeps me awake longer than usual. I actually finish the first 30-minute meditation and have to start it over. Somewhere in the second 30 minutes I drift off to sleep.

∞∞∞

The second thing I do when I wake up is check my Match App. I exclaim, *another message!* My heartbeat quickens again and the butterflies return to my stomach.

Hi Anna,

Were you or are you military? You've lived near a lot of military bases. Where is your sister in Europe? Garrapata is like you heard. Maybe we could hike it together sometime. Sweet dreams and safe travels tomorrow.

Frank

I quickly type a response.

Hi Frank,

Not military. I get that a lot though. Just a school junkie and the schools I went to happened to be near military hubs. My sister is in Germany. Also not military-related. She married German. I'd like to possibly hike with you some time. I'm off to work now. I hope you have a good day.

Anna

I resist the urge to check my Match inbox throughout the day. That doesn't stop me from thinking about Frank. What else does he like to do? Is he from the area? Is he a serial killer? Should I ask for his phone number? Is that too desperate? Does he want kids? Why didn't he put that in his profile? Maybe he has kids? Maybe he can't have kids? I decide on my drive home to review other profiles because I don't want to put all my eggs in one basket. I tell myself, *plus I'm obsessing too much about him and I don't want anything serious.*

The sun is setting and I realize I haven't eaten in six hours. I stop at In-n-Out Burger for dinner. My phone stares at me.

Travis appears reading a newspaper in his recliner. *Just check. There is no harm in checking.*

Mini Monster remains next to his hammock even though his hair is a mess and his eyes are bugging out. *What if he has figured out how to track your phone and he is on his way here now?*

New Part rolls her eyes. *You know you want to check. Give in to the urge. Cling to the man.*

I reach for my phone to unlock it and swipe to the app. Frank sent a message minutes after my last message to him this morning. I instantly feel bad and hope he isn't discouraged since I've taken so long to respond.

Hi Anna,

I lived in Germany. I was in Bavaria. Where is your sister? I hope I don't sound too forward, but would you be interested in exchanging numbers so we can text or talk outside of Match? If it is too soon, no worries. I hope you have a good day, too.

Frank

The now-familiar butterflies return. Without thinking, I reply:

Hi Frank,

My sister is outside Berlin. I've been to Bavaria once, but was sick so didn't see much of it. My number is xxx-xxx-xxxx. I had a good, but long day. I won't be home for another few hours. Look forward to hearing from you.

Anna

My parts are silent, which surprises me. I briefly wonder why and then feel relief. I feel right about the way this conversation is going.

I take my exit off the highway when my phone notifies me of a text from an unrecognized number. I quickly read it while the light at the end of the exit is red. "Hi Anna. It's Frank. Are you home? I didn't want to text sooner in case you are still driving. What are you up to this weekend?"

I turn left toward my house and think about my response. I say to myself, *maybe Mini is right...he could be a serial killer. This is all moving too fast.* I decide to respond after I've been home for an hour.

Twenty minutes later I sit on my couch and scroll through the TV guide. Grey's Anatomy is on again. I say to myself, *the aftermath of Derek's death. Can I handle that right now?* HGTV has a marathon of one of those house flip shows.

I acknowledge, *I really want to text Frank back.*

Travis encourages, *just do it.*

I grab my phone and store his number as Frank Educated Guess. I comment sarcastically, *Should I tell him I have therapy with my dad this weekend?*

Travis's expression questions the seriousness of my comment. *Maybe hold off on that.*

"O.K.," I say out loud. "You're probably right. Too soon for that."

I text, "Hi Frank. I got home about 30 minutes ago. Texting while driving is very tempting, but I try not to do it. My sister is coming in from Germany soon, so I am going to get my house ready for that this weekend. What are you doing?"

I resume scrolling through the T.V. guide. My heart quickens when my phone beeps. I exclaim, *he wrote back already!*

Frank texts, "I'm hanging out with friends and will go to the gym. Glad you didn't text while driving. How long is your sister in town?"

"They are coming for 3 weeks. My sister's birthday is at the end of the month. You lived in Germany, right? Do you speak German?"

"Ja, aber ich spreche hier nicht oft Deutsch. Sprechen sie Deutsch?"

I giggle and copy his message. Then open Google Translate. I set the language from German to English and paste his message. According to Google Translate his message says, "Yes, but I don't speak German often here. Do you speak German?" I say to myself, *he is clever*.

Frank texts before I can respond. "I used to speak German better, but I don't use it here so I've lost a lot of it."

"I was just using Google Translate to tell you in German that I don't speak German. It is on my bucket list. Especially since my niece and nephew are bilingual. You could probably communicate with them in German."

"How old are they? Will they be here, too?"

"Yes, everyone is coming over. My sister, brother-in-law and their 2 kids. They are 3.5 and 1.5. Super cute and fun to be with. Do you have any nieces or nephews?"

I set my phone down and gaze back at the T.V. I wonder again if he wants kids.

Mini Monster holds steady by his hammock, yet remains disheveled. *Maybe he wants to steal Leah and Max and now he knows they will be here, too!*

Travis pulls his newspaper down to look in Mini's direction and rolls his eyes.

I walk to my office to get my computer. I say to myself, *I'll just check in on Match. Maybe there are other potentials.* By the time I return to the couch, Frank messaged.

New Part instructs with a sharp tone. *Do not look at it. You need to play hard to get. You seem too eager.*

I feel angry at this new part. I shake my head and wonder out loud, "What is your purpose?"

To my surprise she answers me. *To help you act like a lady in a man's world.*

I reply to her out loud. "I don't need help acting like a lady. You are all about games. I don't want to play games anymore."

New Part responds with sassiness. *You say that, but really you know you have to play games. Men want one thing- sex- so you have to play the game if you don't want to end up alone with cats.*

I'm seething now. I take deep breaths.

Mini Monster looks like he is about to come unglued. *Cats? Ahhhh. You're allergic to cats. You can't end up alone.*

New Part continues with arrogance and sassiness. *You will end up alone if you keep doing what you're doing. You need to play hard to get. Be mysterious. Lure them in. Be smart, but not too smart. Sexy and seductive. That's what they want.*

Travis stands protectively with his finger pointing at them. *Just stop. Both of you. Anna can be whoever she wants. I will protect her if needed. I am a knight after all.*

I'm tense. I ask with bewilderment, *what the fuck just happened?*

Travis urges, *ignore them. Just ignore them. Push them out of your mind. Look on Match.*

I focus on my breath. I am confused by this exchange with my parts. What activated them? I was calmly sitting on the couch, chatting with Frank, looking at other profiles, and watching-not-watching television. I mental note to talk with Jennifer about this exchange.

My phone notification flashes. Frank Educated Guess wrote two messages while I was hijacked by my parts on the way to get my computer out of my office. I hesitantly unlock my phone. Maybe I do seem too needy and desperate. Maybe that new part is right.

Frank answered, "I have 2 nephews. They are 13 and 15, I think. Maybe 12 and 14. Haha. I can't remember."

His next message asked, "What else is on your bucket list?"

My heart quickens and I feel calmer. I say to myself, *fuck my parts. I am going to chat with him.*

I write, "Haha. It is hard to keep track of those details. Where do they live?"

I type a second message immediately after sending the previous one. "My bucket list includes learning Spanish and German. I also want to write a book someday and travel to places I've never been. What's on yours?"

I power on my computer.

Frank texts, "You might need to add Portuguese to your list.:)"

I ask, "Are you Portuguese? Do you speak it?"

"My nephews live near the Bay Area."

Moments later, he writes "I am Portuguese. I don't speak It, but I do speak Portuguese. ;)"

I smile and exclaim to myself, *he is clever!* I open Safari and click on Match. There are several messages in my Match inbox.

While the messages load, I write, "You're funny! That's so cool that you speak other languages. Are you from the Bay Area?"

I open my Match inbox. To my surprise, Goleta messaged me. I decide to ignore Goleta. I comment to myself, *too much work and feels like a game.* I set the search filters to a 25 mile radius from my zip code and click search.

Frank responds, "No, I grew up in the Central Valley of California. I'm not fluent in any language other than English."

I scroll through the Match profiles from my search. I say to myself, *hmmm...he seems interesting.* I quickly ascertain that he meets my basic criteria. His pictures show a friendly-looking man with blond hair. He works in the foster care system. I send him a brief message.

Hi,

How are you? I'm intrigued to learn more about you. We work in similar fields. What do you do in foster care? I hope you are having a good week.

Cheers,
Anna

I glance down at my phone. I re-read Frank's last message. I ask him in my mind, *why do I already feel like I am cheating on you?* I can't shake the feeling that I am being deceptive by continuing my Match search while talking with Frank.

New Part seems happy. *You are being deceptive. That's good. You want to play hard to get.*

I wonder if I am looking at profiles to play hard to get. *Am I playing a game?*

Travis answers me. *No you aren't playing a game. You haven't met Frank. You don't know if it will work out. You can continue looking for friends for your social life.*

I take a deep breath. I return to my inbox. One message catches my attention. His message is simple.

Hi Return2SunnyCA,

Where are you back from? I like to travel and read, too.
I look forward to hearing from you.

Best,
Alex

His profile meets my basic criteria. I see he has traveled internationally and likes Tuesdays With Morrie and The Alchemist. He lives in San Luis Obispo.

Hi Alex,

I'm back from the South. I lived there for 4 years. Where do you like to travel? Your profile shows you like Tuesdays with Morrie and The Alchemist. Those are great books. What are you reading now?

Cheers,
Anna

I turn my attention to Frank's message. I respond, "Well, good thing we are both fluent in English.:) I am going to turn in for the night. I hope you sleep well and have sweet dreams."

I power down my computer. I think to myself, *I wish I had a cigarette. For some reason I really want one.* I walk to my office and set my computer on my desk. I ask myself, *am I doing something wrong by pursuing multiple people at once?* I turn on the bathroom light and open the drawer with the toothpaste. As I brush my teeth, I look at my reflection. I say to my reflection, *you seem tired and a little agitated.* I sigh. *Yes, to both of those things. I feel so unsure and restless.* I finish my bedtime routine. A message from Frank shows on my phone when I plug it in to charge.

"Sleep well, too. Sweet dreams."

I reply, "J zzzzzzzzz"

I turn on the sleep meditation podcast. I toss and turn. Sleep finally happens at some point during the third meditation.

Reflections ∞ Reactions ∞ Responses

_____

_____

_____

CHAPTER 36

COLLATERAL SESSION
WITH DAD PART 3

I feel weary as I drive to Jennifer's office. Today is hopefully the last session with Dad. Then we can move on to meet with Lindsey, too.

New Part pops in out of nowhere. *It is taking forever to get on with it. It being your daddy issues. You are just like every other girl out there. Daddy issues daddy issues.*

I muse, *I wonder who you are, Part.*

The sun shines over the recently irrigated fields. Water droplets glisten and birds seem to glide effortlessly overhead likely looking for worms and bugs in the moist soil. I say to myself, *or at least it seems effortless. On second thought they look graceful, working efficiently for their survival.* I'm struck by the metaphor to my own recovery. Most people with whom I interact do not know the extent of my mental illness and work towards recovery. I used to feel like I had to perform to hide it, and in performing I was somehow living a lie. Now I feel less like my life outside of therapy is a performance and more like I'm on a path to be congruent in my internal and external worlds.

New Part doesn't miss a beat. She appears tapping her foot, arms crossed and eyes rolling with a look of disdain for my comparison. *Now that's deep. Don't get yourself stuck down in that hole.*

Dad's car is parked near where I park. I say to myself, *he figured out how to get to this level. Third time's a charm.* I pull in to the spot next to him. He waves and smiles. I open the car door and begin climbing out.

"Doc-T-or A," he greets emphasizing the T in doctor. "How was your week, honey?"

I smile at his greeting. "Hi, Dad. My week was long. I was on another work trip. Lots of meetings with the leadership team. And a board meeting. It was a long week. How was yours?"

"Oh, you know. Same old same old," he replies nonchalantly. We walk toward the stairs. "You know I am trying to pull out of all of it. I don't want to deal with the headaches anymore. But I just can't seem to do that."

I look at him out of the corner of my eye. He seems tired like last weekend. His skin sags and wrinkles a little more than I remember. I notice his belly. I think, *his drinking must be up again.*

"Yeah," I nod in agreement. "I know it is really hard to untie from everything. You have been at it for so long and it is like one of the biggest parts of who you are. Leaving it will be both a relief and maybe also a letdown."

We cross the street and approach the steps to Jennifer's office. Pansy paws at the window and yelps a greeting.

"You are right about that, honey." He opens the door.

I greet Pansy and Jennifer with a pat and hug. Dad follows suit. We set our stuff on the chairs and take our shoes off. Jennifer and I settle into our spots on the floor and Dad in the chair. He rests his feet on a bolster. I adjust a blanket under me to comfortably sit cross-legged. Pansy gnaws on a chew toy between all of us. Dad and I look at Jennifer.

Jennifer begins warmly. "So, we seemed to have a break-through last week. Before we start with the note I wrote for you, Charlie, I wanted to check in and see if either of you have anything to share since then."

Dad and I look at each other and shrug our shoulders.

"I don't," I say apologetically. "I was gone all week and had tons of meetings. So I honestly haven't had a moment to really think about our last session."

Confusion flutters across Jennifer's face.

I hurriedly add, "It was a great session, for sure. We weren't able to have lunch because I was away for work all week."

"Yes, it was a great session," Dad concurs. "It started out rocky. But overall it was really good. I was busy, too. We will make time for lunch though. So, what did my note say from last week?"

Jennifer glances down at her notebook. "Lindsey. And then here I wrote 'the girls being open to her.' Does that ring a bell?"

Dad crosses his arms and rubs his chin with his right hand. "Now, let me think about that."

I suppress an eye roll because I know what's coming. My inner commentary booms. *His tone is set for a 'Mr. Talkable lecture' about the role Lindsey plays in our lives and how much she loves us and looks at us as her own children without wanting to take over as being our mom and and and...* I shake my head slightly.

Dad looks up at the ceiling. He continues to rub his chin. Jennifer catches me. She drops her eyebrows silently inquiring what's up. On her cue, I interrupt Dad's thoughts.

"Are you wanting to reiterate how much Lindsey loves us and what a prominent role she plays in our family?" My tone is short. "You've had this same 'talk' with Violet and me many times." I air quote 'talk' with my fingers.

An annoyed laugh escapes from his lips. "What? Oh, you girls. You never want to listen to what I have to say about Lindsey." He turns towards Jennifer. "In fact, this is exactly what I meant by that note about the girls being open. They always blow me off when I try to tell them about including Lindsey. You know, Lindsey does so much for us as a family." He turns his matter of fact lecture tone on in full force. "They don't know how much she does for all of us. She loves them like they are her own. She doesn't have to do half the stuff she does. You know, she never had kids of her own and that's because I already had Anna and Violet. I didn't want to have anymore. They just shut me down and roll their eyes every time I try to bring it up."

Before Jennifer can respond, I exclaim, "Dad! Seriously, what do we need to do to show you that we appreciate Lindsey, we love Lindsey, we know everything she does for us? We include her in everything we can. I mean I took her wedding dress shopping even before Mom. What are you really trying to say? I think this has more to do with your weird guilt around needing to include everybody all the time so their feelings don't get hurt. All I said last week was that I'd like to have lunch, or whatever, with you and only you every once in a while. That doesn't mean I don't value, appreciate, or love Lindsey. I mean really. What is it that you are really trying say?" My cheeks flush.

"Wow," Dad says flatly. "Now there's something there, wouldn't you agree, Jennifer?" He looks at her for confirmation.

I observe to myself, *this is one of his bully techniques…to get confirmation from others and make his point be the RIGHT one.*

Jennifer takes a deep breath. "Yes, there is something here," she says calmly. "Let's try to slow down a bit. This topic is one that has come up a lot for you both. Charlie, why don't you finish what you started saying in the beginning? Anna, will you be able to listen to what he has to say? I need to hear it so I can have a better understanding from him. O.K.?"

I nod. I begin silently counting my inhales and exhales in an attempt to control my frustration and anger.

"Thank you, Anna," Dad taunts in a child-like way.

I silently respond, *I'm surprised you didn't stick your tongue out at me just now.*

I tune back into his words. "As I was saying, Lindsey does a lot for all of us. I mean half the shit I get done is because Lindsey actually does it. I just can't keep everything straight. She loves you guys like you are her own. I just don't think you and your sister give her enough credit."

Jennifer asks, "What could Anna and Violet do to give her more credit?"

Dad looks up at the ceiling and rubs his chin again. "Now that is a good question, Jen. Thank you for asking that." He directs his next comments to her. "You know, they could include her more. It's like even these sessions that we've had without her have been hard for me. I don't like leaving her home on Sunday afternoon. She has been around long enough now that she should be involved in whatever I'm involved in."

Jennifer cuts in before he can continue. "Charlie, can I ask a clarifying question?"

He nods. "Sure."

"I am trying to understand what the core issue is for you here. You started with a note about the girls being open and clarified that you meant open to talking about Lindsey's role in the family. In that, you shared that she does a lot for all of you, even things she doesn't have to do, and that she never had kids of her own. You also said you would like it if Anna and Violet included her more and that she has been in the family long enough to be involved in everything. Am I on track so far?" He nods. "Great. Can you tell us more about what goes on for you coming to these sessions without her?"

His expression shows he is caught off guard. "Well, let me think about that." He looks up again. "I'm uncomfortable coming here without her because I feel like I have to hide things from her that we talk about in here."

Jennifer exaggerates a head nod. "Ohhhhhh. I get it now. You are caught in the middle of wanting to honor confidentiality of Anna's therapy sessions and sharing openly with your wife?"

Dad's face lights up. "Exactly! And it is very uncomfortable for me because I know Lindsey has a lot to add. Especially about the business stuff. I mean she has played a huge role in growing the businesses and getting us to this point. I just don't think the girls understand that. And she's not some greedy gold digger. She doesn't want to hoard it all for herself. She wants to share it with Anna and Violet. So when I come here, I have to leave her and then go home and she asks how it was and I'm like 'ahhhhhh what can I say?'" He shrugs his shoulders.

I jump in before Jennifer can respond. "Dad, when have we ever said Lindsey is a gold digger? Or what gave you that impression that we see her that way? I mean some of your other girlfriends between Mom and Lindsey were definitely like that. And no one was shy about telling you that back then. But Lindsey isn't. She is a super hard worker. I've told her that before. I've told her that I really look up to her professionally. She's made headway for women in agriculture. She's bucked the traditional gender role trend of following the husband's career when she moved out of state to pursue that opportunity for her career and you guys did long distance for many years. I really admire her for that. She's helped me a lot in my career, especially when I flounder. I just don't understand where this thought that Violet and I see her as a gold digger comes from."

Dad opens his mouth to speak, but nothing comes out. He closes his mouth. His lips purse together. His eyebrows dip. He shifts uncomfortably in his seat.

I start in again. "I mean, we do a lot of things with her. Like for Mother's Day that one year, we did an overnight in Los Angeles to see a musical. Whenever we are together in the same city, we do a spa day, well she plans those. We call her. If anything, she doesn't always reach out to us. Especially when she moved away. She was only really reachable during holidays back then...which is totally O.K. It's just where we were." I take a breath to share more when I see Jennifer raising her hand slightly.

"Anna." She startles me. "I am going to interrupt you right now, which I don't like to do usually. Your dad seems like he needs a moment. I'm going to ask you to hold on to your thoughts until he has time to let us know what is going on for him right now. O.K.?"

I nod. "Oh. O.K. I'm sorry about that. I guess I can be Mr. Talkable, too." I grin sheepishly.

Dad quips, "The apple doesn't fall far from the tree or the horse doesn't move far from the carriage, or is it the grape doesn't roll far from the vine. I can't remember. But, yes, Dr. Talkable."

We all giggle.

Jennifer prompts Dad to return to a moment again. "Charlie, just now you opened your mouth to say something and then closed it again before saying anything. Then Anna continued giving examples of ways that she and Violet respect and love Lindsey. Can you get back to that place and see if you can let us know what was going on?"

Dad smiles at her. "Thank you, Jen. Yes, Anna what you said brought up something for me. It pinged something new." He pauses to explain, "Jen 'a ping' means it struck a chord." He pauses again to look up at the ceiling. After a few breaths, he says slowly, "I'm honestly not sure what the ping was about."

"That's O.K.," she reassures. "The meaning behind the ping isn't coming up right away. But you noticed the ping and gave pause to reflect on it. That pause helps guide our conversation. Would it help if I summarized what Anna said right before?"

"Yes, that may help," Dad says softly. "I'm just not good at remembering things."

I wonder if Jennifer notes Dad's self-deprecating comments.

She glances through her notes. "Anna asked you about your belief that she and Violet see Lindsey as a gold digger. Anna mentioned ex-girlfriends who apparently were gold diggers and described several ways in which she and Violet do not see Lindsey that way. Anna shared about admiring Lindsey's professional life and talked about Lindsey being someone who helped her along her own career. Does that help?"

Dad nods. "Yes, Jen thank you. My pea brain couldn't take it all in. What Anna said made me think. I don't think I've ever heard her say those things before. I mean about Lindsey. I'm not really sure where the gold digger idea comes from. Maybe it was left over from an ex-girlfriend."

Jennifer postulates, "So, Charlie if I'm hearing you correctly, you are re-thinking your idea that Anna and Violet think Lindsey is a gold digger?"

He hesitates before he answers. "Well, yes, I guess I am."

Jennifer looks at me. "Anna, what is going on for you right now?"

I quickly answer. "I am glad he is seeing that we don't think Lindsey is a gold digger. I also want to point out that I don't think she minds not being at these sessions and may even like having a few hours to herself. I'm just saying..."

Dad's tone is guarded. "You are just saying what?"

"I'm just saying that Lindsey likes to read, stretch, putter around the house. She likes quiet and down time. You don't necessarily like those things as much as she does. So, I think she is really O.K. with not being here. I also think she trusts this process that I am on and will be available when it's time. Unless you know something I don't know, Dad. Has she said something to you like her feelings are hurt not being here?"

"I think at the beginning we clarified that your Dad feels stuck between honoring your confidentiality and being honest with his wife, right?" Jennifer recalls. "The issue for him isn't actually about hurting Lindsey's feelings by not including her here. Is that right, Charlie?"

Dad looks up at Jennifer. He rubs his chin. "Well, now that you remind me, I am afraid her feelings are hurt by not being included in this. She has been around long enough now."

I shift the bolster under my knees. "This conversation is getting frustrating for me. Dad, she has been around long enough. But she hasn't been around the entire time. She was like 10 when you and Mom got married and 12 when you had me. A lot went down in the 14 years before she came into our lives. In other words, our relationship started 14 years before your relationship with her. That doesn't make our relationship more important or more valuable. It just means there is a separate relationship from her that I want to nurture."

He spits words out of his mouth. "Well, Lindsey doesn't have to spend quality one on one time with her dad."

His comment pierces my gut. I note to myself, *there is that bully tactic again.*

I pause to take a deep breath and focus my thoughts. "Yes, Dad, you are probably right. So, what? My request to spend time with only you every once in a while is not negated by Lindsey not wanting that with her dad. Why are you comparing?"

Jennifer interjects. "I am going to stop you both for a moment. It does seem as if the conversation is going in circles. Charlie, it sounds like you see Anna's request to spend time with only you as somehow weaker or bad compared to Lindsey and her father. You didn't say that outright. Your tone may have implied it and I think Anna picked up on that. Anna, can you tell us where you felt that comment?"

I close my fist and stab my gut. "Right here. It pierced me. I feel like I can't win. And I don't understand what is so wrong with wanting to spend time with you, Dad. I'm not even saying I want to spend all the time with you. I'm saying I want to have lunch or coffee every once in a while. There were also many years between Mom and Lindsey, where it was just you, Violet and me. I just don't understand why this request is so, I can't even find the word because it seems more than wrong. It's like you are repulsed by it."

Dad's eyebrows rise.

Before he can say anything, Jennifer instructs him to be present. "Charlie, let Anna's words sink in. She felt stabbed by your comparison and feels confused and hurt."

Dad's face softens. His shoulders sink away from his ears.

After a moment, she asks gently, "Do you feel repulsed by Anna's request?"

"No," he shakes his head. "I guess I didn't see how comparing might hurt Anna. It is just something new for me."

Jennifer furrows her brow slightly. "I'm not sure the idea or even experience of spending time alone with Anna is new. Maybe your awareness of her need to connect with you without Lindsey is new?"

"Yes, you are right, Jennifer," he confirms.

"O.K." Jennifer sits up taller. "I have a question for you, Charlie. Please let me know if my question is too forward."

He nods. "Yeah, sure."

Jennifer takes a deep breath and slowly exhales. "Is it possible for you to separate your relationship with Anna from your relationship with Lindsey and still value them the same?"

He looks at her quizzically.

"Your love for both of them is apparent," she explains. "And you have a strong desire for them to have a strong relationship, which I have to say I don't see all the time with blended families. I've heard Anna say that she has a close a relationship with Lindsey. You spending time with Anna alone won't diminish the quality of Anna's relationship with Lindsey. And I wonder if that isn't also true with your relationship with Lindsey. I also don't see that the quality of your family relationship will be diminished if you spend time with Anna without Lindsey sometimes."

He emphatically nods his head. "I think I get it! I need to stop worrying that you girls and Lindsey will get along and just accept that you do."

"Yes!" I exclaim. "And also that spending quality time together with just me or just me and Violet doesn't take away from Lindsey. It is a different relationship that needs nurturing. We've neglected it for a long time."

He nods again. "Yes, I get it."

"I'd also like to suggest that you talk with Lindsey about this," Jennifer adds. "We can do that in our session with all 3 of you or you can do it outside of here. Whichever works for you."

I begin nodding, too. "I think we can talk with her outside of here. That way when she is here we can spend the time talking about ways you can help me with the trauma piece. What do you think, Dad?"

"Yeah, yeah that's all fine," he answers hurriedly.

"We've covered a lot together in the last three sessions," Jennifer concludes. "Today we are about at time. It feels like we are at a place to meet with Lindsey, too. What do you think?"

"Yes," Dad and I answer in unison.

"Great. Does next Sunday work?"

I confirm that I will be here either way.

"Per usual, book it and I will talk to Lindsey," Dad says. "If something conflicts, I will let you know."

We make small talk as we clean up the blankets, chairs and bolster, and gather our belongings. I hand Jennifer a check and thank her for helping us. Pansy snuggles against my leg as I walk toward the door. I bend down to pat Pansy's head.

Dad and I walk toward the parking lot. "What do you have going on this week?" he asks.

"I'm having mom, Aunt Tessa and Grandma G over for dinner tomorrow night. Then I leave early Tuesday for a work trip until Thursday. What about you?"

"Oh, I don't know. Let's see….I'm golfing on Wednesday. The usual. Meetings, dinners, you know how it is."

"Are you excited to see Violet and the crew?" We approach our cars.

"Of course," he smiles. "When are we going to get together? With just us. It will probably have to wait until they go back to Europe."

"Yes, you are probably right about that. Maybe you, Violet and I can do something."

We stand by the back of our cars. I reach to give him a hug.

"Yeah, we can try to make that happen," he says. "Have a good week, honey. And thanks again for these sessions with Jen."

"You're welcome, Dad." I feel gratitude. "Thanks for coming to them with me. It has really helped me."

Reflections ∞ Reactions ∞ Responses

_____

_____

_____

CHAPTER 37

PANIC ATTACK NUMBER 89 THOUSAND WITH A DOSE OF SUICIDE

I feel tired and hopeful as I drive to the grocery store from the last collateral session with Dad. I need to pick up ingredients for the pasta dinner I'm serving tomorrow night for Mom, Aunt Tessa and Grandma G.

I say to myself, *maybe Dad and I can finally move on.*

The parking lot at the grocery store is crowded as usual. I park in the last row and walk quickly to the carts. A group of homeless men are sitting under the awning near the carts. My stomach drops.

Mini Monster shoots into my conscious looking frantic. His hammock is nowhere in sight. He yells and waves his arms, *RUN RUN RUN. They are going to attack you. They are rapists. RUN RUN RUN.*

Travis stands with his armor on and sword in hand. *I will protect you. Hold your head high. Make eye contact. Let them know you mean business. You are not to be messed with.*

I increase my pace, hold my breath, smile and nod my head in their direction. They barely acknowledge me. I grab a cart and turn on my heel towards the door. I exhale when the automatic doors open.

I curse, *damn I wish those carts were somewhere else. I just don't feel safe.*

An image of my unconscious, bloodied body lying next to the carts in a muddy puddle covered in urine intrudes into my mind. My heart rate increases. My breath becomes shallow. I race through the grocery store to collect the ingredients for dinner tomorrow night. I grab a rotisserie chicken for dinner tonight.

My inner dialogue races without me deciphering which parts are activated. *Fuck me. Why does this always happen? I just want these anxiety attacks to stop. Where did that image come from? Get out of my head. Get out of my head. You are safe. You are safe. You aren't hurt. You are O.K. Pay and get to your car. Leave the cart inside. Just take the bag of groceries. You can make it.*

I basically run to my car.

Voices continue to spin in my head. *You look like a crazed person. Like someone invisible is chasing you. The boogey man. Everybody is looking at you. I am panicked. The sun is setting. I'm a target. No you aren't a target. You are only a target because you make yourself one.*

That image of my unconscious, bloodied body emerges in my mind again. I throw open my car door, throw the grocery bag across to the passenger seat and hop in. I slam the door closed and hit lock. I grip the steering wheel.

I think I hear Travis. *Steady. Steady. Breathe. You made it. You are safe. You made it.*

Mini Monster and other parts frantically talk over each other. *What if someone is in the car behind me. Oh God. Like those horror stories where someone snuck in the car and as soon as I start driving he will pop up. The boogey man. One of those homeless men.*

I close my eyes and rest my head on the steering wheel. The inner chatter continues. *When you open your eyes, look behind you. If someone is there, hit the horn and scream. 1-2-3. I* open my eyes and turn my head. My eyes dart around the backseat of my car. It is empty. I exhale with relief. *What if they are hiding in the very back against the seat so you can't see them? They could be there. You aren't in the clear yet.* Tears blur my vision. *Why is this happening? I just want to go home. I don't want to be scared.*

I fumble the keys and they drop on the floor. *Fuck.* I reach down and grab them. My hands are numb. *Breathe. Breathe. Breathe.* I listen for any noises that indicate a man is hiding in the back of my car waiting for the perfect moment to take me hostage, rape and beat me. A siren sounds in the distance. I hear a car driving down the row of the parking lot. I notice the stop light changing color. I find my car key and put it in the ignition. I turn it and the radio turns on. I startle. *Turn it off. You need to be able to hear when he sneaks up to strangle you.* I push the volume button to turn it off. I check the rear view mirror. So far, no indications that a boogeyman is in my car. I put the car in reverse and carefully back out of the parking space.

The next thing I know, I am pulling into my parking space at home. *How did I get home? I don't even remember driving.* I say thank you to whoever made sure I didn't get in an accident.

I'm exhausted when I finally close and lock the door of my apartment. I set my groceries down in the kitchen and reach for my phone. Frank messaged. I smile for the first time since I left Dad in the parking lot.

He wrote, "Hi. How was your weekend?"

I say to myself and my parts, *do I tell him it was good except I just had a major panic attack? Oh and that followed a therapy session with my dad. And by the way, I have PTSD.* Tears well up again. *I'm just so tired of feeling this way. No one wants to be with someone like me who can't keep it together.*

I put my phone down and walk to the bathroom. I look at myself in the reflection.

A shrill voice comes into my mind. *This is why you just need to end it. This madness. You can just end it and be done and not suffer anymore.*

Tears flow down my cheeks. "I don't want to die, though," I whisper. "I just want to be O.K."

The shrill voice jeers, *you don't want to die. But you know death is the only sure way to stop these panic attacks.*

I watch my reflection as I begin to sob. A voice instructs, *text the retreat girls. They will know what to say.*

I walk to the kitchen to retrieve my phone. I open my messages. A brief, sad smile dances across my face when I see Frank's message again.

I say to him silently, *you don't want me. I'm a mess.*

I open a new message and select Sasha, Camille and Dusty. I type "Girls, I'm having a terrible panic attack. Now I want to die."

I stop and read it. *I want to die? No I don't. That will scare them. Don't write that.* I delete the last sentence.

I type "Girls, I'm having a terrible panic attack. I don't know what started it. I hate it. I'm so tired. I want these to end. It is the worst kind of out of control feeling. I don't feel sane. I don't feel rational. I'm not lovable."

I stop and breathe. *Delete that last sentence. Too much information.* My breath wavers and tears pour faster down my cheeks. *But it is true. I am not lovable.* I collapse on the floor. *Just hit send.*

My thumb hovers over send. *No, delete this last line. It sounds stupid and weak.* I delete it. Then I hit send before any other part has time to chime in.

Within seconds they respond.

Camille writes, "Oh Anna. These are the worst. It will pass. Are you in a safe place? Want me to call you?"

Dusty writes, "Anna Gem. It is going to be o.k. They do feel out of control and insane. You aren't any of those. You are o.k. You got this girl. We are here with you. You aren't alone."

Sasha writes, "Anna thanks for sharing with us. It will pass. You are brave and lovable. You are not defined by these panic attacks. Just breathe."

I crawl into the living room and pull all of the pillows and blankets onto the floor. I turn the fireplace on and nestle into the pillows and blankets. I re-read their texts until I feel calmer. I don't know how much time has passed.

I respond, "Thank you girls. It is subsiding. I'm really tired. I'm home lying on the floor in front of the fireplace. I feel safer. I don't think I can talk Camille. Knowing you are all here with me helps a lot. Thank you."

I repeat Sasha's words to myself. *You are brave and lovable. You are brave and lovable. You are brave and lovable. You are brave and lovable.* I focus on those words. The flames dance around the fake log in my fireplace. My heart rate is calmer. I feel like a train ran me over. My body is limp. My eyes are heavy. I click on Frank's message. Responding to him gives distance from my panic attack. It allows me to pretend everything is O.K.

I respond, "My weekend was mellow. I went for a run yesterday and cleaned. I have a drawer of toys and things for my niece and nephew that I went through. How was your weekend?"

He responds immediately. "It was good. Mellow, too. I worked out with my friend. You could work out with us sometime if you want. We go to a park and he brings a rope and weights. It is fun."

I fight off the image of being tied up in the park with the rope.

Instead I type, "Sounds like fun. Like workouts from the Biggest Loser. Have you ever seen that?"

"Yes, we do workouts like that, but not as hardcore. What does your week look like?"

"I'm having dinner with family tomorrow night, then a work trip until Thursday night and then my sister arrives. A busy week. What about yours?"

"Oh bummer. I was going to see if you wanted to meet. Mine isn't as busy. Just working and going to the gym."

"Yeah, this week isn't good for me to meet."

I stop typing. A voice says, *plus, you don't even know if you want to meet him. He seems like a nice man. And you don't want to burden him with your madness.*

I shake my head and continue typing. "Yeah, this week isn't good for me to meet. Maybe another time. We can keep texting though."

"O.K. What about a phone call?"

I pause before responding. I just don't know if I'm ready for any of this. "Maybe later this week. Like on Wednesday?"

"That sounds good. Well, have a good night."

"You, too. Talk to you then."

I smile at the flames. I say to myself, *you are going to be O.K.* I drift off to sleep at some point. I wake up with a start. *What time is it?* I look at my phone. 3:00 AM. *Whoops. Didn't mean to leave the fireplace on that long.* I peel myself off the ground and go to the kitchen to get some water. I see the rotisserie chicken sitting on the counter when I switch the light on. I ask myself, *when did I put the other groceries away?* I turn the light off and walk towards my room. I turn the fireplace off. I'm too tired to brush my teeth and wash my face. I crawl into bed and tuck the pillows around my body before falling back to sleep. I don't remember any dreams when I wake up Monday morning.

Reflections ∞ Reactions ∞ Responses

_____

_____

_____

CHAPTER 38

MY COUNCIL OF ANCIENTS INSIDE AND OUT

Work on Monday is grueling. I am tired after yesterday's panic attack. My brain is fuzzy. Concentration eludes me. Mom, Auntie and Grandma G will be here in an hour. I haven't started cooking. I power down my computer and gaze out the window of my home office. I decide to take a shower. I realize I'm wearing the clothes I wore yesterday. They suddenly feel clingy and tarnished.

I peel them off as I walk to the bathroom. I look at my reflection. My eyes are red and strained. My hair is loosely up with wisps of hair falling around my face and neck. I shake my head.

I call myself, *train wreck.*

I stare at nothing while waiting for the water to heat up. The bathroom starts steaming up. I wonder how long I stared at nothing. I step into the shower without testing the water temperature.

I say to myself, *ouch. That is hot!* The hot water hitting my body startles me to the present. Suddenly I feel my feet tingle, the water running down my legs, my hair clinging to my head as it gets wet. I realize, *this feels so good.* I turn and let the water patter on my back and shoulders. I realize how tense they are. I close my eyes.

I ask, *Travis are you there? You can take the armor off and read the paper.* My shoulders slowly fall away from my ears. *Mini if you are there, you can return to the hammock.* Suddenly my lungs open to accept a deep, full breath. I nod at them in the recliner and hammock. *Thank you both.*

I'm warm and calm after the shower. I put on my comfortable black stretch pants and oversized sweatshirt. I decide to wear one purple and one blue sock as I channel my friend Catherine. I say to myself, *Catherine, may your happy-go-lucky, fun, honest, steady ways guide me.* I smile broadly at my reflection. *O.K., it's go time.*

I click the television on and select the top hits music channel. I fold the blankets and return the pillows to their homes on the couch and chairs. I open the blinds. The table isn't set.

I reassure myself, *that's O.K. Just get dinner started.*

I pull the ingredients out of the refrigerator for the pasta sauce and salad. I gather the pots and pans I need to boil water, sauté artichoke hearts, mushrooms and sausage, and heat up tomato sauce. While the water boils I prepare the sauce. My guests arrive as I'm washing lettuce for our salad. I dry my hands and wave to them through the sliding glass door.

I note to myself, *they are always so happy. They even smell happy.* My face smirks. *That's a weird thought.*

Their chatter and footsteps echo as they approach my front door. I open the door to a warm and jubilant greeting.

"Annieeeeee," Auntie sing songs. "Hi, honey."

She comes in first and gives me a warm, strong hug. She smells like lavender. Grandma is next. Her smile lights up the room.

"Hi there!" she exclaims. "How are you? Oh your house looks so good." She hands me a little gift bag. "This is just a little something for you," she whispers.

I accept it. "Thank you. You are so thoughtful."

Mom comes in last. "Hi, honey. Your house smells so good." She gives me a warm, familiar hug. She smells like Dove soap.

I think to myself, *I love the smell of Dove soap.*

Auntie exclaims from the kitchen, "This looks and smells great! Thank you so much, honey. What can I do to help? Anything?"

They gather around the kitchen. I feel the ground under my feet. I say to myself, *I hadn't realized I was floating.*

I respond to Auntie. "Sure, if you want can you finish washing the lettuce while I set the table?"

"Oh, sure." Auntie moves to the sink and picks up where I left off.

"What about us?" Mom asks.

Grandma chimes in. "Yes, is there anything we can do?"

"Well," I look around. "What about the wine? Or water. Can you open and pour that?" I point to a wine bottle on the shelf behind the table.

Mom moves in that direction. "Sure, I can do that."

I walk towards the front door. "And, Grandma, if you want, you can help me get the linens out of the cabinet-thingy by the front door. I can never remember what this piece of furniture is called. A banquet? Entry cabinet? I don't know."

She follows me. "Oh sure. Whatever it is, I really like it. Where did you get it?"

"Pier One," I inform her. "I didn't intend to get something like this when I went there. I was looking for a vanity and jewelry armoire, but it caught my eye and I had to have it. I like the different color woods and the V-shaped design." I run my fingers along the front of the cabinet doors where the wood Vs as I squat down to pull out the linens.

"It's really very nice." She touches the cabinet door, too. "You have a great eye for décor. I just love what you've done with the place."

I hand her striped cloth napkins. "Thanks! How are you?" I reach for the sand-colored linen place mats and stand to face her.

She takes a deep breath. "Oh, I'm doing O.K. My house keeps me busy and I'm planning to go visit my family back east this summer." We turn to walk back to the kitchen.

Mom hands us wine glasses after we set the table.

"Cheers!" We clink our glasses.

"So, Anna, I am dying to hear how Match is going," Grandma inquires. "Have you met anyone?"

A twinkle sparkles in my eyes. I grin. "Well actually, I've been chatting with a few people. It has been really fun."

"Ohhh," they say in unison.

Auntie asks if I have pictures and wants to know more about them.

Mom interjects about dinner. "Oh, I put the pasta in the water. It was boiling. I hope that is O.K."

I nod. "Oh yes. Thanks Momma. I have bread, too."

I walk by Auntie to the cabinet with cutting boards. "The salad looks good, Auntie. Thank you."

"Oh sure, honey!" she exclaims. "Do you want me to make a dressing, too?"

"That'd be great. Let me put this bread on the table and then I'll grab my computer to show you the pictures."

"Where's your olive oil and vinegar, honey?" Auntie asks.

"Oh, yeah." I stop in my tracks. "Right there." I point to the pantry cabinet across from the refrigerator. "And the bowls are right up there." I point to the cabinet above the dishwasher.

Mom and Grandma sit at the table. Auntie brings the salad bowl to the table and returns to the kitchen to make the dressing. I stir the pasta sauce.

"How much time is left on the pasta, Mom?"

"Whoops. I didn't set a timer. Just taste test it."

I use the spoon to get one piece of pasta out of the boiling water. I run cold water over it before tasting it. "Needs a few more minutes. Still a little firm." I set the timer for 4 minutes. "O.K., what was I going to do?"

Grandma reminds me I was on my way to get my computer to show them Match. She grins from ear to ear.

"Oh, yeah." I stop in my tracks again. "Let me grab my phone. That will be faster. I have the app."

We all settle into our seats at the table when the pasta timer goes off.

"Let's just dish our dinner and then I'll tell you all about Match." I feel disorganized.

"Yes, that's fine," they say in unison.

I strain the pasta and toss it in the sauce.

Mom calls from the table, "Don't forget the hotplate. You don't want to ruin your table."

I grab a trivet from the drawer by the oven and place it on the table. I set the pasta pan on it.

"What are we missing?" I ask.

Auntie raises her eyebrows. "Plates?"

"Oh, yeah!" I exclaim. "Duh."

I notice sideways glances between Mom and Auntie. I say to myself, *uh-oh. They sense that I'm off.* In an effort to cover my disarray, I ramble about the busy day I had at work while I gather plates and utensils. I sit down and realize I forgot the parmesan cheese, crushed red pepper, salt, pepper and butter.

I stand up again. "Start dishing. I just have to grab a few more things."

I place the last remaining items on the table and sit down.

"What me to dish you, honey?" Auntie asks.

"Sure, that would be great." I hand her my plate.

We take the first bites of dinner followed by exclamations of "yum" and "so delicious."

Grandma sets her fork down. "O.K., Match. I want to hear how it is going."

"Yes." I swallow a big bite of rigatoni. "So, I've been chatting with a handful of guys. The first we will call Goleta. He seemed cool at first, but then stood me up. Well, he didn't actually stand me up. He canceled on me the morning of. We were going to meet at the nail salon and get manicures."

They freeze and look at me then each other. Then they giggle awkwardly.

Auntie's voice is higher pitched than normal. "Manicures?"

I flash them a playful and knowing smile. "Yes, manicures."

"No wonder he canceled." Mom says between giggles. "He probably didn't think you were serious when he said yes."

Giggling turns into full blown laughter.

Grandma lends her support of my manicure-pedicure idea. "Well, I think that is a fun idea for a first date. Times are so different."

I wipe away a tear that formed while I was laughing with them. "Well, anyway, he said something came up with his family and we kind of fizzled out after that. So, then there is a guy from San Luis Obispo. We haven't met yet. In fact, I'm thinking of seeing if he wants to meet on Thursday for dinner since I will be flying in from a work trip that evening. He seems nice so far. In his pictures, he has a very young face, but his profile says he is my age. He is divorced, too. And he wants kids. So we shall see."

Grandma inquires, "So do you have criteria you use to pick who you talk to?"

I explain the criteria and steps I use to screen potential Matches. First, I look at their income, education, past relationship and kids' status. Then I look at their pictures. Finally, I read their profile.

"Seems very thorough," she nods. "I'm impressed!"

"It seems to be working so far," I nod back at her.

Auntie asks, "O.K., so you have Goleta, Babyface, who else?"

"I just messaged a guy who is in this area who works in foster care. That's the newest." I pause to take another bite.

"Do you like any of them?" Mom seems to hold her breath.

"Well, I haven't told you about the one I like the best." I attempt to smile and chew rigatoni at the same time. "His name is Frank."

They give each other knowing looks.

"He has a name!" Auntie exclaims.

"Yes, he has an actual name." I smile shyly. "Do you want to see his pictures?"

"Of course!" Grandma looks at Mom and Auntie. "Ohhhh, this is so fun!"

I turn around in my chair to find my phone. It is on the kitchen counter. I stand to retrieve it.

Auntie's curiosity gets the best of her. She fires off questions. "So, what does he do? What do you like about him? Do you have a lot in common? Have you been chatting through Match or does he already have your phone number?"

Grandma giggles and Mom takes another bite. I sit down again and sip my wine while the app opens.

"Good questions, Auntie." My homepage opens. I click on my inbox and from there Frank's profile. "I don't know what he does, but I do know he makes as much as I do. From his profile, we both like to read and travel. He asked for my phone number, so we have been texting directly. I like his sense of humor. He is witty and seems kind and thoughtful. Here are his pics. Scroll left."

I give the phone to my mom first. She quickly scrolls through and hands the phone to Aunt Tessa. Grandma leans over so they see the pics at the same time.

Auntie exclaims, "WOW! What a great smile!" She turns the phone to show us the picture she's looking at.

A shy smile creeps across my face. I look down. "I know. That picture is my favorite one. He just has a twinkle in his eye. Like it says, 'if you want to have fun and enjoy life, come to my table and all are welcome.' There is something about that picture that made me make an exception to my criteria because he didn't answer the question about wanting kids." I notice that all 3 of them are staring at me intently as if they see something I don't see. "But, I figure, I am on here to make friends and he seems like someone I'd be friends with."

Auntie returns her gaze to the phone. "Well, I think I'd want to be friends with him, too. Doesn't it look like he is sitting around a table with friends, pleasantly full after a great meal, and laughing over wine? Just like we do in our family. I like him already."

She hands me the phone. Grandma picks her fork up again. I look at Frank's picture one more time before closing out of the app.

Grandma swallows. "Well, I think this is just really fun, you know. I think it is a great way to meet people and I love hearing all the stories."

Auntie looks at my hands. I curse, *shit, she notices that I bit all my nails off.*

"How are you doing otherwise, honey?" Her tone hints of urgency mixed with concern.

Mini Monster bolts into sitting position on his hammock. *Don't tell them…they will definitely think you're crazy and admit you to the looney bin.*

I look down at my hands. I tell Mini, *I'm going to tell them. I'm trying to do things differently and sharing is one way.*

I take a deep breath to calm my nerves. "Well, I wasn't going to say anything but since you asked. I had a panic attack yesterday. It came out of nowhere. I'm feeling better now, though."

Mom's face fills with concern. "Did you reach out to Jennifer? That's really a bummer, Anna. I'm sorry."

"No, I haven't reached out to Jennifer," I say quietly. "I know I probably should. I'm meeting with her next weekend, so I will tell her about it then."

Auntie glances at Grandma who looks confused and concerned.

I turn to Grandma to explain. "I haven't told you about everything since our dinner with the retreat girls last October. The panic attacks have continued. It has gotten better and I'm seeing a therapist every week. I also take an antidepressant every day."

Grandma's smile is gentle and warm. "I've never had a panic attack myself, but I know they can be unbearable." She pauses as if she is deliberating something. "You know, your Grandpa took a little pill every morning. It helped him be himself. If that helps you, that's great."

"Really? I don't know why that surprises me. I guess because generationally those aren't as common." I'm also surprised Grandma shared something so private. She does not usually do that. "Thank you for sharing that Grandma. I really appreciate knowing I'm not the only one in the family that is helped by antidepressants."

I look at the women sitting around me and the empty plates in front of us. Gratitude washes over me.

I say to Mini Monster, *see that was the right thing to do Mini.* I hope my tone wasn't patronizing because I'm practicing how to be in charge of my parts.

"Thank you. It is so fun being so close and being able to share about the Match guys. I definitely want all of your input along the way this time. I don't want to end up in another unhealthy relationship, so be prepared to give your input."

Mom's grin is mischievous. "You mean, like we get to be a council that gets a say in picking your next husband? This could be funny, ladies!"

Auntie quips, "The Council of Elders."

Grandma jumps in. "No, The Council of Ancients like you called us that one time Anna when you drove us around for Violet's graduation. I still am so tickled by that."

Auntie giggles. "Yes, the Council of Ancients on Love."

Mom laughs. "You'll have to add us to your screening criteria. Like if they make it past the first meeting, then you have to have them come to dinner with the 3 of us so we can vet them."

Laughter erupts across the table.

Grandma banters, "We can come up with a set of questions beforehand."

Mom exclaims, "Yes! We can ask how they feel about the in-laws moving in someday."

More laughter. Tears are pouring down Mom's cheeks.

Auntie adds, "Yes, we can serve some really gross food and see if they eat it all. And test their willingness to clear the table and do dishes."

"O.K. O.K." I wipe tears from the corners of my eyes. "The Council of Ancients is officially part of the process."

Our banter dies down. We continue to chit chat about plans for the week and prepare for Violet's arrival while clearing the table. I promise to update them on dinner with Babyface on Thursday.

By the time they leave, I feel completely back in my own skin. I pack for my work trip and get ready for bed. My reflection in the mirror shows a calm and content person.

"Fuck," I say out loud to myself. "I forgot to take the trash out."

Mini Monster startles, *don't do it now. It's dark and late and you never know who will be there lurking in the shadows. You don't want to be the next body found in a dumpster.*

I shake my head. "Stop. I'm obviously not going out there now for all the reasons you said and also because I'm tired and don't want to. I will take it tomorrow on my way to the airport. That way I can have my car headlights on the dumpster and the panic button in my hand. Capiche?"

Mini Monster huffs and stomps for a moment before climbing back into his hammock. Travis nods, which I interpret to mean that he is prepared to help if needed.

"Thank you, Travis."

I say to myself, *seriously, this parts thing is so wild.* I shake my head again. My reflection rolls her eyes.

A voice, possibly the New Part says, *they might admit you to the looney bin if they saw all of us now.*

I smile. *But this parts business is working. I mean Travis and Mini Monster you are much better off, right?* Before they can answer I giggle as I imagine myself explaining about my parts to my Match dates.

"Looney bins," I say out loud before turning off the bathroom light and walking to my room.

Reflections ∞ Reactions ∞ Responses

_____

_____

_____

CHAPTER 39

MATCH MEETING NUMBER 1

I check the time on my phone. I'm sitting at the gate waiting to board my flight back to San Luis Obispo. So far, it is on time. Babyface and I are meeting for an early dinner. I feel nervous and a little scared about meeting him for a full meal.

A voice says, *the good news is the sun will still be out. And you can leave if you don't want to finish your dinner. And if you have to park in a parking garage, you can ask mall security to escort you to your car if you get a creepy vibe from him.*

I ask, *Travis is that you? Are you the voice of reason?*

I see Travis wink from his recliner. *Most of the time nowadays I am the voice of reason.*

I scroll through my messages and re-read the conversation with Frank over the last few days. He shared about his time in the military, in college studying international relations, and growing up on dairy farms. Talking with him is really easy.

I re-read the conversation with Babyface. It seems more formulaic and less familiar. I open the Match app to see if Foster Care

Guy responded to my last message. Nothing from him. The gate attendant begins the boarding process over the loudspeaker. I close the app and black out my phone.

I say to myself, *here goes nothing.*

The flight lands on time. I switch my phone out of airplane mode and see that Babyface texted to confirm dinner. I text him to let him know I landed and plan to meet him for dinner in 30 minutes.

I stop in the restroom before walking to my car. I'm grateful to have my bag with me so I can quickly freshen up. I brush my teeth and re-secure the bobby pin that holds my hair out of my face. I apply lip gloss and look at my reflection in the full length mirror one more time.

I reassure my reflection, *you look fine. He knows you are coming from a work trip.*

I park in a parking garage near the restaurant. It is brightly lit even though the sun has not set yet. I look at myself in my rearview mirror and smile. I repeat, *here goes nothing.*

I walk to the entrance and see him just inside the door. He waves when he sees me. I wave back.

I tell myself, *he really does have a baby face. He could be my little brother.*

He opens the door for me. We exchange pleasantries. He tells me there is a table available inside, unless I would prefer to wait for the patio. He asks how my flight was. I tell him it was uneventful and ask how his day was. He describes it the same way. Uneventful.

I'm bored before we get to the table. We both spend an extra long time looking over the menu, which happens to be long like the menu at Cheesecake Factory. It might be the first time I am not overwhelmed by an extensive menu.

We place our order. An awkward silence settles around us. I ask him about his family and college experience. He asks me the same thing. Another awkward silence. I ask him about his experience on Match. He overshares about his ex-wife and their divorce. Dinner ends with me simultaneously feeling sorry for him and anxious to get on the road.

I call Auntie from the car. She answers after the first ring.

"I was hoping you'd call me," she greets me. "Did you have your date with Babyface?"

"Hi Auntie," I greet her. "Yes, he is really a nice guy. Friendly, safe. He doesn't have a mean bone in his body. Annnnnddddd…I was so bored the entire time. I can't decide if I was just tired from my work trip so I didn't have the energy to carry the conversation or if it just isn't a match. But all I know is I was bored and we spent most of the time talking about his divorce and ex-wife."

"Hmmmm." She surmises, "Well, maybe you were tired. Or are tired. But you know if you clicked with him you probably wouldn't have felt so bored. How was dinner?"

"Oh, it was good. Nothing too fancy. Simple flavors. Really good." I turn right to the on-ramp for the freeway. "So do you think I should meet him again? He said he would come down to my area next time. I couldn't figure out why he would want to do that since I was so bored. I thought for sure he'd be bored, too."

"Well, honey." She speculates, "You are beautiful and I'm sure even though you felt tired you were able to carry the conversation. You are really good at talking with people. You make it easy for people to open up to you. He probably really appreciated those qualities. I'm sure he would want to have dinner with you again. I can't imagine why he wouldn't."

"Thanks Auntie." I hesitate because my approach to dating this time is new. "I just don't want him to waste his time coming all the way down when I honestly don't see us being friends. I mean don't get me wrong. Like I said, he was really really nice. But what would we do together? I don't know." My mind draws a blank on conjuring an image of a potential activity with Babyface. "Maybe he was just really nervous and if I give him another chance it will be a different experience."

"Yeah, maybe he was just nervous," she agrees. "What if you meet to hike or something like that? Or go for a bike ride. Something other than dinner where you can see if you have things in common."

I switch lanes. "Yeah. That's a good idea. I'll think about it. Right now I have to go. There is a lot of traffic and I don't want to be distracted. Sorry about that."

"Oh, that's O.K., hon. I'd rather you be safe, and we can talk more later. I'm glad you called, though. I was a little worried and, of course, curious." I hear her smile through the phone.

"I love you, Auntie. I'll call you later." We hang up.

I turn on the radio. My mind wanders from topic to topic on my way home. *How's Frank? When will we meet? Next session is with Dad and Lindsey. I'm tired. Will this traffic ever open up? Violet gets here soon. Yeah! I have to pee.*

By the time I pull in my parking spot, I'm officially exhausted. I quickly gather my luggage and work bag, stop to retrieve my mail and walk to my house.

I curse, *fuck, I forgot to take the garbage out.* I remember as I am hit by a waft of stale garbage permeating my condo.

I say to myself, *ugh. Gross. I live in a hot musty dump.* I close and lock the door behind me.

Mini Monster appears frantic again. *Now you have to take the trash out and it is dark again. You are gonna die!!!!*

I open the slider to circulate fresh air in my apartment. I take a deep breath and count to five.

I tell Mini, *I am going to be fine. I will take the panic button and a flashlight. It will be fine. The dumpsters are well lit.*

I reassure myself with each step that brings me closer to the dumpster. *I am safe. I can protect myself. I am safe.*

I throw open the gate to the dumpster. A quick glance shows it's empty. I push the gate door open as wide as possible. I notice one of the dumpster lids is already open. I am standing in front of it in three strides. I heave the bag over the top and turn back to the entrance before I hear it hit the bottom. I slam the gate door closed harder than I intend and am halfway back to my apartment in less than a minute.

I reassure Mini, *see, I told you it would be alright.*

I feel relieved and proud that I did not have another panic attack. I decide to take a long hot shower. I don't unpack. Sleep comes and stays until my alarm goes off Friday morning.

I reach for my phone to shut the alarm off. I notice I have an unread text message. It is from Frank.

He writes, "Good morning Anna. I hope you have a good Friday."

I reply before getting out of bed. "Thanks and good morning. I hope you do too. What are your plans this weekend?"

"Nothing much. I'm going to spend time with friends and workout. You?"

"My sister arrives on Monday and I'm meeting up with my dad and step-mom on Sunday."

"That's right. I remember you said your sister is coming in."

I kick the covers off my legs.

I say to myself, *I wonder if he wants to ask me out. What's taking so long?* I feel groggy. *Coffee first.* I get my single cup drip maker out.

Travis peers in again from his recliner. *He probably thinks they will take up all your time?*

Frank texts before I respond. He asks, "Are they staying with you?"

Travis exclaims, *see that's what he thinks!*

I respond to Frank. "No, they are staying with our dad and step-mom for part of the time. Then we are all going to our cabin and then they will stay with our mom and step-dad. I have 2 bedrooms, but it is too small for all four of them to stay comfortably."

Frank replies, "Gotcha. Well, let me know if you can break away to meet."

I pour almond milk into my coffee cup.

I cheer to myself, *he does want to meet. Yay!!!*

I open my calendar app to confirm I'm not traveling next week and see when I have scheduled meetings. I took Thursday and Friday off to go to the cabin with Violet and the family.

I type, "Yes, that would be great. Maybe Wednesday?"

Frank responds immediately. "Great. I can make a reservation for dinner."

Mini Monster jumps up and down. *What??? Dinner??? Oh no. Too soon.*

I write back, "Oh I'm sorry I can't do dinner. Could you possibly meet for breakfast or lunch? Sorry about that. We have dinner plans every night while Violet is here."

"That's no problem. I can adjust my schedule Wednesday. Want to meet at 11 at Café Tuscany?

"That works. Thanks for understanding."

"I'm the new guy on the block. I get it.:)"

"J yes, you are. When my sister is here I try to spend as much time with her as possible. Have to get ready for the day and start work. Have a good day. I look forward to meeting."

"That's cool that you and your sister are so close. I hope you have a good day, too."

Friday flies by. Babyface messaged at lunch time to see if I made it home safely and ask if he can come down on Sunday. I close my computer and contemplate how to respond. I consider making up an excuse, but decide to be honest.

I text, "Hi! I did make it home. There was a lot of traffic. I will be honest. I enjoyed dinner with you. Unfortunately, I don't feel a connection and I don't want to waste your time. I wish you the best of luck on your search. Thank you again for dinner."

Babyface responded a few minutes later. "I'm glad you made it home safe. Thank you for being honest. It isn't easy. I appreciate you did not blow me off or waste my time. Best of luck, too."

I text, "J."

I glance outside and see that it is still light outside. I change into my running gear and head out for a quick jog. My step is light. I intentionally keep my heart rate down so as not to trigger a panic attack, which means sometimes I walk. My body feels in sync. I think about the men I have met through Match.

I say to myself, *it has been fun this time around. Not pressured.* I feel confident and secure in myself. I tell myself and my parts, *everything is going to be O.K.* I return home without incident.

Reflections ∞ Reactions ∞ Responses

_____

_____

_____

CHAPTER 40

COLLATERAL SESSION
WITH DAD & LINDSEY

Sunday starts slowly. The fog is in. May gray. I lift my phone off the night stand. 9:25 AM.

I say to myself, *today is the day with Dad and Lindsey.*

I stare at the ceiling. Images of Lindsey walking to the couch to hold me when I told them I was suicidal float to my consciousness. Her facial expression was soft and caring. I say to myself, *she can be so nurturing.*

Next, I see the image of her standing in the kitchen fuming when she accused me of perpetuating Dad's alcoholism. I note, *what a contrast.* Her face was stone-cold and hard. Her eyes danced with fury.

I think to myself, *I wonder what today will bring.*

I climb out of bed to make coffee and put bread in the toaster. I open the blinds even though it is still foggy. Quiet mornings like these give me too much space to worry. I busy myself with laundry and cleaning until it is time to leave. Of course I leave later than I intended, so I am running late.

Critic appears out of nowhere. *Fuck, why did that happen? You didn't have anything to do this morning. You really shouldn't be late. You are just like your dad. Always late. Can't leave on time.* I shake my head.

I ask, *Travis, what did you call him? Brute?*

I imagine Travis standing to attention. *Yes, ma'am.*

The interesting thing about Brute is he is only a voice. My other parts appear in images. Brute's voice is loud, his tone sharp. The sound of his voice makes me shudder.

I say to myself, *interesting that Brute is here today.*

My chest begins to tighten and anxiety bubbles in my stomach. *Hi Mini Monster.*

I see Mini standing on the sand next to his hammock. He jumps up and down frantically waving his arms. *Brute's here. RUNNNNNN. HIDE. TAKE COVER.* Mini shrieks.

Brute's voice bellows out of the darkness. *You WIMP. Don't listen to that little twerp. He doesn't know how to step up to the plate. You don't want to be weak like him.*

Mini begins to cry. He sits down in defeat. *Brute, you are mean.*

Out of nowhere, Travis appears in full armor. He stands in front of Mini and waves his sword towards Brute's Voice. Travis is calm and firm. *Stop it both of you! Enough. You will both be quiet and let Anna drive in peace.*

My shoulders and back are rock solid. I'm wearing Travis's armor. I feel tired even though I haven't done that much today.

To my dismay the roads are packed, so I arrive ten minutes late. I immediately sense tension in the room. Lindsey sits in a chair next to Dad. Her facial muscles are clenched in such a way that she doesn't look at all like herself. I've never seen her so guarded, stone-like. I think, *maybe she has a Travis, too.*

Dad makes friendly conversation with Jennifer. Pansy is lying down with her hind legs ready to burst forward at any minute. Her entire body is touching Jennifer's thigh. I've never seen her in such a protective position, ready to pounce if needed.

New Part appears with her arms crossed and one foot out tapping while casually leaning against the wall of a house with a lot of windows. *Well, this should be interesting.*

I settle on the floor in my usual position with bolsters and blankets under me. I ask if we've tried to call Violet and Franz because they are going to join via FaceTime. No one has. I pull out my iPad to dial them, but FaceTime won't connect. Dad offers to call them on their landline and put them on speaker phone.

The entire session feels disjointed and tense already. I look to Jennifer with wide eyes. Her expression returns my uneasiness with a hint of reassurance.

She looks at Dad. "How is it going, Charlie? Are you able to get Violet and Franz on the phone?" She turns towards me. "Anna, does this work for you?"

"Hi guys." Violet's voice floats through the phone. "I don't know why FaceTime isn't working. I'm sorry. Will this work?"

Dad flings his phone on the floor in the middle of us. "Violet, honey, can you hear us if I put the phone there?" He points to the floor where his phone landed.

Violet and I giggle. Dad's eyes widen. "Oh, you guys. Don't start ganging up on me already."

"We aren't ganging up on you," I clarify. "It's just that Violet can't see where you put the phone, so pointing at it and asking her if she can hear with it there was funny."

"Yeah Dad, I can't see where there is," Violet agrees. "I can hear just fine. Thank you for your concern, though, Dad."

I notice that Lindsey's face remains stone-like, reflecting no emotion. I wonder, *what is she thinking?*

Brute answers, *she's thinking you guys are ridiculous and you are wasting her time.*

Jennifer must wonder the same thing. She squares her body and face to Lindsey. She doesn't completely match Lindsey's facial expression, but she does sit up taller and firmly holds eye contact with Lindsey. "Lindsey, is it O.K. that I call you Lindsey or do you prefer something else?"

"Lindsey is O.K."

"O.K.," Jennifer smiles. "I think this is the first time you and I are meeting. I've spent time with Violet, Franz and Charlie before. So let me explain a little about what we are doing here." She pauses to look at her notes. "Well, let me start by asking if you have had experience with therapy? You don't have to give details."

Lindsey's inhale is sharp. "I've been to therapy on and off for years. I'm familiar with the process." She sits up straighter.

Jennifer nods. "O.K. Good. So you are familiar with confidentiality. It means that what we say in here stays in here. It isn't meant to be discussed with people outside of this group. The purpose of these family sessions, sometimes called collateral sessions, is to help build Anna's support system outside of therapy. Family sessions can take on many different forms. For today, Anna has asked that we talk about trauma in general and share about specific ways

Anna's trauma affects her and ways you might be able to help. Does that make sense?"

We nod.

Jennifer makes eye contact with me. "Anna, did I capture that correctly?" I nod before she continues. "O.K., I should also say that if at any time any of you feel like we are moving in an unproductive, unhealthy or scary direction, please let me know. In fact, Anna and Charlie came up with a safe word." She looks to Dad and me. "Do you want to share with Lindsey about that?" She quickly adds in a slightly louder voice, "And Violet and Franz, do you know about the safe word? This goes for you, too."

Dad and I look at each other as if to give permission to the other to tell Lindsey about the safe word. We start speaking at the same time.

"Go ahead, honey." Dad adds dismissively, "This is your deal."

Brute's voice bellows out of the darkness. *See, even he thinks you are weak and he doesn't want to be associated with your deal. Where are you Travis? Piss poor job stopping her from feeling that knife.*

I inhale sharply and force myself to mirror Jennifer's poise. I square my body to Lindsey and hold steady eye contact. "So, I think you know the purpose of the safe word. Anytime any of us needs to step back and take a break, we say Pansy. Dad came up with it, actually."

Mini Monster jumps up and pumps his arm in his new cheer-leader role. *Nice zinger. You tell him!*

Dad shifts in his seat and shoots Lindsey an uncomfortable glance. "Yes, I think you are right about that." His tone attempts to imply that he just remembered that he was a part of 'this deal' before now.

Violet's voice rises from the middle of the circle. "Sorry, it broke up. What was the word?"

In unison, we say, "Pansy."

"Oh, O.K. The dog is named Pansy, right? Is that where it came from?" she asks.

Jennifer looks at the phone. "Yes. That is right Violet." She looks at me. "O.K. we are going to move on to the part about trauma. Violet, Franz and Charlie, I know you have heard this before. So for you it will be a review. Lindsey, I'm not sure if you are familiar with this." Before anyone can respond, Jennifer turns her notepad over and draws a triangle. "This is Karpman's Triangle." She scribbles as she talks. "Up here in the top corner is Perpetrator. Down here is Victim and over here is Bystander or sometimes people say Rescuer." She looks up to see that we are looking at her. "Violet and Franz, I'm sorry you can't see the drawing, but hopefully you remember it from last time we were on FaceTime.

"So, the idea is that when someone is traumatized, they internalize the triangle and take on these roles. They bounce between perpetrating, being a victim, and less frequently being a bystander or rescuer. They could perpetrate against themselves or others. So, for instance, you might recall times when Anna is more aggressive than normal either in berating herself, being too hard on herself, or coming off really strong and even verbally attacking others."

Dad and Lindsey nod. The phone is noticeably quiet.

"As the victim, Anna might be weepy, sad, down, and depressed. Or she might be stuck in a rut and express the whoa-is-me outlook. Like everyone is out to get me. As the bystander or rescuer, she may jump in to save others or she may freeze and not take any action where action is warranted. Anna may jump between these roles in one sitting, too. The idea is that when Anna doesn't seem like herself, she could be caught in the triangle. Usually, someone who is traumatized gets triggered by something and that propels them into the triangle. It is really hard, especially in the beginning of doing trauma work, for someone to know they are in the triangle. Does that make sense?"

Lindsey's head nods up and down quickly. "Yes, yes," she says with impatience.

Jennifer's expression indicates she is caught off guard. "Oh, O.K. Have you seen this before Lindsey?"

"Well, no," Lindsey replies. "It makes sense though, which is what you asked."

Pansy jumps to action, barking and scurrying across the room to the front windows. She jumps up and down frantically barking at the window.

Jennifer hastily sets her notepad down and springs up after Pansy. "I'm so sorry. She gets really protective when she sees squirrels and birds. She must have seen one," Jennifer explains over her shoulder.

She reaches out to pick Pansy up. "Pansy, it is O.K. We are all safe. It is O.K. Thank you for watching out for us." Jennifer returns to her seat and holds Pansy in her lap. She pets Pansy's back until Pansy noticeably calms down. "Where were we?" Jennifer asks.

I use this question as a cue to share more about my experience. My hope is Lindsey will soften when she realizes this session isn't about family bashing or whatever fear she has that's got her so stonewalled.

"So for me, the important thing, well several important things, is that learning about Karpman's Triangle helped me to begin seeing when I'm not being myself. Like I can feel myself shift between these roles when I think back to situations where I got caught in the triangle.

"I haven't yet figured out how or when I'm going into the triangle and I haven't figured out how to get out of it yet. But the goal, or one of the goals, is for me to be able to step out of the triangle when I get caught in it. Like right now it is like a tornado that sucks me in with little awareness. But after, I can look back at the weather report and see that a tornado just happened. It helps me orient the trauma response so the clean-up happens faster. Or maybe not faster, but I can separate myself from it. And that helps. I don't know if any of that makes sense." I feel tongue-tied and at a loss for how to make them understand.

Brute criticizes, *of course you are tongue-tied. And you sound crazy.*

Dad's phone rings from the center of the circle. Violet Home flashes across the screen. I lunge forward to answer it, grateful for the distraction.

"Hi Vi," my voice booms.

"I'm so sorry." She sounds frustrated. "Our connection is just really bad and the kids won't go to sleep. I think they are excited about coming to California tomorrow. We've only caught bits and pieces. I think we have to go. I know what you are doing is important and I want to be there. Can we set up a time when Franz and I are there in the next few weeks to meet in person? I know that means you have to explain it all over again, so if that is too much, Anna, I understand."

"No, not a problem at all," I assure Violet. "It just isn't working out this time. We will set up a time when you guys are here. That will be better. Then you can see the pictures."

"O.K." Her voice sounds sad. "I love…" The call drops.

Silence billows from the center of the circle. My jaw clenches. I remember the words I heard when Julia massaged my jaw on the mental health retreat. *Your sister saved your life.*

Jennifer looks at me with raised eyebrows. "Are you O.K., Anna?"

"Yes," I say too quickly. "I wish it worked for them to be here, but that's the way it goes." I consider sharing about what happened on the massage table.

Brute's voice drips with sarcasm. *Oh yeah, like that will help them understand. You hear voices. That's woo-woo.*

Dad tries to move his phone closer with his foot, but his leg is too short. "Honey, can you help me with that? I just don't want to forget it on the floor."

I lean forward and slide the phone towards him. It stops directly in front of him.

"Nice shot!" He has a goofy grin on his face.

Lindsey's shoulders soften ever so slightly. Her face seems to thaw, too. "Annie, I think what I'd like to hear is what we can do to help you. Like what do you need from us?"

Jennifer jumps in before I can answer. "That is really import-ant. Before we go there, I want to make sure Anna doesn't have any-thing else to share or need anything else from us about Karpman's Triangle." She shifts so her body faces me. "You looked like you were about to tell us something else after Violet dropped off."

"No, I didn't have anything else to say."

To Brute I say, *maybe you're right.*

Jennifer raises her eyebrows. "Are you sure? You also were trying to describe what happens for you with Karpman's Triangle." She turns her attention to Dad and Lindsey. "Actually, I want to hear from you both a recap of what you heard Anna describe. I think she needs to hear that you understand what happens for her. That is really important because this is an area I anticipate she will ask for help."

Gratitude fills my chest. I didn't realize I need to hear from them what they heard from me, but I am so relieved that Jennifer asked them. I often question whether or not they hear me. My gaze bounces from Dad to Lindsey and back.

Brute's voice fills the silence. *See they weren't paying attention because you aren't important. They don't believe what you are going through.*

Doubt replaces the gratitude and relief I felt a moment ago. Jennifer must have sensed that because she asked Dad to recall what he heard since this is the second time he's heard it.

Noticeably uncomfortable, Dad stalls. "Hmmmm." He slouches in his chair and looks up. "Let's see. I think what you said, Anna, is that when you get stuck in the triangle you can't get out and you need our help." He looks at me for validation. "Did I pass the test?"

"I'm sorry," Jennifer apologizes. "I didn't mean to put you on the spot and make it sound like I'm testing you. This isn't a test. We were interrupted by the poor connection and I want to make sure that Anna was heard. If not, that's O.K. She can start again." She looks at Lindsey. "What about you, Lindsey?"

Lindsey smiles for the first time. "I appreciate that you are having us go back to that point." She looks at me. "What I heard you say, Annie, is that you are getting better at seeing when you've been in the triangle, but you still don't always know in the present time when you are in it. Knowing about the triangle has helped you orient your…triggers. Is that the word you used?" She continues without a pause. "You want someday to be able to not let the triangle take over. So to learn to stop it before it starts."

Relief floods my chest again. I say to myself and Brute, *she was paying attention. Then what's with the hard expression?*

"Yes! Thanks, Lindsey. Dad your description was on par, too."

"Let me talk a little about triggers, and possibly re-enactments before we move on to talking specifically about Anna's trauma," Jennifer suggests.

I nod. "Yes, that would be helpful."

Jennifer faces Dad and Lindsey. "I feel like a teacher. I hope I'm not coming off as too preachy." They shake their heads no. "O.K. Well please tell me if I do. I don't want you to feel like we are testing you. This is all meant to help Anna by helping you to better understand trauma."

She looks at her notebook. "So triggers are those things that happen that make someone who has been traumatized feel the trauma again. Triggers can be environmental, related to anniversaries, smells, specific people, noises, dreams, places. When someone has been triggered, they might take on one of the roles in Karpman's Triangle; they might dissociate, they might have a flashback, they might become hypervigilant, they might freeze. Any number of things could happen when someone is triggered. People commonly describe feeling not like themselves when they've been triggered. O.K.?" She nods towards Dad and Lindsey.

They nod back. Lindsey says, "O.K., that makes sense."

"Re-enactments are when someone repeatedly gets into similar situations as the trauma to re-enact it and see if they can change the outcome. It's a nasty little trick the mind plays on us because it never works out."

I notice Pansy sitting between Jennifer and me chewing on her toy, as if she is now a member of the group. Jennifer sees me looking at Pansy and a smile dances across her face.

I say to myself, *Pansy doesn't feel threatened anymore. The ice has thawed.*

Sure enough, Lindsey's face is soft and filled with concern and care. "Annie, what can we do to help you?"

"Well," I start and then stop. We are moving to unchartered territory. Territory that in the past resulted in family blow ups.

"O.K., so I know that Violet and I always get mad when you invite your friends to family functions." I turn to Jennifer to explain. "Dad does this thing where he invites his friends to everything. To him his friends are his family. But to us, they are not. But whenever we say something about it, Dad gets mad, blows us off, doesn't listen, or whatever. It isn't good."

I turn back towards Dad and Lindsey. "So, I'm going to try to explain why it is so hard for me to be around your friends. I don't want to bash you. And I'm not saying that I never want to be around them."

I look to Jennifer for reassurance. She smiles and nods with encouragement. "So, Dad when you are around your friends, you are different. You are more likely to make gross, crude comments about women and sometimes you specifically put me on the spot. For instance, the dinner you guys had a few months ago with the usual cronies, you were standing on the patio with your male friends and I walked out of the slider past you guys towards the other end of the table and you turned and said really loud 'Wow, Anna, you really look good.' It was almost like a catcall. Like I felt all those men turn their eyes to my body and check me out. That's disgusting and wrong on so many levels. It makes me really uncomfortable. It makes me feel like a sexual object. In other words, not human. It makes me feel unsafe and dirty. I get really angry and really sad. Sometimes I dissociate. Like that memory I just described I'm watching myself from above walk across the patio. It is a dissociated memory. It triggers me. It's not just things directed at me. You and Jason discussed your sex lives and your penises in front of us." I quickly add, "No offense, Lindsey."

She shakes her head. "None taken. You are right, that does happen."

Jennifer inquires with curiosity. "So, Lindsey, you have also seen what Anna describes?"

She nods.

Jennifer continues to press. "And does it bother you?"

Lindsey shrugs. "I mean, yes and no. It is just the way they are. So I don't let it affect me. I don't take it personally."

"Oh, I see." Jennifer glances at her notes.

I imagine Jennifer is trying to control her anger. I say to myself, *after all she is a feminist.*

Jennifer looks up at Lindsey. "Have you experienced objectification as a woman before?"

"Well, yes," Lindsey hesitates. "In the produce industry, it is male-dominated. I've experienced some…stuff." She glances sideways at Dad who is looking at her reflection in the mirror behind Jennifer.

I'm suddenly very annoyed. "Well, it does affect me." I spit the words across the room with more force than intended. "I mean, it actually drives me crazy. I think it is rude, disrespectful, inconsiderate, degrading, dehumanizing. It sends me into one of two places-either my militant feminist comes out or I dissociate."

I look at Dad. "You don't behave that way when you aren't around your friends. I like you better when they aren't there. You don't have to perform." I pause and take a deep breath. "That's one piece of the friend thing. The other is specific to Jason and Kayla. I know they are your best friends and to you they really are family. And despite what I said a moment ago about them, I do believe they are less sexist than most of your friends. That said, their son was friends with the rapist in high school. The first time I had a flashback I was walking on the beach with Mom passed their son's apartment that I think the rapist lived in, too? Maybe not, but I know he was there a lot. Every time I see Jason and Kayla, my mind goes down a rabbit hole that ends with the rapist's face. I wish it was different. But they specifically take me to him every time. It is a battle for me to stay present."

"Wow!" Jennifer exclaims. "I didn't know any of that. Is this new stuff?"

"No," I say softly. "It is the first time I have been able to articulate all of it so clearly." I turn to Lindsey. "You've seen the impact it has on me. You've held me through panic attacks, like that one time when Elizabeth was there. You can tell when I get really aggressive about male privilege, misogyny, and sexism. It's like this thing comes over me and I can't stop it. I'm filled with hatred and rage." I take a sharp, quick breath and let it out with a puff. "So that's probably the biggest thing you can do. Just limit the time we have to spend with Dad's friends. At least let me know when they are coming to functions, so if I want to come I can get my game face on. When I have the energy to hold up the shield, I, too, do not take it personally. But I have to have advance notice. Also, I can't go to the Country Club. The rapist is a member there. I have no desire to see him or any of his friends. And for whatever reason, Counting Crows is off limits, too. He played Mr. Jones in high school all the time and now whenever it comes on the radio, I cringe and have an internal battle to get him out of my head."

Lindsey turns towards Dad. "Charlie, I need to know that you heard Anna. We can help her by having family dinners without inviting everyone. But you have to be on board because you have a hard time not including everyone."

"I know, I know." Dad rolls his eyes. "Growing up, our door was always open. Everyone came and went. Mom never limited who could come. It was one big party. I'm just not used to it. But I'll try."

Lindsey turns towards me with an expression of love in her eyes. "We can do this. I have a better understanding now and I'm sorry for all those times in the past when we didn't know."

Jennifer scribbles something on her notepad and looks up with a grin. "Wow!" she exclaims again. "You just did some incredible work together."

Lindsey leans forward in her chair. "I can see how Anna gets in the triangle based on what she just described." She directs her comment to Jennifer. "Thank you."

"Is there anything else, Anna?" Jennifer asks.

"Only that if you sense I am not quite myself, it is O.K. to ask me about or share your observation with curiosity and non-judgment. And the anniversary of the rape is MLK weekend in January, so you can acknowledge that without sending me over the edge, because that is a hard time for me anyway so chances are knowing I am not alone and others remember it, too, will help."

We wrap up the session. Jennifer and I schedule the next two weeks. I'm looking forward to meeting with her alone next week and then with Violet and Franz the following week. I have so much to share with her.

On my drive home, I realize Brute is no longer activated. *I wonder when he went away?*

Reflections ∞ Reactions ∞ Responses

_____

_____

_____

CHAPTER 41

VIOLET, FRANZ AND FRANK

Violet, Franz and their kids arrived yesterday. We gather around the computer on my coffee table. I log into Match to show them the profiles. I don't tell them Frank is my favorite. Instead, I gauge their reaction to each profile without my influence.

Franz leans back on the living room floor to stretch his back after we finish looking through the profiles. He moves his right leg over his left and twists his torso. "I like this guy Frank the best. He has a good name." Franz winks and we giggle.

Violet shakes her head. "What are the chances?" She clicks on his profile again. "He seems so friendly in his photos and you guys have a lot in common. I mean he likes to read! You bring your library everywhere we go."

"I know!" I exclaim. "Remember the Europe trip with me, you and Mom and I lugged 5 books all over the Continent. I read them all, though. I just can't give up my books."

Franz switches sides so his left leg is over his right. "Yeah, just like me," he says sarcastically.

We all laugh again.

"Riiggghhhttttt," I exaggerate. "How many years have you been reading the surfer book?"

"At least 10." He grins playfully. "I'm still on chapter one."

Violet logs out of Match. "So, what do you think, Annie?"

Excitement crosses my face. "Well, Frank and I are having coffee on Wednesday. And maybe lunch. He wanted to do dinner, but it is Ben's birthday. Plus I don't want to do dinner as a first meeting."

"Oh, cool," they say in unison.

"Like tomorrow?" Violet inquires. "Isn't today Tuesday?"

"Shit!" I exclaim suddenly nervous. "You are right. I totally lost track of the day. So yeah, tomorrow."

"What are you going to wear?" Violet asks.

"Hmmm…" I speculate. "I think it is supposed to rain, so probably jeans, boots, shirt and rain coat. With a scarf, of course." I feel safe bundled up with a scarf.

"Good idea," Violet concurs. "Cute and casual. I like it."

Leah and Max run out of my bedroom. "We found a jump rope! And a teddy bear! And rocks shaped like a heart." They bubble with excitement.

Violet raises her eyebrows at me.

I smile and nod. "Yes, I have a jump rope in a circle under my bed. You guys are such good treasure hunters! You can bring them out here to play if you want."

They scurry back to my bedroom to retrieve their treasures.

Violet asks, "Is that jump rope part of your healing?"

I feel shy. "Yes, and the teddy bear and the rocks. I know it probably seems stupid, but the idea is to cultivate a sense of safety in myself and those items help me feel safe."

"No, not stupid at all. It makes sense. The jump rope made me feel safe when I was little." She leans her head on my shoulder. "You've come so far Annie. I'm so glad. I know it hasn't been easy."

Later that night, I text Frank to confirm the time and place. He promptly responds that I have the correct details. I have trouble falling asleep because of my excitement.

∞∞∞

Rain blankets my windshield as I drive to Café Tuscany to meet Frank. Nervous questions float through my mind. *I wonder what it is going to be like? Will he look like his pictures? Will we have enough in common to carry a conversation? Will I recognize him?*

I glance at the clock. Brute's voice says, *of course you will be a few minutes late.*

Traffic is slow going in the rain. I park across the street in a 90 minute space.

I say to myself and any parts that might be listening, *that is a good amount of time. And if I need an excuse to leave, I can always say I don't want to get a ticket.* I imagine Travis approves of this plan, although he is quiet.

I put the car in park and turn off the ignition. One more glance in the rearview mirror confirms that my lipstick didn't move on the drive. I open my mouth to make sure it didn't transfer to my teeth either. I take a deep breath to calm my nerves. These are butterfly nerves, not anxious nerves. I say to myself, *here goes nothing.*

I pull my hood over my head and step out of the car. There aren't any cars coming, so I jaywalk across the street. I see Café Tuscany's awning ahead of me. My step quickens. I pull out my phone and see that I am three minutes late. I reassure myself, *oh well.* I take a deep breath and pull open the door.

The moment I step inside, I see him look up at me. He flashes the same warm, friendly smile from that one picture on his Match profile. My nerves instantly calm. He casually sits on the chair. I notice he's wearing a tie.

"Hi," he says. "You are Anna."

"Yes, I am." I smile. "You are Frank."

The conversation flows with ease over lunch. He is just as witty in person as in text. His questions show interest in my life. He shares more about his family, school, time in the military. He says he works from home and lives alone.

I tease, "So you put on a tie in the morning to work from home by yourself?"

He chuckles. "No, I have to go out in the field most days to meet with people."

"Ohhhh," I nod slowly. "I thought you put on a tie for coffee with me. I certainly don't get dressed up when I work from home."

We chuckle.

After about an hour, reluctantly we stand to leave. He opens the door for me to step out first. I observe, *wow I don't even mind that he does that.* I mental note to talk to Jennifer about not caring that he opened the door for me. In the past that behavior seemed to be chauvinistic, which I saw as a turn off. *It probably triggered me, too.* We walk in the same direction towards my car and his house. I stop when we reach my car across the street.

I turn to face him at the same time as stepping backward off the curb. "Thank you so much." I smile again. "I really enjoyed meeting you."

He returns my smile. "Yes, me too."

I glance over my shoulder and see the street is clear.

He asks, "Would you like to meet up again? Maybe for dinner?"

I step my other foot off the curb and begin to turn to cross the street. "Yes, I would like that a lot." I begin jogging across the street before I remember I will be out of cell phone range this weekend. I turn to yell across the street over my shoulder. "I'm going to be at our family cabin this weekend without cell phone service or internet, so don't be alarmed if I don't respond."

"O.K. Thanks for telling me," he shouts. "I'll add it to my calendar."

I giggle softly. He watches me climb in my car. I wave one more time before putting the key in the ignition. When I look up again, he is walking up the street. My body feels warm and happy. My mind is empty of anxiety, confusion and anger. I call Violet on speaker phone.

She answers with a question. "So, how was it?"

"I really like him," I declare.

"Does he want kids?"

I cringe. "Doh. I forgot to ask. But we are going to have dinner so I'll ask him then."

We confirm details for Ben's birthday dinner later that night and hang up. I'm on cloud nine the rest of the day.

∞∞∞

The following Tuesday, I sit on the couch of my hotel room going through my inbox. I'm on a work trip. It is almost 9:00 PM. My phone lights up with a notification that Frank messaged me. The warmth I felt when we parted ways spreads across my chest.

He writes, "Hi. How was the weekend at the cabin?"

"It was great. We just remodeled it, so it was our first time staying there with everyone. We had a blast. How was your weekend?"

"It was good. We did a little winetasting and I went to a spa."

I type, "What spa?"

I say to myself, *I love spas. This guy is better and better with each conversation.*

He writes, "It's a spa-type place with different saunas and pools and silence."

I respond, "Sounds relaxing."

"It was. What does your week look like?"

"Well, I'm on a work trip right now. I'll be back on Thursday. What about you?"

"Oh bummer, you are away. I was going to ask if you wanted to grab dinner. I'm just working."

"I'd love to grab dinner. What about Saturday?"

"I'm supposed to go camping with my friend this weekend. Let me see if we can shorten it."

"Don't change your plans for me. I'm around all next week and weekend, too. My sister leaves this Friday."

"No that's O.K. I've been camping at this place we are going before. We can go for one night instead of two."

I look up from my phone. Happiness and joy fill my body.

I respond, "O.K. that sounds good to me. Where should we go?

"You tell me."

I suggest, "I've always wanted to try Passion. Have you been there?"

"No, I've heard it's good. I'll make a reservation. Does 6:30 work?"

"Yeah. I don't have any plans, so any time works."

"O.K. I'll let you know what they have available."

"Sounds great. Thanks!"

He asks, "Thanks for what?"

"For organizing it."

"You're welcome."

I look up and realize I'm grinning from ear to ear. I stand to go to the bathroom.

I say to myself, *he is just so…likeable.*

I daydream about our dinner date. He will pick me up. I will wear my skinny jeans and a cute top with heels. I'll even straighten my hair.

Mini Monster pipes up, *what? You will have him pick you up? He will know where you live! Don't do that.*

I frown. *Ugh Mini. It is going to be O.K. He is sincere. He won't hurt me.*

To my surprise Mini Monster does not respond. I am relieved because I don't want to have a panic attack over this. Another message notification from Frank shows on my phone when I return to the couch. I decide to shut my computer down.

I say to myself, *these emails can wait until tomorrow.*

I also decide to get ready for bed before reading his message. Once I am comfortably in bed, I open his message.

He writes, "By the way, in case you are wondering, I don't have PTSD or anything like that."

I'm stunned. I say to myself, *that's out of left field.* I re-read the message.

Travis appears. *He must get that a lot since he was in combat.*

I inhale sharply. I ask Travis, *should I tell him about me?*

Travis quickly responds, *YES.*

My fingers feel light and free when I type my response to Frank. "That's cool. I happen to have PTSD."

I hold my breath as I wait for him to respond.

New Part jeers, *he is never going to write you back. No one wants a crazy lady. He will see you as damaged.*

Mini Monster shakes his head frantically. *Ahhhh. Why did you do that? Now he knows everything about you. He is going to take advantage of you.*

Frank responds, "I have a lot of friends from the military with PTSD. It is a really private experience. Whatever you want to share with me I'm open to hear it. I have a lot of respect for people who live with PTSD."

Tears well up in my eyes. My parts are stunned silent. I re-read his message.

Mini Monster recovers first. *He is smooth. He is just saying that to take advantage of you.*

New Part pouts, *humph.*

Travis looks up from his chair with a twinkle in his eye. He nods, but doesn't say anything.

I ask, *how should I respond to Frank?*

Travis answers, *honestly*

I write, "Thanks for saying that. I'd like to tell you about it sometime, but not yet."

We continue chit chatting for a few more minutes via text before saying good night. Even though I still don't know if he wants kids, I have a good feeling about him. I sleep peacefully.

Reflections ∞ Reactions ∞ Responses

_____

_____

_____

CHAPTER 42

TRIGGERED KARPMAN'S PERP

Summer is here. Frank and I have been dating for several months. I can't stop weeping. I feel so ashamed by my behavior last night. Thankfully it is Sunday, which means a session with Jennifer. I take an extra-long shower. The hot water feels good against my skin. I focus on the hot water in an attempt to block images from last night entering my mind. A heavy weight settles on my chest. It suffocates me with guilt and remorse. I try taking deep breathes. Nothing works.

The moment I see Pansy from the sidewalk, tears spring to the corners of my eyes. Jennifer's familiar smile greeting quickly turns to a concerned frown.

"Oh, my." She reaches to give me a hug. "Come in. You aren't alone."

Tears begin pouring down my cheeks. My chest opens.

"You know just what to say," I whisper.

We settle on the floor. I sit with my legs crossed, rest my elbows on my knees and slouch my shoulders and head over my hands.

She begins with tenderness in her voice. "Do you want to tell me what's going on? I haven't seen you this weepy in a long time."

I nod, but can't get words out. I'm overwhelmed with shame.

"You don't have to if it is too much," she continues. "We could start with grounding or safe place. Do you want some blankets?"

Pansy gently nudges my knee and elbow. She looks at me with pure concern. I reach down to pet her. Tears fall faster down my cheeks.

"Let me get you some blankets." Jennifer's tone is soft yet firm.

I don't object. She walks to the storage closet. I lie on my side and fight the urge to curl in a ball.

She calls from the door of the storage closet. "It's O.K. to be in the fetal position. If that is comforting to you right now, then do that."

She gives me permission to take care of myself. She places three blankets over me. She and Pansy sit with me while I sob for several more minutes. Even though I haven't said anything, I feel supported in my pain.

I remind myself, *like the night Violet wrapped her little arms around me.*

I take a shaky breath. "I am so embarrassed." I force the words out of my throat. I can't make eye contact.

I hear Jennifer's voice tell me it is O.K. to be embarrassed and reassure me that she does not judge me. My throat constricts every time I try to tell her what happened last night. I begin to feel frustrated that I cannot get the words out. Jennifer's voice reassures me again that she will not judge me and that I can take my time. She even says she has no one after me if we need to go longer.

After some time, I find the words to start. "It all began with Counting Crows." I look up at her.

She nods knowingly. "So you were triggered."

"Yes," I whisper. "Frank and I met at his house before going out to dinner. He lives near a restaurant lounge place that is popular right now. They play music really loud. So from his balcony, we were out there smoking a cigarette, I heard a Counting Crows song come on. I immediately saw Evan's face. Then I went into pep talk mode where I just kept telling myself to ignore it, it's just a song, don't be ridiculous, just have willpower, pretend you are normal. The usual things I say to try to make it all O.K."

I look at myself in the mirror behind Jennifer and see a tortured soul looking back at me.

"The song passes. I don't want Frank to know that I'm crazy and can't hear Counting Crows without going into a full meltdown, so I go to the bathroom. I'm not sure how, but I managed to get it together. If he noticed anything, he didn't say. We went to dinner and had a really good time. As usual, being with him is just easy and nice and calm. We went to his favorite bar after and had some drinks. I was pretty drunk when we got home. So was he. He wanted to just go to sleep, but I wanted to have sex."

I stop again. My neck and cheeks redden.

"I don't even know why I wanted to have sex. I usually don't like having sex when I'm drunk. For me, drunk clitoris doesn't have orgasms, so why do it."

I stare at the floor between us.

"Anyway, he rolled over and said he was tired and didn't want to. He said we could do it in the morning. I wouldn't let it go and I climbed on top of him and began aggressively kissing his neck and cheeks. He laughed and said, 'O.K. fine then.' We started having sex when all of a sudden I was like he's right this is a dumb idea. I mean neither of us were in sync. So we stopped. I said sorry and we both went to sleep.

"I woke up and wanted to crawl into a dark hole. He was in the kitchen making us coffee. He brings me coffee in bed every time I stay with him. It is one of my favorite things about him. He even has these mugs that say things like 'You're Wicked Awesome' with Disney villains etched in them."

I pause my story long enough to notice my reflection looks less tortured.

"Anyway, I just feel so ashamed. I mean, I never want to put someone in a position where I push them to have sex. I mean that is so gross. That is so not like me. It really came out of left field."

Jennifer's tone is firm. "You were triggered, Anna. It did not really come out of left field when you stop and think about it. You were in Karpman's Triangle playing the perp role. Feeling ashamed and embarrassed makes sense. You also said he laughed and agreed to have sex, so I'm not too worried that you forced him against his will. Don't you think?"

My face scrunches. "I guess you are right. I told him I was sorry for my behavior and hoped that I didn't make him do anything he didn't want to do this morning. He said not to worry about it and laughed again. He said if he really didn't want to do it, then he would not have done it."

"And do you trust him?"

My face relaxes. "Yes, I do. He is very self-assured. I am just more ashamed because I…" I struggle to find the words to describe why I feel so ashamed.

Jennifer hesitates before posing a question. "Do you want to know what it sounds like?"

I nod.

"O.K. It sounds like you have an excessive amount of shame that isn't yours that's been triggered. It is the shame from your rape and everything else that you've seen and experienced that is degrading towards women that has been put on you. So your response to this interaction is perhaps more intense than it would be otherwise." She stops and stares intently at me for a moment. "I mean, what you described is a situation you didn't feel good about, so you repaired it as soon as you could when you woke up. And he seems fine with everything, based on what you shared."

"I can see that," I whisper. "But is that me passing the buck on my past? I mean, I did behave poorly. I don't want to behave like that ever again. It feels like I am blaming my rape and daddy issues when I am a grown adult who should be able to take responsibility."

"There is a difference between those things." She looks at her notes for a moment. "Like I said a moment ago, that behavior is out of character for you. It is not what you would ever normally do. Yes, you did it. You are responsible for it. And part of how you are responsible for it is by becoming aware that you were reacting from the shame dumped on you by those who perpetrated against you. Does that make sense?" I look skeptical. "You aren't blaming your rape and daddy issues in a way that allows you to continue behaving that way. You are here talking about it. You are weeping because you feel bad about it. You want to make sure you never do it again. Am I right?"

"Yes." I am still skeptical. "I guess I see what you are saying. Anna without being triggered would never have behaved that way. But because I was in a trauma response, I acted in ways that just weren't me. I was a little proud of myself because I apologized to him instead of just ignoring it. I mean he definitely didn't seem to think twice about it so it must not have bothered him."

"I'm wondering if you want to do a little IFS around this?" Jennifer suggests. "It seems like you are ready to unburden some of this shame."

"O.K., we can do that." I close my eyes and roll onto my back.

She giggles softly. "You know exactly what to do to start. I don't even have to tell you anymore. O.K. go inside and let me know when you have found your little girl. We left her in the house with the garden around it, right?"

I take several deep breaths. I see her sitting on the porch. The sun is out. The house looks a little more dilapidated than it did when I left her. She looks at me with sorrow in her eyes.

"O.K.," I whisper. "I found her."

"Good. What is she doing?"

I describe her and the house. "My chest feels tight like I failed her."

"Can you ask her if she feels like you failed her?"

I nod. When I ask, she responds softly. "She says she was afraid I wasn't coming back."

"Can you thank her for telling you that?"

I thank her. "She smiled."

"How do you feel toward her?"

I scan a mental list of emotion words. "I feel guilty that I left her a long time and haven't checked in in a while and now the house is a little dilapidated."

"Can you tell her that?"

I nod. "O.K. I told her."

"What did she say?"

"She said that's O.K."

Jennifer asks, "Where are you in relation to her?"

"I'm standing on the walk path leading up to the stairs. She is sitting on the top step. There are four steps that go up to the porch."

"O.K. Can you ask her if it is O.K. if you sit next to her?"

I ask. "She says that's fine." I walk up the steps and sit next to her. We both stare into the meadow. The sun is setting.

"How do you feel towards her now?"

"I love her and feel grateful that she didn't give up on me."

"Can you tell her that?"

I tell her. "She said she feels grateful that I didn't forget her."

"Can you tell her that you are 37 now and you won't forget her?"

I tell her. "O.K."

"O.K. you will tell her or she said O.K.?"

"She said O.K."

"Do you think she believes you?"

I ask her if she really believes me. She looks at me for the first time. "She said yes, she believes me."

"How do you feel towards her now?"

"Love. She is brave and forgiving."

"Can you tell her that?"

I tell her. She reaches out and grabs my hand. "She grabbed my hand when I told her."

"Good. Can you thank her for being here and doing this with you?"

"O.K," I say. "She said you're welcome."

Jennifer gives longer instructions. "O.K. now think about the shame. Think about what color it is. What consistency it is. Its smell. And let me know when you've identified it."

Black tar starts oozing out of the garden. It is thick and sticky. It shines and shimmers in the sunlight. I describe it to Jennifer.

"O.K." Jennifer checks in on my location. "Are you still sitting next to your younger self?"

She sits next to me gripping my hand. Terror flashes in her eyes. "Yes, she is holding my hand really tight and looks really scared."

"Can you reassure her that you are in charge and you know what you are doing and she is not alone?"

I reassure her. I tighten my grip on her hand, too, but not so tight that it hurts. "O.K., I told her."

"What did she say?"

"She said O.K. and her eyes look less scared. She asked if she could sit on my lap."

"Did you tell her yes?"

"Yes, she is sitting on my lap now." Her little body feels fragile in my arms.

"How do you feel towards her?"

"I feel like she is so brave and strong. She has such courage. She trusts me."

"Can you tell her that?"

I tell her and she settles deeper into my lap. "O.K."

"Now, I want you to imagine all that black tar, all that sticky, thick, gross shame goes away. You can do it however you want. You can bury it, hose it down, whatever you want. And let me know when you are done."

I imagine a bulldozer coming through and scooping it up out of the garden. It is a big, yellow bulldozer with a huge scooper. "O.K., it is being picked up in a bulldozer."

"Oh, good," Jennifer encourages. "Now, instruct that bulldozer to put it somewhere. Anywhere, but somewhere where it doesn't bother you anymore."

The bulldozer freezes, almost like it breaks down. I begin to panic a little bit. Questions swarm my mind. *Where can it go that it won't bother me anymore? Is there really such a place?*

Jennifer asks, "Is it moving the tar away from you?"

The bulldozer turns away from the porch towards the sun. "O.K. yes, it is driving away."

"O.K." Jennifer instructs, "Put it somewhere where it will be safe. Where it won't bother you or anyone else. Like maybe bury it somewhere."

All of a sudden we are looking up at the mountains near the cabin. Way up at the top where there are boulders and thick brush, I see the bulldozer dig a hole to bury the tar. I'm a little confused because we weren't at the cabin a moment ago, but I go with it.

"O.K.," I tell Jennifer. "We are now at the cabin watching the bulldozer bury the shame up on a mountainside. It is far away from us."

"Let me know when it is done," she instructs.

After several minutes, I tell Jennifer the bulldozer is gone. "You can't even see a mound, it is buried deep in the mountain."

"Is your little girl still with you?"

"Yes, she is still in my lap."

"How do you feel towards her?"

"Empathy, gratitude, love."

"Did you tell her that?"

"Yes, she is holding a purse now. She wants to play." My little girl is standing in front of me with a purple purse holding My Little Ponies. She is smiling and invites me to play with her. I tell Jennifer.

"Can you go with her to play?"

I follow her. She takes me inside my grandma's living room and begins pulling out the My Little Ponies. "O.K. we are playing at my grandma's house."

"Good," Jennifer says. "Can you let her know that you need to leave and that you will be back to play with her?"

"O.K., I told her."

"Can you also thank her for today?"

"O.K. I thanked her and gave her a hug. She said she will see me soon."

"Let me know when you are away from her and ready to come back here."

I walk backwards toward the front door. I watch her play. She is so innocent and free spirited. When I reach the door I hesitate because I don't want to lose her again. I tell her I will be back one more time. She looks up and waves. She says, *I know*. I tell Jennifer I am ready to come back.

"O.K., start slowly wiggling your hands and toes. We did a lot of work today, so come back as slowly as you need."

I start moving my fingers and toes. I inhale, filling my lungs and belly. I move my head from side to side, stretching my neck. Next my legs extend further out from my hips. I open my eyes and blink several times. I wonder how long that took. I turn and see

Pansy sitting on her hind legs staring at me with her tongue out and eyes smiling.

Jennifer's face is filled with kindness. "You just did incredible work. How are you?"

"I feel lighter that's for sure. And not so weepy. In fact, I don't feel weepy at all." I start to roll on my side to get up.

"Wait." Jennifer stops me. "Are you O.K. to do a little movement?"

"Sure, why not?"

Her expression questions me. "If you are sure, would you go back to the fetal position you were in earlier, and slowly with deliberate movement, stretch out of that position until you are standing tall?"

I curl back into the fetal position on my left side. Then I slowly uncurl my legs and put my right hand firmly on the ground. I lift my body onto my hands and knees. I slowly walk my hands towards my knees, rounding my back and tucking my chin to my chest. I pause when I am sitting up on my knees. Next, I firmly plant both hands on the ground. I imagine I am a flower blossoming after a long winter. As I begin standing and rolling up vertebrae by vertebrae, I see the stem of a flower unfolding in my mind. When my chin starts untucking, I raise my arms slowly above my head until my fingers are reaching towards the sky. I see the flower petals fully extended, reaching towards the sunlight. I open my eyes and look at Jennifer.

Her eyes gleam with delight. "Wow, that was so beautiful."

I take a deep breath and drop my arms. "I feel like giving myself a hug. Is that weird?"

"No!" She exclaims. "Let's do it."

She reaches her arms around herself and I do the same around myself. I feel a little foolish, but mostly I feel so much gratitude for believing in this process.

"I'm glad I believed and trusted you that this process would be worth it in the end, even though it has sucked so much of the time. And I know it is not over." I hope my expression and tone reflect the sincerity of my reflection on our work together.

She laughs her knowing laugh. "I know. It really does suck and it takes a long time to heal trauma. But it can be healed. We still need to free your 22 year old self. We will get there in time."

Reflections ∞ Reactions ∞ Responses

_____

_____

_____

CHAPTER 43

JOURNAL ENTRY[71]

November 18, 2015

I haven't written in a while. Things are going so well and usually I write when things are falling apart.

I recently went off my medication. Jennifer was not happy that I did it cold turkey. I have to be honest- she is right. That wasn't the best decision. But I haven't had suicidal ideation ever since the unburdening session we did over the summer.

Frank and I are doing really good. He is a good man. He actually agreed to come to a counseling session with me. It took some convincing but in the end he realized it is to help me and he actually wants to do that. He even told me that he admires my willingness to work through everything. He said "you are one of the most emotionally stable and aware people I know." And here

---

71 The journal entry in this chapter was written for the purposes of this book. I did not write it at an earlier date. I made this decision to capture the relevant points related to healing while honoring the privacy of my relationship with Frank. Also, this story is getting long.

I was afraid he would think I was crazy if he really knew everything.

I think the night he slept over when I woke up from my dream screaming HELP had something to do with changing his mind. It was a nightmare really. For the first time I was glad I wasn't alone when I woke up from that nightmare and I actually fell back to sleep pretty easily.

Anyway, I am very grateful for him. It is so refreshing not having to hide my PTSD from him. I spent so much energy hiding it, or maybe hiding from it, for so long. We've talked about moving in together and possibly buying a house together. I asked my family- including the Council of AncientsJ- what they think about this idea, too, because I do NOT want to make another mistake. They are my litmus test. They gave a unanimous, resounding yes to moving forward in our relationship. Of course, they all said to treat buying a house as a business decision together and make sure it is all documented in some sort of contract. I agree and fortunately, so does Frank.

As for the meds, so far so good. I haven't really experienced any issues. I'm still smoking. I told my family that I was going off my meds and asked them to be aware of any changes they might see in me. I also told them they can tell me to go back on the meds if they think it is necessary.

It's so nice to have them as extra eyes and ears. I used to feel so weak when I thought about needing that kind of help. Now I am just so grateful that I don't have to be alone in this world anymore. And funnily enough,

I don't feel weak. I feel whole. It is a fragile whole-
ness though. Like at any time it can all crumble. But
this time, I have so many more supports in place than
I ever have in the past. For instance, Dad and Lindsey
have actually limited times when I have to be around
their friends! And we haven't had major family blow-
ups, either.

I feel like the healthiest version of myself. I'm actually
looking forward to this holiday in fact. Holidays in the
past have been absolutely awful for me. But this year, I
feel like I can say when I need a break from family. Or
maybe not say it, but just do it. I am excited to spend
New Year's at the cabin with my cousins and sister,
Franz, Frank and all the babies. It is a really special
time in my life.

I've even thought about stopping therapy for a while.
But I know from my training that stopping while the
going is good is a bad idea. So I'm going to cut back.
That's all for now.

Reflections ∞ Reactions ∞ Responses

_____

_____

_____

BEING HUMAN

A conversation with my 6-year-old niece and 5-year-old nephew captures human-ness in 2018.

"What does it mean to be human?" I ask.

"Auntie…what do you…" Leah starts slowly. "Do you mean like a skeleton?"

"Yes! What else goes into being human?"

Their voices become louder and their words come faster. "Muscles, hair, fingers and hands. Leeeeggggsss. Arms. Mouth. Eyes. Ears. Nose. Voices. Skin. Ouchies."

Giggle's escape from Max. "Farts, poop and pee." Leah adds. "Boogers." More giggles.

"Auntie, what about crying?" Leah asks thoughtfully.

"Yes, humans cry," I affirm.

Max asks, "Auntie have you seen crying for happy? Like when you cry it can be because you are happy. Not just sad or when you have a ouchy."

"I have seen happy tears." I smile at Max.

He giggles again before returning to what it means to be human. "Eating cake. And ice cream."

Leah exclaims, "Yeah! And watching movies. And playing."

CHAPTER 44

CABIN HEALING

The eve of New Year's Eve is here again. Frank and I are at the cabin with Violet, Franz and their kids Leah and Max. Our cousin, Zach, and his wife, Emily, are visiting from the East Coast with their daughter. She is one year younger than Max. Zach's mom was my Aunt Lisa who died by suicide in 2003 and visited me in spirit on the massage table last year with Phora. Zach, Violet, Zach's sister and I spent many days and nights at the cabin when we were younger. There is something special about bringing the next generation here together. Tomorrow Aunt Tessa's children, our cousins Kate and Bradley, will be here to bring in 2016.

Everyone is asleep. I sit on the deck stairs outside our bedroom. The mountain air is brisk and pure. The creek flows over rocks and swirls around trees and brush dangling in from the water edge.

I recall, *Aunt Lisa used to paint rocks right here where I sit.* This bedroom and deck were added after Aunt Lisa moved to the East Coast.

I close my eyes. I say to myself, *inhale slowly. Exhale slower. Wiggle your toes. Feel your feet on the ground. Hear the water moving steadily. The water and mountains are where I buried my shame for safe keeping. Breathe in. Breathe out.*

I feel my chest rise and fall. I hear the wind singing through the leaves. I feel at peace. My body is soft. My senses are focused. My mind is calm.

A voice declares, *suicide has left your body.*

My eyes shoot open. I'm startled. Did I hear that right? It was not the usual shrill voice that accompanies suicidal ideation. It also didn't sound like Travis. The voice sounded like the one that commanded me to put down my phone, go to sleep, and tell my family in the morning that I was about to attempt suicide.

The voice states louder, *SUICIDE HAS LEFT YOUR BODY.*

My chest opens. I feel energy flowing from my body into the creek. Energy that used to protect me from my suffering by urging me to end my life.

I say to myself in awe, *wow the creek is taking my pain. My body is releasing it.*

With each exhale, the energy leaves my body, joins the water and flows away from me. A smile spreads across my face.

I reflect to myself, *that was profound. Something big just happened. Am I really rid of suicide?*

The voice repeats, *suicide has left your body.*

I respond, *it actually feels like it has left my body.*

After one minute or so, the energy transfer stops. My chest remains open and my body feels lighter and fuller. I return to the sound of the creek's water flowing over the rocks and wind rustling the leaves of the trees. I look up to see hundreds of thousands of stars in the vast dark sky. They seem to be twinkling more than usual, but I'm sure they always were that way and now I see them for the first time.

I know my Aunt Lisa is here with me again like she was when I first started working with Phora. *Thank you, Aunt Lisa.*

∞∞∞

The first five months of 2016 brought a lot of excitement, and with it a lot of change. Frank and I bought a house together, of course with consent of the Council of Ancients, Dad, Lindsey, Violet, Franz and Samantha. The actual move was really stressful, especially because Frank's job took him out of town for three weeks during that time. Mom took a risk to tell me she noticed signs that I was sliding into another possible mental health crisis and instructed me to go back on Zoloft. She isn't usually that firm and direct, so when she is I tend to listen. It was the right move. Another example of how grateful I am for my increased support system.

I had a panic attack right before Frank and I moved in together. It happened at his friend's house. I was so embarrassed. Of course, Frank was calm and understanding. He has come to counseling with me a few more times to help us learn how to live with PTSD in our relationship. I think the panic attack had to happen that way because I was nervous about moving in with him without him having actually seen me have one.

It is finally Memorial Weekend. Frank and I invited Catherine and her family to the cabin for the long weekend. Catherine and I have been friends since our first study party at a coffee shop in August 2003. I was in their wedding. She encouraged me to go to the EMDR counselor back in 2006 or 2007. She reminded me that I don't need to worry about my ex-husband and instead encouraged me to focus on myself getting better right after my suicide crisis. Her words- *you need to stop hiding in the bathroom*- guided my early recovery efforts.

Catherine continued to leave me cheerful voicemails and invite me to join her and her family for different occasions over the last few years. I've declined almost all of them. Being around kids and a happy, functioning family was painful for me. I enjoy spending time with her and her family at the cabin this weekend.

Catherine and I decide to go on the ridge walk, which takes us halfway up the mountain where my little self and I watched the bulldozer bury our shame during an IFS session. I'm overcome with relief and gratitude as we stand at the pinnacle and look down on the cabin, creek and trees.

Catherine glances sideways at me. "What's going on?"

We step back to begin ascending the ridge walk trail. Love washes over me. A lump catches in my throat and tears well up in my eyes.

"Catherine, I..." The words jumble together in my mind. "Hold on. Let me collect myself."

I wait a moment to feel my emotions and allow my senses to experience the present. She waits patiently. We step in unison, gravel crunching under our feet.

"I don't really know where to begin," I start slowly. "I want to apologize because I haven't been the friend that I want to be in a long time. I know I've been absent. And I'm sorry."

She hesitates before responding. "I've felt it. And I know you've been struggling. I didn't know if it was me or..."

"No, not you," I interrupt. "I haven't been able to be around most people for the last several years. It's a symptom of the PTSD and the trauma recovery work I've been doing. My energy level is just different and my need for downtime has grown exponentially."

"I figured that is what it was. I felt so bad because if I was closer and also if I didn't have kids I would have come down and plopped on the couch with you. I just couldn't do it. I couldn't be the friend I know you needed, either."

Tears pour down my cheeks. "Yes, but Catherine you never gave up on me. You never pressured me. You never got angry with me. I can't tell you how much gratitude I feel that you never lost faith in our friendship. Thank you for not giving up on me." I pause for a few steps. "Sadly, I've lost some friendships and family relationships during this ordeal. Those hurt my heart."

She reaches her arm around my shoulders for a sideways awkward hug-while-walking. "You are welcome. I knew you were in a fight for your life. I just wish I could've done more in the trenches."

I shake my head. "Fight for my life is right. It was gnarly for a while. And you were there. You never stopped calling and texting, even when I couldn't respond. And your words that day when I told you I was getting divorced...they stick with me. I have learned how to stop hiding in bathrooms."

We giggle.

"Yeah, Anna, that's good. Because bathrooms are stinky." She scrunches her face.

"Yes, yes they are," I concur.

The rest of the weekend passes too quickly. Their children enjoy the pool, game room, and lake. They collect water skeeters in the creek. We only get a few mosquito bites. Before we say goodbye on Monday, we promise to see each other more regularly.

Reflections ∞ Reactions ∞ Responses

_____

_____

_____

CHAPTER 45

JOURNAL ENTRY[72]

July 8, 2016

I can't believe Trump secured the nomination! BARF!
This might be the only area that Frank and I have
arguments about. He insists that he is not for Trump
or Clinton. I wish he was more supportive and understanding of why Clinton's nomination is so profound
for women. But we will get there.

Everything else in our relationship is great. We have
developed a nice routine together. We share most household chores. I really don't like taking out the trash, so
that one he does more often than me. Who am I kid-
ding? He always does that one. But otherwise, we are
pretty gender neutral when it comes to the household
duties. We also decided to start trying to have a baby.
I've never tried for one before and haven't ever been

---

72 The journal entry in this chapter, like in Chapter 43, was written for the purposes of
this book. I did not write it at an earlier date. I made this decision to capture relevant points
related to healing while honoring the privacy of my relationship with Frank. Also, this story
is getting long.

pregnant, and neither has he, so who knows how long it will take.

Mom and I went to a session with Jennifer together earlier this month. I've been healing wounds from early childhood emotional neglect. This area is hard for me because I am fiercely protective of Mom. I know she did the best she could given Dad's alcoholism and addiction, and Violet's eye birth defect. The only thing I remember hearing about me as a 2-year-old was that I lost all my hair. Mom thinks it happened because I spent so much time in my car seat driving to LA for Violet's eye specialist 3 times per week. She said chunks of hair fell out and left bald spots on my head. Well, I also remember circling Mom, Dad, and Violet in jump ropes when they had to put the contact lens in Vi's eye.

Anyway, I digress. The session with Mom was really healing for us. She agreed that she probably wasn't able to give the emotional support that I needed back then. I asked her what she enjoyed doing with me when I was little. She always talked about how much she loved mornings with Violet before anyone else woke up. She gave me a big hug and told me she loved the evenings with me when Vi was asleep and Dad was out of town. That was her favorite time with me. I asked her about why she never brought up my rape again after I told her it happened and described how she seemed shell shocked by it. She agreed that she was shell-shocked and was flooded with anger and sadness that she couldn't protect me from it. She promised that she'll be more present in giving emotional support in the future.

Even though I always said I never, ever wanted to live in my home town again…I'm so excited to be here now. Especially with the possibility of having a baby.

Reflections ∞ Reactions ∞ Responses

_____

_____

_____

CHAPTER 46

2016 ELECTION TRAUMA
RESPONSE WITH DISSOCIATION[73]

I lean against the counter in our kitchen and stare absentmindedly out the window. Our daughter grows inside me. I feel flutters of her movement in my body. Donald Trump's voice is a broken record in my mind. *I just grab them by the pussy.* Stop. I can't stop thinking about the latest debate with Hilary Clinton. *Donald lurks behind her.*

A voice demands, *get that image out of your head.*

Another voice jeers, *like a shark circling his prey.*

Chills sprint up my spine. My chest tightens. My mind plays on repeat the excuses people give on the news- *Boys will be boys. Locker room talk.*

I say to myself with desperation, *so many people discount his words...these are the words that perpetuate rape culture. Who can I*

---

73 The sections within this chapter lack transitions. I wrote it this way on purpose. When I dissociate, the flow to my daily activities becomes disrupted. I pop in and out of presence. My intention for not writing better transitions between sections is to give the reader a sense of what dissociation feels like for me.

trust? Who will protect me and my daughter from this locker room talk? Why don't the men in my life get the gravity of this situation?

My mind floats back in time. I'm really young. At a party with my dad's friends. Their tongues are wagging like dogs salivating as the women, their women mingle around them. How do their women ignore this? I feel it. The lust. The hunger for sexual satiation. They prepare to pounce. They egg each other on. Their chests puff up as they reveal their conquests. Their women continue to smile, chit chat, laugh, and refill the chip bowls as if everything is normal. And not at all predatory.

Baby kicks hard. My mind pops back to the present as my hand lands on my pregnant belly.

I talk to her, *hi Baby Girl. I'm sorry I got lost in that memory. I'm scared for this world we are bringing you into.* A smile spreads across my face. *You are already using your voice for good...bringing me back to now.*

I put my mug in the sink. It is time to start my day.

∞∞∞

"I've been floating a bit Phora, ever since the pussy grabbing video came out." I have trouble making eye contact. "I don't think I can handle stretching and deep tissue today."

Phora fills her office with comfort, warmth, and safety. The lights are dim. The room is filled with a clean aroma. "How's Baby Girl? You are all belly!" She smiles and her voice is gentle.

"She is good. She is already helping her mama." My voice catches in my throat. "I'm worried about her. About hurting her because I'm dissociating again."

"Well let's get you on the table. We will work on grounding. You are doing the right things. You are taking care of yourself. She is in good hands with you."

∞∞∞

It's 2:48 AM. Frank sleeps peacefully.

A voice urges, *don't get on your phone. Try to go back to sleep.*

It's 4:12 AM.

Fuck. I'm never going back to sleep. Might as well continue the battle on Facebook. How can people not see the sexism, misogyny, racism…the hatred in this candidate? In themselves? How can societal awareness happen? We have to make the fish see water and the human see air. Hatred can't be in the top office. Hatred can't be in power.

My eyes scan articles, links and posts that might help this effort. My fingers dance on my screen to a frantic rhythm that begs people to connect hatred-in-power to my rape. Hatred-in-power to war. Hatred-in-power to violence, pain, and suffering for all people. My eyes grow heavy. It's 5:23 AM. Sleep for an hour. The day starts again.

∞∞∞

"How are you?" Jennifer and I settle into our places on the pillows on the floor. The mirror behind her jumps out at me.

"Well, I've been having a hard time with the election. Especially since the pussy grabbing video came out. I mean I am infuriated by the majority of what spews from his mouth about immigrants, Veterans, Muslims, and women. But something about that video pierced me. Like a new fear is born. Plus Brock Turner only getting 6 months. It is just so mindboggling and terrible. How this behavior is not only protected, but also rewarded and encouraged. I am just so sad and so fearful." My hands go instinctively to my belly.

"Is it a new fear or an old fear?"

"Good question." I catch my reflection in the mirror. "It's a deeper fear. It's old and new. It's old because clearly it reminds me of my rape. It's new because I'm now remembering other times I've been on the receiving end of sexual assault and harassment. From innocent friends who honestly didn't know better. It's new because if a person in the highest office of power does it- just grabs women by the pussy and sticks his tongue down their throats on purpose just because he can, even if the woman doesn't want it- what's going to stop others from doing it? And other men, and women for that matter, excuse it with an eye roll or egg it on with a verbal pat on the back because it's just locker room talk. Well then that behavior can only then be justified and continue, probably at greater rates."

"Are you dissociating right now?"

I pause. I can't focus on my reflection anymore. My eyes blink several times. I try to take a deep breath and can't. Her voice seems far away.

"Yes. My eyes are fuzzy."

"O.K. Anna, I want to talk more about the election and this fear you are describing. First, I want you to be safely in your body. Triggers can take you outside your body and your executive functioning brain isn't in charge anymore. Remember that?"

Jennifer is calm, yet firm. Her gentle concern sounds closer. I nod.

"I'm going to walk us through a grounding exercise. Remember we have done this before." She looks straight at me. Her gaze feels secure.

I nod.

"O.K. Can you lie back and close your eyes? If not, sit up and close your eyes."

"I can lie back. Well, on my side. I can't lie on my back anymore because it's bad for the baby and my circulation."

"Do you need any more pillows or a blanket?"

"No. I'm O.K." I feel suddenly very tired.

She adjusts her position. "O.K. when you are ready, take a deep breath. Close your eyes. Good, breathe. Exhale slowly....good. Do that a few more times."

I hear Jennifer breathing, too. I startle when Pansy snuggles against my back.

"Oh, Pansy. Is that O.K. Anna? I can move her."

"It's O.K." I put my hand on Pansy. I feel her snuggle deeper into my back as if she is supporting me and Baby.

"O.K. Check in with your parts. Which one do you see?" Jennifer guides me through IFS.

I smile. *Why didn't I think of this?*

"The little girl on the picnic bench. She is back on the picnic bench. Only this time she looks like she is waiting to see if she needs to go inside for protection. Not like before when she was already inside and wanted to come outside."

"Can you go to her and remind her that you are in charge and that she is safe? Remind her that you've got this, and you aren't a little girl anymore. That you will take care of her and keep her safe."

I walk through the gates to the inner court where she is sitting. The sun is out. She looks so all alone. And tired. Her expression says 'don't worry, I got this.' I ask if I can sit across from her. She looks down, shyly. Her hands clasp in front of her on the table.

Tears form in my eyes.

"What are you seeing? Are you able to go to her?" Jennifer gently inquires.

"Yes. I'm sitting across from her." I don't open my eyes. Pansy barks. I jump.

"Oh Pansy. Stop." Jennifer giggles. "I'm sorry about that. Are you O.K.?"

"I'm fine. Pansy knows what's going on." I smile.

"O.K. Can you tell her that you are sorry she felt so afraid and let her know she is not alone?"

I take another deep breath and nod.

'I'm sorry,' I say. 'I know you have had to deal with a lot of this on your own in the past. You don't have to anymore. You are so brave. We can be brave together now.' She looks up at me. Her hands are still. Her eyes are searching for truth. They seem to say are you sure you won't abandon me again? Tears flow down my cheeks now.

"What is happening?" Jennifer asks.

"I told her we can be brave together."

"Good. Ask her if there is anything else?"

'Is there anything else?' She reaches her hand out to mine. She says, 'I want to go back to Grandma's house.' I reach my hand back. 'O.K.,' I say. 'Let's go.' She hops down from the bench. She clutches her teddy bear.

"What's going on now?"

"We are walking through the gates together. There is a green grassy hill and some oak trees beyond the gates. The sun is beginning to go down. There is a warm breeze. We are going back to Grandma's house."

"What do you feel towards her now?"

"I feel love and hope."

"Good. When you are ready, open your eyes."

I slowly wiggle my toes and stretch my back. I see them walking hand in hand together. They are just beyond the gates. I open my eyes.

"How do you feel?"

I take a deep breath. "Much better. Calmer. Inside myself." I see my reflection in the mirror.

"You seem grounded."

"Yes, I am."

"Good. You can do this by yourself, when you feel yourself dissociating." Her eyes are hopeful.

∞∞∞

Election night. I dropped my absentee ballot at the poll nearest my house earlier today. I'm jittery with excited anticipation for our first female President of the United States of America.

∞∞∞

The next day, Frank stands in front of me in our kitchen. He reaches his arms out to give me a hug. I forcefully put my arms straight in front of me to block his hug.

"Don't touch me," I scowl. "I can't even look at you. I don't know where I am right now. I need space."

I've been dissociated since the election results last night. Samantha's text told me I was in a trauma response. I told her I was going to leave Frank over this Election. He laughed at me when I told him we'd have to move to Canada. He didn't realize that I was serious. I am scared again. I don't know who to trust. Everyone around me could've voted in this perpetrator. *Perpetrator in Chief.*

Frank's face falls. His eyes fill with concern. He glances at my belly. I know he is worried about Baby. *Well, you should've thought of that before you made fun of my need to escape to Canada.*

"I'm meeting with Jennifer on Sunday." I hope sound actually comes out of my mouth because I'm having trouble hearing myself. "Maybe you can come?"

"Yes, of course," Frank responds immediately. "Is there anything else I can do?"

"I'm sorry, no there is nothing." I can't make eye contact. *Get away from him.* Hatred pulses through my body. *Or is it anger?* "Actually there is something. Please give me space. Also, make sure I don't have to interact with any family members who voted for that perpetrator. And make sure I eat."

∞∞∞

By Sunday, my anger, hatred, fear, disappointment, betrayal, and sadness are no longer pulsing through me. They are at a low-grade hum. I slept in our bed last night for the first time since election night. I don't think Frank is one of *them* anymore, but I am still angry that he doesn't understand why I've been in the throes of Karpman's Triangle since election night. We drive to Jennifer's office in silence.

Jennifer and Pansy greet us at the door. Concern spreads across her face as soon as she sees us.

"We have a lot to talk about today, Jennifer." I walk absentmindedly to the blankets on the floor.

"Anna is having a hard time with this election," Frank states flatly.

He sits next to me on the floor. Jennifer settles on the floor with her back against the mirror. Pansy sniffs around the blankets between us. I catch my reflection and notice Frank for the first time since Tuesday. My expression is blank. Frank sits upright, almost like he is ready to stand to attention. His eyes are wide and bewildered.

"Anna, are you here, in your body?" Jennifer's words seem to float through the air.

I shake my head. "I don't think I've been in my body since Tuesday around 6:30PM." I begin to cry. *Where did those tears come from?* "I don't know why I am crying. I don't know where those came from. I've been wandering around aimlessly. I really shouldn't drive. I just don't trust anyone. I can't believe I live in a country that would elect a perpetrator." My voice cracks and I crash back into my body with huge, heaving, sobs. "I am so afraid, all over again," I whisper between sobs. "Like all the work we have done here is undone. It is gone. Ripped apart. I feel so defeated."

I'm not sure how much time passes. Jennifer hands me a box of tissues. Frank gently rests his hand on my shoulder. Eventually my tears stop falling and my breathing returns to normal.

"O.K., I'm here now." I make eye contact with Jennifer and nod my head. "I guess I needed to release something." I still can't bring myself to look at Frank.

"Are you sure you are safely in your body, Anna? Because it is O.K. if you aren't and want to do some meditation to help with grounding." Jennifer leans forward to show her concern.

"Yes, I am here now." I reach my hand to my belly to feel Baby. "We need to talk about what happened so Frank can understand."

Jennifer looks at Frank. "Yes, this must be hard for you to see Anna like this."

"Yes, it is. And honestly I don't understand what happened." His shoulders soften. "One minute we were sitting on the couch watching the election results and the next minute she was gone."

Jennifer raises her eyebrows. "Oh, I see. That's what it looked like for you? Anna, do you think you can tell us what happened for you?"

I nod and take a deep, slow breath before starting. "You laughed when I said we needed to move to Canada."

He interrupts. "That's what all this is about? My laughing? It was a joke. So many people are saying that and they don't really mean it."

"Well, I meant it," I snap.

He opens and closes his mouth before words could come out.

"See, he just doesn't get it," I'm exasperated. "I feel like it is so obvious why I am triggered and he just doesn't see it."

"You are right," he says with bewilderment. "I don't get it. I made an innocent comment. I didn't have any idea it would lead to this reaction."

Jennifer nods towards me and shifts to face Frank. "Let me give this a try." We nod. "Do you remember when we went over Karpman's Triangle when we met before?"

"Kind of," he responds.

She quickly draws the triangle on the back of her notepad. "Remember, perpetrator, victim and bystander or rescuer?" Her pen shifts around the triangle as she names each role. "When Anna is triggered, she gets sucked into the triangle and takes on one or more of these roles. It sounds like this time she is in the victim role. Is that right Anna?" I nod. "O.K., so Frank, Anna's trauma is in the driver's seat right now. She really feels intensely afraid and her solution is to actually move to Canada. Anna, when you made that comment, did you seriously mean it?"

"Yes, I did. I know it is farfetched and extreme, but I literally don't know how I will survive here. Like I don't know who to trust and who not to trust. My radar tells me that everyone I encounter is a rapist, sexist pig. I am afraid of what is the inevitable…I will likely be raped again since our President condones behavior consistent with rape culture. And…"

"Hold on," Jennifer interrupts. "I don't like to interrupt you, but what you just said is important and I want to make sure not to overwhelm Frank." She turns to address him. "So, Anna is serious. I know it sounds like a farfetched and extreme plan, like she just said. In that moment on election night and since then Anna's parts have been in the driver's seat. To Anna, this solution was, maybe still is, the only one that will ensure her safety. Is that right, Anna?"

"Yes," I say softly. "Right now, as I listen to these words pouring out of my mouth, I realize how extreme they are. And ridiculous. But there was a fierceness in how logical that solution was and when Frank made fun of it, I took it really personal and felt really alone. We are having a daughter. If I can't keep myself safe here, then how will we keep our daughter safe?" After a silent pause I add, "Being pregnant definitely adds to my fear. Thankfully, Samantha pointed out I was operating from a trauma response and urged me not to make any rash decisions. So I've just avoided Frank for most of this week. And he's been really great." I turn toward him. "You really have. You gave me space, you didn't push or question me. You made sure I had food. I know it hasn't been easy."

"No, it hasn't," he agrees. "I just didn't get it. It was an innocent comment. Had I known it would cause all this, I never would've said it."

"And now that is another thing I am afraid of." I look back toward Jennifer. "Frank goes into shut down mode. Like he is now going to not say anything because he doesn't want to trigger me, which is good that he doesn't want to trigger me, but not good because he can't decipher what is triggering. Does that make sense?"

Jennifer nods. "Yes, I can see the cycle and it is a hard one. I also can see that you both have a lot of love for the other. Anna, you mentioned that once Samantha pointed out you were in a trauma response, you purposely avoided Frank, right? What might you have done differently had Samantha not pointed that out to you?"

I sit up straighter. "Well, I would've exploded on him and told him he was just like everyone else who condones that horrible behavior. I probably would've made some awful comments about how Baby wouldn't stand a chance to be protected by him because he is clearly part of the sexist, misogynistic cesspool…"

"O.K., I'm interrupting you again, Anna," Jennifer raises her hand to signal stop. "I'm not sure you saw Frank when you shared what you would've said. He was visibly affected. My question was not meant to hurt you or Frank and I don't think hearing the words will benefit. If it's alright with you, I'd ask that you try to summarize how you were different without saying potentially hurtful things."

I see his reflection in the mirror. His expression is confused and hurt. "I am so sorry. I didn't actually say those things because I didn't and don't actually believe them. I am so sorry I said them just now. I feel horrible." I turn to Frank. "Babe, I am awful. I avoided you because I didn't want to unleash that fury on you. Please believe me that I don't actually believe those things or think those things."

He stiffens. "Jennifer, she said them, though. How is it that she can think them and say them, but not actually believe or think them?"

"Frank, that is a great question," Jennifer encourages. "When I work with families of someone struggling with PTSD this is one of the hardest pieces to understand and not take personally. Because Anna's words are hard not to take personally. The thing with trauma is that triggered-Anna is not Anna. Let me see how I can explain this because it is really important." Jennifer pauses to contemplate her next words. "O.K., let's go back to the triangle. When Anna is inside the triangle, she is acting one of these parts. Sometimes she may be bouncing between parts. Like she is playing a role in a theater play. She is acting as if she is a victim or as if she is a perpetrator in that moment. You see what I mean? When the scene is over and she isn't in the triangle any longer, she is Anna who does not actually believe those things."

His shoulders soften, but he continues to look skeptical.

"I don't think I've understood what happens as clearly as I do right now," I state assuredly. "I hesitate because I don't want my trauma to be a quick excuse for all my ugly behavior because sometimes I can just be a brat. Usually when I'm hungry. But what you just said makes so much sense about acting. It's like I enter a movie set. Sometimes when I dissociate, like over the last few days, I actually feel like I'm watching my life on a movie screen."

Frank's expression shifts from skeptical to curious. "How can I know if she is acting or if she is being real Anna?"

Jennifer chuckles softly. "That is why this piece is so hard for loved ones. Oftentimes, Anna doesn't even know herself when she is in the triangle. So, she can't tell you in advance."

"That would be nice," Frank states plainly. "Is it ever going to be possible for her to be able to know before she is in the triangle?"

"Honestly, maybe," Jennifer responds. "We are working toward that. It takes time. It involves layers and layers of healing and rewiring of her brain." Jennifer turns towards me. "Anna, what is going on for you right now?"

"You mean, listening to you talk about me in the third person while I'm sitting here?" I ask with a grin. "It's a little weird to be honest, but I also appreciate you both. Frank, especially you. You don't have to do this with me. You don't have to be here. You can simply wipe your hands clean and walk away because this is really hard."

"I know I can walk away," he says softly. "But I don't want to. I love you. I think this is just part of being in a relationship with you. I have my things, too."

My eyes well up with tears again. Only this time, my tears are full of love and gratitude for this man sitting next to me. "I just feel so grateful for you. I've never had someone be willing to work through this with me. I promise I will keep working. I don't want it to hurt you or Baby."

A quiet silence settles around us. Pansy lies on her belly with her head resting on her front paws. Her eyes shift from Frank to me and back to Frank. Her posture and expression remind me of a wise old person who has been here before and seen love at work.

I add, "I guess we both need to give each other the benefit of the doubt. When you made that comment, instead of automatically clumping you together with the evil perpetrators of the world, I could pause and say to myself 'no, that's not how he is.' Because it's not. You aren't like that. It is one of things I fell in love with about you and one of the reasons I feel safe with you. And you could say to yourself 'Anna isn't sounding like herself' when you see me being off. Because you know I don't ever want to hurt you."

"Yes," Jennifer chimes in. "Do you think when you notice something that just doesn't seem right about the other person, that you could alter how you might interact?"

"I'm not sure what you mean," I say with furrowed brows.

"Well, I mean how could you let the other person know that something just doesn't seem right in a way that isn't hurtful?" she rewords her question.

"Oh," I nod. "I get it. Well, I could try to pause before closing down or lashing out and say, 'what did you really mean by that?' Or I could try to be more aware when I am in a trauma response or moving towards one and give him the heads up. That one feels like a tall order to me though because I really don't know most of the time. I am getting good at seeing it after the fact, but catching it up front is really hard. Like I don't know if that is possible."

"It can be possible, with time and work." Jennifer repeats, "It just takes time and continued work. Frank, what about you? Is there anything you can do to let Anna know that something is off?"

"I don't know how I can possibly read her mind," he says defensively. "I mean I want to try, but I also don't want to say the wrong thing and trigger her."

"Babe," I implore. "Do you think you could say, 'Anna, you don't seem like yourself. Is everything alright?' And if you can, I will do my best to take your question to heart and not respond harshly to it."

"I mean, I can try," he agrees. "But again, I just was so caught off guard. It is so out of left field, that I'm afraid by the time I catch on, it will be too late. But I will try."

Later that evening, I watch Frank load the dishwasher from our dinner table. *He really is a remarkable human.* "Babe, I love you. And I am really really sorry again about the last week."

"I love you, too." He puts a glass in the cupboard. "I wish…" His voice trails off. He seems to be weighing something.

"You wish what?" I try to sound open and curious, even though I feel nervous and fearful. *What if he is going to say, 'I just wish you weren't tarnished' or 'I just wish I didn't know you' or 'I wish we weren't having a baby together.'* I shake my head and brace myself for the worst.

"I just wish you could tell me before you are triggered." His voice is sincere. "I am really worried about hurting you without even knowing it. Like I am walking blindly through a mine field."

Sadness fills my heart. "I know. I wish I could tell you, too. I wish I could tell myself because maybe then I could stop a trauma response before it starts. Wouldn't that be great?!"

He asks softly, "Why can't you? I just don't understand."

"Babe, what color is the air?"

He stops, his arm frozen in midair with a plate in his hand.

"I'm sorry. Was my tone sarcastic? I don't mean to be. I really mean, what color is the air around you?"

He stacks the plate on the shelf and closes the cupboard door. "Well, I don't know. I can't see it."

"Exactly. I can't see trauma responses, either. They just happen. Like air is just there for our body to automatically breathe. You can't say, 'watch out, there's the air, it's going to get you.' Because air is everywhere and you can't see it. My world is full of potential triggers, a few that I'm aware of, but many that I'm not. I can't anticipate them. I can't see them. And they are potentially everywhere."

A light bulb seems to turn on in his head. His eyes widen and he slowly nods his head. "O.K., I guess I hadn't thought of it like that before. I think I get it better. The way you just explained it helped me understand."

"I will try, Babe. I promise, I want nothing more than to be able to be proactive instead of reactive. Well, the only other thing I want more is for Baby to be healthy." I stand and walk to him in the kitchen. "Can I get that hug now? The one you offered the day after the election that I pushed away?"

His arms reach around my body. My head rests on his chest. I inhale one of my favorite smells- his detergent mixed with him. "I love the way your shirts smell," I whisper.

I feel safe again.

Reflections ∞ Reactions ∞ Responses

_____

_____

_____

APRIL 2018

Our daughter sleeps in her crib. Her first birthday was last month. Parenting with Frank is one of the greatest gifts, second only to our daughter. We got married in the Fall last year. Our daughter was our flower girl.

Tonight I feel anxious, like a panic attack is lurking around the corner. *I haven't felt this way since before Baby's arrival.* I focus on my breath. I stretch the inhale to 3 counts. *Shit.* The movie Frank and I were watching ends.

"Are you going outside?" I ask him. Usually he smokes one last cigarette before bed.

"Yeah, I think so." He takes his wine glass to the kitchen sink. "You want to come?"

Thankfully, I haven't had the urge to smoke since I found out I was pregnant. But I still like to breathe in the cool evening air from time to time when he smokes at night.

"No, I'm going to get ready for bed."

I stand and walk 15 feet down our hallway, through our bedroom and into our bathroom. I know before I turn on the light that a panic attack is underway. *Just breathe. Get through this. You haven't had one in so long. You can do it.* I reach for my toothbrush. *Just do your routine.*

I look at my reflection. My eyes are bright red, as if I'd been crying all night. My breath count shortens to a half second in and half second out. *Shit. I am hyperventilating.* My vision becomes fuzzy. *No, don't go out. Hang on. Let me get help.*

I riffle through our medicine cabinet for the Ativan I was prescribed after Baby was born. Back then, I broke into full-body hives and the ER doctor prescribed Ativan to help me sleep and prescription-strength Zyrtec to decrease the hives[74]. *Shit, it's the generic names.* I reach for my phone, open Safari and key in the generic name off the first bottle. My vision is blurry. Tears collect in my lower eyelids. *Fuck. Hang on.* I see that this bottle is the generic for Ativan. I manage to see the dosage is really low. I tell myself out loud, "Take one pill now. And tell Frank to give you another one if it doesn't pass in 20 minutes."

I stumble out of the bathroom door and reach for the dresser to steady myself. I'm hyperventilating now. I feel light headed. My vision is blurry. I keep one hand on the hallway wall.

"Frank," I whisper loudly so as not to wake Baby. "Frank."

He peeks his head around the corner from the kitchen. Concern spreads across his face. I'm standing in front of him now. I hand him the prescription bottle. My chest rapidly rises and falls with shallow breaths.

---

74 I used this prescription for a purpose other than what it was meant for. I do not recommend misusing prescriptions. Instead, I should've worked with a psychiatrist to prescribe an antianxiety for panic attacks. I knew from my training that Ativan is a medication for panic attacks. I also knew the dose was low, so I made a decision to use the medication in that moment.

"I'm having a panic attack," I gasp. "I need you to be with Baby tonight. If she wakes up. I took one of these pills. I don't trust myself holding her. Can you be with Baby? Even though it is my night?"

My chest heaves up and down. Tears steadily stream down my cheeks. We usually take turns consoling Baby when she wakes up at night. Tonight is Friday and Fridays are usually my night.

"Absolutely." He reaches for the bottle. "What happened?" His eyes are wide with concern.

"I'm not sure," I say between gasps. "I know this will pass. Just give me another pill in 20 minutes if it doesn't."

"O.K., yes. For sure." He stands in front me like a pillar of support. Even though I know he is concerned, I feel secure in his steadiness. "Is there anything else?"

I continue to hyperventilate. I recall pillow forts and the words of one of the therapists on the mental health retreat. She said having someone embrace you tightly can help slow your nervous system. *Will that help?*

"Yes, can we go lie in bed and will you hold me really tight?" I continue to gasp. "I'm going to be O.K. I know I'm going to be O.K. You just have to take care of Baby. I can't do it tonight."

"Yes, yes. Of course, I can take care of Baby and hold you tight."

Eight minutes later, the panic attack subsides.

"Wow." I am incredulous. "It has really only been 8 minutes. I can't believe it. That has never happened before."

I snuggle deeper into Frank's chest. His arms tighten a little more around my body.

"That's good." His voice is calmer, but still concerned.

"I feel almost giddy. Which is weird going from that hyperventilation, blurry vision place to feeling calm and giddy. Thank you, Babe. Thank you."

I reflect on events leading up to tonight that may have triggered that panic attack. Ideas float through my mind. Before I realize anything conclusive, I fall into a restful sleep.

Saturday morning. The sunlight filters through the window blinds. Frank's chest rises softly under the covers. Baby sleeps in her crib. I wonder if she woke up at all and I missed it, or if she slept through the night. Frank stirs. He lifts his head up and opens one eye.

"Are you awake?" he asks.

"Yes," I whisper. "I didn't mean to wake you. Did baby sleep through the night?"

"She woke up once, but went right back to sleep as soon as I picked her up. She didn't wake up again when I put her back in her crib." He rests his head on his pillow. "Are you feeling O.K.?"

"Yes, I feel surprisingly well." A smile spreads across my face. "Are you?"

"I'm O.K., too. I didn't sleep great. I was worried about you." He rolls on his side to face me. "Do you know what that was about? It really caught me off guard. When I went to smoke, you seemed fine. And five minutes later, you were in a full blown panic attack."

I close my eyes and recall my reflection right before I feel asleep. "The Bill Cosby verdict was part of it. I am so happy with the verdict, but I read a bunch of articles about it and inevitably, details of the rapes and sexual assaults were in them. That was a bad idea. I was just so happy that he was convicted. I wanted to read for myself."

"Yeah, I can see that." Frank rolls on his back.

"And that movie we watched. The part where the dad told the daughter that had he known someone beat her up, he would've done something to protect her. That part struck a chord in me. A father protecting his daughter. And then it didn't help that I had 3 iced coffees yesterday. The strong ones."

Frank turns his head quickly to face me. "Ohhhhhh," he exaggerates. "That's enough to do it right there."

"I know," I say sheepishly. "The next big verdict, you are going to have to read about it and report back to me. And I won't drink that much coffee again. It has been so long, though. Over a year since the last panic attack. And this one only lasted 8 minutes. We were such a good team!"

He smiles. "Yes, we were."

"I'm so scared that will happen when you are on a work trip and I will be alone with Baby."

He reaches his hand to cover mine. "You will call your mom, or your dad, or Lindsey or Tessa. They are all close enough to help you." He squeezes my hand in reassurance.

"Yes, that's a good point."

Baby's sweet voice calls from her room. "Maaaamaaaa. Paaaapaaa."

"I got this," I say. "You go back to sleep. Thank you, again."

I lean over to kiss Frank, throw the covers off and walk to greet our Baby Girl.

∞∞∞

The following Thursday, I prance across the street to Jennifer's office. My excitement bubbles out of my body. I see Pansy waiting at the door. A smile erupts ear to ear. Jennifer holds Pansy's collar and I open the door to walk inside.

"Wow!" Jennifer exclaims. "You are full of joy."

We hug each other in our usual greeting. I pat Pansy's head.

"I know!" I say with exuberance. "I have some awesome things to report."

"Well, let's hear it." Jennifer sits facing me with her notepad in her lap. She smiles eagerly.

"I had a panic attack!" My grin widens when I see her eyebrows furrow. "I know that doesn't sound like something to be so excited about. Let me explain." I take a deep, satisfied breath. "So, I haven't had one since Baby Girl was born. I think since the election actually. On Friday, it seemed to come out of nowhere." I recall what happened and how Frank and I handled it together.

"Wow, again!" She grins. "Only 8 minutes! Frank was really there for you. You were in charge. You didn't let the parts hijack you. Anna, this is really, really great."

"I know!" My smile remains. "And there is more. You know how we are going on vacation tomorrow?" I don't wait for her to respond. "Well, I desperately needed to get my nails done because we are going to a resort and I just like having my nails done. So, I'm sitting in the massage chair soaking my feet and I start singing along to this song. I think to myself, 'I really like this song. Which one is it?' And you'll never guess. It was a Counting Crows song! You know how much those songs used to trigger me. I'm telling you, Jennifer, it was quite a moment. I felt so overjoyed. I almost started crying in the chair."

"Anna! That's amazing. And like, unheard of." Jennifer's head shakes and nods at the same time.

"I know! Me either. And I honestly don't know if it will ever happen again. Once I realized it was a Counting Crows song, I did think about how it used to be a trigger. But it didn't have the same effect on me. Like, none of my parts were activated."

"Yes, I've never heard of this happening for anyone. But it doesn't mean it can't happen. And even if this is the only time that you aren't triggered by one of these songs, that's O.K. What do you make of all this?"

"Well, I've been thinking about it. I think all of our work together, and all of the other things I've done are actually working. I think my brain has new pathways. I think IFS and movement combined made a huge difference. Having a support system with family and friends who keep trying and learning with me to find ways to help me cope. Using meditation, massage and medication… my brain is calm. I can regulate emotions. I can keep myself safe."

I take another deep, satisfying breath. I move my arms over my head to stretch and drop my hands behind my neck. I rub the base of my skull and think about Phora. Pansy brushes against my legs and sits gently against my feet. I look at Jennifer.

"Anna, you did this." She seems to be glowing. "You really stuck to it, through all the pain. All the shit. All the layers. You have turned a corner."

Reflections ∞ Reactions ∞ Responses

_____

_____

_____

APPENDIX A[75]

LETTERS TO MY PARTS

Dear Travis,

You are the first part I think I really came to understand and develop a healthy bond with. You were born as a protector and your job is to keep me safe. You literally wear a knight's armor suit. Over time, I think your armor became permanently fused into my muscles. I'm so grateful that you were willing to tell me what you wanted to do. And I was so surprised that you are an old man with gray hair and kind eyes. I mean, a fit old man. Hahaha. You know what I mean.

I've come to trust that I can call on you when I need you. And I appreciate that very rarely you put your armor on without me asking. My favorite moments are when you

75 These letters were written during the first quarter of 2018 before the Epilogue took place. I drafted the letter to New Part for a homework assignment from Jennifer. The exercise was cathartic, so I decided to draft letters to other Parts to be included in this book. Letters address each Part that I am aware of at the time of publication, although not each Part with letters are mentioned in the narrative. I fear this book would never end if the discovery of each Part was included in the narrative. The IFS process used with Travis, Mini Monster and Little Anna is the same process used with each Part addressed in these letters.

pull your newspaper down to say something or flash a look to command something. You are very wise.

You seem to be a leader of a lot of my other parts, like Brute, the New Part, and especially Mini. You and Mini seem like you've been through battle together. I think Mini looks up to you. You naturally have a sense of calm that Mini has to work for.

Anyway, thank you for being with me through all my pain and suffering, and for being with me now. Please let me know if you need anything else to stay comfortable in your retirement. Here's to reclining chairs!

Big hugs and love,
Anna

∞∞∞

Dear Mini Monster,

You bring the biggest smile to my face now! I never thought I'd be able to say that about anxiety. When I imagine you- your cute-little-but-fierce self with your wild hair under your sombrero on the hammock at the beach- I just can't help but smile.

You have been my biggest firefighter. You have fought fires from the outside and from other parts on the inside. I don't know how you held up energy for so long to do that day in and day out. I do know that I am forever grateful for you. You kept me alive, even when I wanted to die. Well Suicide wanted me to die.

I love where you have chosen to retire. The palm tree on the beach painting that has moved with me since 2003 is currently by my bed. I imagine your hammock is somewhere on that beach. I know we are still learning how to work together when you are activated so that you stay in retirement unless I ask you to help fight a fire. We drew a circle in the sand around the hammock so you have a clear boundary when you are activated. So far that seems to work. You have a space to jump up and down and wave your arms and get the energy out. But you don't have to overrun me in the process.

I also love your job as my cheerleader. You have the energy for it! And you have really helped me more recently when Self-Doubt is activated. You jump up and down and cheer me on. You remind me to take breaks and rest on the hammock. You are really good at your new role.

Thank you for being with me so long and sticking with me now. Please let me know if you need anything else to stay comfortable in retirement. Happy hammocking!

Lots of love,
Anna

∞∞∞

Dear Young Exiled Self,

You are simply remarkable. I know you stayed locked away in that prison-like institutional place for so long. You had to survive on your own without the comfort and love you deserve. And you held on to teddy bear and waited for me to come.

You have been my primary motivation to become a trustworthy adult. Through you, I learned that cultivating inner safety is where trustworthiness starts. From there, making decisions that consider safety comes next.

I've failed many times since I first met you. And I continue to make mistakes here and there. Like right now, I'm writing this letter when I should be sleeping since I have strep throat. But I'm so close to finishing the book and I'm in the flow.

You have been understanding with my missteps. You are always there looking to me for guidance, direction and protection. You are always willing to keep trying as I learn how to be trustworthy.

You also give me a reason to play. I love spending time with you in Grandma Ophelia's living room. Oh how much fun I had in those days when I was your age. And you have helped me bring this playfulness to my relationship with my daughter. Thank you!

Your bravery, courage, hope, and resilience are truly remarkable. Please continue to work with me.

With a heart full of love,
Anna

∞∞∞

Dear Brute,

I'm still learning about you. I know you are a young part, and maybe even one that I inherited because you shared that with me. I know your criticisms are meant to protect me from disappointment, rejection, and shame. You first appeared in my mind as a one-dimensional cartoon character. Like one of those burglars in an old school cartoon.

More recently, you've revealed more to me. You actually became human in the shape of a young boy. That surprised me because you seemed so big and scary and thief-like before. You said it was your costume you put on to hide from pain. I am impressed with your ability to become one-dimensional. That's a very crafty disguise!

I look forward to working out more details for your new role. Right now you and the New Part are together on a tropical island retreat taking it easy. New Part seems like a big sister-figure to you. Is that right? I had a dream that you, she and I were tied together with a belt in a swimming pool and I cut myself free from you both. We all floated to the surface, me alone and you with New Part. That's why I think you may be related. I'm also curious about your relationship to Travis and Mini?

Thank you for being with me for so long, like maybe even since pre-verbal times. Please keep sharing as you feel comfortable so we can continue building trust in each other and learning how to work better together.

With love and curiosity,
Anna

∞∞∞

Dear Imposter (a.k.a. New Part),

You live in my brain. Specifically the front part of my brain, behind my forehead. I imagine there is quite a posh living space set up in there. You are fantastic. You are witty, sassy, straightforward, coy, sly, cute, flirty, sexy, playful, funny, and fun-loving. You are a protector of others- at times a staunch protector- especially of women who fall victim to misogyny and sexism and hatred for no reason or fault of their own.

You know how to outsmart 99% of the people on this planet, especially men. You came up with the tool-on-stupid-men game we played in graduate school. Those poor bastards didn't know what hit them. The game- you hooked them and then ran. Poised, calm, collected, mysterious, mischievous.

You helped me exist in the world after the rape. I spent so many nights hysterical, sobbing, flooded with such pain that I didn't know how to survive. I drank too much, slept with too many men, tried drugs. I was so self-destructive in an attempt to avoid that pain. You rescued me from it. You helped me regain control. You kept me moving forward with school and my career, with buying a house. You kept me socially desirable. You kept my pain at bay.

Although, at times, you colluded with alcohol- aka the party girl, which led to suicidal ideation. And my exiled 22 year old self would come with the suicidal ideation. Those deep sobs boiled up in my throat, usually accompanied by actual vomit and hysterical calls to my sister where I would try so hard to express what was going on. But you wouldn't let me. You waited patiently, at times dialing her number and holding my hair back, for me to wear myself down to a dreamless sleep instead of form the words- I am a victim of a terrible crime. I was invaded. My body became a cum receptacle of a predatory rapist whose day job was a happy-go-lucky funny goofy party guy/big brother.

You reasoned with me. Who will believe you? He comes from a family of lawyers. Who will ever see you as a clean, honest person ever again with the shameful poison rotting your core? These questions were so confusing, I just couldn't ever get out what I needed to get out.

All that said, I am grateful to you and for you. You kept me moving forward. You kept me believing I could do great things. I think you effectively managed Brute- the sexist pig inner critic who is actually a young boy. You helped me adapt in the world.

Now I need 22-year-old me to be seen in full so I can help her heal. I need you to be here, still, too. You can help her feel beautiful again after her bruises heal. You can help her with self-care- spa days, safety pillow fort nights. You can help her feel sexy again. And playful. I need all those things, too. You can help me ask for what is pleasurable in my romantic relationship with my husband. Yes, you read that right. I have a husband who is truly, genuinely, sincerely loving and support- ive. I want to be able to enjoy sex with him consis- tently. I want to feel passionate. I want to be patient with my vagina and clitoris and all the other pleasure nerve endings as they come back online. I don't want to feel impatient and rushed, embarrassed and guilty for not instantly responding to his or my touch. Or grossed out by the thought of his thinking I taste dirty. I don't want to feel dirty, annoyed or anxious in anticipation of another failed attempt where I coax a pleasure response from my body that is sincere in intent but unable to be authentic in response. I think you can help with those challenges because I really miss mind blowing sex, pleasurable flirty sex, and beautiful love making. I miss the multidimensionality of it all. Most of all, I miss con- necting with my husband.

I also think you need a name other than New Part. You can stay in residence in my brain if you want. But you can't live in a Truman-show like façade house of cards that keeps 22-year-old me exiled. You have to get an actual place of your own so she can stay on that beautiful beach. I think you will get bored with that life anyway. What about Anna for a name?

In your debt and with much gratitude and love,
Anna

∞∞∞

Dear 22-Year-Old Exiled Self,

It has taken a very long time to meet you. New Part was exceptional at protecting you and keeping you in exile. She meant well. In fact, I think New Part and you fragmented from my Core Self the night I was raped. You bore the brunt of that violence by yourself for a long time.

When I first met you, after New Part's imposter role became clear, you were sad and weepy. You were lying in a dark room, forgotten. The darkness hid your pain. Only your tears glistened on your cheeks when sunlight entered your room at just the right angle.

At first I did not know how to approach you. I was afraid I would say or do the wrong thing. I felt paralyzed by the mix of emotions I felt towards you. I felt love for you that was clouded by a deep sadness that reached to the depths of my soul. I felt angry at the man who did this to you. I felt afraid of that anger because it conjures a hatred so intense it could melt iron. I felt helpless. I felt anger with myself for abandoning you.

The words came to me though and you patiently waited while I stood at the door. "You are not alone." I looked up at me and I saw your eyes for the first time. I saw hope in your face. Your hair fell softly around your face and draped over your shoulders. You sat up and asked if you could go out of the room. It turns out we were in a spa-type place. The room adjacent to your dark room was full of windows and natural light. White sheer curtains waved gently with the breeze. It was the perfect temperature. The house was surrounded by a big lawn and the ocean was just at the end of the lawn. There were comfortable couches and fresh fruit. You wore soft light blue pajama pants with a matching button down shirt that hung loosely off your body.

You asked if you could stay here for a while. And when I said of course, you reached for an orange and settled into the couch. You pulled a light blanket over you. Your eyes glimmered with hope. You said you want to heal here. You want your bruises to be seen.

I felt very afraid at that moment because I was not sure if I would be able to be trustworthy enough to hold that space for you. I wanted to face your pain, too. I wanted to see your bruises. That meant talking about being a victim of a crime. A violent, invasive and life-crushing crime. That meant seeing helplessness in me for the first time. There was nothing we did to warrant being raped. I've known that on an intellectual level for a long time. But actually believing it on a visceral level meant grappling with victimhood.

You were patient. You operated at your own pace. For weeks you stayed in that beautiful, cozy room. Eventually, you started drinking tea on the veranda. You watched the waves for hours. You leaned back in the comforts of the oversized chairs and put your feet up on the veranda railing. Your bruises changed color. They were healing. Surprisingly…or maybe not…I actually ended up with random bruises on my legs during that time. One was from the paw of a super friendly big dog who jumped on me as a greeting. It left a 4 inch bruise from the top of my thigh to almost my knee. I think it helped me to keep you present in my awareness.

Most recently, you asked me if you could go outside to the beach and play with children. You were wearing a sundress. You looked at peace. Fragile, still, but at peace.

You are beautiful. Thank you for helping me hold the insufferable pain of that night for so many years. Your courage and strength are remarkable. I look forward to continuing to heal with you. Please know I will do my best to be a trustworthy leader of our inner family so you may continue to heal.

With much love and gratitude,
Anna

∞∞∞

Dear Suicide,

Thank you for leaving my body. You were really good at what you did. I hope you enjoy your new life as water in the creek. Maybe you will be evaporated and become rain clouds and give water to plants and animals. You will be nourishment for life.

Love,
Anna

P.S. A friend who read this letter noted you may also rain on all the perps, and release them from this planet.

∞∞∞

Dear Parts-in-Progress,

You are all waiting your turn. Or maybe you are masters at hide-and-seek, so it is taking a longer time to find you. Or maybe I need to continue showing that I am trustworthy and can be a leader before you will appear. Whatever the reason, I will wait and once you appear I look forward to meeting you. I think the Parts-in-Progress consist of:

- Alcohol

- Hypervigilance

- Dissociation

- Confusion

- Self-Doubt

- Anger

- Numb

- Pre-verbal exile

- Paranoia

- Work-aholic

Some of you have appeared before, but in small snippets. Perhaps other parts needed attention more urgently.

Anyway, thank you for protecting me. I look forward to re-purposing your role in our inner family.

Love, Anna

INTERNAL FAMILY
SYSTEMS GRAPHIC

Reprinted with Permission from Dr. Richard C. Schwartz, Ph.D., Founder of Center for Self Leadership

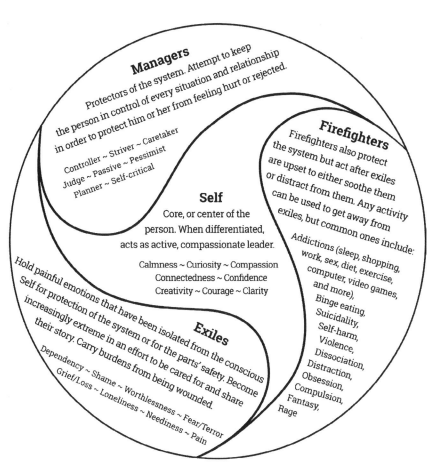

Managers

Protectors of the system. Attempt to keep the person in control of every situation and relationship in order to protect him or her from feeling hurt or rejected.

Controller ~ Striver ~ Caretaker
Judge ~ Passive ~ Pessimist
Planner ~ Self-critical

Firefighters

Firefighters also protect the system but act after exiles are upset to either soothe them or distract from them. Any activity can be used to get away from exiles, but common ones include:

Addictions (sleep, shopping, work, sex, diet, exercise, computer, video games, and more),
Binge eating,
Suicidality,
Self-harm,
Violence,
Dissociation,
Distraction,
Obsession,
Compulsion,
Fantasy,
Rage

Self

Core, or center of the person. When differentiated, acts as active, compassionate leader.

Calmness ~ Curiosity ~ Compassion
Connectedness ~ Confidence
Creativity ~ Courage ~ Clarity

Exiles

Hold painful emotions that have been isolated from the conscious Self for protection of the system or for the parts' safety. Become increasingly extreme in an effort to be cared for and share their story. Carry burdens from being wounded.

Dependency ~ Shame ~ Worthlessness ~ Fear/Terror
Grief/Loss ~ Loneliness ~ Neediness ~ Pain

Text adapted from *Internal Family Systems Therapy* by Richard C. Schwartz, Ph.D.
Graphic by Janet B. Mullen, LCSW

ACKNOWLEDGEMENTS

I have gratitude, appreciation and sincere thanks for many people who have supported me on my healing journey, and specifically, in writing this book. Jennifer Lazar has been with me since September 2014. She read this manuscript multiple times and provided edits, feedback and questions that improved the accuracy and relevance of the therapeutic process. She answered emails and text messages to clarify her notes, sometimes late at night. She encouraged me along the way when I faltered. She reminded me to slow down when the writing process overwhelmed me. She encouraged me to write with self-care and compassion in the forefront, so as not to retraumatize myself. Jennifer is a role model for trauma-informed practitioners. Her skill, knowledge and authenticity are…I'm having trouble identifying the word that captures the immense reverence I have for her as a board-certified dance/movement therapist and Ph.D. in clinical psychology. She is a gift, a miracle worker. She also brought Pansy into my life. Who knew I would connect with an animal the way I do with Pansy!

Phora Crane is another miracle worker who came into my life in September 2014. She physically healed my body and helped me learn to accept love through touch. I was numb and disconnected when I started working with Phora. Her skill, knowledge and intuition…again, I am having trouble identifying the word that captures the immense admiration and gratitude I have for her as a massage therapist. She taught me about my body with patience, compassion, steadiness and love. She also helped me in the writing process. She read the manuscript, wrote feedback in the margins, shared resources about her field and encouraged me along the way.

Dr. Richard C. Schwartz, founder of Internal Family Systems and his brother Mr. Jon Schwartz, Executive Director of the Center for Self Leadership met with me several times. They read the manuscript and offered feedback on it and the publication process. I am grateful for their guidance, expertise and encouragement.

There are other professionals whom I want to acknowledge. The staff at the mental health retreat held space for me to delve deeply into my pain. Their commitment to providing a safe space with a variety of opportunities to explore suffering, feel pain and express it kick started my healing. I still incorporate art regularly, although not as frequently and in different forms, like we did on retreat. My primary care doctor and her staff helped me with medication, even at the end of the day on a Friday when I was feeling desperate. My OBGYN and his staff supported me and my husband through my pregnancy with a trauma-sensitive approach. The meditation teacher you met in Chapter 31 opened my eyes to the power of meditation to aid in recovery and healing. The facilitators of the dream retreat in Chapter 5 helped me explore my inner world. None of these professionals read this manuscript. However, without their care, concern and expertise, I'm not sure I would've been able to write it.

My friends, many of whom are part of this book, are a big reason I am alive and well today. Samantha, Catherine, Elizabeth, Camille, Dusty and Sasha kept me alive, reminded me of who I am, of what life could and would be like again, forgave me, loved me unconditionally and never gave up. Despite limited interaction today, my friends in Chapters 2 and 5 were pivotal in my healing at a time when I was not ready to engage in trauma recovery work. Another group of six women whom I met after the 2016 election kept me writing when I felt self-doubt, inner critic, boredom and discouragement. Their instant text messages of encouragement and reassurance motivated me to keep writing in those moments. One woman from this group designed the cover of this book. Two women with whom I used to work are now friends. One reminded me of the importance of this story for mental health training. She encouraged me to keep writing and helped me stay connected to my professional identity. The other helped me craft the trigger warning for readers who are survivors at the start of this book. She also helped me remain connected to my feelings while writing this story. Another friend with whom I've been friends since high school consistently sticks up for me, challenged my rapist and offered to read the manuscript. She is also in the mental health field and helped me professionally while I wrote this book. Lastly, a neighbor shared her wisdom and resources about the healing properties of crystals and rocks. Most of these women are survivors of sexual violence. These women have keen insight and awareness of patriarchy, sexism and misogyny. Ten of the 18 women mentioned here read and gave feedback on all or part of this manuscript. They also helped select the cover. These friendships enrich my life and contribute to my recovery every day.

My family made the publication of this manuscript possible. They gave their permission to publish it. Each of my immediate family-of-origin read all or part of the manuscript. Even with the use of a pseudonym and changes to names of people and places, there is a risk for discovery. They graciously agreed to make this story public, despite this risk. They also spent countless hours reviewing the manuscript and, at times, re-living painful memories to provide feedback on accuracy, timeline, grammar, flow and more. I am grateful for my family. Like my friends, they never gave up on me. They continue to express a desire to help me heal that their actions support. Their love and willingness to walk through this journey with me makes me the woman I am today.

My husband and our daughter are the greatest evidence of my recovery. My husband's unconditional love for me and our daughter, his willingness to learn and grow together, to see me and not PTSD first…he is a wonderful man. Even when we struggle, he shows up consistently with love and compassion. He read part of the manuscript and offered insight and feedback. He is a staunchly private person. When deciding whether to publish this manuscript, I asked him what it would be like to have the details of our private life available to the public. He was firm in his response: "You need to publish this. It is your story to tell, so tell it." Our daughter and her future gave me determination to finish this book. I've been asked if I will let her read it. My answer is always yes, when she is ready. I hope in publishing this story, her experiences in the world will be safer than mine.

Lastly, I want to express my gratitude and appreciation for all victims and survivors of sexual violence who have courageously spoken out. Ms. Tarana Burke, Dr. Christine Blasey Ford, Dr. Anita Hill, Ms. Andrea Constand, Ms. Emily Doe; the US Women's Gymnastics team members; the accusers of Harvey Weinstein, Matt Lauer and other perpetrators; Ms. Oprah Winfrey, Ms. Stefani Joanne Angelina Germanotta (a.k.a. Lady Gaga), Ms. Kesha Rose Sebert (a.k.a. Kesha), Ms. Taylor Alison Swift (a.k.a. Taylor Swift); and, those who posted #MeToo in response to Ms. Alyssa Milano's tweet in 2017. Your courage and strength in coming out publicly to press charges and share your experiences with sexual violence paved a path for me to follow. Thank you.